THE CHRISTIAN COUNSELOR'S COMMENTARY

THE GOSPELS OF MATTHEW AND MARK

JAY E. ADAMS

MID-AMERICA
INSTITUTE FOR NOUTHETIC STUDIES

Institute for Nouthetic Studies, a ministry of Mid-America Baptist
Theological Seminary, 5640 Airline Road, Arlington, TN 38002
mabts.edu / nouthetic.org / INSBookstore.com

*The Gospels of Matthew and Mark: The Christian Counselor's
Commentary*
by Jay E. Adams
Copyright © 2025 by the Institute for Nouthetic Studies,
© 1999 by Jay E. Adams

ISBN: 978-1-949737-97-4 (Paper)
ISBN: 978-1-949737-98-1 (eBook)
Old ISBN: 0-889032-09-3

Editor: Donn R. Arms

Library of Congress Cataloging-in-Publication Data
Names: Adams, Jay E., 1929-2020
Title: *The Gospels of Matthew and Mark:
The Christian Counselor's Commentary*
by Jay E. Adams
Description: Arlington, TN: Institute for Nouthetic Studies, 2025
Identifiers: ISBN 978-1-949737-97-4 (paper) | OCLC: 41379163
Classification: LCC BS2575.3 .A465 | DDC 226.2

Published in the United States of America

Introduction to
The Gospel of Matthew

Of all the Gospels, Matthew is the one that holds the most possibilities for counselors. In it, for instance, is the so-called Sermon on the Mount, which is full of instruction that might—in another place—provide the basis for an entire, in-depth book on counseling. Because of this fullness, many things one would like to treat in detail must be handled only in a cursory manner, but not with neglect. Every effort has been made to be thorough, if not complete.

The Gospel was written to demonstrate to Jews, by His words and works, that Jesus Christ is the Messiah of Old Testament prophecy. To learn how Matthew admirably achieves this end, under the guidance of the Holy Spirit, is one of the benefits of studying the book. It is also one of the reasons why a counselor should have more than a passing acquaintance with it. Many counselees are weak in their faith and need the sort of buttressing that this Gospel can give them. It is a faith-strengthening book and should be recognized and used as such by counselors.

The relationship of this Gospel to the other three is not within the purview of this series of commentaries and may be best left to those critical works that devote themselves to such matters. The Gospel will be taken straightforwardly for what it says, dealing with matters that arise within the scope of the work, but rarely going outside to raise issues not altogether pertinent to its interpretation.

That Matthew's method is different from that found in other Gospels is apparent to the thoughtful student. Matthew frequently treats subjects topically rather than chronologically. In chapters 5 through 9, for instance, we have a section containing sayings and healings (the former in chapters 5:1-7:29; the latter in chapters 8:1-9:35). In chapters 23 through 25 he groups eschatological material, some of which is spread out in a more chronological manner in the Gospel of Luke. Chronology, except in the broad sense, is not a vital concern for Matthew.[1] There is nothing wrong with this method; every writer is entitled to frame his book in the manner that seems to him best suited to accomplish those ends that he has in view. After all, Matthew makes no pretense at writing a biography of Jesus any

---

1. For details on Matthew's triplets and other groupings that are found in his book see Alfred Plummer, introduction, *The Thornapple Commentary*, Baker (Grand Rapids), 1982.

more than do the rest of the gospel writers. Each has selected the data he thought important for his purposes and has written from a perspective that the Holy Spirit "moved" him to adopt. It is not our place to attempt to require of Matthew, or any other biblical writer, that he compose his book according to canons that seem more helpful to us. On the contrary, if we believe that the Spirit inerrantly worked in the writers of the Bible so as to produce works that at once are both His and that of the writer, we will be anxious to discover why the Spirit caused a writer to compose as he did and *learn* from Him rather than criticize his method (as too frequently modern commentators seem desirous of doing).

All-in-all, the Gospel of Matthew will challenge the understanding of counselors, as well as raise issues that they might not encounter else-where. Like all Scripture, it offers insight that a counselor cannot afford to do without. I hope that as you peruse its pages you will agree that it is eminently worthwhile to know and to use in counseling practice.

CHAPTER 1

1 A genealogical record of Jesus Christ, son of David, son of Abraham:

    2   Abraham was Isaac's father,

           Isaac was Jacob's father,

           Jacob was the father of Judah and his brothers,

    3   Judah was the father of Phares and Zerah by Tamar,

           Phares was Hezron's father,

           Hezron was Ram's father,

    4   Ram was Amminadab's father,

           Amminadab was Nahshon's father,

           Nahshon was Salmon's father,

    5   Salmon was the father of Boaz by Rahab,

           Boaz was the father of Obed by Ruth,

           Obed was Jesse's father,

    6   and Jesse was the father of David the king.

           David was the father of Solomon by Uriah's wife,

    7   Solomon was Rehoboam's father,

           Rehoboam was Abijah's father

           Abijah was Asa's father,

The title of this Gospel, like the titles of the others, was not a part of the original document that Matthew composed. The book actually contains a record of the sayings and the works of the Lord Jesus Christ during His ministry of 3 1/2 years.[1] But at the outset it does include something of His heritage and early days. Matthew was careful to include only that which served his purposes. There are no "interesting details" about the infancy of Christ, but there is a detailed genealogy (grouped in three sections) that leads the reader back to David and Abraham, showing His rich heritage and His royal line. It is interesting that such persons as Rahab, a prostitute, and Ruth, a Moabitess, are not omitted. That there is a place for repentance from sin and conversion from Paganism before God is surely emphasized by these inclusions.[2] It might be worthwhile mentioning this fact to counselees who, because of their sin, see little in their future to

---

1. The Gospel *emphasizes* the speeches and sayings of Jesus as compared to the things that He did.
2. Genealogies, which were of great importance to Jews, did not have to be complete; often they included only those persons who were significant to the

8	Asa was Jehoshaphat's father, Jehoshaphat was Joram's father, Joram was Uzziah's father,
9	Uzziah was Jotham's father, Jotham was Ahaz' father, Ahaz was Hezekiah's father,
10	Hezekiah was Manasseh's father, Manasseh was Amos' father, Amos was Josiah's father,
11	and Josiah was the father of Jeconiah and his brothers, at the time of the Babylonian exile.
12	After the Babylonian exile Jeconiah was Sheattiel's father, Sheattiel was Zerubbabel's father,
13	Zerubbabel was Abiud's father, Abiud was Eliakim's father, Eliakim was Azor's father,
14	Azor was Zadok's father, Zadok was Achim's father, Achim was Eliud's father,
15	Eliud was Eleazar's father, Eleazar was Matthan's father, Matthan was Jacob's father,
16	and Jacob was the father of Joseph, the husband of Mary, who was the mother of Jesus Who is called Christ.

look forward to.

According to verse 16, Joseph, whose lineage is recounted in the genealogy, was considered the father of Jesus only in the legal sense. The fact that he is designated **the husband of Mary**, rather than the father of Jesus (at the conclusion of a genealogy throughout which the phrase **the father of**[1] was dominant) is truly significant. Jesus was born of Mary, not Joseph.

That Jesus is unique is, thereby, signaled from the outset. Indeed, Matthew goes on to say that He was **called Christ**. The name **Christ** is the Greek translation of the Hebrew translation Messiah; both titles mean "The Anointed One." Prophets, priests, and kings were all anointed as a sign of induction into their respective offices. *The* **Christ** for which the

---

writer. These women could have been excluded, but were not. Obviously, Matthew had a purpose in mind in making sure that they were in this list.

1. Literally, so-and-so **begot** so-and-so.

17 So then, there were, in all, fourteen generations from David to the Babylonian exile, and fourteen generations from the Babylonian exile to Christ.

18 Now the birth of Jesus Christ happened this way. His mother Mary was engaged to Joseph, but before they began to live together, it was discovered that she was going to have a baby by the Holy Spirit.

Jews waited was the Anointed One *par excellence.* The term was used in both the Old Testament (cf. Psalm 2) and in intertestamental writings. The problem was that the Jews expected someone who would drive out the Romans and set up the Hebrew nation as the preeminent one in the world. Jesus had come for a different purpose—that is one of the factors that Matthew will be anxious to maintain. But, writing to Jews, he puts right up front the fact that Jesus was **called** the **Christ.** By stating it that way, he makes it clear that in this book he will set forth the truth about the Messiah. It is his intent to discuss this issue about which they had heard. He will take up Jesus' claim to Messiahship: is He the **Christ** or is He not?

It is normally proper to exhibit one's purpose at the outset. Counselors may learn from this—a practice that they will find to be the ordinary way in which biblical writers present their material. It seems that they often go out of their way to be up front about what they are doing. There should be no manipulation. Counselors correctly may withhold judgment on many issues at the beginning of their sessions (after all they must gather data before making judgments; cf. Proverbs 18: 13), but there is one thing about which they should be clear from the outset: they are about to engage in *Christian* (i.e., truly biblical) counseling. Counselees, like the readers of Matthew, should know from the beginning what it is they are getting into.[1]

In verses 18 through 25, we have an account of **the birth of Jesus Christ** from Joseph's point of view (just as Luke records the event from Mary's perspective). Interestingly, Matthew makes no bones about his belief that the claim of Jesus' Messiahship was valid; here, he clearly calls Him **the Christ** (v. 18). Matthew goes on to explain the extraordinary wording of verse 16. The reason for the unusual wording in this verse was

---

1. Not that one can say all that there is about such matters, but enough should be said that at some later point the counselee is not suddenly surprised about them. One way of doing this is by handing out a counseling agreement to be signed by the counselee that plainly states the overall purpose and method of the counseling to which he is committing himself.

19   Joseph, her husband, a just man, didn't want to make a public example of her, so he decided to divorce her secretly.

---

that a truly extraordinary event had occurred. Matthew then relates the facts about this event.

Mary and **Joseph** were an **engaged** couple who, according to the proper practice of the Jews, were not living together as man and wife (v. 18). But during the nine month period of the engagement it was discovered that Mary was pregnant. Ordinarily, this would lead to a divorce or her stoning. But this was an extraordinary event, as we noted: the child was a **baby by the Holy Spirit**. The title **Holy Spirit** was not unfamiliar to the Jews; not only was the Person of God so described in the Old Testament, but also throughout the intertestamental period. This designation made it clear to every Jew who read, that Matthew was attributing the pregnancy to the power of God rather than to any mere human agency. Counselors, too, must be sure that the language they use in counseling sessions is intelligible to their counselees.

This claim of a virgin birth needed to be explicated. And that is precisely what Matthew does. **Joseph** loved Mary, and though he must have been deeply hurt by what he learned and Mary's obvious denials, nevertheless he determined not to make a **public example** of her, deciding to **divorce her secretly**. There is something not only charitable about Joseph, but also tender in his treatment of Mary. Perhaps, though we are told nothing about it, he was mildly troubled by Mary's undoubted protests that she had not had sexual relations with anyone. How one would go about secretly divorcing another we do not understand (though the ordinary procedure is related in Deuteronomy 24), not knowing enough about the customs of the period. That a divorce was needed, and that it was possible among the Jews for infractions of God's law such as that which this was supposed to be, is certain.

Joseph's contemplated action is commended as **just** by the Holy Spirit writing through Matthew. That all **divorce** is wrong, therefore, is certainly not biblical. Counselors may use this passage to make that point. The erroneous "no divorce" view was propagated in post-New Testament times during the Middle Ages; the Bible knows nothing of it. That it was necessary for engaged couples to obtain a divorce in order to break the engagement, shows that in the understanding of the times an engagement was as binding as marriage itself. In fact, it seems that it was considered

20 But during the time he was reflecting upon these matters, by a dream an angel appeared to him, saying, "Joseph, son of David, don't be afraid to take Mary, your wife, because what is conceived in her is by the Holy Spirit.
21 She will give birth to a Son, and you must name Him Jesus, because He will save His people from their sins."
22 Now all this happened in fulfillment of what the Lord spoke by the prophet, saying:
23   **The virgin will conceive and give birth to a Son, and they will call Him by His name Emmanuel** (which means "God with us").

---

the first stage of a marriage.[1] While we have no command to follow this Hebrew custom, counselors might point out how serious it is to break an engagement. It is better not to get engaged in the first place than to break it and treat it as lightly as many do today.

Joseph **reflected** on what he had been told by Mary, and seemed reticent to proceed with the divorce (v. 20). Rather than storming off in a rage, as many counselees might, he gave mature thought to what was going on. And he was rewarded for this by the visitation of an angel who, in a dream, explained what had happened. The angel confirmed the fact that Mary had not had intercourse with anyone, but that the child Mary was carrying was **conceived by the Holy Spirit**. There was to be no **fear**, therefore, on his part, about taking Mary, **his wife**, to live with her as husband and wife. When God gives directions, regardless of how difficult they may seem, regardless of the consequences (social or otherwise) a counselee is to obey. God won't send messages to your counselee by angels, but all they need to know for life and godliness as found in the Bible. If the Scriptures command, one must obey. Joseph obeyed (v. 24).

Not only a clear explanation of the particulars of Jesus' conception but also some directions about the baby were given to Joseph. The baby was to be given a name, **Jesus**, which means "Yahweh saves." As the angel explained, the purpose of Jesus' coming into the world is summed up in this name: **He will save His people from their sins** (v. 21). A simpler statement of the good news is hard to find. It is always appropriate to see if a counselee understands the gospel. He ought to be able to put it in terms like these.

Then the angel referred to the Old Testament prediction of this marvelous event: **A virgin will conceive and give birth to a Son, and they**

---

1. That is why Mary could be called Joseph's **wife** (v. 20).

24 When Joseph woke from sleep, he did what the angel from the Lord ordered, and took Mary, his wife.
25 But he had no sexual relations with her until she had given birth to a Son, Whom he named Jesus.

---

will call Him by His Name Emmanuel (which, Matthew explains to those who were no longer familiar with Hebrew, means **God with us**). Matthew records the revealing words of the angel that this is no ordinary birth just as plainly as John does in his prologue, in which Jesus is said to be God manifest in the flesh. The Child was conceived directly by God without a human father, and He would be, according to the second Name given to Him, **God** coming to be **with** His people to save them from their sins. The reasons for Jesus' birth and His advent are clearly set forth here. The "good news" did not originate with Paul as some have theorized. The message first was spoken by an angel echoing Old Testament prophesy!

Joseph's obedience to the angel's several commands is noted in verses 24 and 25. The compliance of this man under these trying circumstances tells us that counselees, faced with problems, unresolved questions, and deep hurt, need not wait to obey God's commands until such a time as they "feel" like it. The record makes it clear that he did what he was directed to do immediately. That sort of cooperation from counselees makes counseling a breeze; difficulty comes when counselees hesitate, linger, and prolong obedience. When they offer excuses for delay, counseling then takes a different turn. Now counsel is needed about why it is sinful to delay rather than obey. Joseph's example demonstrates that obedience is possible even in very trying circumstances.

CHAPTER 2

1 Now after the birth of Jesus in Bethlehem of Judea, in the days when Herod was king, Magi from the East arrived at Jerusalem, asking,

2 "Where is the One Who is born to be King of the Jews? We ask because we saw His star in the East and we came to worship Him."

The second chapter is about the Lord Jesus' early days on this earth. It is an exceptional chapter in that it weaves together Old Testament prophecies as they relate to the events of these days and shows us something of the ways of God with men. The coming of the Magi and Jesus' escape from the clutches of Herod are of great importance to understanding the Lord's early background.

That **Magi** (astronomers and astrologers of the period from Persia or Babylon) came at this time is understandable. Presumably, they put together the widespread notion that a Ruler of the world would come from the Jews[1] at this time (an idea that was abroad in all the East) with the appearance of a "star" that they associated with Him, calling it **His star** (v. 2). First, it is significant that Daniel, who predicted the coming of Christ (Daniel 9), was in close touch with Babylonian Magi of his time. From his Book, as the prophecy was passed down through the ages, they learned of it, probably looked forward to its fulfillment, and spread the idea abroad. Then, as they studied the stars and encountered an extraordinary light in the sky (that they called a **star**), a phenomenon that they could not otherwise account for, they assumed that it heralded the coming of the expected Ruler. It is possible also that some other revelation was given to them about which we know nothing—but the text seems to indicate that it was the star that motivated them to begin their journey. That it was no ordinary star is clear from the fact that it went before them and then stood over the place where Jesus was (v. 9).[2]

In this story (vv. 1-12) we see how God provided for everything. Joseph and Mary were humble peasants. Doubtless they had little money, the bulk of which they had already expended in traveling to Bethlehem. Now it would be necessary for them to relocate and live for a time in Egypt, a trip of some 75 to 100 miles away (depending on where in Egypt

---

1. See Suetonius, *Vespasian* ch. 4; Tacitus 5:13.
2. Obviously, no ordinary star or conjunction of planets explains this action of the light.

3   But upon hearing this, King Herod became upset, and all Jerusalem with him.
4   So he assembled all the chief priests and scribes of the people and inquired of them where the Christ was to be born.
5   And they told him, "In Bethlehem of Judea; this is what the prophet wrote:
6   **And you, Bethlehem, of the land of Judea, are in no way least among the rulers of Judah; since out of you will come a Ruler Who will shepherd My people Israel."**

---

they ultimately resided). How would they do so? The coming of the Magi, foreshadowing the coming faith of the Gentiles when the gospel would go into all the world, also provided the wherewithal necessary for Mary and Joseph's flight into Egypt. The **gifts** that they brought to Jesus were expensive and could later be sold for quite a sum of money to finance the trip to and the subsequent stay in Egypt.

When things seem desperate to a counselee, he should remember the gracious ways of God toward His own. He often provides in a manner that one least expects. From this account they also could be shown how God ties many things together in order to bring about His will. God is not an absent God Who started it all only to go off to do His own thing. The Bible doesn't teach deism. Ours is a God Who not only superintends His creation, but also guides His story His way for His purposes. Often in the most unlikely and unexpected ways, He brings about events that just exactly meet the needs of His children. With a God like that, no Christian counselee should despair or doubt. He should rather expect and look for God's providential workings in his life. Show counselees that the Christian life should be an exciting adventure one takes with God.

Herod was a wicked man who was jealous of his position. He was so afraid of losing the kingship that he put his own two sons to death to prohibit them from taking the throne from him. That he was capable of killing the few two-year-old children in Bethlehem is not surprising given his character. His lies to the Magi and his duplicity were typical of him as he is known from sources outside of the Scriptures.

The interesting thing is that the religious leaders of Israel also knew where Jesus was to be born (vv. 5, 6), yet they made no effort to find Him or worship Him. It was pagans who were drawn to Him by God at His birth. So often similar things happen today. Counselees will sometimes find that the very people who ought to be helping them learn and do what the Bible requires, know God's will but refuse to follow through on that

7   Then Herod secretly called the Magi and asked them to tell him at exactly what time the star had appeared.

8   Then he sent them to Bethlehem and said, "Go and make careful inquiries about the child, and when you find him, report to me so that I too may come and worship him."

9   After listening to the king, they started out on their trip and, there it was—the star that they had seen in the East. And it went before them until it stopped over the place where the Child was.

10   When they saw the star they were thrilled with joy.

11   Entering the house, they saw the Child with His mother Mary, and fell down and worshiped Him. Then, opening their treasures, they offered to Him gifts of gold and incense and myrrh.

12   But because they were warned by a dream not to return to Herod, they departed for their country by another route.

13   Now when they had departed, an angel from the Lord appeared to Joseph by a dream, saying, "Get up and take the Child and His mother and escape to Egypt, and stay there until I tell you otherwise; Herod is about to look for the Child to destroy Him."

14   So he got up and took the Child and His mother during the night and departed for Egypt.

---

knowledge. It is disconcerting to discover that it is sometimes humble, new converts to which one must turn to find help and direction in such circumstances rather than to those steeped in biblical lore. But if it is biblical, a teaching is correct, regardless of the source. Herod and these Jewish leaders were **upset** (already the religious leaders were beginning to have problems with the coming Messiah), and as the word got around, **all Jerusalem with them** (v. 3). Yet we read nothing of a mass exodus to Bethlehem (such as that which attended the preaching of John the Baptist) to see and worship the Lord. The enthusiasm of new converts often is stronger than that of those who think that they know all that they need to know. They think that they have it made; they need no one to upset their neat little packaging of the facts. Counselees should be made aware of this and not be disturbed by it. They should, however, take care not to soon join these persons in their lethargy and self-satisfaction. Counselors will run up against these sinful traits in counselees and will discover that until repentance occurs, no progress can be made in other matters.

The flight to and return from Egypt paralleled the coming of Israel **from Egypt** (v. 15). After Mary and Joseph heard of the death of Herod, it was time for them to return to Palestine. But Archelaus, who was not much better than Herod, was now in power, so Joseph took his little fam-

15 And he stayed there until Herod's death. This happened so that the Word spoken by the Lord through the prophet when He said, "I called My Son from Egypt," might be fulfilled.

16 Then, when Herod saw that he had been tricked by the Magi, he became extremely angry, and he sent out orders to kill all the boys in Bethlehem and all of the territory that surrounds it, who were two years old or less, in keeping with the time that by his exact inquiries he had heard from the Magi.

17 Then what was spoken through the prophet Jeremiah was fulfilled:

18   **A sound was heard in Ramah,**
    Wailing and loud mourning;
    Rachel weeping over her children,
    and refusing to be comforted
    because they are gone.

19 At Herod's death, an angel from the Lord appeared to Joseph in Egypt by a dream, saying:

20 "Get up, take the Child and His mother and go into the land of Israel; those who were after the Child's life are dead."

21 So he got up, took the Child and His mother and went to the land of Israel.

---

ily to Nazareth ("the place of the shoot, or root," a name that spoke of the Messiah) in Galilee, which was not under Archelaus' jurisdiction. Jesus grew up here and was thus called a **Nazarene**.

As I have indicated, God was in control. That one great fact is clear in the passage. Another is that no matter how the devil and his crowd attempt to block the work of God, they eventually are thwarted by His control over life and its happenings. God is still working out His will among men. He will not be hindered by anyone or anything. Assure counselees of this fact. Finally, note how God perfectly arranged things to bring about all that He wished in the infancy of Christ. Help counselees understand that God is in control of their circumstances—whether this is immediately apparent or not.

New Gentile converts came out of heathen religions and worshipped the Savior at His birth (either on the occasion or two years later), instead of the religious leaders of Jerusalem, the city of God; this is sad but prophetic of the great change that was coming. There is no reason to doubt that He came to His own, but His own people received Him not. Yet, to as many as received Him He gave the right to be called the sons of God (John 1:11, 12). The same is true today. But it is also true that, as Paul warned, the unnatural branches may be broken off because of pride and

22 But when he heard that Archelaus was ruling Judea instead of his father Herod, he was afraid to go there; and being warned by a dream he departed for the regions of Galilee.

23 When he arrived, he settled down in a city called Nazareth, so that the Word spoken by the prophets, "He will be called a Nazarene," was fulfilled.

---

unbelief (Romans 11:21). Knowing this about people will help counselees understand why there are so many faults among those in the church. The prevalence of such unbelief excuses no one, but it should help them to look not at the leaders who may let them down, but at the Savior Who never does. Often counselees will use the failures of church leaders to excuse their own failures saying, "If he can't, how do you expect me to?" That line is to be utterly rejected. Instead, make it clear that each one is to accept his own responsibility before God—regardless of what others (even leaders) may or may not do. And God can raise up others as He wills—even "Magi" (the least expected persons you could imagine)—to accomplish His purposes. The makings of a philosophy of history are in this chapter. If you can only grasp the principles behind what Matthew writes, you will greatly encourage your counselees in sessions where everything seems to be going haywire. In brief, history is His story!

CHAPTER 3

1 Now in those days John the Baptist appeared preaching in the Jordan desert, saying:
2 "Repent, for the empire from the heavens is at hand."

In chapter three we encounter **John the Baptist**. John's mission was to prepare the way for Christ. The fact that God raised up an "advance man" to go before the Messiah and alert the population to His coming once more signals the *importance* of the One Who was coming. But more than that, it was His call for a people who would be ready to hear the words of life that He would proclaim. John readied those people by **preaching in the Jordan desert** a message that commanded men to **repent, for the empire from the heavens is at hand** (vv. 1, 2). As Plummer says, it was as if John excommunicated the entire nation and called them into God's continuing (but different) rule from the **heavens** through the acknowledgment of their sins and the need to turn from them to the Savior.

Repentance (the New Testament word which means "to rethink, to change your mind" together with the Old Testament term that means "to turn around") is the act by which John commanded people to think differently about God, themselves, and the way of salvation. It was the solution to the problem highlighted in Isaiah 55:8 where we are told that our ways and our thoughts are not God's ways and thoughts. We must change both and bring them into conformity to His Word. God will not change His thoughts and ways to conform to ours!

The reason for John's call was that the coming fifth world **empire** of Daniel's prophecies was **at hand** (cf. Daniel 2, 7). This was the empire which came **from the heavens**: one that is not like those that preceded, which existed for only a time and then were given over to others. This would be the everlasting rule of God in the hearts and minds of men. It was the empire that would be given to His Son by the Ancient of Days, the empire which eventually would fill the whole earth that would be like a **stone** not carved out by hands, but by God. John clearly taught that with the coming of the Messiah a new era was dawning.

The preparation of counselees by repentance, which is essential for making any change that pleases God, is necessary for counselors to understand. People who come for counseling rarely come expecting to be called

3   This is the one about whom Isaiah the prophet spoke, saying:

> **A voice shouting in the desert: "Prepare the road for the Lord; make His paths straight."**

4 Now about the man himself—John had clothes made of camel's hair, and around his waist was a leather belt, and his food was locusts and wild honey.

5   At that time Jerusalem, all Judea and the whole Jordan River region went out to him,

6   and were baptized by him at the Jordan River, confessing their sins.

---

upon to repent of their lifestyles. Even "Christian" counseling books rarely mention repentance. Too often counselees blame others for their problems. Too often they stand pat in their ways. But if they can be shown that their **ways** are not God's ways, and that their **thoughts** are not God's, then they may be ready to repent. It is the counselor's task to call counselees to repentance whenever this is appropriate.[1] To bring people to repentance often requires the sort of message that we shall see recounted below.

Matthew quotes Isaiah (v. 3) who predicted that John's ministry would resemble a **voice shouting in the desert**. While Jesus was the *Word*, John was but a *voice*. That he was **shouting** meant that he must awaken people to their need. The voice of the counselor is also often an awakening voice for lethargic Christians. That John preached in the **desert**, wore rugged **clothes**, and lived off of an austere diet spoke of the desolate spiritual condition of the people to whom he was sent. The man himself was a message. The congregation to which he preached, as a whole, was a virtual desert. Others, who had any life at all, lived a skimpy spiritual diet. Many in the church today might be described similarly. John's message, like his appearance, was a rugged one, as we shall see.

The results of his preaching were phenomenal. He was a huge success (vv. 5, 6). Counselors today, who are willing to "tell it like it is," will also find success among members of the church who have been awaiting a message of the sort. Too many today pamper and pander to their counselees rather than tell them the truth about their lives before God. John was not a man to cater to people or to trim God's message for the sake of popularity. In the end, of course, you must remember, John lost his head for his frankness in preaching. Counselors, likewise, are not exempt from reprisals that may come their way for telling the truth.

---

1. Of course, not every counselee needs to repent. But many (perhaps most) do.

7 But when he saw many of the Pharisees and Sadducees coming for baptism, he said to them:

You brood of vipers—who warned you to flee from the wrath that is coming?

8   Bear fruit that is in keeping with repentance.

John's task was to **prepare the road for the Lord; to make His paths straight** (v. 3). The picture in those words is of a pick and shovel crew going out to prepare the road that an emperor was about to travel. Gullies would have to be filled and bumps smoothed out. Similarly, the bumps of pride and self-satisfaction and the potholes of sin would have to be dealt with so that the Messiah could ride smoothly into the hearts of the people. Repentance requires the confession of sins (cf. v. 6[b]). When John baptized people who **confessed**, the baptism symbolized their purification from sin.[1] In this way it was a negative baptism. However, One would follow, Who would also baptize with a Spirit baptism that would unite men to Him in His new Empire from the heavens.

What John said to those who came for **baptism**, that led either to repentance or rejection of his ministry, is recalled in verses 7 through 12. As I have been saying, John did not trim his sails. He preached judgment. The message to the religious leaders was straightforward; John called them a **brood of vipers** (v. 7). That is strong language. Jesus would echo it later on (ch. 23). John Broadus says it describes the **Pharisees and Sadducees** as "odious." To that description I would hasten to add that they were also characterized by this description as dangerous; their teaching was poisonous—deadly. There comes a time when a counselor must confront those who spread lies and falsehood and who live hypocritical lives. Perhaps some will believe (John seems to hold out hope even for *them* as he exhorts them to a new, genuine lifestyle: v. 8). He is amazed to find religious leaders among those seeking baptism. He intimates by his question (v. 7) that destruction would soon come upon the nation: the **wrath** of God would be poured out in a few short years on Jerusalem. And at death, they would find the eternal wrath of God awaiting them. There is a place in counseling for warning about God's judgment when you suspect that the counselee may not be a Christian after all. Too much so-called evangelism consists of trying to meet "felt needs" or adding Jesus as a helpful adjunct to one's life. John makes it clear that coming to Jesus as Savior is

---

1. Cf. John 3:25, 26. Purification (or cleansing) was an Old Testament ritual.

9   Don't think that you can say among yourselves, "We have Abraham for our father." I tell you that God can raise up children for Abraham from these stones!
10   Even now the axe is laid at the root of the trees, so that every tree that doesn't bear fine fruit is going to be cut down and thrown into the fire.

---

a matter of shaking up one's entire life. When that is needed, counselor, don't settle for less.

Furthermore John says: **Bear fruit that is in keeping with repentance** (v. 8). I have pointed out that repentance has two fundamental elements: a change of mind leading to a change of lifestyle. Here John shows that the two are inseparable. If repentance is genuine it will inevitably lead to the **fruit** of the Spirit, which means a life that is consistent with a change of mind. Counselees who are willing to settle for Jesus as a mere addition to their lives will not happily hear this. They will want to go on living as they have in the past with whatever Jesus can contribute to make their lives more pleasant. That is not His way. When He truly changes a person's thinking, the change is so vital that it always leads to a radical change in a person's living.

The religious leaders (and because of their false teaching, the people also) believed that all Jews would be saved merely because of their heritage. John begs to differ (v. 9). He says that to think one is saved by being a lineal descendent of Abraham is erroneous. Salvation is an individual thing; it is not corporate. To believe that because he is a member of a denomination or congregation a counselee will be saved is an illusion. Anyone who thinks that way must be told otherwise. As John said, "**God can raise up children for Abraham from these stones.**" He is not dependent upon those who have grown up in a church, who are of a particular ethnic background, or anything else. God can raise up His family of faith out of the most unlikely materials (here described as **stones**). Indeed, He would soon do just that; to the astonishment of the Jews, He would bring Gentiles into His church. Counselees who think that they are God's gift to the universe should be told to think again. He needs no one. He is dependent on none of us. Rather we need Him; we are utterly dependent on Him!

Verse 10 speaks of the coming judgment on Jerusalem (70 AD). This is clear from the fact that John saw the judgment of which he speaks as right around the corner: *Even now* **the axe is laid at the root of the trees**.

> **11** I baptize you with water upon repentance, but the One Who is coming after me is mightier than I; I am not worthy to carry His sandals. He will baptize you with the Holy Spirit and fire.
>
> 12 His shovel is in His hand and He will thoroughly clean up His threshing floor. He will gather His wheat into the barn, but the chaff He will burn with unquenchable fire.
>
> **13** At that time Jesus arrived from Galilee at the Jordan to be baptized by him.
>
> 14 But he tried to stop Him, saying: "I need to be baptized by You; and You come to me?"
>
> 15 But Jesus answered by saying to him, "Allow it to take place for now, since it is proper for us to fulfill all righteousness." Then he allowed Him to come.

The image here is that the woodsman is about to strike the tree a deadly blow (to chop out the root is to kill the tree). The axe is laid at the place where the blow will be aimed. The lumberman would then raise it and bring it down on the place that he had thus indicated. Time for repentance runs out. That is John's message. There can be no delay. **Even now**, or as we say "even as I speak," the woodsman is taking aim. This is no time to procrastinate. There is often a need to stress urgency in counseling. Many counselees want to put things off. When God commands, it is time to obey (as we saw in the first chapter with Joseph).

Judgment is, as always, based on works (v. 10). If there is no fruit, the tree will be cut down and burned. The believer is saved by grace through his faith. But his saving faith will be evidenced by his works (fruit). That is exactly what James says. No one is saved by works, but no one who is saved will fail to exhibit it by his works.

John contrasts his baptism with that of Jesus Christ (v. 11). John's was with **water** on the basis of **repentance**. Jesus' baptism will be **with the Spirit and fire** (cf. Acts 2 where we read of the first fulfillment of this promise). The one baptism was negative, having to do with purification through repentance; on the other hand, Jesus' also contained a positive element, having to do with being baptized into Christ and His church (cf. Romans 6:3; I Corinthians 12:13). John's baptism, therefore, was not equal to the baptism of Christ.[1] Again in verse 12 an urgent warning is issued: note that Christ's **shovel is *in His hand***. That is to say, He is ready

---

1. That is why at Ephesus the disciples of John needed to be rebaptized (Acts 19:1-5).

16 Now when Jesus was baptized, He immediately went away from the water, and then the heavens were opened, and He saw God's Spirit descending like a dove, coming upon Him.
17 Then there was a voice from the heavens, saying: "This is My Son Whom I love, in Whom I am well pleased."

---

to use it to separate the **wheat** from the **chaff**; this is another allusion to the destruction of Jerusalem which, unlike eternal judgment, *was* at hand.

We turn now to the baptism of Jesus Christ (vv. 13-17). John rightly understood that Jesus needed no cleansing and therefore needed no baptism of repentance. But Jesus had something else in mind in seeking baptism from John. He was about to undertake His ministry. He had to be set aside for it, and appointed as the Messiah. This was what He meant by **fulfilling all righteousness** (v. 15). The anointing with the Spirit that immediately followed the baptism with water indicated that this baptism was more than a ritual. John's baptisms prior to this led to no such effect. Here, however, God was doing something exceptional. In addition to the water that symbolized it, the Lord sent His Spirit upon Jesus to consecrate and empower Him for the ministry that would follow. This was no baptism of repentance. There was no confession of sin; rather, the Father sent the Spirit upon Jesus and the Father verbally confessed His pleasure in His **Son** Whom He now officially constituted as the Messiah (v. 17).

The chapters that follow will have even much more to offer than these first three wonderful ones. But those that follow will have much more to offer. Recognizing that, we shall now turn to them with eager anticipation.

CHAPTER 4

> **1** Then Jesus was led by the Spirit into the desert to be tested by the devil.

The **Spirit** did it! The very same Spirit Who set Him aside and empowered Him for ministry **led** Jesus **into the desert to be tested by the devil.** It is possible, therefore, that prior to embarking on some worthwhile activity for the Lord He will lead you, or your counselee, into temptation too. One answer to the "Why?" a counselee may pose could readily be "Possibly because God has some important task(s) for you to perform." That should make a counselee sit up and take notice. If the Lord Jesus was not exempt from temptation, why would His disciples think that they should be? That is a question to put to those who wonder.

But, of course, the Lord Jesus went on to do the many things that He accomplished *only after He successfully passed the test!* That too is important to stress. It was, doubtless, the Spirit Who **led** Who also enabled the Lord Jesus to **withstand** the temptations that came His way. Your counselee possesses the very same Spirit. Remind him of that fact as well.

The word translated **testing** is the same word that in other places is translated "temptation." The translation depends on the context. Because there is only one term that is used to set forth both ideas we may learn something from the biblical usage that is important to our understanding of temptation (testing). Every test is also a temptation; every temptation is also a test. It all depends on whether you view the event from the purpose and perspective of the Lord, or whether you view it from the purpose and perspective of the devil. God is testing your counselee in order to strengthen him for future service. If he passes the test he will be more able to enter into work ahead. At the same time the devil wants to bring him down in the test; he is tempting him to sin in order to weaken him so that he will be unable to accomplish those tasks. That is the important understanding to have in mind. Because of the Lord's purpose, your counselee can say with James that he counts it wholly joy whenever he falls into various temptations (testings). A clear explanation of this is often very helpful to counselees so they can understand what they are enduring. Of course, if the trouble they encounter is of their own making, they cannot say that they are merely being tempted by Satan or tested by God

2   After fasting forty days and forty nights, He was hungry,

3   and the one who was testing Him came and said, "If you are God's Son, order these stones to become bread."

(cf. James 1:13). That is another matter altogether. And, remember, the devil is but an (unwilling) agent of God, whom He uses providentially to serve His ends. Nothing that he does is out of the control of the heavenly Father. All that he does God ultimately turns to His own glory and your counselee's good.

As you can see from the fact that the sinless Lord was **tempted**, temptation is not sin. One sins when he yields to temptation. First the yielding is a matter of the heart, in which the sinner gives assent to the temptation. Whether he follows through or not, he needs to repent of the sin of giving assent to sin. If the sin is a heart matter alone, he is to deal with God alone. If he goes on to sin outwardly in concert with the heart sin, he may also have to seek forgiveness from those whom he has wronged. If, for instance, a counselee has sinful sexual thoughts toward another, but has made no advances toward her/him, the matter must be dealt with before God. He should not go to the other party who is unaware of the fact to confess to her/him. That could cause more trouble than it settles. But if there were outward advances (words, actions) of which the other person was aware, then seeking forgiveness of that person is required.[1]

In addition, we learn in Matthew 4 that the devil tempts at the point of human need; it was after forty days of fasting that the temptations took place (cf. vv. 2, 3). When in a weakened condition, therefore, a counselee should be especially wary of his vulnerability. Times of sleeplessness or sickness, financial setbacks or sorrow, ought to be seasons of special watchfulness for temptation. Counselees need to be made aware of this strategy of the evil one. At such times, for instance, a counselee may protest, "I don't feel like coming for counseling." You, or your secretary who answers the phone, must insist that this is precisely when he needs the most to come. In such times you can best instruct, encourage, and strengthen him—which is what he needs.

Notice also that the temptations took place in the **desert**. The word refers to a lonely place. There was no one else to whom the Lord could turn for encouragement except to His heavenly Father. Counselees will

---

1. For details about forgiveness, see my book *From Forgiven to Forgiving.*

4   But in response He said, "It is written, **A person can't sustain life on bread alone, but he must live on every Word that comes from God's mouth.**"

---

find themselves tempted in similar situations.[1] At such times they too must learn to turn for help to God and for directions to His Word. Notice that Jesus met every temptation with an appropriate biblical passage. His constant rejoinder was **it is written** (vv. 4, 7, 10). After Jesus fully resisted the devil, he finally left Him (v. 11). It was only then that God sent angels to minister to Him. Often the help one wishes for comes only after one successfully has dealt with temptation. That, too, ought to be communicated to a counselee.

Consider each of the three temptations themselves. The first was the temptation to make bread out of stones (vv. 3, 4). This temptation was leveled at the Lord in His present physical condition having fasted for forty days. Jesus responded scripturally that there are two kinds of **bread**: that which sustains the body and that which sustains the spiritual life. The latter is God's Word. Many counselees are weak and emaciated spiritually because of their lack of spiritual nourishment. Getting counselees into regular Bible study is, then, of the utmost importance to their lives.[2] You might recommend that from the first session counselees begin to engage in a regular study of the Scriptures.

Notice, too, that Jesus didn't say, "Wait a minute until I look up the pertinent Scriptural passage" when responding to temptation. He knew His Bible well enough to be able to pull out the appropriate passage to meet the temptation. Learning the Bible, so as to turn it into portable truth, is important. I have written elsewhere about the use of proverbs, which are of special help in this regard.[3] Divine principles are compacted into a brief proverb that is often attached to one picturesque application of that principle that makes it easy to retain and carry with you. Here the verse that Jesus quotes is similar; it pictures a person eating spiritual food. For that reason it was not only memorable but also appropriate because the particular temptation had to do with hunger and food.

---

1. Perhaps in a motel with the availability of pornographic movies.
2. One means of doing so is by encouraging them to use the book, *What to do on Thursday,* which is a Bible study guide that teaches a method of moving from problems to biblical solutions. One needs to know his Bible in times of temptation so that, like Jesus, he can call up appropriate Scripture to meet it.
3. See my commentary on *Proverbs* in this series.

5   Then the devil took Him into the holy city and stood Him on the wing
of the temple
6   and said to Him: "If you are God's Son, throw yourself down; it is
written, **He will give orders to His angels about You and they will hold
You by their hands so that You won't strike Your foot against a stone**."
7   Jesus said to him: "Again, it is written, **You must not put the Lord
your God to the test**."
8   Again the devil took Him to a very high mountain and showed Him all
the world's kingdoms and their glory:
9   and he said to Him, "I shall give you all of them if you will fall down
and worship me."
10   Then Jesus said to him, "Get out of here, Satan! It is written, 'You
must worship the Lord your God, and you shall serve Him alone.'"

Many temptations counselees face will pertain to the needs and
desires of the physical body. The devil is really rather dull. While it is true
in superficial differences that the truth is one but error has many forms,
beneath that error you can discern the same old tactics that the devil used
in the Garden of Eden. Here we see his appeal to the desirability of food
as he did when confronting Eve. Handling desires for physical satisfaction, so prominent a motivation in our day, is one area in which counselees must be shored up. Mention such matters and discuss them in the light
of this passage, the temptation in the Garden and I John 2:16.

In the second temptation (vv. 5-7) the promises of God would unnecessarily be put to the test. The devil, taking his cue from the Lord, also
quotes the Scriptures. Make a name for yourself, he says in effect, by
throwing yourself from the wing of the temple and showing how God will
rescue you from harm by His angels. The Lord counters with Scripture
that teaches one must not take unnecessary risks. Yes, the promise is
there, but it is not to be presumed upon. One must not put himself in
harm's way unnecessarily, thus **putting God to the test**. The desire to
exalt one's self by heroics in the face of artificially structured risks in
which the promises of God are relied upon in ways He never intended, is
taboo. We are not to put ourselves in dangerous positions that can be
avoided. This is especially true when we do so to gain the applause of
men.

The third temptation is to gain good ends by evil means. Only God is
to be **worshipped**. One cannot bow to the devil in any way, shape or
form—even to attain a "good" result. Jesus had come to bring people
from all the world into His kingdom *through the cross*. The devil offers to

11 Then the devil left Him, and angels came and waited on Him.

12 Now when He heard that John had been arrested, He departed for Galilee.

13 Leaving Nazareth, He came to Capernaum beside the sea, in the districts of Zebulun and Naphtali, and lived there,

14 so that Isaiah's prophecy might be fulfilled:

15   **Land of Zebulun and Land of Naphtali, along the road of the sea, beyond the Jordan, Galilee of the Gentiles;**

---

give Him these kingdoms of the world in an easier way—by means of a detour around the cross. That Satan had the right to grant this is clear. It was a genuine temptation that Jesus faced. Since wresting Adam's dominion from him, the evil one had become the "god of this world." Jesus would regain that dominion by His death, resurrection, and ascension (cf. Colossians 2:13-15). Had He agreed to the devil's arrangement, in the long run there would have been no worldwide kingdom of Christ, since no one would have been saved. Because He successfully resisted the devil, he left. When a counselee does this as well, he too will discover that the evil one will leave (cf. James 4:7).

Every counselor should be familiar with the subject of temptation. He should know well what James says about it, what John teaches in his first letter, what happened in the Garden, and what took place here. Knowing these passages cold will fortify him for most counseling experiences that involve temptation.

Matthew now turns from the temptation narrative to the **preaching** of Jesus (vv. 12-17). **John the Baptist** was arrested and imprisoned, eventually to be put to death—all over the bitterness, fear, licentiousness, and violence of persons whose sin he had exposed. Hearing of John's arrest, Jesus went North to Galilee where He settled, making **Capernaum** His headquarters. This was the most important city in the lake district. It was a center for the fishing industry and was located on an important road. There were many Gentiles in the area mingled among the Jewish population. From here, His popularity spread far and wide (vv. 24, 25).

His move to the region was also another **fulfillment** of **prophecy** (vv. 14-15). There was **darkness** of sin and ignorance and death which He, as the **Light** of the world, began to dispel. He brought the light of truth and salvation by His preaching, like the dawning of daylight upon travelers who were hunkered down somewhere in danger of death, having been overtaken by **darkness** before reaching their destination (v. 16).

It is interesting that the message that Jesus preached was identical to

16   **the people sitting in darkness have seen a great light, and on those sitting in a land of the shadow of death a light has dawned.**

17   From that time Jesus began to preach and say, "Repent; the empire from the heavens is at hand."

   18   As He walked along the Sea of Galilee, He saw two brothers, Simon (who is called Peter) and his brother Andrew, throwing a net into the sea (they were fishermen).

19   And He said to them, "Come, follow Me and I will make you fishers of men."

20   Immediately, they left their nets and followed Him.

   21   Now, going along from there, He saw two other brothers, James, Zebedee's son, and his brother John, in a boat with their father Zebedee, mending their nets. And He called them.

22   Immediately, they left the boat and their father, and followed Him.

---

that of John: "**Repent, the empire from the heavens is at hand**" (v. 17). There is a consistency here that is not to be missed.[1] How strange today that so little is said about repentance! How sad that people who need to repent are seldom told to. In your ministry of counseling be clear about the need for repentance. Moreover, how little is said about the church (the empire from the heavens), which Jesus came to found. Since the Darby-ites the church has been looked down upon as hopeless and ineffective, an institution almost to be despised. But we shall see in chapter 16 that Jesus thought differently about it. In all your counseling be sure that you emphasize the need for counselees to become faithful members of a congregation of God's people who serve and worship Him corporately. They must also submit to the authority of Christ vested in the elders of His church (Hebrews 13:17).

   The calling of the disciples to full time discipleship is recorded next (vv. 18-22). Two pairs of brothers who were fishermen are mentioned at this time. Notice how, in what are now famous and memorable words, He tells them to leave fishing for the greater catch: "**Come, follow Me and I will make you fishers of men**" (v. 19). Their immediate response, putting Him before work and family, is noted in verse 22. One wonders whether those nets that they left ever got mended (v. 21)! It is interesting that Jesus

---

1. When we come to the book of Acts, we shall see that the apostles also preached the kingdom. The only difference is that what John and Jesus preached as at hand, after the death and ascension of Christ to the throne, they preached as having come.

23 And He went all over Galilee, teaching in their synagogs, preaching the good news about the empire and curing every sort of disease and illness among the people.
24 A report about Him went out to all of Syria, and they brought to Him all the sick who were suffering from various diseases and painful illnesses, demoniacs, epileptics and paralytics, and He healed them.
25 Large crowds from Galilee, the Decapolis, Jerusalem, Judea, and from the Jordan followed Him.

---

called none of the religious leaders, none of the intellectuals of the land. Those He called were principally working men, what we would call blue collar types. This call to discipleship was a call to constant companionship with Jesus, by which the disciples would learn by being with Him every bit as much as by learning what He taught (cf. 11:28).

Sometimes the intellectuals will hem and haw in response to the truths that you teach them. They will debate and argue. They will spend a lot of time "thinking" about their responsibilities—and accomplish nothing. While it is not true of every intellectual, that is his temptation. On the other hand, the more simple, uncomplicated mind of the working man may respond more readily. At any rate, watch out for the pondering hesitation of the intellectual which, at the end of the day, may turn into an excuse for not responding at all. Remember I Corinthians 1:26-28.

In verses 23 and 24, along with verse 9:35, Matthew gives us summaries. These summaries bracket the collection of material that we call the Sermon on the Mount and the record of numerous healings. Together they form a powerful section of his gospel that provides much helpful information for the Christian counselor. Mark this twofold section in your Bible, especially the first portion of it.

CHAPTER 5

1 Now when He saw the crowds, He went up into the mountain, and when He sat down His disciples came to Him.

Chapters five through seven contain the so-called Sermon on the Mount. Whether Matthew grouped materials here or whether they were all delivered on one occasion is not my concern in this book. Doubtless, Jesus said the same things on more than one occasion (for instance, He spoke of cutting off the right hand, etc., in different contexts); so this could be explained either way. All good counselors use examples, certain felicitous phrasings, over and over in different cases—just as preachers do.[1] If you don't, you are making a huge mistake.

At any rate, the words that follow were spoken to Jesus' disciples (v. 1). It is important to see how much of what He did and said was designed to train them for the work that they would be doing after He left them. Similarly, the training of counselors is important. Too few pastors are given proper instruction about counseling in seminaries. If anything, they are mistrained to refer counselees to psychiatrists and psychologists rather than to deal with them themselves. The sufficiency of the Scriptures for counseling is rarely upheld. Every nouthetic counselor should consider it an obligation, therefore, to help as many ministers as he can to learn to counsel biblically.

That people need training is certain; but that those who have wrong views must be *retrained* is something that many fail to see. Yet in the training session that follows (chs. 5-7) much of what Jesus has to say is a matter of disabusing the disciples' minds of the teaching that they had heard from the Pharisees and the Sadducees, in order to teach them properly. As you proceed, note how much of His teaching consists in *re*training, not merely teaching *de novo*. The idea of contradicting what some self-created "authority" taught, while presenting the truth, is so foreign to many counselors that it is necessary to emphasize it here. Much of what you will do in teaching other counselors will be setting forth a biblical system *over* and *against* a non-biblical one. If Jesus thought it necessary to launder the minds of the disciples, then we also should make the effort.

---

1. Perhaps even more than preachers do. The next counselee has not heard what you said in the last case.

2   Then He opened His mouth and taught them, saying:

3   Happy are the poor in spirit, since theirs is the empire from the heavens.

First comes the beatitudes. Like the list of responses in Romans 12:14-21 this list is contrary to sinful human nature. That is why the items on the list stand out in such utter contrast to most popular thinking. They are arranged in such a way to set forth that contrast most vividly. Consider printing these in a handout form useful for counselees to carry with them in their pocket or purse.

The beatitudes speak about happiness. The first word that Jesus utters, when He **opens His mouth** to speak, is **happy**. What a way in which to begin a message![1] He is talking about the very sort of happiness your counselees need: a happiness that doesn't depend on happenings. Is a counselee discouraged, defeated, ready to throw in the towel? Well, that is because he has been robbed of some happiness based on happenings. It is time for him to appropriate the happiness that comes from trusting Christ. Because Jesus emphasizes happiness, it would seem that happiness should characterize His followers. Your counselees need to know that God wants happy, joyful children in His family. Most counselees are unhappy. Unhappiness is what drives many to counseling. You are able to hold up the possibility of happiness before them.

The beatitudes are designed to fly in the face of conventional thinking. The world has its beatitudes too: "blessed are the wealthy," "blessed are the famous," "blessed are the powerful." The world laughs at those who are happy because they are **poor**, because they **mourn**, because they are **persecuted**. Yet this strange viewpoint that Jesus is setting forth is exactly the point. He is showing that man's ways and man's thoughts are not God's ways and God's thoughts (cf. Isaiah 55:8). The Lord wants His disciples to help counselees to see that Christianity involves a radical reinterpretation of life. The person that Jesus sketches in the beatitudes is one who, like Himself, stands out from the crowd. He is different. Make it clear that the counselees who succeed (and, of course, there are some who don't) do so because they catch this radical spirit and proceed to deal with problems in Jesus' unique way. They are truly happy.

Show your counselee that it isn't what happens *to* him or *around* him that counts, but what happens *in* him. That is the secret of understanding

---

1. And not a bad way to begin a counseling session either!

and appropriating happiness. Happiness depends on the condition of his heart. It is found only—but always—when certain inner qualities are present. The structure of the beatitudes is important: they are not set forth as commands. Rather they *describe* the qualities found in a person who is truly happy. The rest of the Sermon on the Mount tells how to develop those qualities. They grow in those who follow Christ's commands. So first, there is the description; then the means for attaining to it.

Yet, it must be understood that you can't attain to happiness by being poor, mourning, or stepping into the midst of persecution. These things, in and of themselves, surely don't produce happiness. God is the one Who *makes* you happy by the provisions He gives you to enable you to meet these problems and needs. He sums up these provisions in the first and last beatitudes by saying that He will give you **the empire from the heavens**. It is in this gift that the rest of the requisite qualities are found. The beatitudes are the standard by which you may measure happiness or the lack thereof. They constitute the rule by which you may test your growth as a believer. Counselees who like to set up lists of dos and don'ts might be well advised to replace those lists with God's list (not of do's and don'ts, but) of qualities that lead to genuine happiness.

Poverty will not make you happy. Julian, the Apostate, confiscated the property of Christians, sarcastically saying, "This should make you happy." Like many, he misunderstood the first beatitude. Some ascetics in the church throughout the years have thought by taking vows of poverty they would find happiness. They too were wrong. Conservative congregations sometimes have said, "Keep your preacher poor and you'll keep him humble and happy." Rarely does that work. A deeper poverty than the absence of money is what Jesus had in mind.

The **poor in spirit** are not necessarily poor financially. Many who are poor financially are anything but happy. Sherwood Anderson writes in his biography of picking up coal along the railroads which he resented for the rest of his life. Being poor *in spirit* is an inner attitude that is the opposite of the current craze, shown especially in sports, of shouting "we're number one!" To serve Christ properly, with true happiness, the disciples would have to become humble by recognizing their spiritual poverty.

The phrase describes an attitude of humility that emerges from a correct evaluation of one's self. True believers must come to the place where they are willing to admit their utter spiritual poverty. They have nothing to offer God for their salvation ("nothing in my hand I bring"). Indeed, they are like pleading beggars who must come to God holding out the empty hand for Him alone to fill. All those who think that their lives are "not so bad after all," or who go around repeating the pop saying, "I'm a good person," fail to realize that the prerequisite for salvation and the subsequent mercies of God is an acknowledgment of utter spiritual poverty. Christian counselees also need to come to God in the same way when dealing with their problems and needs. They may demand nothing. This inner attitude is essential to all that follows and, therefore, is presented by the Lord at the outset.

When he achieves something (even something for the Lord) a counselee must be taught to watch for pride rearing its ugly head. Like a poisonous snake, it must be crushed at its first sight. It cannot be allowed to grow. How does one subdue pride? By remembering that it is Christ Who makes every achievement possible and, instead of glorying in one's self, by thanking Him for it. Again, counselees must be warned about the nasty tendency to compare themselves with others (cf. Galatians 6:3, 4). Tell them, "You can always find someone with whom you can compare favorably. If you must compare, then compare yourself with the Lord Jesus. That will help you become poor in spirit."

Such a person is **happy** (or blessed) because he will receive something from God—**the empire from the heavens**. That is, he will become a member of Christ's spiritual kingdom, the church and all that it offers will be made available to him. He should rejoice in becoming a subject of this royal kingdom. After all, he now belongs to a kingdom where everyone, including himself, is wealthy—spiritually. There are no spiritually poor in Christ's world empire. God is no piker. To the poor in spirit He gives all—the whole thing!

What is the empire of God like? What does one get when he receives it? Paul says it consists of "peace, joy, and righteousness" (Romans 14:17). These all are items that money cannot buy. And they are precisely those things that the average counselee so desperately seeks. But, once more, they are for the humble "little flock," to whom the "Father is pleased to give the kingdom" (Luke 12:32). So, when counselees complain about how little they have, remind them of the truths taught here.

Like Christians in the church of Laodicea, many counselees are poor spiritually, but do not recognize it. It is this very fact that is hindering them from experiencing the true happiness that is available to the believer. Refer them to Revelation 3:17-19. It would also not hurt to draw a contrast with the church in Smyrna (Revelation 2:9[a]).

There are very few who really believe the words of the second beatitude: **Happy are those who mourn**. Happy at funerals? Happy when you grieve over the loss of a job? Of your health? The words seem almost con-

4   Happy are those who mourn, since they will be comforted.

---

tradictory—happy *mourners*? The prevalent view is that "if I can be free from sorrow and grief, my life can be beautiful." But there is no contradiction here; not even paradox. Rather, Jesus is propounding a great truth; an all-important principle of happy Christian living. This beatitude cuts through the superficiality of much modern thinking.

Of course, mourning, sorrow, and grief, in and of themselves, are no straight path to comfort or happiness. There are various kinds of grief and different reasons for mourning; even the right sort of sorrow can be wasted. Counselees must learn to mourn properly. The **mourning** verse 4 speaks about is the sadness of those who come to realize the tragic world situation in which they live. It is grief over sin. There is no need to talk about wickedness in high places or low; to those who have been redeemed, these things are apparent. If the loss of loved ones who did not know Christ doesn't make one mourn for their eternal state, something is wrong with their understanding of the gospel. If the pain and sickness that we experience in this life because of Adam's sin doesn't add a dimension to that mourning, again, something is missing. If the hatred, misunderstanding, false accusations and the tragic human relationships that he sees all around don't cause mourning, then once more, there is reason to question the genuineness of a professed believer's faith.

So, in this life, there is much that brings mourning to the heart and soul of God's children. Most of all, he mourns over his own sins. Here he is, one who has been redeemed by the blood of Jesus Christ, yet he still acts in ways that displease Him. This is the "godly sorrow" of which Paul wrote in II Corinthians 7:10. It is sorrow over having offended our loving heavenly Father. It is sorrow that leads to repentance. Such sin, alone, is sufficient reason for mourning

It is often true that a counselee's problem lies right there. There is very little sense of sin left in America, since sin has been psychologized away. Christians have been influenced by this erosion. One reason why the Word of God has so little effect is that when it is sown it so often falls on stony ground! A growing Christian will have a growing sense of sin. Ask your counselee, "When did you last grieve over your loose tongue? Over your lack of self-control? Over your stubbornness and pride? Over your lack of concern for others? Over your failure to honor God?" Perhaps those questions—and others like them that fit a particular counseling

5   Happy are the meek, since they will inherit the earth.

---

case—are exactly what your counselee needs to consider.

But the beatitude continues: **they shall be comforted**. Proper mourning will bring comfort to a counselee. We are not talking about a false comfort that comes from avoiding the truth about himself. True comfort comes when one faces up to the sin in his life.[1] That comfort is available now in the promises of the Word of God. But it is incomplete. It is comfort that comes from forgiveness, but the believer knows that before long there will be more in this life to confess and be forgiven of. Yet, it is wonderful to know that one need not go around with the guilt of his sin as a burden he must carry. He has a loving heavenly Father Who forgives and Who has made His Son a Counselor-at-law Who intercedes for him. The **comfort** of which Christ speaks is comfort in the midst of mourning, in the midst of tears and pain. And with every temporal comfort that he receives there is also a reminder of the kingdom promises about the ultimate, once-for-all comfort of a sinless life on the other side of death. That is a life in which all pain, tears, and suffering will be gone. All misunderstandings will be cleared up. No one will hurt another (cf. Revelation 21:4). These truths may be effectively communicated to counselees. We shall live with other glorified believers in the presence of our risen Lord. There is comfort now in knowing that these promises will all be a present reality some day. Counselees must learn to lean on the comforting promises of the Scriptures. True, lasting, and satisfying comfort is found nowhere else.

The next beatitude extols the **happiness** of the **meek**. Meekness involves an attitude rarely sought by those outside of the church. Most think that meekness means weakness. The believer knows otherwise. His very strength comes from meekness. But it is the aggressive, self-assertive leader that the world applauds—not the meek! This is an extremely unpopular beatitude today. A. W. Tozer once said that a fairly accurate picture of the human race could be drawn by turning the beatitudes inside out. If that is true of any, it certainly is true of this one!

The meek person is kind in heart and action, making it his purpose to

---

1. There is a false, self-aggrandizing moaning and groaning that some engage in. It is false because they are proud of their "deep conviction." That is certainly not what Christ spoke about.

do nothing that harms or offends others. He is willing to let others have what he might otherwise attain for himself through roughness or toughness. He will forego much in order to help rather than harm. Someone said that meekness grows out of the ashes of self-love and the grave of pride.

Meekness is not spinelessness. Jesus was "meek and lowly" (Matthew 11:29) but He was not weak. Moses was the "meekest of all men" (Numbers 12:3), but he was strong in trusting not in himself but in the Lord. That is just the sort of man God uses (cf. Numbers 12:6-8). The power that a meek person has is power over himself that leads to power over others. He walks softly and talks gently because he wants to please God.

As a result, he will receive everything: he will **inherit the earth**. That seems out of sync with the facts. Isn't it the aggressive, who push and elbow their way through the crowd, who gain life's possessions? Doesn't the self-seeking person with a string of scalps hanging from his belt as he climbs over others bear rule? Jewish ideas of the day were similar to such thoughts. They thought driving out the Romans and setting up a kingdom that will rule the world was what would be the zenith of the Messiah's reign. But Jesus spoke of something far greater. It was to Him, the meek and lowly One, that "all authority in heaven and in earth" would be given. He would rule over a new, eternal heavens and earth in which righteousness would be at home. To inherit that new land would be far more than to inherit the land of Palestine. The meek have this inheritance to look forward to. It comes not by force of conquest, or political pressure, but as a gift of God's grace. It is the **inheritance** given to all who trust in the One Who died for them. And it is as good as if they had it now. Paul wrote of "Having nothing, but possessing everything" (II Corinthians 6:10, cf. I Corinthians 3:22). One may draw upon the riches of grace in that land even now.

There is nothing worthwhile that will not be available to the believer throughout the years of eternity. Often counselees are unwilling to have anyone transgress their "rights." The meek person is willing to have that happen if it will help rather than harm. He knows that getting "all that is coming to him" now means nothing by comparison to what is coming to him forever! Convey that to those aggressive counselees who are out to get all they can in this present life. (On this point, see my commentary on Ecclesiastes.)

Those **who hunger and thirst for righteousness** are also **happy**. Discontent! That's probably as large a problem as any other. Running

6   Happy are those who hunger and thirst for righteousness, since they will be satisfied.

---

from one supposed source of happiness to another is characteristic of people today. "If I get a new job!" or "If I can only find the right church" or "If I had a new marriage partner:" these are the thoughts that go through the minds of so many. They hunger for something, but it never satisfies. When they make the changes, in time, they find that the new is no better than the old. That is because dissatisfied Christians hunger for all the wrong things. Like the world, they **hunger** for temporal things (cf. Matthew 6:25-32). All their planning and scheming efforts are, as the writer of Ecclesiastes said, "in vain." Why is this? It is because they confuse the by-product with the product itself. To seek happiness is to have it elude you. Those who are missing it have never learned the truth of Matthew 6:33.

The Christian also should hunger for true satisfaction, that Spiritual satisfaction which comes only from His Word. The Spirit is the One Who creates proper hunger and thirst through that Word. Then, by the same Word, He satisfies all who hunger for the righteousness to which it directs them.

These are people who recognize their lack of spiritual nourishment. They know that man lives not by bread alone, as Jesus reminded the devil. They cannot get enough of the words that come from God's mouth. They devour the Bible. They don't *read* its pages; they *study* them. When they don't know how to study, they find someone to teach them how. They join a church where the Scriptures are taught; and they are faithful in their attendance. After a time, they begin to find **satisfaction**. But it isn't the sort of satisfaction that causes them to sit back and take it easy. It is like eating potato chips or pretzels—the more they eat, the more they want. And there is no danger in consuming all the spiritual food they can swallow. There is no such thing as spiritual gluttony. Eventually, the **righteousness** that flows from the biblical understanding of God's will, as it is put into effect, brings genuine satisfaction.

Your counselees' righteousness will be incomplete in this life. That is why they must still hunger and seek for it. But some day, full, 100% righteousness will be theirs in heaven. That will be the ultimate satisfaction. Counselees, having problems here, often attempt to find satisfaction in ways other than in the application of the Bible to their lives. That, you may tell them, is one reason why they have ended up in counseling. If

7   Happy are the merciful, since they will be shown mercy.

---

they learn the truth of this beatitude in an experiential way, they most likely can avoid future counseling and begin to help others instead.

Stress to counselees that spiritual hunger and thirst are not like going on a strict diet in which you give up everything that is tasty and good. Rather it is like changing from an unhealthy diet of bitter and poisonous food to eating chicken and turkey and steak! After getting one taste of such food, a counselee hungers and thirsts for more! Call on him to "taste and see that the Lord is good."

Note, too, that under the figures of hunger and thirst Jesus speaks of the inner desire to be righteous. His emphasis is on the *desire* to be righteous (that is, to live by God's standards). This is something for all. It is something that can begin at the very next counseling session. It is something you, as a counselor, need to instill in your counselees. But the desire must be for real. When it is like true hunger or thirst, then money, power, fame and everything else becomes insignificant. One who is starving or dying of thirst, would give away millions for a crust of bread or a cup of water. The Lord Jesus is speaking of this kind of compelling passion for righteousness.

Merciful people also are **happy**. Defeated and unhappy counselees must realize this and begin to show mercy to others. Mercy is a word seldom used today, and when it is used, often it is misunderstood. There is a sign on a convent wall in Baltimore, Maryland that reads,

SISTERS OF MERCY
Trespassers will be prosecuted to the full extent of the law

"Prosecuted to the full extent of the law!" It would seem that those who supposedly have dedicated themselves to mercy have forgotten what it means.

There are so many who come to counseling angry—even enraged. They seem to have forgotten that those who received the mercy of God in Christ ought to exhibit the same to others. If they wonder why others never show them any mercy, read the latter half of the beatitude to them. That should stop them in their tracks and make them consider their own attitudes toward others. What a powerful tool this beatitude can be in counseling!

The Greek word from which mercy comes meant *pity plus action to*

8   Happy are the clean-hearted, since they will see God.

---

relieve misery. It was not merely the feeling, but also the act that was in view. The Westminster catechism says that man fell into a state of "sin and misery." Grace is directed toward that sin; mercy is directed toward that misery. Mercy means helping those who are hurt by sin. It does not mean overlooking sin, but looking beyond sin to the misery it occasions. The man who hungers after righteousness reaches out beyond himself and extends mercy to others in need of it.

Jesus gave us two examples of mercy. One example is of the unmerciful servant who received mercy but would not give it (Matthew 18:23-35), and the other is of the good Samaritan ((Luke 10:37). So important is mercy to God that He wrote through Hosea, "I desire mercy, not sacrifice" (Hosea 6:6). Your counselee needs the "wisdom from above which is full of mercy" (James 2:17). Many counselees are hardened to the misery of others; they have grown cold. This happens when they begin to think only of themselves. Be aware of this and counter it whenever you meet it in the counseling room. Without mercy, we have seen, there is no mercy. Fatherly mercy is dependent on mercy given to others. Gladstone commended an embarrassed accountant who had made a mistake for making only one! He even found a way to express mercy in *that* situation. A father at a little league game does not berate his son for striking out, he encourages him for the next time at bat. He shows mercy, remembering Psalm 103:13.

When we really come to understand ourselves, we come to see that there isn't a person alive who doesn't need mercy from both God and man. Christ came in mercy; He also died in mercy. Mercy impelled him forward in spite of hardship. We, as Christians, are to emulate the mercy which we have received. If a counselee refuses to show mercy, it is conceivable that he isn't really a child of God (cf. James 2:13). The Pharisees became so concerned about minutiae that they neglected the weightier matters of the law, one of which was mercy (Matthew 23:23). Remind counselees about this when they demand from others absolute conformity to some extra-biblical standard.

No one can **see God** unless his **heart is clean**. God requires clean hands and clean hearts in His presence (both the outer and the inner must be in sync). The Lord Jesus will take no one to Himself whose heart has not been cleansed by His blood. And **happy** believers are those who by righteous living and confession of sin keep their hearts (not merely their outward actions) pure.

Clarity of spiritual vision comes through purity. As this is true of windshields and eyeglasses so it is also true of counselees' inner sight. The **heart** is the inner person. It is that from which all else flows. It is man as he really is, not as he wants others to see him. Man looks on the outer appearance, but God looks on the heart. He is called the Heart-knower. He knows what each man thinks, desires, knows, believe in his heart. He may hide his heart life from others, but a man can't hide it from God.

A pure heart does not mean an innocent heart. That is not possible. That was lost with the fall. Nor does it mean mere freedom from impure sexual thoughts. Purity of heart is more than that. It means a heart free from hatred, bitterness, unbelief, doubt, pride, and the works of the flesh (Galatians 5). Purity, as used in the Scriptures, involves two things: cleanliness (that which is free from pollution) and singleness (that which is free from impurities). Both are mentioned in James 4:8. There are many problems that come from a divided heart. Doubtless, this is the source of hypocrisy. The slave with a single heart is the one who serves wholeheartedly (cf. Colossians 3:22). Jesus spoke clearly of the importance of the single eye (Matthew 6:22, 23). There can be no dividedness in living for Christ. When there is, it begins with a divided heart. To remedy the condition, one must remove whatever it is that shares his interest with his interest in Christ.

Many have polluted hearts. Their spiritual blood is contaminated with spiritual HIV. God requires "kosher" (clean) hearts. And it is He Who will purify your counselee's heart. David cried out "Create in me a clean heart, O God" (Psalm 51:10). Encourage counselees to pray that prayer.

Seeing God is the beatific vision. It means to come to see the Savior (no one can see the Father at any time) in all of His divine wonder and glory as the God-man crowned with heaven's honors. That, in itself, is sufficient to thrill every believer. Ghandi said "What I have sought and yet seek is to see God face to face." Tragically, he did not seek God through Jesus Christ. His Hinduism, Fabian socialism, liberal Christianity, Janism and Vishnuism could not cleanse his heart so as to see God.

Seeing God is seeing Him in His works, in His words and in His Son. Psalm 24:3-6 speaks of those who "seek God's face" (i.e., the light of His countenance). That means to seek His favor. David said, "I have beheld You in the sanctuary, to see Your power and Your glory" (Psalm 63:2). In those ways, counselees may see God now. Eventually, they will

9   Happy are the peacemakers, since they will be called God's sons.

---

stand in the presence of the God-man, Jesus Christ.

Sally storms out of choir practice when a solo part in an anthem she thought she "owned" is given to Mabel this year. Jon leaves First Church when he is not included on the remodeling committee. It has always been that way. Husbands and wives, siblings, church members, neighbors have been at each other's throats since the Garden. Even Paul and Barnabas quarreled in a hot dispute over John Mark.

Nevertheless, Christ wants you to be a **peacemaker**. That there is such a need is clear from the very idea inherent in peacemaking. Sin leads to many things, one of the nastiest of which is conflict. That Jesus requires peacemaking of His disciples means that it is possible. Wherever your counselee is involved in conflicts (and many are) he can learn, instead, to make peace. Hold that biblical ideal before him.

If **peacemaking** is an activity that the Christian is required to pursue (cf. Romans 12:18), he ought not to continue arguments and fights. He ought never to instigate them. He must be willing to step in and mediate between those who quarrel. He will wait to hear all sides of an issue and, without compromising truth, will back down on anything that would unnecessarily cause or lengthen trouble. Peacemakers are called **God's sons** because, like Him Who sent His Son to make peace, they reflect the heavenly Father's attitudes and actions. Counselees, however, often have the opposite attitude. They are most unhappy as the result of trouble making. **Happiness** stems from peacemaking. Assure them of that fact.

What is this peace of which Jesus spoke? What was the Hebrew concept of *shalom?* Does it mean bringing conflicts to an end? Yes. Deuteronomy 23:6 uses the word that way. But that is only one side of *shalom*. It is much larger. In addition, it refers to a positive state of harmonious personal and social well being. In Deuteronomy 23:6 it is linked with prosperity. It is not merely "learning to war no more," but also "every man sitting under his vine and fig tree." God's way is always to replace, not merely to remove. God has called us to peace (Romans 12:18). So, your counselee must be taught to desire and to work at bringing both spiritual and other kinds of prosperity to others as a peacemaker.

Peacemakers want to live a quiet life (cf. I Thessalonians 4:11). They avoid trouble makers and avoid being troublemakers themselves. They don't interfere in matters that are not their own (Proverbs 26:17); they

| 10 | Happy are those who are persecuted, because of righteousness, since theirs is the empire from the heavens. |
| 11 | Happy are you when people insult you, and persecute you and tell all sorts of evil lies against you because of Me. |

don't ask for trouble. They return "soft answers" to those who speak roughly (Proverbs 15:1). Whether something causes peace among church members is the factor by which they judge their actions (Colossians 3:15). They are always willing to be reconciled (Matthew 5:23).

This, however, is not peace at any cost. It is not appeasement. It is not the compromise of God's truth (cf. Matthew 10:32-37). James put it this way: first purity, then peace (James 3:17). One is called a **son** because the Hebrews thought "like father, like son." Since God is the Peacemaker *par excellence*, peacemaking on the part of counselees identifies them with God. They are like Him in that respect. And, because of that, people will recognize the fact (**you will be *called* the sons of God**).

Persecution is the lot of the Christian who is living **righteously**. It is easy to *become* a Christian, but living out Christianity as it should be lived out is not a bed of roses. Many misrepresent Christianity as an add-on religion in which Jesus makes life easier. That is hardly the way that Jesus represented it. Jesus was realistic. He wanted and wants His servants to know what they are getting into when they seek to serve Him. Counselors, too, must be open about all that they do. It is not a paradox to say that one can be happy under persecution. Paul was. Your counselee can be too. Nor is there even a hint of masochism here. But one must not even think of inviting persecution as some did during later times. Paul called on his Roman citizenship to avoid it.

Christians will find comfort, help, and acceptance from the people of God in Christ's **empire**. The interesting thing is that this beatitude continues for two more verses. It is so difficult to get counselees to see that there is happiness in persecution that Jesus found it necessary to devote more space to a consideration of this point than to the other beatitudes. Jesus explained: "**Happy are you when people insult you and persecute you and tell all sorts of evil lies against you because of Me.**" That last note—that others **lie** about you *because you are a servant of Christ*—is the key. It is persecution as the result of one's faith that is in view. A counselee must not cry "persecution" when he has done something that brings retaliation from others. It is not persecution that comes from trouble-making that is in view. Because they cannot get at Christ anymore to persecute

12   Be joyful and glad, since your reward in heaven is great; they persecuted the prophets before you in the same way.

Him, sinners turn to His church (cf. Revelation 12:5, 13). And Jesus
doesn't apologize for the persecution that comes when Christians act as
they should. Instead, He says, "Congratulations!" (v. 12: **be joyful and
glad**).

What can make one **glad** about persecution, slander and lies? In
verse 12 we are told: **your reward in heaven is great**. And, as an added
incentive to hanging in there in the right way He adds, **they persecuted
the prophets before you in the same way**. The disciples were being
classed with the Old Testament prophets. Those who endure today for the
sake of Christ today find themselves among an illustrious company of
prophets and apostles! Remind counselees of that fact. Remembering the
reward that is coming in the next life may help too. Counselees should
endure out of the highest motives (to please God; to honor Him), but the
lower ones are not wrong. Jesus threw them in as well. Sometimes, it
seems, people must be led through lower motives to the higher ones.
Don't disdain either in counseling.

The beatitudes are powerful for use in counseling. I trust that you
will spend time thinking about them and their many uses so that you will
be ready to haul them out in various situations. Notice that they sum up
many of the things that Christ would go on to teach in the rest of the Sermon on the Mount. But because they are so important as a unit, it would
be well to print them off on a card to hand to your counselees.

The Sermon first sets forth the beatitudes as a description of the sort
of persons Jesus expected His disciples to become. The qualities mentioned, for the most part, are descriptive of what a person should look like
within. They describe qualities of the heart. Now, following the beatitudes
is a description of what the disciples were to look like outwardly—in the
world. They are described as **salt** and **light**. By these figures of speech He
intends to show the disciples that their task is to influence those around
them. Counselees should be told to take note, so that they too might learn
to exhibit these vital elements in their relationships to unsaved persons.
After all, counseling is done primarily to honor God, secondly to make
Christians useful in church and the world and lastly to benefit the counselee. Do your counselees know that, or are they bent on simply getting
something for themselves at the expense of all else? If so, counseling will
surely fail.

13 You are the salt of the earth. But if the salt goes flat, how will it be salted? It is too weak for anything except to be thrown out and trodden under people's feet.

In Matthew 5:13 Jesus said, "**You are the salt of the earth**." Salt exists not for itself; it benefits something else. Like salt, the Christian is to bring zest to the earth. Salt is an essential to life. Its importance is seen in the fact that soldiers were paid in salt in ancient days (that's where the word "salary" comes from). Salt preserves. It was rubbed into fish and other meats to keep them from putrefying. While adding a certain tangy zest to life, Christ's disciples also deter the corruption of any community. A decadent community is one that is devoid of salty persons. It is Christians who make the earth palatable. Life alienated from God is drab, dull, meaningless. It is flat like food that needs to be salted to bring out its flavor.

A counselee should be helped to recognize the significant role that God has accorded him; he should then strive to fill it. The significance is not for himself but to make the gospel message attractive to a world that knows nothing of the taste of true life. Ecclesiastes describes life with no salt. The Christian and the church come into a community to bring meaning, purpose, excitement, and zest through the Gospel. Each counselee should be taught that he is a grain of salt that God sprinkled somewhere for those purposes. It is his task to provide flavor to life wherever he is.

But salt can lose its saltiness. Then it becomes worthless, is thrown out, and is trodden on by people in the streets. There are Christians who become weak, insipid: worthless for the purposes stated above. Many counselees are virtually tasteless; they have lost sight of their purpose in life. They are supposed to help others find the zest Christ brings to living. Instead, they themselves are miserable and dull. That is because they have focused on themselves. Along with whatever else you do for counselees, be sure that you tell them that they are receiving help primarily for the glory of God and the blessing of others. If they don't see that and accept it, they will be back in counseling in no time.

How did salt lose its savor (saltiness)? It became mixed with impurities, especially gypsum (which looks salty but isn't). Christians lose their saltiness in a similar manner—by mixing with worldly people from whom they adopt worldly thoughts and ways. Warn counselees about this problem. They are to preserve life by inhibiting corruption, not by being corrupted themselves. A believer, himself weakened and corrupted, can add

41

> **14** You are the light of the world. A city situated on a mountain can't be hidden.
>
> 15   Nor do people light a lamp and put it under a measuring pot, but on a lampstand, and it gives light to everyone in the house.

---

little to life and have little influence. Your task is to help Christians to remedy the situation. If they will not change, the church must discipline them: they will be **thrown out and trodden under people's feet**. In Luke 14:34 and following we read of salt that is not even good enough for the manure pile where salt was used to retard fermentation and kill weeds. Surely your counselees will sit up and take notice when you clue them in on this evaluation of the unsalty life!

The world needs **light**. As we saw in chapter four, people are pictured as sitting in darkness awaiting daylight (vv. 15, 16). Jesus was the Light of the world that dawned upon them. But Jesus did not plan to remain on this earth. He would leave His apostles and His church behind to spread the Gospel into dark places. For this reason, He enlightened His disciples of whom He said were then to be **the light of the world** (v. 14; cf. Psalm 36:9). Everywhere the Bible pictures sin and its consequences under the figure of **darkness** (cf. Colossians 1:13; Ephesians 4:17, 18).

The purpose of light is to illumine that which is invisible. Darkness hides truth; light reveals truth. Darkness hides evil deeds; light brings them to one's attention. What Jesus says to His disciples is not that they *ought* to be light, but that they *are*. That is to say, they have come to know the truth, and they have acknowledged their sins and their need of a Savior. Every true believer is a light shining in darkness like his Lord (John 1:4-9). In this dark world, Paul says, believers "shine like stars" (Philippians 2:15).

If the purpose of light is to illumine that which otherwise would remain dark, it is necessary for a counselee to **let his light shine** (v. 16). A city situated on a **mountain** is clearly visible. When a **lamp** is **lighted** and placed on a **lampstand, it lightens the entire house.** Like the disciples, your counselee must think of himself as a **lamp** to be placed on a **lampstand**. If he hides his light under **a measuring pot** it will do no one any good. He is to bring men and women to Christ, thus **glorifying God**. This will happen only by letting his light shine. Fundamentally he does this through **fine deeds**—deeds that are well done as well as good—that the world may see and believe (I Peter 2:12).

This does not mean that you tell your counselee to make a show of

16   In the same way, let your light shine in the presence of people so that they may see your fine deeds and glorify your Father Who is in the heavens.
17   Don't think that I came to abolish the Law or the Prophets; I didn't come to abolish but to fulfill.

---

his works for the Lord. Of course not! How he does good deeds in the presence of unbelievers is all-important. If these are done in Christ's Name, then he takes no credit for them himself. Moreover, if he does them out of true concern for others and for the Lord, he will not push himself forward in that holier-than-thou manner that so disgusts the world. The beauty of a white, limestone village (like Nazareth) gleaming in a bright, Palestinian sun calls attention to itself without making a point that it is doing so. It is attractive rather than repulsive.

The word **fine** refers not merely to good deeds (those that are according to the biblical standard), but to deeds that are noteworthy. The word means, literally, noble, or beautiful. It is the *manner* in which these works are performed that makes others take notice of them. The believer is to do what he does in a manner that is worthy of one who serves a great God. He is to do nothing in a perfunctory manner, but with fervor and zeal. He is to do nothing in a slipshod manner, but with care and concern that it be done rightly. In short, he is to act with finesse.

Too many counselees miss the joy of winning the lost to Christ because their lives exhibit little that is different from those around them. They are like a misused lamp placed under pots. Help counselees to uncover the lamps and place them on lampstands that others may come to the Light. Ours is a derived light; Jesus is the Original. Help them to see how they can be a light publicly (like a city on a hill) and privately (like a lamp in a room). Counselees should seek to shine!

Jesus went on to discuss the life of righteousness that would make one salt that has tang and a lamp that guides to the true Light (vv. 17-20). To begin with, Christ pointed to the Scriptures as the Standard by which His own could become salt and light to achieve their purposes (v. 15). He made it clear that the Word of God would stand; He did not come to **abolish the Law and the Prophets**. Rather, He came to **fulfill** them. Indeed, He observed, **not the smallest letter or the smallest part of a letter will in any way pass away, until everything has taken place**. Fulfilling the Law and the Prophets refers to "filling them to the full." It is like when we say, "That meal fulfilled all my expectations." Christ fulfilled all God's

18   What I say to you is certain—until heaven and earth pass away, not the smallest letter or the smallest part of a letter will in any way pass away from the law until everything has taken place.

19   Therefore, whoever relaxes one of the least of these commandments, and teaches people to do so, will be called least in the empire from the heavens, and whoever does and teaches them, he will be called great in the empire from the heavens.

expectations in keeping the law. That is, He demonstrated by His life all that the Law and the Prophets were intended to achieve. He fulfilled it by understanding and living according to its inner meaning. He showed what love (which is the fulfillment of the Law) means. He taught the Bible perfectly. Believers are to understand the Scriptures in the same way today—they are to note just how Christ did this and to emulate His example.

For example, they are not to **relax** the law, or teach others to do so. Rather, they are to adhere to the commandments of God in both life and teaching (v. 19). In sum, their **righteousness must exceed the righteousness of the scribes and the Pharisees**. That is to say, it must stem from within and not be hypocritical. It cannot be a surface "righteousness" where one merely conforms outwardly. A real danger in counseling is for counselees to conform outwardly *in order to obtain something* without heart conformity. While you cannot look at your counselee's heart to discover what is there, you can discuss the matter with him and assure him that God can and does see his heart. God knows the thoughts and the intents of his heart (Hebrews 4:12, 13). He cannot deceive God. Make that clear from the outset.

The Pharisees **relaxed** the commandments by misusing, misinterpreting and misapplying them. They shaped the commandments to make them say whatever they wanted them to say. As Jesus went on to show in this sermon, the religious leaders relaxed prohibitions and extended permissions. Counselees still attempt to make the Bible say what they want it to say (some integrationist counselors do the same). Watch out for this tendency. Adhere to the Scriptures firmly; allow no one to mold or shape them according to his predilections. Develop exegetical skills and insist on exegetical accuracy. Otherwise, counselees may deprive themselves of the better things of the empire from the heavens (v. 19). They will become **least** in the **empire**: second class citizens. This is dangerous territory. To add or subtract from God's Word can even lead to exclusion from the empire. This was true for the Pharisees who misused the Scriptures making them teach salvation by works (v. 20).

20   I tell you that unless your righteousness exceeds the righteousness of the scribes and Pharisees, you will certainly not enter into the empire from the heavens.

   21   You have heard that it was said to people long ago, **You must not murder**; and whoever murders will be liable to a court trial.

But how does one "exceed" the righteousness of the scribes and the Pharisees? The Jews counted 365 prohibitions and 248 commands in the Old Testament, a total of 613. Is, then, doing 500 of the 613 when the scribes did only 450 what Jesus meant by **exceeding** their righteousness? Is it a matter of your batting average? Certainly not. There is nothing mechanical in what Jesus said. This wrong thinking was exactly the Pharisee's problem.

Then what does Jesus mean? You must help your counselee to **exceed** not in quantity but in quality. The Pharisees, as a matter of fact, did not do even one deed righteously. The *kind* of "righteousness" they offered God was wrong. Paul comments on this in Romans 10:3: "Out of ignorance of God's righteousness, and by trying to contrive their own, they didn't submit to God's righteousness." Counselees must be taught to exceed the righteousness of the scribes and Pharisees by conforming not to their contrived righteousness, but by submitting to God's. This conformity is a pleasure, not the burden that the Pharisees made it (cf. Matthew 12:28-30). As the sermon continued Jesus provided several examples of this **greater righteousness**.

Again and again in the examples that follow Jesus used the phrase, **You have heard that it was said**, or words to that effect. He was referring to the oral law that, among the Jews, had become the standard for faith and life. The overlay of this oral tradition annulled the commandments of God. In contrast to this again and again Jesus replied, "**But I tell you**," or similar words. He opposed His standard—something that He had every right to do as God manifest in the flesh—to theirs. What was the basis for evaluating each? The written Word of God would never be out of accord with the spoken Word of God. It might be—and indeed, was—out of accord with Jewish oral tradition. Jesus was infallibly interpreting the divine commandments which had been **relaxed by** the religious leaders.

Counselor, you too must correct misinterpretations. Of course your interpretations are not inerrant. But you ought to learn how to properly interpret the Scriptures so that you may retrain counselees and counselors alike in how to use the Bible. All you need to do is to read a small slice of

22   But I tell you, whoever is angry with his brother will be liable to a court trial; and whoever says to his brother, "You're stupid," will be liable to a trial before the Sanhedrin; and whoever says, "You're a fool," will be liable to the fiery Gehenna.

---

writing by Christians in the area of counseling to see how the Scriptures have been tortured to support the views of these writers. If your counselee (or some counselor you are attempting to train in nouthetic counseling) has been imbibing such materials, you will have your task cut out for you. But it is not an impossible one; Jesus demonstrated that retraining the disciples could be done. Study how He does so in this chapter and you will be in a position to attempt something of the same.

Many think, along with the Pharisees and the scribes, that they have not violated the sixth commandment if they have never put anyone six feet under. That is not how the commandment was intended to be understood, nor is it how Jesus interpreted it. That is **relaxing** the commandment by failing to reach through it to its inner intent. In adding a rider that those who murder become liable to a court trial, the Jews trivialized the commandment. The rider made both the offense and the penalty external.

Every town in Palestine with a population of 120 or more had a sanhedrin (a court of 23 men). This sanhedrin had the power to pronounce the sentence of capital punishment. That is what the religious leaders had in mind by this addendum. They said that those who murder are liable to be handed over to the sanhedrin for trial. That was all that they thought of when they thought about the commandment, and that is all that many today think about in relation to it. They must be taught that though the external aspect of the commandment certainly holds (even though some doubt that today), there is an inner aspect to the commandment too. I John 3:15 says that "everybody that hates his brother is a murderer." John, who had listened to Jesus, understood this and was helping those to whom he wrote to penetrate more deeply into the commandment's meaning.

In verse 22, Jesus set forth the true breadth of the sixth commandment. Jesus talked about being **angry** at one's brother and calling him names as serious violations of the commandment. While He did not set aside the rider or the punishment, He traced the outer sin to its inner motivation in the heart. He moved from the act to the attitude, where murder is born (cf. 15:19). **"Whoever is angry with his brother"** [without cause[1]],

---

1. Not in some manuscripts, but certainly gives the true intent. At times, Jesus

46

23 So then, if you are offering your gift at the altar, and there remember that your brother has something against you,

24   leave your gift right there in front of the altar, and go first and be reconciled to your brother; then come and offer your gift.

Jesus said, "deserves the same court trial as those who commit physical murder!" He was speaking, of course, about how God reckons murder. He was concerned not only about outer but also about inner murder. Moreover, He continued, "If you say *raca* (the translation of which is something like "stupid") to your brother, you deserve to be brought before the great sanhedrin" (of 72 persons) in Jerusalem—the body that tried the highest crimes. And, to go even farther, He said, "if you call your brother *more* ("fool," in the sense in which the word is used in Proverbs of one who is not only silly but an enemy of God) you deserve not only to be put to death, but also to be thrown into Gehenna, rather than to be buried."[1] Jesus was saying that anger wrongly aroused and expressed and anger that is out of control deserve death by one or the other of these gradations or executions. He was not calling for literal court trials on the basis of heart murder; He was showing how God views unrighteous anger.

Clearly, then, the commandment extends beyond physical murder to anger in the heart. Every counselee bearing anger in his heart, ought to be made aware of God's estimate of his condition. "Who," a counselee might ask, "can keep the commandment?" Certainly neither you, nor I, nor your counselee. That is why Jesus came: to redeem us from our sin and to help us put away sinful anger and hatred. One may grow in keeping the commandment, as love more and more replaces hatred; but in this life, he will never attain sinless perfection in this area or any other.

Verses 23 and 24, however, give direction about dealing with the problem of anger. They both show how to deal with anger the right way. Both stress the need for immediate action. Note the words: **go first** (v. 24) and **quickly** (v. 25): reconciliation takes precedence over worship; settle before you get to court. That is the way God views the matter. In other words, one must not let the sun go down on his anger (Ephesians 4:26).

Himself was angry (Mark 3:5).

1. Here, He refers to the temporal Gehenna (the valley of Hinnom) S.E. of Jerusalem where the bodies of the worst criminals were disposed of rather than the eternal punishment of hell that is the *everlasting* Gehenna (compared to this refuse dump) where the fires are never extinguished and the worms (maggots) do not die.

> **25** Quickly come to terms with your legal opponent, while you are with him on the way; otherwise your opponent may hand you over to the judge, and the judge to his officer, and you will be thrown into prison.
>
> 26 Let me assure you that you surely will not get out of there until you have paid the last cent.
>
> **27** You have heard that it was said, You shall not commit adultery.
>
> 28 But I tell you that whoever looks at a woman with the intention of desiring her already has committed adultery with her in his heart.

Some let many moons wax and wane. Anger must be dealt with as soon as it is given expression. If it is not, it will lead to resentment, bitterness and unreconciled conditions that harden into enmity.

This section on anger is preeminently important to counselors. There is no way in which a counselor can avoid dealing with anger. He will find it in many (most?) of the cases with which he deals. So it is important to get a firm grasp on Jesus' teaching. What He said, in a nutshell, is this: anger, in God's sight, is as reprehensible as murder (you deserve the same punishment for it). So, if you become angry at someone, deal with it as soon as possible. Better still, of course, is to learn to replace anger with mercy and love. But Jesus is eminently practical; He assumes the reality of a sinful society where many will get angry and then tells them what to do about it. That is the reality that counselors face most of the time.

The seventh commandment may not be **relaxed** either. That is what Jesus taught in verses 27 through 32. Surely the commandment not to **commit adultery** pertains to the act as does the command not to **murder**. But that is not all. Jesus showed how there is much more to the commandment. The religious leaders of His day had **relaxed** the commandment so as to make it apply *only* to the external act. Jesus' interpretation revealed all that God had in mind. Jesus reached to the lust behind the act, that gives the act its impetus (v. 28). The essence of what He said is that God prohibits all sexual impurity (of heart and body); sexual relations are to be restricted to marriage alone.

Counselees get into trouble exactly as Jesus indicated: they **look at a woman with the intention of desiring her**. This may or may not lead to the physical act of adultery. Either way, it is adultery in the sight of God because the adulterous desire is there in the **heart**. We live in a society in which not even a bar of soap can be advertised unless it is accompanied by a woman who tempts the viewer to look at her lustfully. If there ever

29   So if your right eye causes you to stumble, tear it out and throw it
      away from you; it is to your advantage to have one of your mem-
      bers perish than for your whole body to be thrown into Gehenna.
30   And if your right hand causes you to stumble, cut it off and throw
      it away from you; it is to your advantage to have one of your
      members perish than for your whole body to go away into
      Gehenna.

---

was an age in which a commandment applied, this is the age and this is
the commandment. Many counselees who have never committed adultery
physically, are ruining their marriages by filling their minds and hearts
with lustful thoughts. They indulge in pornographic videos, magazines,
and internet presentations. But it is not only those who go in for hard core
porn that are guilty; it is all those who look at the milder (?) forms of
temptation and lust. The phrase *look and lust* sums up Christ's warning.
That is where the problem lies. In II Peter we read about *"eyes* full of
adultery." David *"saw"* and *"beheld"* Bathsheba. If he had turned away
rather than continuing to look he would never have committed adultery in
the heart or otherwise.

Those who see billboards that tempt them to lust, or who watch com-
mercials (interspersed even with the news) that are designed to catch the
eye, soon discover that everything seems to be geared toward lusting.
How, then, can a person refrain from breaking the commandment? The
answer is: none can. We all sin. But we can begin to grapple with the
problem and overcome it more and more. In order to do so, the *look and
lust* formula is important to keep in mind. "But how can one avoid seeing?" He can't. But he can avoid looking. David didn't have to continue
looking and neither does anyone else. We must do as Job did. Job tells us,
"I made a covenant with my eyes not to look on a young woman" (Job
31:1).

Once more, Jesus added two appendices to this discussion of adultery in the heart (vv. 29-30 and 31-32). First, he urged all to do radical
amputation—cut off the limb or pluck out the **eye** by which one sins.
Even the most important limb or eye (the **right** one) is to be sacrificed for
this purpose. Of course, Jesus did not intend for anyone to literally maim
himself. The virus of lust works too deeply for surgery! Besides, that
would do little good. The point is to eliminate anything that leads to sexual sin. If a person has videos in his possession that do so, he ought to get
rid of them. If he travels a certain route to work in order to pass by the

> **31** And it was said, Whoever divorces his wife must give her a written record of the divorce.
>
> 32 But I tell you that everyone who divorces his wife, except on the ground of sexual sin, makes her commit adultery, and whoever marries a divorced woman commits adultery.

house of a certain woman, hoping he will spot her, he should change his route. Press counselees to learn what it is that occasions sinful thoughts and urge them to "amputate" them. After all, says Jesus, it is better to be maimed than to have the entire body thrown into Gehenna (about which, see above).

So, Jesus is telling us to take radical action to make us aware of the danger into which we are about to enter (if you have cut off your foot, for instance, you become aware of the fact that you are heading in that direction because you must hop rather than walk), and to make it more difficult to do that which stimulates lust. The trouble is that we get into sinful habits that need shattering so that we will not unconsciously drift into temptation. Therefore, to avoid lust, we must develop new biblical habits to replace it.[1]

The next example shows a complete distortion of the seventh commandment. The Pharisees misstated and misused Deuteronomy 24:1-4 to get around the commandment. They quoted but a part of the passage (cf. v. 31). Deuteronomy speaks only of a *sinful* divorce,[2] one that, while valid, was obtained on the wrong basis. The view of Hillel, which was prevalent, was that a divorce for neglect of household duties, burning the toast, even preference for another woman was okay. The phrase *erwath dabar* (literally, "a thing of uncleanness") that occurs in Deuteronomy 24 was understood by Hillel to mean that anything distasteful or disturbing was a ground for divorce. The rule in Deuteronomy 24 was set up to avoid serial marriages in which one might divorce and remarry the same person if he didn't prefer someone else whom he married for a while in the meantime. The **bill of divorce** simply describes what he does in the process; it was not prescribing divorce. There is no *command* to divorce. People of the day, however, took it to mean that all that was required to obtain a divorce was to rightly go through the process of handing one's marriage partner the bill.

---

1. See *The Christian Counselor's Manual* for more on this matter.
2. One by which a divorcee became "defiled" (Deuteronomy 24:4).

33 Again, you have heard that it was said to people long ago, Don't fail to keep your vows, but carry out your oaths to the Lord.

34 But I tell you, don't swear at all, neither by heaven—because it is God's throne,

35 nor by earth—because it is the footstool for His feet, nor by Jerusalem—because it is **the city of the great King,**

36 nor by your head—because you can't turn one hair white or black.

37 But let the word *yes* mean *yes* and the word *no* mean *no* when you speak it; anything more than this comes from the evil one.

Jesus tightened things up. He made it clear that there is only one cause for divorce among God's people: sexual sin.[1] Divorce for sinful reasons causes a divorced woman to commit adultery. It is important in this day (when divorce is rampant) to know the ins and outs of divorce. A counselor cannot avoid dealing with the subject. Learn all you can about the matter.[2] You will not be able to counsel effectively unless you do.

In verses 33 through 37 it is not only one commandment that Jesus said was being **relaxed**. Oath taking and truth telling involve two commandments: the third (taking God's Name in vain) and the ninth (giving false witness). The Pharisees weaseled out of their oaths and thought that they were not lying or taking God's name in vain when they did so. Jesus showed how they were violating the commands and how a believer ought to have a high regard for the truth. His word alone, without an oath, ought to be sufficient. Counselees regularly get into arguments over who is telling the truth, so that this section is quite apropos.

An oath is a form of bearing witness; when you take an oath you bear testimony to something. You maintain that what you have to say is true, and call upon God as your witness. Behind the taking of every oath is God, who is called on to back up your word. So, when someone under oath lies, he is also lying about God. He has called on God to lend His authority to his falsehood. Thus he attempts to make God a party to the deception. That is to take God's Name in vain, *plus*! Oath taking in the proper circumstances is permitted in Deuteronomy 6:13. But while oath taking of that sort is fine, it may be misused. Oath taking that is not in an

---

1. Fornication includes all forms of sexual sin. Through Paul God added one other reason for divorce: desertion by an unbelieving partner (I Corinthians 7:15).

2. For details on this and other passages, see my *Marriage, Divorce and Remarriage in the Bible.*

38 You have heard that it was said, **An eye for an eye and a tooth for a tooth**.

official setting is warned against (cf. Deuteronomy 23:21).

The Jews said that only breaches of religious oaths were perjury. No oaths, unless made in Yahweh's Name, were considered binding. Other oaths need not be kept. Some were even circumvented, as in the practice of Corban (see Matthew 15:5, 6; Mark 7:11). But Jesus' point was this: if oaths meant nothing, and could be violated with impunity, then words meant nothing.

Oath taking ought to be unnecessary for the Christian in ordinary situations because of his reputation for truth telling. His word should be so dependable that his simple assertions or denials should themselves have witness-bearing force without the need for backing. After all, whatever we say is said in God's presence. If a person has a reputation as a liar it does him little good to add God's Name, or some synonym (God's throne, footstool or Jerusalem[1]) to his assertion. Even lesser things ("**by your head**"—you had no control over its color; these were the days before Grecian formula!) are of no need and of no avail. The simple import of these words was that the disciples were to be trustworthy. Their word was to be their bond, as we often say.

Jesus' words are of great significance to those who deal with counselees, some of whom feel quite free to put a spin on the truth. There are counselees who are better spin doctors than those in Washington D.C. Counselors should warn counselees who have a tendency to distort truth in their own favor—even swearing that it is true at times—that this is not a matter of indifference. Jesus was concerned enough about the matter to speak these penetrating words. Every counselee must be urged to let his yes be yes and his no be no, without any additions.

The *lex talionis* (law of retaliation) is discussed in 38 through 42. An eye for eye and a tooth for tooth might seem cruel to many, but if they lived in Christ's time and in Old Testament times, they would have considered it merciful. This law was not an attempt at vengeance but a prohibition of exacting judgment greater than the crime. It was a graphic way of saying that the penalty should match the crime. Many law codes of the past were unequal. Hammurabi's famous code, for example, required that a child's hand be cut off for striking a parent.

Jews misused this law (Leviticus 24:19, 20) in order to take personal

1. Cf. our expressions "by heaven" and "By all that's holy."

39   But I tell you, don't oppose persons who do evil to you. Rather, if
       anyone slaps you on the right cheek, turn the other to him also;
40   and if anyone wants to take you to court and take away your shirt,
       let him have your coat also.
41   and if anyone forces you to go one mile, go two miles with him.
42   Give to anyone who begs for something, and don't refuse to lend
       to anyone who wants to borrow something.

---

revenge. Their attitude was like that of many counselees today—"don't get angry; get even." But see Proverbs 20:22; Romans 12:19; Leviticus 19:18; Proverbs 24:29. It was not to be taken literally; fines were levied, exile was practiced, and imprisonment was used to punish. But these were to be equal to and not heavier than the weight of the crime committed. The law, in fact, was a blessing.

Again, take a look at the fuller meaning (v. 39): **Turn the other cheek**. To slap another on the cheek was the height of an insult. It was most extreme, a punishment reserved for slaves. Not too long ago in America it could lead to a duel. What Jesus meant was to respond to insults—even extreme ones—gracefully. In verse 40, the disciple is told to let a spoiler **take his coat** in addition to whatever else he can get through a lawsuit. The **coat** in view was the expensive outer garment, not the cheaper inner shirt. Once more, a believer is to handle such matters well, whether they happen by violence (Luke 6:29) or by law (Matthew 5:40). There are many today who would have a hard time doing this (but cf. I Corinthians 6:7). How a counselee takes injustice tells a lot about his faith. Make the point from this passage.

Going the second **mile** (v. 41) was a good example of an onerous task. The Roman army was allowed to impress people (cf. Simon of Cyrene). The disciple was to take up this burden graciously even if it was ungraciously required.

He is also to give when he is asked to lend (v. 42). That doesn't mean to give to every lazy scoundrel (cf. II Thessalonians 3:10), but to those truly in need. It is not the refusal to give or lend that, in itself, is condemned, but the refusal out of selfishness.

Obviously, these words are not literal any more than those about radical amputation. But principles are best understood when pushed to an extreme. That is what Jesus was doing here. These four examples inculcate an attitude of love and its expression toward wrong doers *instead of revenge* (cf. Leviticus 19:18). They stress a willingness to take it on the chin (or cheek) when necessary. They are just the opposite of the modern

> **43** You have heard that it was said, Love your neighbor and hate your enemy.
>
> 44 But I tell you, love your enemies and pray for those who persecute you,
>
> 45 so that you may be sons of your Father Who is in the heaven's; He makes His sun rise on the evil and the good, and pours out rain on the just and the unjust.
>
> 46 If you love those who love you, what reward will you get? Isn't that something that even the tax collectors do?
>
> 47 If you greet only your brothers, what more are you doing than others? Isn't that something that even the Gentiles do?
>
> 48 So then, you must be perfect as your heavenly Father is perfect.

---

self-centered teaching that is propagated in the public schools and elsewhere. There is much here for the counselee who is ready to exact the most severe punishment against an offender to consider.

In verses 43 through 48 we encounter the last illustration of how God's law included a much fuller fulfillment than was supposed. The Pharisees added "and hate your enemy." They restricted the command to love to literal neighbors—other Jews who lived next door. But in response to the question "who is my neighbor?" Jesus told a story that made it clear that one becomes a **neighbor** whenever he is in need (Luke 10:25-27; 36-37). They also removed the words "as yourself" which was a big reduction since we love ourselves so much! That is a dangerous way to treat God's Word.

Even enemies must be loved (v. 44). How important that truth is. Remember that Jesus died for you when you were an **enemy** (Romans 5:8). God in His general benevolence sends sun and rain on both the good and the evil (Acts 14:17). By loving an enemy, one emulates His heavenly Father. How should you encourage your counselees to do so? Tell them to shine their love and pour out their goodness on the just and the unjust alike. This is done by meeting the needs of an enemy (cf. Romans 12:20, 21). Can they do that? Of course; they can meet needs whether they feel like it or not. It is no great thing to love those who love you, Jesus noted. Even pagans do that (v. 47).

One may be **perfect** (literally, "complete") by taking heed to these teachings of Christ and beginning to do them. No one will be perfect in the sense of achieving sinlessness in this life. But all can be complete in the sense of dealing with all of the areas that have been covered by Christ. Counselees must not be allowed to avoid or ignore any of them.

CHAPTER 6

1   Be careful not to do your righteous acts in front of people, so that
     you will be seen by them. Otherwise, you will have no reward
     from your Father Who is in the heavens.

With this chapter comes a change. We begin to encounter a series of
instructions in which Jesus showed how *not* to do something, and then
explained *how* to do it. We also have set forth for us a contrast between
the world's philosophy of life and the philosophy that the disciples are to
adopt. This is a most powerful chapter for counselors to understand and
use.

Counselors should learn from the "how not to" and the "how to" that
follow to provide direction for counselees. It is not enough to tell them
what to do, there is also a need to suggest biblical ways of doing it. Many
counselees want to do the right thing, but they don't know where to begin.
When they begin, they don't know how to get into gear. Help them with
implementation, and you will find the success rate of your counseling
soar.

Verse 1 sets the theme for much that follows: **Be careful not to do
your righteous acts**[1] **in front of people so that you will be seen by
them. Otherwise, you will have no reward from your Father Who is in
the heavens.** That says it all. There are people who are ostentatious about
giving, who love the applause of men—and if they don't get it, you can be
sure they will let you know it. They want to be rewarded; that is the motivation behind their acts. They are interested in the accolades of men.
However, as Jesus pointed out (and you should do the same when dealing
with counselees of this type), in seeking an earthly reward they are giving
up a heavenly one. It is a bad bargain!

Is this verse in conflict with 5:16? Is there a contradiction between
the two? Was Jesus so inconsistent that He refuted himself within the
compass of one sermon? Of course not. In 5:16, the point is that you must
not hide your light. It is to shine in such a way that it directs men to God.
You are encouraged to glorify *God*—not *yourself*. Shine your light on
Him! That is the essential difference. All of this is apparent from the contexts but also from the two words used for "seeing." In Matthew 5:16 you

---

1. The word here is "righteous acts," not alms, which is too narrow a translation.

> 2   Therefore, when you give charity, don't blow a trumpet before you, as the hypocrites do in the synagogs and in the streets so that they may be praised by people. Let Me assure you, they have their reward.

---

have the ordinary word for **seeing**. But here, in 6:1, the word used is *theathenai* from which we got our word "theater." When you do righteous acts in order to "put on a show" you may expect God not to count what you do toward a heavenly reward. As Jesus said at the end of verse 2, people who thus put on a show and play to the audience **have their reward.** They got what they sought—the applause of men. How could they even think of asking for more?

Notice, in grace, God rewards righteous acts. He, Himself, gives the incentive, the wisdom and the ability to perform them,[1] yet He rewards these works of grace. It is like a father who gives his son the money to buy him a father's day gift, then thanks him for it. The counselee has no reason to complain if he gets no reward; he has no reason to boast if he does.

This issue raised by the Lord Jesus is not a casual one. He said **Be careful** about it. The strong warning in those words should be heeded by Christians. Here He unmasked the hypocrite. The hypocrite's heart isn't right; his motives (at best) are mixed. He has no eye singled to God's glory. He puts on a mask for the sake of the show. He really isn't interested in the poor to whom he gives. He is interested in himself! You probably will hear such counselees recounting their spiritual exploits—for God? No, for themselves. Such people like to slip a word here and there into whatever they are saying about their good deeds, hoping that you as a counselor will reward them. Don't fall prey to any such shenanigans. Indeed, when you hear it happening again and again, you will soon have enough ammunition (if you jot down quotes in your notes) to make a case for the charge of self adulation.

Jesus mentioned three areas in which people fall into this sin. These are the areas of *giving* (vv. 2-4), *prayer* (vv. 5-15) and *fasting* (v. 16-18).

Consider the first. Jesus certainly isn't against giving. Indeed, in the passage, He assumed that the listener will give. But He also assumed that there are two ways people give: the right way and the sinful way. Some expositors take verse 2 literally. I think this is a mistake. Much of what

---

1. Cf. Philippians 2:13.

3   But when you give charity, don't let your left hand know what your right hand is doing,

4   so that your charity may be given secretly and your Father, Who sees what is done in secret, may reward you.

5   And when you pray, don't be like the hypocrites, who like to stand and pray in the synagogs and on street corners so that they may be seen by people. Let Me assure you, they have their reward.

6   But when you pray, enter into your room, and when you have shut the door pray to your Father Who is in secret, and your Father Who sees what you do in secret will repay you.

7   And when you pray, don't use needless repetitions, as though you were stuttering, like the Gentiles do. They think they will be heard because of a lot of talking.

Jesus says in this sermon is hyperbolic.[1] Blowing trumpets seems to be a strange thing to do **in the synagogs**. Rather, it seems that He is speaking much as we do when we talk about someone who "toots his own horn." Most likely, he was referring to people who *boasted* about their giving.

Here, we note once more that God will not reward them with eternal benefits when they have settled for a temporal one instead. So much for the "put off" (the way *not* to give). Now for the "put on" (the way God wants you to give). How does one avoid ostentation in giving? In verse 3 Jesus said, **"Don't let your left hand know what your right hand is doing."** That is, give and think no more about it. It is those who dwell on what they have given who are liable to fall into the sin of ostentation.

Next, notice the principle at work in prayer (vv. 5-15). Two instances are noted (each stressing the put off and the put on). The first has to do with those who "just happen to be caught" on the street corners at the hour of prayer, or who pray ostentatiously in the synagog. They do so **to be seen** (the word used means "manifested" or "marked out") by others. Hypocrites are like this. God doesn't like it! What is the put on? The disciple is to enter a storage room (literally[2]), shut the door and talk to God privately. That is the way to pray. In other words, if a person has a problem with his public prayers, he should pray privately. The passage is not against public prayer. Jesus prayed publicly.[3]

There is a second way of praying wrongly (vv. 7-15). Prayer that is

---

1. Jesus often exaggerates, uses shocking figures of speech, etc., in order to awaken.
2. Probably one without a window
3. There is also a danger in praying about private matters publicly.

8		Don't be like them. Your Father knows what you need before you ask Him.
	9	So then, pray in this way: "Our Father, Who is in the heavens, May Your Name be holy.
10		May Your empire come, May Your will be done on earth as it is in heaven.
11		Give us today our daily bread.
12		And forgive us our debts as we also have forgiven our debtors.
13		And don't bring us into testing, but rather, rescue us from the evil one."
14		Now if you forgive people their trespasses against you, so too your heavenly Father will forgive you;
15		but if you won't forgive people, neither will your Father forgive your trespasses.

ostentatious because of its length or repetition displeases. The **Gentiles** sound as if they are **stuttering** when they pray. Why? They say the same thing over and over again thinking that they will be heard for **a lot of talking**. They are like the prophets of Baal in I Kings 18. Believers don't need to pray that way. When Elijah prayed once, briefly, that was enough. The fire fell! God hears the first time; He doesn't need to be awakened or be persuaded by incessant begging.

How often have you heard believers pray for the very same thing that someone else has just finished praying for? Rather, they ought to simply say "amen" and go on to something else. The "how to" that Jesus offered over against long, repetitive prayer is the so-called Lord's prayer. It is a brief, substantive, non-repetitious prayer. It is a model of what prayer ought to be like.

I shall not go through the prayer commenting verse by verse; there is a lot of material available on it already. There is, however, a footnote on one of the clauses in the prayer that does need comment. To pray for forgiveness *as* one has forgiven others needed further explanation. So Jesus gave that explanation in verses 14 and 15. He was not talking about the *judicial* forgiveness that was granted once for all when a believer put his faith in Christ. Rather, He is speaking here about forgiveness *after* that forgiveness. Rather than *judicial*, the forgiveness Jesus discussed is *fatherly* forgiveness. It is the forgiveness that a father grants his son.[1] For

---

1. The word "Father" is emphasized in the context (cf. vv. 9, 14, 15).

> **16** Now, when you fast, don't look gloomy like the hypocrites, who disfigure their faces to show others that they are fasting. Let Me assure you that they have their reward.
>
> 17 But when you fast rub oil on your head and wash your face
>
> 18 so that you don't appear to people to be fasting, but only to your Father Who is in secret. And your Father Who sees what you do in secret will repay you.

---

instance, he will allow him to borrow the car when (and only when) he gets matters straightened out with his sister. That is the sort of thing Jesus is saying here. In effect, God is saying, "Don't expect me to listen to your prayer for forgiveness until you forgive your brother or sister."

Counselors must make this point clear. How foolish are those who say to a husband and wife who are unreconciled, "Well, pray about the matter." Peter applies Jesus' principle in I Peter 3:7 differently. There he makes it clear that their prayers will be interrupted until they are reconciled to one another. Get this straight, counselor, and you will not be likely to make the false moves that many do make.

The final example of the principle set forth in verse 1 has to do with **fasting** (vv. 16-18). Again, those who make a show of the fact that they are holy because they fast, by **disfiguring their faces and rubbing oil on their foreheads** for others to see, clearly seek human approval. Jesus probably fasted twice a week, but He made no show of it. Christians may fast occasionally (unlike the Jews, we have no stated fast days), but they must be careful not to do so in ways that call attention to it. Jesus advises the one fasting to wash his face (God has seen). There are many other ways in which one can attempt to look good before others by the way they **disfigure their faces**. Many put on a **gloomy** expression to appear holy, when they feel quite different inside. Counselees will even put on such a show for a counselor. I have had a man get down on his knees, grimace, and pathetically say, "I've given the best years of my life for that woman." Then getting up, he immediately attempted to verbally tear his wife to pieces. All such hypocrisy must be counteracted by counseling.

The remainder of the chapter, in harmony with the antithetical nature of the rest of the Bible, consists of four areas in which choices must be made between God's way and the world's way. It is a powerful section for counselors to know and to use. These sections are as follows: verses 19 through 21 call the disciple to choose between two *treasures*; verses 22 and 23 call upon him to choose between two *conditions*; verse 24 calls for a choice between two *masters*; verses 25 through 34 call on the counselee

> **19** Don't store up treasures on earth for yourselves, where moth and rust ruin them and where thieves dig through and steal.
>
> 20 But store up treasures in heaven for yourselves, where neither moth nor rust can ruin them, nor thieves can dig through and steal.
>
> 21 Where your treasure is, there is where your heart will be too.

to choose between two *philosophies* of life.

First is the choice between two **treasures**. One is an earthly treasure, the other is a heavenly one. Christ commands you and your counselee to choose the right one (vv. 19, 20). Many counselees are making the wrong choice. That fact contributes to their present difficulties. Once again, the put off is contrasted with the put on. In setting forth the antithesis, Jesus has helpfully told us what not to do as well as what to do. He is concerned with both the what to *and* the how to.

Jesus said, **"Don't store up treasures on earth for yourselves** (v. 19) . . . **But store up treasure in heaven for yourselves"** (v. 20). That is as clear as directions get. There are **treasures** in both places. You must choose between them. Note, Jesus didn't say it is wrong to have treasures on the earth, but that it is wrong to **store up** those treasures. He was opposed to building bigger and better barns to store one's earthly treasures. If God providentially sends treasure your way, that is another thing. But the storing up process to which He referred is done by those who are *trusting* in the "uncertainty of riches" (I Timothy 6:17). There is nothing wrong with riches *per se*; it is when one thinks that security lies in them rather than in God that he is in trouble. It is when he determines to get rich that he will pierce his own heart with many sorrows (I Timothy 6:9, 10). Rather, he should enjoy the riches God gives him, as well as use them generously, to help others by means of that wealth (I Timothy 6:17, 18). However, there isn't anything wrong with storing up a little for emergencies, for your children's welfare, and so on. I Timothy 5:8, for instance, makes it plain that one ought to "provide for" his own (and see especially, II Corinthians 12:14).

Jesus' point is laid out simply, but powerfully, in verse 21: **Where your treasure is, there is where your heart will be too.** That principle is broader than this one application. Certainly, it fits the situation in which one trusts in money. But it also fits all sorts of other situations. If a counselee says that he has given up his adulterous past, but keeps thinking about the "other woman," he still has some investment in her—that's where his treasure is. Check if he still has a picture of her, if he sees her

22 The eye is the lamp of the body. So if your eye is single, your whole body will be lighted,

23 but if your eye is not single, your whole body will be darkened. So then, if the light in you is darkness, the darkness will be great!

---

now and then, if he still possesses a key to her apartment or still retains some love letters. All of these things need to be disposed of. He must close out the account in her name and must, instead, invest deeply in his wife. Where his treasure is, that's where his heart (his inner concerns and interest and love) will be. One focuses on that which he considers a treasure.

Instead, the counselee must store up treasures **in heaven**. The reason given is a very practical and solid one. The one is temporary, the other eternal; the one is corruptible, the other is not. A person who believes this would be a fool to make the wrong choice. Clearly, the latter, heavenly option has it all over the former, earthly one. Why, then, does a counselee choose wrongly? When you boil it all down, it is a lack of faith. If he really believes what Jesus says, by God's grace he will overcome the habits and ways that he developed in the past. But if his faith is weak, he doubts. So he wants to be sure of future security in this world by his own way of securing it—storing up earthly provisions for the future—rather than trusting in God and storing up heavenly provisions for the heavenly future. He can see, feel, and taste the present, earthly world; he has no such sensuous grasp on the heavenly one. It is by *faith* that we "see" the things that are invisible (cf. Hebrews 11).

The second choice that one must make is between two *conditions* (vv. 22, 23). One is the condition of defective eyesight; the other is good eyesight. Jesus says that the eye is the lamp of the body. That is to say, it is through the eye that one is able to see those things that light makes visible to us. He represents it as something like a window that lets light (and sight of all it illumines) into the body. Defective eyesight hinders one's capability to do so. It may distort or, in the case of blindness, allow no light into the body. It is like pulling a shade across the window to block out what is going on outside the house.

The expression **if your eye is single** (note also its contrary) means "if it is healthy, sound." When it is you will see well. You will be able to focus on and distinguish an object for what it is. There will be no distortion. Diplopia, or double vision (v. 23), obscures, dims, confuses. If you press on the side or top of the eyeball the world breaks in two (try it if you

> **24** No one can serve two lords as a slave; either he will hate one and love the other, or he will be attached to one and despise the other. You can't serve God and mammon.
>
> **25** Therefore I tell you, don't worry about your life, what you will eat or what you will drink; or about your body, what you will wear. Isn't your life more than food and your body more than clothing?
>
> 26 Look at the birds of the sky; they don't sow or reap or gather into barns, and yet your heavenly Father feeds them. Aren't you more valuable than they?

never have, and you will see what I mean). Now, suppose that is how you saw all the time. That is like a double, divided heart. It is a heart that tries to ride the fence (to store up treasures in both places just to be sure). The single heart by faith puts all the eggs in God's basket. Many counselees don't have a single eye.

Jesus also talked about serving two masters (v. 24). In that verse He made it perfectly clear that you can't ride the fence. You can't root for both teams. You can't serve two masters—you will end up tilting to one side or the other. You will love one and hate the other. A person can't serve (be a slave to) both God and mammon.[1] Jesus would have no divided allegiance among His disciples. The Bible teaches that we are to love God "with *all* the heart, *all* the mind and *all* the soul." There is to be no half-heartedness. Calling counselees to put implicit faith in God is essential to good counseling. Calling them to singleness of trust is a prerequisite to giving them the sort of help that honors God. Calling them to jump off the fence, to reject the lordship of mammon or any other thing in which they seek to place their trust in addition to God, is crucial. Whenever one tries to divide his interest between the two, he ends up serving mammon rather than God!

Finally, what Jesus was teaching in this section all boils down to a choice between two *philosophies* of life (vv. 25-34). One is the pagan (Gentile) philosophy (v. 32); the other is the Christian philosophy (v. 33). One leads to a life of **worry** about **things**. The other leads to a life of joy as one places his faith in Christ and His provisions. **Worry** is useless. By it a person can't add a single hour to his life (v. 27). But worry is inevitable when *things* are what he lives for. Living for things and worry are tied

---

1. This is an Aramaic word for that which one puts his confidence in that probably means "one's pile" (much like our kindred expression). To trust mammon is to trust in the pile of money or provisions that one has stored up.

27	Now, which one of you by worrying can add an hour to his life-span?
28	Why are you worried about clothing? Consider the lilies of the field; see how they grow? They don't labor or spin,
29	yet I tell you, Solomon—in all his glory—wasn't clothed like one of them!
30	But if God clothes the grass of the field that is here today and thrown into the oven tomorrow, how much more certain is it that He will clothe you! You have so little faith!
31	So then, don't worry, saying, 'What will we eat?' or 'What will we drink?' or 'What will we wear?'
32	It is all these things that the Gentiles zealously seek. Your heavenly Father knows that you need all of these things.
33	But seek first His empire and His righteousness, and all of these things will be added to you.

together so closely that they cannot be separated.

The Christian way of life means dependence on God; it is based on the fact that He will take care of His children and provide for their true needs (not those that they may think are needs, but are not). The problem today is that we have been taught that we need all sorts of things that we really do not. There is only one fundamental need—Christ Himself. As God provides food for the birds (v. 26) and clothes the lilies of the field (v. 28), so too will He provide food and raiment (the two essentials for physical life) for His own.

Christian counselees torn apart by worry do need to have their worries removed—worry has no place in the Christian life (cf. Philippians 4). But it cannot be removed apart from abandoning pagan thinking and replacing it with godly thought. As I have been saying all along, it is a matter of faith. Jesus points His finger to lack of faith (v. 30). The worrying counselee needs an increase of faith (which comes ultimately from the Word; cf. Romans 10:17). Focus his attention on Matthew 6 in order to help him rethink his values.

What must he do when he recognizes that lack from the Word? Obey. He will begin to **seek first** God's **empire and His righteousness** as Jesus commanded (v. 33). And in time, as he makes the right choices that Jesus has outlined in this chapter, he will find coming his way—as a by-product—all the necessary things he previously sought. In the end, it is a matter of what one seeks as his goal in life—the reality, or its by-product. When he chooses correctly, he will find it possible to live day by day,

34   So then, don't worry about tomorrow; tomorrow will worry about itself. Each day has enough trouble of its own.

---

peacefully handling *that* day's problems (which are all his shoulders were designed to carry at one time) rather than worrying about tomorrow (v. 34)

     This chapter was designed to deal with major problems of counselees. Master it and use it to the full in counseling.

CHAPTER 7

1	Don't judge, or you will be judged;

We come now to the concluding chapter of the Sermon on the Mount. This section begins with a passage that has frequently been mis-used by counselors and others. Doubtless, when you have pointed out sin you have had someone respond, "Judge not!" Jesus did not forbid judg-ing; He condemned the wrong kind of **judging**. What He had in mind is that sort of judging in which one judges another improperly—in ways that the one doing the judging would not care to be judged. Far from advocat-ing never judging in any way at any time, the purpose of the passage is to show His own *how to correct others correctly*. The passage provides *instruction* in judging.

Note, first, that elsewhere Jesus commands us to judge: "Judge a righteous judgment" (John 7:24). Later on in this chapter of Matthew the disciples are encouraged to judge who is a **false teacher**. In that place, a proper basis for making the judgment is given (not by trying to judge someone's motives, but by judging the **fruits** of his teaching; cf. vv. 15, 16, 20). And, even more immediately, Jesus' words in verse 6 demand that a judgment be made about who is a **dog** or **pig**. So, counselor, it cer-tainly doesn't mean that you cannot form an opinion of people. Indeed, if you are going to counsel at all, one of your principal activities will be making judgments about people. But if you heed Jesus' warning here, you will make sure that your judgments are based soundly on factual evi-dence.

To judge rightly, among other things, means that you will take the time to carefully gather data.[1] You will make no snap judgments. For instance, you will take the observation in Proverbs 18:13 seriously. You will not guess. You know that your own conclusions, unaided by the guidelines laid down in the Scriptures, are bound to be flawed. You will lovingly give the benefit of the doubt (I Corinthians 13:7). You will believe a counselee until the evidence proves otherwise. All this and more is summed up in the statement, "Don't judge unrighteously" (John 7:24). Notice from that exhortation that a wrong judgment isn't merely a mis-take, it is a sin (it is "unrighteous"). So what you do is a serious matter.

---

1. See the chapters on data gathering in *The Christian Counselor's Manual*.

2	the same sort of judgment that you use in judging will be used to judge you; and the same sort of measure that you use in measuring will be used to measure you.
3	Why is it that you can notice a speck in your brother's eye, but can't see the log in your own?
4	Or, how can you say to your brother, "Let me take the speck out of your eye," when there is a log in your eye?

You may not take it lightly.

In the parallel passage in Luke 6:37 an additional word is added to the word *krinete* ("judge") which is used here. It is *katadikazete*, "to condemn." Another way of judging wrongly is evaluating others from a fault-finding, censorious attitude in which one is ready at the drop of a handkerchief to pick him to pieces. That sort of thing is likely to characterize some of those you counsel. Even the best efforts of a wife or husband are condemned by a spouse who, when this attitude is present, can do nothing rightly. More than likely, you will also find such a person judging motives (trying to steal God's task from Him; *He* is the one who judges hearts). In this sense, Paul asks, "Who are you to judge another man's servant?" (Romans 14:4). And James asks, "Who are you to judge your neighbor?"[1] (James 4:11, 12).

The Lord Jesus told the one who is passing judgment on another to first judge himself. He went on to say that he will be judged by the very same standards that he uses to judge others (v. 2). This is a strong warning. It amounts to an application of the golden rule to the matter of judging.

How, then, are you to judge? By judging yourself first, you will be able to learn to judge properly. If you are careful to preempt any judgment of you that would be according to unrighteous standards, you will be extremely careful about how you judge another. That is the background for learning to judge rightly. As you judge another, all the while you ought to be asking yourself, "Would I think it fair and right to be subjected to this sort of judgment?" If you keep that question in mind, you will find yourself steering clear of making unrighteous judgments.

Jesus went on to speak (as usual) in a hyperbolic fashion about **logs** and **specks** in the eye. Picture the situation: here is someone trying to remove a speck from the eye of another when he has a log sticking out of

---

1. James is probably reflecting Jesus' words here in Matthew, as he frequently refers to the Sermon on the Mount about other matters.

5   You hypocrite, take the log out of your own eye first, and then you
        will see clearly enough to take the speck out of your brother's eye.
   6 Don't give what is holy to dogs; and don't throw your pearls
        before pigs; otherwise they may trample them with their feet and
        turn on you and attack you.

---

his own eye! Absurd? Of course. That's the point. That big log would
keep him from even getting close enough to remove the speck from
another (as, indeed, the spiritual log should). Moreover, it is absurd to
think that one should be concerned about a tiny speck in another's eye
when he has a log in his own. He must first remove his log before he can
help another. That principle ought to be applied first to the counselor and
then to the counselee. People who are able to see the speck in the eye of
another are not always too swift at detecting the log in their own. That is
why counselors are to be Nathans with respect to the Davids who come
for counseling (cf. II Samuel 12).

Does that mean one is never to be concerned about specks in the eyes
of others? Of course not. But one must not be **hypocritical** about it. Having removed the log, he will be able to **see clearly** (v. 5). Seeing clearly,
he will be able to help others with their sins.

But there is one other caution in this matter of helping others rid
themselves of **specks**. In verse 6 Jesus warns against feeding holy meat to
scavengers (**dogs**). Being the garbage collectors of the time, dogs were
considered unclean. To feed meat from the altar to dogs was a sin. This
meat was to be eaten by the priests or burned. The dog who ate such meat
would give no thought to the fact that it came from the altar. He would
make no distinction between it and any other meat. Likewise a **pig** would
care nothing about the value of pearls. He would simply **trample** them
underfoot, **turn on you and attack you** because what you gave him was
not edible. Neither the dog nor the pig will appreciate what you have
done. You won't gain anything by your gifts; neither will thank you for
the precious gift nor glorify God.

So, Jesus was saying, you should not attempt to remove specks from
the eyes of unbelievers. You will only unnecessarily aggravate them. They
will not appreciate it. You will lose your witness to them. It is not your
task to try to reform unbelievers. Those who are in the flesh cannot please
God (Romans 8:8). Why waste effort in turning them from one lifestyle
that displeases Him to another that displeases Him? Your task with unbelievers is never to counsel, but only to precounsel them (that is, evangelize

> **7** Ask and it will be given to you; seek and you will find; knock and it will be opened to you.
>
> **8** Whoever asks will receive, and whoever seeks finds, and whoever knocks has it opened to him.
>
> **9** Is there any one of you people who, when his son asks for a piece of bread, will hand him a stone,
>
> **10** or if he asks for a fish will hand him a snake?
>
> **11** So then, if you (even though you are evil) know how to give good gifts to your children, how much more will your Father in the heavens give good things to those who ask Him?

them). So, counselor, spend your time correcting *believers*—correctly.

Has what Matthew recorded been getting you down? Well, it need not. There are words of encouragement which, doubtless, Jesus knew that at this point in the sermon the disciples needed (vv. 7-12). But even these are not without a word of exhortation (the same principle is found in v. 12 that we encountered in v. 2). Counselors who have been in tense conversation with counselees ought to know when to sit back and throw out a word of encouragement. Jesus did.

Jesus knew that the disciples, hearing all that He had been saying, might have been thinking, "Where would we ever get the strength to overcome worry, stop being censorious, . . . ?" Again, remember that all of Jesus' commands are also encouragements. He never commands His own to do anything that they cannot do by His wisdom from His Word and by means of His strength. He even helps us pray (Romans 8). So we should not despair at His commands.

The answer is to come to Him in prayer (v. 7ff.). Three words—**asking, seeking, knocking**—are laid out before the wondering disciples. You **ask**. If God seems remote, **seek**, and even if He seems to have locked you out, **knock**. In other words, keep on praying until you get the wisdom and strength you need. These verbs teach persistence. They are not verbs that express actions but verbs that express habits: keep on asking, keep on seeking, keep on knocking. God answers all prayers. But He does so according to His timetable. When you are ready to receive (you may *think* that you are when you aren't), He is ready to give. And He gives what He wants, in His way (sometimes through difficult experiences that when handled rightly make us strong). That is the sort of thing to explain to counselees. Often they will complain that their prayers are not answered.

Teach counselees about God Himself. Many think because God acts

12   Therefore, whatever you want other people to do for you, that is
      precisely what you must do for them; this is what the Law and the
      Prophets are all about.

---

sovereignly, as I have indicated above, that He is unconcerned for them.
But Jesus asked them (as you also should) to consider whether God is less
concerned about His children than an earthly father is. If a son asks for
bread his father will not give him a **stone**.[1] He pointed out that if he asks
for a wriggling **fish** he will not give him a wriggling **snake**. He goes on to
say that if evil[2] parents give good things to their children, the righteous
Father will surely do every bit as much (and more) for His children. The
loving Father has a disposition to give His children good things. The problem is in us. We want them when we want them; we want them to come
our way and in our time. And we want the very thing we ask for when He
has something better to give us. Counselees who complain about unan-
swered prayers should be taught the truth contained in these words. They
should be told that continued complaints can be considered nothing but
sin in the light of Jesus' explanation. God's answers to His children's
prayers are always good. There is never reason for complaint.

In verse 12, Jesus drew out a further implication. In judging, and in
giving, you should be like the Father in heaven. Here is a form of the
golden rule. Why should one do so? Because it is the loving thing to do.
That love is **what the law and the prophets are all about**. Fulfilling
God's commandments is a matter of doing to others what you would have
them do to you. For some counselees the idea of doing for others what we
would desire to have done for us (apart from some intellectual response)
is a totally **foreign** notion. They have simply *never* looked at life that way.
Having grown up in a self-oriented culture, they have always operated on
the principle of putting themselves first. They must be *taught* the golden
rule!

Why is this so important? Because doing this is **what the law and
the prophets are all about**. If a person is about to serve God by keeping
His commandments in the Bible, he will find himself putting others in the
place where formerly he put himself. If he follows this simple instruction
of the Lord most of the problems that he has with others will evaporate.

---

1. Bread was made flat and round, pita-like, and looked somewhat like a rounded
   river stone.
2. Note Christ's assessment of human beings: they are **evil** (v. 11).

> **13** Enter in through the narrow gate; the gate that leads to destruction is wide and broad, and there are many who go through it.
>
> 14   But the gate is tight and the road is narrow that leads to life, and only a few find it.
>
> **15** Look out for false prophets who come to you in sheep's clothing, but within they are greedy wolves.

Therefore, it is a wise counselor who, noticing that self-interest seems to dominate a counselee's concerns as expressed in his conversation, his actions, and his goals, lays out verse 12 and its implications before him.

The remainder of the Sermon on the Mount deals with three antitheses. These are spoken of as two **gates** (vv. 13, 14), two **trees** (vv. 15-23), and two **foundations** (vv. 24-27).

Before closing, Jesus reminded the disciples that there are two, and only two, **gates** that people enter to obtain eternal life. One is **narrow**, the other **broad**. The narrow gate and the **road** leading to it are narrow because there are so **few** who enter that way. Yet it is the way to eternal **life** (v. 14). Most people enter the broad gate, which needs to be **wide** because there are so many who enter it. Yet it is the way to everlasting **destruction**. George Barna, in a recent poll, discovered that 99% of Americans think they are going to heaven. How deluded they are! Be sure your counselees do know the way to life through the gospel of Jesus Christ. In a way that is just the opposite from our civil law, in which a person is presumed innocent until proven guilty, Christians know that a man must be presumed lost and headed to hell unless proven saved. That is because all begin life as lost sinners, and unless they find forgiveness in Christ they will go on through life walking the broad road to finally enter the wide gate to hell. This reminder to the disciples ought also to be a reminder to every counselor. He is an evangelist as he confronts counselees whose lifestyles give little or no evidence of the new life in Christ.

In verses 15 through 23 Jesus issued a strong warning about **false prophets** ("**Look out for** them," He says; v. 15). It is appalling that so many counselors have been taken in by the false prophets of psychology. These people who ought to be leading and directing others according to the Scriptures have themselves been seduced into feeding the flock on more of the unhealthy teaching that led them into the problems that brought them to counseling in the first place. This is like trying to put out a fire by spraying gasoline on it!

That false prophets are **greedy wolves** who **come in sheep's cloth-**

16	You will know them from observing their fruit. Grapes aren't gathered from thorns or figs from thistles, are they?
17	So too every good tree produces fine fruit, but every rotten tree produces bad fruit.
18	A good tree can't produce bad fruit, nor can a rotten tree produce fine fruit.
19	Every tree that doesn't produce fine fruit is cut down and thrown into the fire.
20	So it is from their fruits that you will know them.

ing is an important insight (v. 15). The greediness that many of them have for money and prestige is clear from the prices that they charge for their wares and from the haughty attitudes that they assume. They are quite anxious to enlist the clergy in sending them more and more people to enrich their coffers. That ministers of the Word have fallen for their deceptive ways, according to them the place of **sheep** when they are actually **wolves**, is evidence that the warning has not been heeded.[1]

If they come looking like members of the flock (dressed in **sheep's clothing**), then we have the task of discerning who is and who is not a false prophet.[2] Jesus went on to give directions about detecting them. He said, "**You will know them by observing their fruit.**" All judgment is made by looking at the results of one's life. Here, Jesus enunciated that principle. The tree's produce tells you what sort of tree it is (vv. 16, 17). **Good trees** produce **good fruit, bad** ones **rotten fruit** (v. 17, 18). It can't be otherwise (v. 18). So, He said, inspect their fruit. That is how you will be able to distinguish the false from the true.

Verse 19 speaks of the seriousness of people leading God's sheep astray by insinuating themselves into the flock, pretending to be sheep; they will be **thrown into the fire** (here, the meaning is probably hell since these false teachers are represented as unbelievers: they have only the *clothing* of sheep). Warn counselees about the danger of following them.

How can you recognize a false teacher? Once more—look at the effects (fruit) of his teaching. Are people drawn closer to Jesus Christ? Does he lead them to follow His Word more faithfully? Does what he teaches accord with the Scriptures? Carefully examine the harvest. For

1. Of course, Jesus referred to all sorts of false prophets, not merely to those in counseling.
2. For additional help, see A *Call for Discernment* (1998), TIMELESS TEXTS, Woodruff, SC.

71

21	Not everyone who says to Me, "Lord, Lord," will enter into the empire from the heavens, but only the one who does the will of My Father Who is in the heavens.
22	Many will say to Me in that day, "Lord, Lord, didn't we prophesy in Your Name, and didn't we cast out demons in Your Name, and didn't we do many miracles in Your Name?"
23	But I will declare publicly, "I never knew you; **get out of here, you workers of lawlessness!**"

example, some persons wanted to know the effects of Calvinistic teaching, so two hundred years after the death of Calvin they examined the lives of the people of Geneva and the effects his teaching had on the city. They found that this city, which before Calvin came was one of the most wicked in Europe, had radically changed for the better under his teaching and, two hundred years later, was still one of the most righteous.

Why do these false teachers produce rotten fruit? They are unsaved (along with their works they will be thrown in the fire). Their profession of faith is false. They are false through and through—from beginning to the end. They are liars who present falsehood as if it were the truth. Their profession is merely verbal; they talk a good game. But there is no reality behind that talk. They *say,* "**Lord, Lord,**" but they take His Name in vain. (v. 21). Not everyone who *professes* to believe **will enter the empire from the heavens**. This warning ought to awaken every counselor so that he is not duped into believing that every one who professes, or every teaching of supposed believers, is to be accepted. There are liars abroad. Even in counseling!

They may seem quite sincere. They may have become so involved in what they teach that they, themselves, have become deceived. The worst form of error is self-deceit. Such persons will have a rude awakening when they stand before the Lord in the day of judgment (v. 22). Jesus will say to them (and to all who are within hearing distance), "**I never knew you**" (v. 23). He will tell them to depart from His heavenly empire for all eternity.

False teachers may even have been among those who had possession of the special gifts granted to the members of the early church (v. 22). Such gifts are not clinching evidence that God is with a teacher. It is not gifts or looking like sheep that impresses the Lord. There is but one thing in view in assessing them: do they **do the will of the Father in the heavens** (v. 21). If their faith and their message is true, they will. That is what you must look for. All else is irrelevant.

24 So then, whoever hears these words of Mine and does them may be compared to a wise man who built his house on the rock.

25 And the rain came down, and the rivers flooded, and the winds blew and beat against that house, but it didn't fall because it had been constructed on a foundation of rock.

26 Whoever hears these words of Mine and doesn't do them may be compared to a foolish man who built his house on the sand.

Finally, Jesus closed the sermon with the parable of the two **foundations** (vv. 24-27). The parable is too well known for me to take the time or space to retell. Besides, the record is so clear that one cannot miss the point or—to think again—can he? Well, many have. The parable is often interpreted as an evangelistic message. And certainly the gospel is present in this parable as it is in all of the Scriptures. Nothing can be treated rightly without reference to the saving work of Jesus Christ. But its application, given by the Lord Himself, is not evangelistic. It has to do with the obedience to which He called His disciples (of that day, and of every era since). Hearing Christ's words is not enough. They must lead to obedient action: that is what He is saying. Unless one has a foundation of obedience, when troubles and difficulties come in like a flood, when winds of adversity blow, he will not be able to withstand them.

Counselees who have been swept away by the floods of life may often be in their sad condition because they have failed to build their lives on the solid teachings of Christ. Oh, they may be able to articulate them; but the fundamental question is whether they have been putting those teachings into practice. In other words, the very things that Jesus taught will lead to a solid life that cannot be overthrown by the trials that come on as a flood. Teach this to counselees. Probe to find where they have failed to appropriate Christ's teachings, thus weakening the foundation by which their lives are supported. You might even quickly go through the sermon with a counselee, expositing it, and asking after each thrust Christ makes, "Have you built your life on this? If you haven't, no wonder your world has collapsed." In other words, examine the condition of the foundation of the lives of counselees.

That this great sermon was heard by more than the disciples, though principally directed to them, is clear from verses 28 and 29. What **astonished** the crowds was that Jesus taught with **authority**. When a counselor does so today, that still astonishes people. There is so much weak teaching in the church it is almost like it was in the days when teachers said, "Hillel

27   And the rain came down, and the rivers flooded, and the winds blew and beat upon that house and it fell, and it was totally destroyed.

28 Now the result was that when Jesus finished these sayings, the crowds were astonished at His teaching

29   since He taught them as an authority and not as their scribes.

---

says so and so, but Shammai says thus and thus." People were left to take their choices. Magazines and books today are published with opposing points of view, even giving five views of this or that. If five views are presented, at least four of them are wrong! Why don't Christians decide what they believe to be true and teach it—with biblical authority? Counselees who come for help (not those who pretend to do so) will appreciate it if you counsel with authority. Most have been looking for an authoritative Word from God. But, of course, you must be sure that when you tell a counselee, "This is what God requires," you are telling the truth! In other words, every counselor must counsel authoritatively, but he must acquire that authority from careful, accurate study and application of the Bible at all points. That is biblical counseling, and nothing else is.

CHAPTER 8

> **1** When He came down from the mountains, large crowds followed Him.
> 2   And, there, a leper came and knelt before Him, saying, "Lord, if You want to, You can cleanse me."
> 3   So He stretched out His hand and touched him, saying, "I do want to; be cleansed." And instantly he was cleansed of leprosy.

In this chapter we are introduced to Jesus' mighty healings and power over nature, a concern that carries over into the next chapter.[1] Once more, it seems, Matthew has grouped his materials for effect. And what an effect it is!

In verse 1 we see that **large crowds** have begun to **follow** Jesus. While preaching to the multitudes was part of His ministry, there was also a problem connected with these massive gatherings. They so called attention to Him that it was possible that the envious officials would seek to kill Him before the time. Jesus was on a schedule ("My hour has not yet come"), and He would not depart from it. For this reason He cautiously sought to avoid all unnecessary publicity (cf. vv. 4, 18; 9:24). Yet His fame spread. Counselors who help many soon find that they are deluged with calls for help. They discover that advertising is not only unnecessary, but can become a problem. Indeed, they will come to a conclusion that they are unable to do everything themselves, and they will soon begin to train others to assist them. That is what Jesus did (cf. chapter 10).[2]

The first healing was a cleansing from leprosy (vv. 2-4). The faith of this leper is seen in his words: **"If You want to You can cleanse me."** Jesus declared, **"I do want to; be cleansed."** And **instantly, he was cleansed**. When counselees come with that sort of faith in Christ, fully assured that He has the answers to their problems in His Word, when they believe that what you tell them cannot fail and do that which they are commanded by the Lord in the Scriptures, they too find that their problems can be dealt with fully and quickly. The healing here was a miraculous one, of course. You will not perform miracles in counseling. But

---

1. Chapter 9 should end with verse 35. Together 4:23 and verse 35 bracket the great teaching and healing sections. The matters mentioned in 9:36, 37 are introductory to what follows so that chapter 10 ought to begin with verse 36.
2. Likewise, Jethro advised Moses to seek help.

75

4 Then Jesus said to him, "See that you tell no one, but rather go show yourself to the priest, and offer the gift that Moses commanded, as a testimony to them."

5 As He was going toward Capernaum a centurion came to Him, pleading with Him and saying,

6 "Lord, my servant boy is lying at home paralyzed, in torturous pain."

7 And He replied, "I will go and heal him."

8 But the centurion said in response,

> Lord, I am not worthy to have You come under my roof. All that You need to do is to say the word and my servant boy will be healed.

---

solid faith in Christ's Word followed by obedience will lead to lasting results that the world knows nothing about. I have seen, for instance, depression lifted in a day that way, and, by continued obedience to Christ, lastingly avoided in the years ahead. Assure your counselees that what God says is true; and that for those with faith it is effective.

Verse 4 indicates how Jesus tried to avoid unnecessary publicity (as I pointed out above) and how He also conformed to the law. In order that the cleansed leper might become a part of society again, he had to pass the test for cleansing that was commanded (Leviticus 13:12, 13). While He didn't want undo publicity from crowds, for the sake of the leper, Jesus did urge him to show his cleansing to the priests **for a testimony to them**. The conformity to God's law, showing the disappearance of the disease and giving the thank offering (the gift), was a **testimony** to the priests that Jesus had come not to abolish but to fulfill the law. Was it because of this evidence (here a sample of what must have happened many times over) that later, when scribes and Pharisees failed to do so, a number of the **priests** believed in Him (Acts 6:7)? They had the proof presented to them in concrete form. Would it not be powerful to send some of the counselees you have helped back to talk to the psychologists who could not help them to show what *God* did for them—as a **testimony** to them?

In verses 5 through 13 the healing of the centurion's **servant boy** clearly demonstrated the **authority** and power of the Lord Jesus. Again, also, the faith of this pagan centurion is front and center in the narrative (cf. v. 10). The power of Christ was shown by Jesus' merely speaking the word and the servant's being healed—at a distance (v. 13). The **faith** of the centurion is evidenced by his humble belief (vv. 8-10). The centurion said, **"All that You need to do is to say the word"** (v. 8). Show counselees from this passage that for the Lord to solve their spiritual problems is

9   I am a person under authority, and I have soldiers under me. I say to one, "Go," and he goes, and to another, "Come," and he comes, and to my slave, "Do this," and he does it.

10 When Jesus heard this, He was amazed and said to those who were following Him,

       I assure you that I haven't found anyone in Israel with such faith.

11   Now I tell you that many will come from the East and the West and will sit at the table with Abraham and Isaac and Jacob in the empire from the heavens.

12   but the sons of the empire will be thrown out into the darkness outside where there will be weeping and grinding of teeth.

13 Then Jesus said to the centurion, "Go, as you have believed let it be done for you." And the servant boy was healed at that very hour.

---

every bit as simple. Remember the story of the man who was let down from the roof (cf. 9:2-8)? There, Jesus said that He would demonstrate His authority to deal with spiritual matters (forgive sins) by His authority over physical illness. The same is true here.

Jesus' **amazement** at the centurion's faith—reasoning from his own to Christ's greater authority—became the occasion for Him to compare and contrast it with that of the people of Israel. Indeed, He even took the opportunity to look ahead to the era in which the Gentiles would comprise the new element in the church (empire) and in which Old Testament believers would form one body with New Testament believers, making, as Paul put it in Ephesians, one new man (vv. 11, 12). The sad fact that the unbelieving Jews would be **thrown out of** the empire and replaced by Gentiles is noted (v. 12). This would also mean their suffering the torments of eternal **darkness** apart from the Father of Lights. Erstwhile counselees who do not exercise faith in Christ's Word have not only the continuation of **torturous pain** in this life to look forward to (v. 6) but also the sorrows of loss in the future (v. 12[1]). That God leaves some behind, who fail to exercise faith—for whatever reason—is apparent. Thus, you will have to give up on some such as well. There is a time, after all attempts are made,[2] to go on to those who do respond in faith.

How important, then, it is to help counselees—many of whom are fearful to step out in faith—learn to trust the Word of God. The problem with many is not fear so much as it is doubt (about which see James 1:6-

---

1. If, indeed, they are not believers and reject the gospel they will suffer hell.
2. The Lord Jesus gave the Jews forty years before the utter destruction in 70 AD.

> **14** Now when Jesus arrived at Peter's house, He saw his mother-in-law lying in bed with a fever.
> 15 So He touched her hand, and the fever left her, and she got up and served Him.
> **16** When evening came, they brought to Him many demoniacs, and He cast out the spirits with a word, and healed all who had illnesses.
> 17 So the word spoken through the prophet Isaiah was fulfilled: **He Himself took our sicknesses, and bore our diseases.**

8). This centurion recognized authority when he saw it; that is what counselees must do. Help them to understand that whenever God speaks, He speaks with **authority** (cf. 7:29), and that authority means that He is to be obeyed implicitly. So much agony could be avoided if only counselees exercised the obedient faith of this centurion.

In verses 14 through 17 we read of the healing of Peter's **mother-in-law.**[1] The fever she had must have been severe. She was bedridden. But with a mere touch she was healed completely. That fact is made clear in that **she got up and served Him**[2] (v. 15). The importance of this incident, so briefly noted, seems to be that this was a healing in which a member of a disciple's family was involved. Anyone who doubted could talk to Peter about it. He could even check out the lasting results of the healing. It is always helpful to have a few people at hand who have been helped by biblical counseling to whom you may send doubters. Perhaps you could make a list of such persons—who were counseled for various problems—who would make themselves available for such purposes.

Note in verse 16 (as elsewhere in the gospel accounts) that demon possession is distinguished from disease. Those who say that demon possession is but a primitive way of explaining illness are simply not playing fairly with the New Testament text. The writers knew the difference, Jesus knew the difference, and the difference is set forth clearly. Explaining things for the benefit of those who wonder about the faith and its power to overcome problems is often hindered by those who are fuzzy about their language. Using the language of the psychologists, for example, rather than biblical language can obscure the real problem. In writing, lack of careful distinctions and biblical language frequently muddles things for the reader. If you speak or write about counseling, please think carefully about how to express what you say.

1. As an aside, note that Peter (the supposed first pope) was married!
2. Presumably, something to eat.

18 Now when Jesus saw that a crowd had gathered around Him, He gave orders to cross to the other side.

19 But one scribe came and said to Him: "Teacher, I will follow wherever You may go."

20 And Jesus responded, "The foxes have holes, and the birds of the sky have nests, but the Son of Man doesn't have a place to lay His head."

Matthew referred to Isaiah 53:4 as a prediction that was being fulfilled by the many healings of Christ. The word used by Isaiah means **sicknesses** (though the Septuagint has "sins"), literally, "things that wear us out"—as sicknesses do. It is important to understand that the whole complex of human difficulties[1] was dealt with by the cross. Jesus demonstrated temporally through these healings what He would do eternally by His death for poor sinners (cf. Revelation 21:4). He still demonstrates the perfect eternal reconciliation that will occur in the new Paradise of God by the healings of relationships with God and man that take place through counseling today.

In verses 18 through 27 two incidents are folded together. To avoid the crowds (see above) Jesus **gave orders to cross to the other side** of the lake.[2] Certainly, this is not what the crowd wanted. But, unlike many today, Jesus was never governed by the will of the crowds. He did not operate according to what the polls indicated. He didn't even wet His finger and hold it in the air to see how the wind was blowing. His agenda was set by Him and by the Father, and He operated solely according to it. Too many counselees want to tell the counselor how and when he should do what; too many counselors are governed by what they are told. A counselor ought to be able to set his own priorities and adhere to them.[3] How can he instruct counselees to get control of runaway schedules when he fails to follow his own?

The first incident involved two would-be disciples (vv. 19-22). Interestingly, the first is said to be a **scribe**. He was making a commitment apart from a true understanding of what it would involve when he declared that he would follow Jesus **wherever** He would **go**. Jesus set him straight by telling him what that would involve (v. 22). This respected teacher who was enamored with Jesus and His teaching presumably had

---

1. Sin and all its effects brought into being by Adam's transgression.
2. See verse 4 for information on why Jesus wanted to escape from the crowds.
3. Always allowing in that schedule time for meeting true emergencies, contingencies, etc.

> 21 And a different disciple said to Him: "Lord, let me first go and bury my father."

never had to suffer any hardships. To **follow** Jesus literally meant to become a wanderer, with no place to put down roots. That was quite contrary to the sedentary life of the scribe, who was basically an academic. It was almost like asking a present day seminary teacher to become a traveling evangelist. He would have to leave his study, his books, and his friends behind. This scribe, who may have meant well, had not thought through what following Christ would be like. He had not gathered relevant data and then counted the cost.

Counselees will similarly agree too quickly to follow some biblical path of action. Stop them in their tracks and, as Jesus did, point out what doing so involves. Frequently counselors are delighted with the immediate favorable and enthusiastic response of counselees. They send them out to accomplish tasks that, once they become aware of what these tasks are like, they will not (or can not) accomplish. Better from the first to let a counselee know what a task entails so that he will not fail for lack of knowledge.

Commitment is a word that is seldom unpacked. So far as I can see, it consists of five elements that must be satisfied in order to accomplish the task to which one commits himself. The first is the one that Jesus calls this scribe to consider. They are as follows:
1. Understanding what it is that one is committing himself to do.
2. A desire to do it (basically, a desire to do it to please God—even if the task itself is not desirable).
3. The ability, skills and resources to bring it off.
4. A schedule, with short term goals, that he intends to follow by which he will accomplish the task.
5. Following through (actually keeping the schedule).

There are many ramifications of each of these points about which I could say more, but these are suggestive enough to indicate that commitment is not so easy as this scribe thought. If any one of these five elements is missing, the task will not be done. Jesus needed only to point out the first to stop this scribe from blundering ahead.

The second would-be disciple said he too would follow Jesus but added a proviso: **let me first go and bury my father**. The first would follow too hastily; the second too slowly. To bury one's father seemed like a reasonable request. But it was not according to Jesus, Who gave the reply

22 But Jesus replied, "Follow Me, and leave the dead to bury their own dead."

23 So He got into the boat and His disciples followed Him.

24 Suddenly a great storm arose on the sea, so that the boat was being swamped by the waves, but He was sleeping.

25 So they went and woke Him, saying, "Lord, save us, we are going to die!"

26 He answered: "Why are you afraid, you men of little faith?" Then, getting up, He rebuked the winds and the sea and it was very calm.

27 The men were amazed, saying, "What sort of man is this that even the winds and the sea obey Him?"

---

that is found in verse 22. Was this a harsh response? Not at all. He was about to send out disciples on a task that couldn't wait. He wanted people who were immediately available to go where He sent them and to do as He directed them. This person was putting his own conditions on his willingness to do so.

There are counselees like this man today. They will do as God directs in His Word—*so long as* certain conditions are met. God will have none of that. Neither should you. If someone says "I'll break up my homosexual relationship if and when my partner agrees," that is unacceptable. He must do so because he wants to please God, not because he wishes to please his partner! The principle taught here is that whatever God requires one to do *now*, must be done now.[1]

The second incident is recorded in verses 23 through 27. In it, Jesus demonstrated His authority over nature itself by **rebuking** the **winds** and the **waves**. That this was a very severe storm seems apparent since fishermen, who doubtless had weathered many other storms, were fearful for their lives (v. 25). That Jesus could sleep during it also tells us something about His perfect confidence in the protection of His heavenly Father. Jesus asked a question (v. 26): **"Why are you afraid, you men of little faith?"** The question was not asked to gather data. Like most why-type questions it was asked to make them think. Good counselors ask why-type questions for the same purpose. The question elicited the right sort of response as is evident in the question that they contemplated (mentioned in v. 27). Why-type questions put people on the spot (something that you

---

1. Of course, as counselors, we have no right to demand immediate compliance to a task unless the Bible does. According to Numbers 19:11-22, to participate in a funeral made one unclean for 7 days. He was asking for a week's delay.

28 When He came to the other side, to the country of the Gadarenes, two demoniacs came from among the tombs to meet Him. They were so violent that no one could travel along that road.

29 And they began to shout, "What do You want with us, Son of God? Have You come here to torture us ahead of time?"

30 Now there was a large herd of pigs feeding some distance away from them,

31 and the demons begged Him, saying, "If You cast us out, send us into the heard of pigs."

32 He replied, "Go!" So they came out and went away to the pigs. Then, suddenly, the entire herd rushed over the precipice into the sea and died in the water.

33 And the herdsmen fled and went away into the city and reported everything, and all about the demoniacs.

34 So, right away, the whole city came out to meet Jesus, and when they saw Him they pleaded with Him to depart from their borders.

---

don't want to do when gathering data[1]).

The final incident in the chapter (vv. 28-34) deals with the reaction of unbelievers to Jesus' miracles: they chose swine over souls. Again, the **demoniacs**, like the storm, were of the most violent type[2] (v. 28). The demons had knowledge about their future. They **begged not to be tortured ahead of time**. Even though they knew their final destiny, they still kept on doing wickedness. How like many counselees!

The city, composed largely of Gentiles,[3] made a choice. It was a bad one. It was based on fear and economics. Watch out for the same factors in counselees who make bad choices. Ask them what were the determining factors in a bad choice. Use this passage to show how people **plead** with Jesus to get out of their lives (v. 34). Most counselees who are in trouble because of their lifestyles arrived at the point where they need counsel through a series of poor choices. Mention this, unearth any such choices, make it clear how these choices led them into sin and its consequences, and help them to develop proper attitudes toward decision-making in the future.

---

1. Or they will give you quick answers to get you off their backs.
2. Matthew chooses incidents that could never be explained by any normal process.
3. That is why there was no problem with their herding pigs.

CHAPTER 9

1   So getting into a boat, He crossed over and came to His own city.

2   And, there, they brought a paralytic to Him, who was lying on a mat. When Jesus saw their faith, He said to the paralytic, "Take courage, child; your sins are forgiven."

3   Immediately, some of the scribes began to comment to each other, "This man is speaking blasphemy."

4   But Jesus, knowing their thoughts, said,
    Why are you thinking evil things in your hearts?

5   Which is easier, to say, "Your sins are forgiven you," or to say, "Get up and walk"?

6   But so that you will know that the Son of Man has authority on earth to forgive sins,"

He said to the paralytic, "Get up, take your mat and go home."

The ninth chapter of Matthew is a continuation of sample healings and other miracles by Jesus that were begun in the previous chapter. The city noted in verse 1 was Capernaum, the place that Jesus made His headquarters. The story of the paralytic found in verses 2 through 8 has been mentioned in the previous chapter. In order to demonstrate that He had the power and the **authority** to forgive sins, Jesus healed the paralytic (v. 6). This silenced those who called Jesus' forgiveness **blasphemy**. The question in verse 5, about whether it is **easier to forgive** sins or heal, is intriguing. The scribes thought the claim to forgive was easier since it could not be proven—it did not immediately result in noticeable effects. They would have replied, "I'm from Missouri; show me." The fact is that God used others over the years to heal, only One could **forgive sins**. And the cost was enormous! Counselees often reason with the scribes: "If I do not have tangible evidence, then I will doubt." It is a matter of faith—as demonstrated by the incidents recorded in the previous chapter. The man of faith takes God's Word for it; he believes even when he cannot see (cf. Hebrews 11:1). Counselees must often do the same. They must take the Scriptures for what they say whether or not they see immediate, visible results. To bring them to such faith is the work of the Spirit of God, of course. You cannot do so. But you can present the facts to them, call upon them to exercise faith, and show them passages such as this in which faith was rewarded. So much of what a counselor does depends on faith in God's Word. Learn all you can about faith and its hindrances.

7   And he got up and went home.
8   But when the crowds saw this, they were afraid and glorified God because He had given such authority to human beings.
9 Now as Jesus was going along from there, He saw a man named Matthew sitting at the tax collector's desk, and said to him, "Follow Me." And he got up and followed Him.
10 Now as Jesus was sitting at the table in his house, a number of tax collectors and sinners came and sat at the table with Jesus and His disciples.
11 But when the Pharisees saw this, they asked His disciples, "Why does your teacher eat with tax collectors and sinners?"
12 When Jesus heard this He said,
> It isn't those who are well who need a doctor, but those who are sick;

Notice, as an aside, that it was in their **hearts** that the scribes were **thinking evil things**. Never represent the heart as standing for emotion, as it does in modern Western society. In biblical terms, the heart is the place where everything internal (including thinking and planning) goes on. Always read it so in Scripture.

Verses 9 through 13 record the calling of Matthew, the writer of this Gospel, and the reaction of the religious leaders to the events connected thereto. Matthew had been a tax collector. Tax collectors were hated (and excommunicated) for several reasons. There was the natural antipathy to those who take away your money. The system was corrupt and those who operated within it usually were too. Tax collectors were considered traitors; they collaborated with the hated Roman government for the sake of money. You can see how they were classified with **sinners** by the Pharisees (v. 11); both were considered outcasts—respectable people didn't eat with them!

But Jesus wasn't interested in the respect of the Pharisees who cared nothing for the lost sinners whom Jesus had come to save. Jesus cut in on the conversation between the Pharisees and His disciples and said, "**It isn't those who are well who need a doctor, but those who are sick**." That said it all. Counselor, that too spells out your ministry: go and help those who are **sick**. You will find that those who acknowledge their needs will be forthcoming for counseling; those who do not, who think that they have none, will not. Like Jesus, Who came not to call **righteous people, but sinners,** you are called to mingle with the unlovely. They will not always be the most gentle, refined, or sophisticated. Many will come with sin clinging to their very garments. But Jesus ministered to them. If you

13   so go, and learn what this means: **I want mercy and not sacri-fice**. I didn't come to call righteous people, but sinners.

14 At that time, John's disciples came to Him, asking, "Why should we and the Pharisees fast, but not Your disciples?"

15 Jesus replied:

Can the wedding guests mourn when the Bridegroom is with them? The days will come when the Bridegroom is taken from them, and at that time they will fast.

16   Now nobody puts a patch of unshrunk cloth on an old garment because the patch will pull away from the garment and the hole will be larger.

17   Neither do they put new wine into old wineskins; if they do, the wineskins will burst, the wine will run out and the wineskins will be ruined. Rather, they put new wine into fresh wineskins, and both are preserved.

---

want only a "respectable" clientele, you will fail in your ministry to those in need of the "doctor."

Notice that Jesus responds to the Pharisees in terms of the Scriptures, sending them off to study the verse, **I want mercy and not sacrifice**. Detractors sometimes are best dealt with in this way. You may say to them, "Go study the Scripture that says. . . ." Send them off to study the Bible. That, of course, is precisely what the Pharisees needed to do. They had taken from the Bible only what they wanted to take; they ignored other passages.

Next, in verses 14 through 17 an important discussion between Jesus and some of John's disciples is recorded. They sided with the **Pharisees** (v. 14) in pointing out that both **fasted** and Jesus' disciples didn't. They wanted to know why. Jesus replied with three illustrations designed to teach them. A **wedding** is a time of feasting and joy, not **mourning**. It is like a wedding for the disciples to have Me with them. Besides, **unshrunk cloth** isn't used to **patch old garments**. Why not? It will cause a **larger hole** in the end because it will rip more of the cloth. The old ways will not do. I am introducing a new era. Don't try to **patch** the old ways onto the new. And there will be new ways of living, new **wineskins** that alone can contain new fermenting wine. Old ways cannot contain something that is volatile, expanding, fresh. They have had their day, but will now crack under the new pressures.

Counselees sometimes fail to realize that ways that were right for the time are no longer so. Yet they cling to them when they should adopt new

18 As He was saying these things to them, a ruler appeared and came and knelt before Him and said, "My daughter has just died. But come, lay Your hand on her and she will live."

19 And Jesus got up and followed him, and so did His disciples.

20 But just then, a woman who had suffered a hemorrhage for twelve years came up behind Him and touched the border of His garment.

21 (She said to herself, "If only I can touch His garment, I shall be healed.")

22 Jesus turned around, and saw her and said, "Take courage, daughter, your faith has healed you." And the woman was healed from that hour on.

---

ones. For instance, the use of the King James version as a fixed doctrine and practice is foolish. The Scriptures themselves are enough to learn and understand; why should new converts be required to learn an ancient and outmoded language as well? The Bible was written in the language of the people and should be translated in each era for those who live in it. What is a "besom"? Do you know? The King James version uses the word. Why not translate it "broom?" The word "let" meant "hinder" in 1611; today it means "allow"—just the opposite. Why confuse people by this language? Moreover, poor translations sometimes led to ecclesiastical views such as "after Easter" (Acts 12:4). The Greek text read in 1611 the same as it does today: "after the Passover." In its day, there were those who didn't want to accept this new KJV. Thus the writers spoke in its preface about people who will accept nothing but what is "hammered on their own anvil." That is a pretty powerful description of some today who will not change as they should. John's disciples had that sort of problem.

In verses 18 through 26 we read about a healing incident within another incident. Jesus' complete control over the situation stands out. He was in absolute command of His time and his activities. Interruptions did not disturb Him; He handled them. Counselors must learn not to be irritated or thrown off their schedules by interruptions. They must allow for such happenings in the planning and the pursuit of those schedules. Fudge factors should be built into the weekday schedule. Counselors who are in a hurry, all caught up in activities and stressed out by them, set a poor example for their counselees. Jesus was in no hurry. For those who follow Jesus, there is no "burnout!" That is a modern excuse for poor planning.

Moreover, we see that Jesus played no favorites: the unknown woman was as important as the ruler and his daughter. A person's status had nothing to do with the service that He rendered. So should it be with you. If some person has more influence or wealth, you must never give

23 When Jesus came to the ruler's house and saw the flute players and the crowd making a racket, He said,
24 "Get out! The girl hasn't died; she is sleeping." But they laughed out loud at Him.
25 Now, after the crowd had been put outside, He went in and took hold of her hand, and the girl got up.
26 And the report of this went into all of that land.
27 Now as Jesus set out from there, two blind men followed, shouting, "Have mercy on us, Son of David!"
28 So when He went inside a house, the blind men came to Him, and Jesus asked them, "Do you believe that I can do this?" They said, "Yes, Lord."

---

him preferred treatment (cf. James 2:1-4).

The **ruler** came, pleading with Christ to raise his **daughter** from the dead. In his statement, "**lay Your hand on her and she will live**," we see remarkable faith exhibited. The healing of the woman who touched the border of Jesus' garment shows something of the humble faith that He honors. She did not think it right to touch *Him*; she was willing to settle for something that was His. She was unworthy; yet she knew to Whom to go for help. And, of course, she found it. Counselees come sometimes with a sense of self-importance. They want things now, they want them their way and they want. . . (you name it). The way to receive something from Jesus is to come asking for His *gracious* help—help that He gives to which, in and of yourself, you are not entitled.

The raising of the ruler's daughter demonstrated once more the absolute control of the Savior over all things. The waves and the seas were at His command, and death itself was under His control. He excluded the mourners, who in that culture made a great show of death (vv. 23, 24). He said, "she **hasn't died**." The professional mourners laughed at Him for making such a statement. But it was He Who had the last laugh. There are those who laugh at the suggestion that people's lives can be changed by the Scriptures alone, apart from psychology. The time will come when the tables will be turned. To treat the teachings of the Bible with scorn is dangerous. Once more we see Jesus' fame growing (v. 26) as the result of this remarkable incident.

The story of the **two blind men** (vv. 27-31) shows again how Jesus was willing to be delayed in His plans (obviously having made time for such delays; another such delay occurs in v. 32). As He was **setting out** the blind men approached Him. Note, too, how each event led to Jesus'

29   Then He touched their eyes and said, "What shall happen to you will be in keeping with your faith."

30   And their eyes were opened. Then Jesus sternly warned them, saying, "See that you don't let anybody know."

31   But they went out and spread His fame all over that whole land.

32   As they were leaving there some people appeared who brought a dumb demoniac to Him.

33   And after the demon was cast out, the dumb man spoke and the crowds marveled, saying, "Never has anything like this been seen in Israel!"

34   But the Pharisees said, "He casts out demons by the ruler of the demons."

35   Now Jesus went about all the cities and villages, teaching in their synagogs and preaching the good news about the empire, and healing every sort of disease and every kind of illness.

---

greater popularity (v. 31).

Jesus asked them if they **believed** He could heal them of their blindness. They said, **"Yes."** Then Jesus set forth this important principle: **"What shall happen to you will be in keeping with your faith"** (v. 29). It might be worthwhile to frame that statement, set it forth in a brochure, or otherwise display it to a counselee. At the outset of counseling it is important to stress the crucial place of faith in the promises and ability of the Lord Jesus to deal with their problems. If this chapter and the last teach anything, it is the crucial nature of faith on the part of the one whom Jesus helps. From time to time ask the same question that Jesus did, **"Do you believe?"** That puts the main issue up front and center. If a counselee has little or no faith that Jesus can solve his problem, he can expect little or nothing in return.

Verses 32 and 33 record the healing of the **dumb** man who was possessed by a demon. Two evaluations of the healings of Jesus are given in verses 33 and 34. The crowd's evaluation was that what happened was uniquely wonderful. The Pharisees, who were jealous, concluded that Jesus was in league with the devil! There is nothing new about these two widely varying assessments. While the wording may differ, there are always those who react positively and those who react negatively to the work of Jesus Christ. Expect it in the results of your counseling as God blesses His Word by helping people get out of their troubles. Amazing as it may seem, not everyone will respond joyfully to the help you give to counselees.

Verse 35 ought to be the last verse in Chapter 9 as it is the bracketing

36 And when He looked at the crowds He felt pity for them because they were harassed and helpless like sheep without a shepherd.

37 Then He said to His disciples, "The harvest is abundant, but the workers are few.

38 So ask the Owner of the harvest to send out workers into His harvest fields."

---

verse for the teaching-healing section that began in 4:23.[1] Chapter 10 ought to have begun with the words of verse 9:36 since, along with verses 37 and 38, they provide the background for the important account of the sending out of the twelve presented in chapter ten. After speaking about the extensive tour that Jesus made around the cities and villages in the North, and after telling us again and again about His growing popularity, Matthew tells us that Jesus took steps to reach even more with the message of the kingdom. It was obvious that He could neither preach to everyone nor help all of those who needed healing. So, as He recognized this fact, He began to **pity** the **crowds**. They were **harassed and helpless like sheep without a shepherd**. That is to say, they were deeply troubled about life and its problems, but had no one to whom they could turn to find answers.

Do you counsel because you also recognize this problem? Certainly our situation has not changed radically from what we see happening then. There are crowds of people who are in the same condition. You, counselor, have what they need. How are you going to meet that need? You cannot do it all. If you are a solid, biblical counselor, you know that most of the pastors and "Christian" counselors in your area simply do not counsel biblically—if they counsel at all. I encourage you to help others learn how to counsel. Train them; let them sit in on your counseling. Hold courses. Set up seminars. Give out books. You should concentrate on doing whatever it takes to multiply yourself.

Jesus did. Saying to His disciples that **the harvest is great, but the workers are few**, He urged them to ask the **Owner of the harvest to send out** (literally, "thrust out") **workers into his harvest field**. The first step is to get those very persons who are concerned about the lack of solid, biblical workers to pray that God will raise them up to reap the harvest. Here, of course, the concern is about spreading the gospel of salvation. But in the salvation that Jesus offers, one is not only saved from the pen-

---

1. Notice that the two verses are virtually the same.

89

CHAPTER 10

1   Then He called His twelve disciples to come forward, and He gave them authority to cast out unclean spirits and to heal every sort of disease and every kind of illness.

2   Now these are the names of the twelve apostles: First, Simon, who is called Peter, and his brother Andrew, and James, Zebedee's son, and his brother John,

3   Philip and Bartholomew, Thomas and Matthew (the tax collector), James, Alphaeus' son and Thaddaeus,

4   Simon the Canaanean and Judas Iscariot (who betrayed Him).

---

alty of sin, but also goes on to be saved from the power of sin. That is what counseling is all about. It is a part of the process of sanctification.

The interesting thing is that from those who were urged to pray for workers, He then selected twelve to become such workers. Presumably, these twelve were among those who were praying for harvesters. God answered their prayers by making them such. Those concerned to pray earnestly for counselors in areas in which they are few may also find themselves called to this work. Every pastor, by the nature of pastoral work as it is described in the Bible, ought to be a counselor. A counselor is one who can truly shepherd the sheep. He is one who can help those who are **harassed and helpless** with no one to tell them what to do and where to go to find help. The sad picture today is that many pastors do not counsel because of failure to understand this, because of laziness, or because they have been taught rather to refer counselees.

In verse 1 we read that Jesus **called His twelve disciples** (that is, those who were to become the **twelve**) to be teachers and healers as He had been. They would multiply the work that He was doing. In calling them Jesus equipped them for the work. He did two things: He gave them **authority** (v. 1), and He gave them explicit **instructions** (v. 5ff.). For official counseling,[1] counselors need the same. The authority Jesus granted them was to teach, heal, and cast out demons. Interestingly, Jesus' concern was for teaching when He saw the crowds distressed. Healing was

---

1. All Christians should counsel unofficially. But every elder of the church is called to counsel officially as a part of the task of ruling the flock as a shepherd. For details, see my book *Competent to Counsel*. His authority is twofold: the authority of the Bible and of the office to which Christ has called him and to which the church has ordained him (set him apart).

5   These twelve Jesus sent out with the following instructions:
    Don't go into any Gentile territory, don't enter any Samaritan city.
6   Rather, go to the lost sheep of the house of Israel.
7   And as you go, preach, saying, "The empire from the heavens is at
        hand."
8   Heal the sick, raise the dead, cleanse the lepers, cast out the
        demons; you received without cost, give without cost.

---

there, but preaching predominated. The twelve are named in verses 2 through 4.

The instructions that Jesus gave were detailed. First, He made it clear that things must be done in the proper sequence and order according to His timing. That is why He forbade them to go into **Samaritan** or **Gentile** areas (v. 5). Rather, they were to go to the **lost sheep of the house of Israel** (v. 6). The gospel had to be preached to the Jew first (as Paul also pointed out). People in the church who need help are those who ought to hold priority for the counselor (cf. Galatians 6:10). Many from the outside may wish to come; and there is room for them to receive counsel after they are successfully evangelized (precounseled) and become a part of the church. But a pastor can spend all of his time trying to evangelize others and never get around to caring for the harassed sheep. Evangelism is the work of all the members of the church (Acts 8:4 makes that clear), not merely the work of the pastor. Indeed, his principal work is to deal with the flock, as the word pastor ("shepherd") means.

Verse 7 indicates that the message was the same as that which John the Baptist preached and Jesus after him. The message about the coming of the fifth empire of Daniel (the church) into which all who trust Christ as Savior may enter is maintained throughout the New Testament with absolute continuity.[1]

While the laborer is worthy of his hire, the Christian preacher is careful to take nothing from those to whom he preaches the gospel. He must be supported by God's people alone (cf. III John 7, 8). Churches too often have been known for grabbing and grasping for money. That is entirely wrong. They should be known for *giving*. Jesus' words are powerful: **you received without cost, give without cost** (v. 8). So, while they were not to charge for the gospel, they were to accept food and hospitality from those to whom they preached on the basis that **the workman deserves his**

---

1. In the last verse of the book of Acts we see that Paul also is still preaching the
   same message.

9   Don't take gold or silver or brass in your belts;
10   take no wallet on the trip, or second coats or sandals or staff. The workman deserves his food.
   11 Whenever you enter a city or village, find out who in it is worthy, and stay there until you leave.
12   Now as you enter a house give a greeting,
13   and if the house is indeed worthy, let your peace come upon it; but if it isn't worthy, take back your greeting of peace.
14   Whenever anyone doesn't receive you or listen to your words, go outside that house or city and shake the dust from your feet.
15   Let Me assure you that it will be more tolerable for Sodom and Gomorrah on the Judgment Day than for that city.

---

food (10). It is clear from the fact that they were not to take money for expenses or supplies for general needs (vv. 9, 10) that these things were to be provided by those who **received** them. How that translates into the counseling situation varies according to the circumstances at hand. But it certainly excludes getting rich off of counseling people in need.

Matters regarding their reception are also spelled out. They were to look for a person who was **worthy** (v. 11; that is, someone who was honestly open to the gospel). They were to live in his home until they left the city. They were to pronounce a blessing on a house as they entered. But whenever they discovered that those within were unworthy, the greeting *shalom* (peace) was to be rescinded (vv. 11-15). Indeed, they were to make it clear that they didn't want to take even the dust of their city or home with them as they left (to indicate that they had nothing more to do with them, they were to shake the dust from their feet). Since **Sodom and Gomorrah** had not had the opportunity to hear the gospel from Jesus' disciples, it would be **more tolerable** for them **on the Judgment Day** than for those who rejected the disciples' message. Counselors must remember—and make clear to their counselees—that it is dangerous to reject the Word of God.

Jesus wanted His disciples to know what they were getting into. So He spoke quite openly about the persecution that they would receive (on this trip and throughout later ministries). Indeed, He goes into quite some detail about the issue. Counselors must be equally as candid. Problems will be solved if a counselee follows God's directions in the Bible, true, but not always by the most pleasant means. There may be hard tasks to perform, such as scorn from unbelievers or rejection by family. The counselor should make every effort to describe some of the scenarios and pos-

16 Consider this: I am sending you out like sheep in the midst of wolves. So become sensible as snakes and as simple as doves.

17 Be on your guard against people; they will deliver you up to councils, and lash you with whips in their synagogs,

18 and you will be brought before leaders and kings for My sake, to testify to them and to the Gentiles.

---

sible consequences of acting biblically. That is what Jesus is doing here.

In general, Jesus made it clear that the world is like a pack of ravenous **wolves**, ready to tear apart Christians who act like the **sheep** God has called them to resemble (v. 16). His words, **consider this**, were intended to make them pause and think about what this mission was to be like. Sure, it would have its thrilling, joyous moments. But for the most part, it would be hard work and unappreciated by many. Indeed, there would be those who would seek to bring it to a halt by contrary and destructive actions.

The contrast of **sheep** with **wolves**, however, was inadequate in explaining how complete the contrast is. In the same verse, Jesus went on to contrast **snakes** and **doves**. A Christian ministering the Word is to be like each. While he is to learn and use all the sensible wariness of snakes, he is (at the same time) not to emulate their cunningly dangerous qualities. The two elements of open simplicity and sensible wariness are not to be blended, so as to reduce the full strength of each. Rather, he is to be as fully the one as he is fully the other. True balance means equality.[1]

In verse 17, the wariness of the snake comes to the fore: **Be on your guard against people**. Few warnings could be more appropriate for the counselor. Those he seeks to help are also those who often turn on him the most quickly when they are crossed and don't get their ways. Here, He warned about those who would drag them up before legal authorities, and even call for physical punishment.[2] They would be betrayed to the hated Roman government officials as well (v. 18). In each case, when this happened, they were to **testify** about the truth of the gospel. On such occasions, as we see the apostles doing so in the book of Acts. Opportunities should be seized to witness for Christ. Counselors should keep this in mind.

In verses 19 and 20, the twelve are told that they will be given divine

---

1. See my book *Maintaining the Delicate Balance.*
2. The Jewish synagog had the right to flog those it condemned.

19   But when they deliver you up, don't worry about what you will say or how you will say it, because what you must say will be given to you in that hour.

20   You aren't the ones who will be speaking, but the Spirit of My Father speaking in you.

21 Brother will deliver up brother to death, and the father his child, and children will rise up against parents and put them to death.

22   And everybody will hate you for My Name's sake, but whoever endures to the end will be saved.

23 Now, when they persecute you in one city, flee to a different one; let Me assure you that you will not have gone completely to the cities of Israel before the Son of Man comes.

---

inspiration in speaking to rulers and authorities and that they should not be concerned about what to say. Of course, we have not been promised the same ability. So we should think *beforehand* about what to say in these (or lesser) situations. Interestingly enough, these verses do indicate what a preacher or counselor should be concerned about when speaking for Christ. There are four things that the Holy Spirit seems to care about: the right thing, spoken in the right way, at the right time, in the right words. Effective counselors work hard on each of these elements. After all, communication is of the essence in what they do.

The issue of persecution is so deep that it even divides families (v. 21). Often counselees will put good relations with family members before good relations with God. Whenever that is a problem, this entire section will prove beneficial.

Verse 22 indicates that people will **hate** those who serve Christ and that the hatred will be universal. That is not a very pleasant prospect—but it is realistic.

There is to be no unnecessary risk-taking, however. One is to avoid all persecution when doing so in a God-honoring way (even to the point of **fleeing**: v. 23). And certainly there is to be no seeking of it—as some did later on in the history of the church. There is to be no self-inflicted danger or persecution at all. That is why the wariness of the snake is necessary and why one is to be on his guard against people. As Jesus said, there was no need to linger in a city that refused to hear; there were plenty more cities to cover before it was too late and Jesus would come in judgment on Israel (70 AD).

Verses 24 and 25 reveal the cause of this persecution (as did the phrase **for My sake** in v. 18). The disciples would be persecuted because

24 A disciple is not above his teacher, nor is a slave above his lord.
25   It is enough for the disciple to be like his teacher, and for the slave to be like his lord. If they have called the Head of the house Beelzebub, how much more the members of His household!
26 So then, don't be afraid of them; nothing is covered that won't be uncovered, and nothing is hidden that won't be made known.
27   What I tell you in the dark, speak in the light; and what you hear whispered, preach on the housetops.

---

they had taken up their **Teacher's** cause and His ways. The more one becomes like Jesus (v. 25), the more he can be expected to be treated like his Master. He doesn't have a greater, or more isolated status than the One he imitates. They said truly evil things about the Lord, calling Him **Beelzebub**, the prince of demons. If they so treated Him Who is the Head of the household of faith, why should the **members of the household** expect better treatment (v. 25)? It will not happen. Counselees must be told that when they identify with Christ and do His will they can expect to be treated by many the way in which He was treated.

But Jesus went on to exhort the disciples not to fear the opposition (v. 26). All the lies spread about them would, in the end, be **uncovered** as such. All the truth would ultimately be **made known** (vv. 26, 27). Jesus told them that the things that they alone had heard from Him must be proclaimed openly. Nothing must be **whispered** or kept in the **dark**. The Christian faith is an open, public faith—it is not a private mystery designed to be understood by some esoteric body alone. As Paul put it, "These things were not done in a corner" (Acts 26:26). The truths of our faith are to be **preached from the housetops**.

In dealing with the fear that was likely to arise when facing persecution and possible death, Jesus told the disciples that death of the **body** was not to be compared with destruction of **both the body and the soul**[1] **in hell (Gehenna,**[2] v. 28). God will care for His own, even if it comes to their physical death. That is what He goes on to say in the following verses (vv. 29-31).

---

1. There are some who think that **soul** always means "life." Clearly, in this passage it cannot mean that since those who kill the **body** *cannot* kill the **soul**. They take away life, but they cannot destroy one's internal entity variously termed soul, spirit, heart. Only God can *destroy* (ruin, not kill; notice the change in terminology) **both in Gehenna**.
2. **Gehenna** was a valley (the valley of Hinnom) south of Jerusalem in which refuse was disposed of. It was the most horrible sight that Jews encountered. It

28	Don't be afraid of those who kill the body but can't kill the soul; rather be afraid of the One Who can destroy both soul and body in Gehenna.
29	Aren't two sparrows sold for a cent? And yet not one of them will fall to the ground without your Father's concern.
30	Even the hairs of your head are all numbered.
31	So don't be afraid then; you are more valuable than many sparrows.

Jesus points out that if God is concerned about the **sparrows** that fall, and if the **hairs** of one's head are numbered by Him, He is surely concerned about you. The concept of self-esteem is wangled in here by some who want to find support for their unbiblical teachings. To be said to be **more valuable** than a sparrow was not spoken to boost self esteem! If **two** are **sold for a cent** and, in contrast, you are more valuable than **many sparrows**, of what value does that make you? The coin was worth 1/3 of a denarius. Take the **many sparrows** to be 500 sparrows, for the sake of argument. Then you are worth more than $2.50 (which would be the price of 500 of them)! Double the **many**, and you would be worth more than $5.00! Obviously the Lord is not teaching about your great value. If He was, He would not say something so unflattering, that would, indeed, defeat the very point He made. The point of the passage is not man's worth, but God's providential care: if God cares for something lesser, He will care for something greater. The point is not how great we are, but how great *He* is to be concerned about such insignificant matters as the number of hairs on one's head. God's concern for His own should lead to confidence and assurance of His care. That, in turn, should relieve one of the fear of men (vv. 26, 31). So counter all attempts to twist this passage into some sort of support for the false self-worth teaching of Maslow and others.[1] Use it for the purpose for which it was given.

There was danger. To **deny** Christ rather than **confess** Him in times of trial means that He will respond in kind (vv. 32, 33). There are counselees who may not be genuine in their profession of faith. When it is safe to

became a fitting symbol of the place of eternal punishment. Fires burned there and worms and maggots abounded. In speaking of hell, Jesus called it a Gehenna where the worm never dies and the fires are never put out. As bad as the earthly Gehenna, the eternal one would be infinitely worse!

1. For further help, see my book *Self Help, Self Worth and Self image in the Bible.*

32	Therefore, whoever confesses Me before people, I will confess before My Father Who is in the heavens.
33	but whoever denies Me before people, I will deny before My Father Who is in the heavens.
34	Don't think that I came to bring peace on the earth; I didn't come to bring peace but a sword.
35	I came to **divide a man from his father, a daughter from her mother and a bride from her mother-in-law**;
36	and **a person's enemies will be the members of his own household**.
37	Whoever loves his father or mother more than Me isn't worthy of Me, and whoever loves his son or daughter more than Me isn't worthy of Me.
38	And whoever doesn't take his cross and follow Me isn't worthy of Me.

---

do so (before a congregation) they confess Christ; when it is dangerous to so (before persecutors) they deny Him. It is that insincerity of which He was speaking. Judas and many of the other disciples who eventually forsook Him were in view when Jesus made this statement. It has certainly been true throughout the ages that persecution separates the true from the false. That is what He meant in verses 34 through 39 when He spoke about sending a sword rather than peace. The sword divides, cutting between people. Love for Christ must supersede love for all else—indeed, even for everyone else, including the most intimate family members. To love others more than Christ means one **isn't worthy** to be His. This is serious business, as is His teaching in the rest of this chapter. Be sure that counselees who are hesitant about claiming Christ or doing His will understand what He was saying here. Stress this especially with those who want to put close earthly relations before the heavenly one.

One who fails to **take up his cross** (put to death his own interests and desires) and **follow** Christ (to do His will instead of one's own) **isn't worthy** to be confessed by Him on Judgment Day. The opposite of what sinful people think is true: **whoever finds his life** (that is, does that which he thinks is best for himself) actually **loses his life** thereby. And those who **lose it for His sake** (who are willing to follow Him, even to death if need be) will **find it.** Sinners have everything turned around. It is the task of the counselor to help them set things straight.

There is another point in the chapter that concerns their preaching mission; to receive the disciples into a city or into a home is, in effect, to

39   Whoever finds his life will lose it, and whoever loses his life for My sake will find it.

40   Whoever receives you receives Me, and whoever receives Me receives the One Who sent Me.

41   Whoever receives a prophet because he is a prophet will get a prophet's reward, and whoever receives a righteous man because he is a righteous man will get a righteous man's reward.

42   And whoever gives a cup of cold water to one of these little ones because he is a disciple, let Me assure you, he will not lose his reward.

---

receive Jesus Himself since He sent them. To reject them is to reject Him (v. 40). In verses 41 and 42, Jesus extended His discussion of the point. For one to receive a prophet (i.e., care for him in the way one should) is to be counted as if he too were out doing the work of the prophet (thus receiving an equal reward). The practical outworking of this principle is found in III John 8, where those who support the traveling missionaries are called "fellow-workers for the truth." They are viewed as if they too were preaching side-by-side with those they entertained in their homes. The **righteous man** and the **disciple** (**little one**) are mentioned to indicate that the reward one receives for helping is commensurate with the sort of activity carried on by the person helped.

This is a powerful chapter about ministry for Christ. The authority, the hazards, the assurances and the comforts are laid out. Every counselor ought to be familiar with it and be challenged and encouraged by it. Those who endeavor to assist counselors also ought to be encouraged by the fact that they too are included in the rewards of service.

CHAPTER 11

1 Now when Jesus had finished giving directions to His twelve disciples, He left that place to teach and to preach in their cities.

2 But when John heard in prison about Christ's deeds, by his disciples he sent and asked Him:

3 "Are You the coming One or should we expect someone different?"

Jesus did not turn over the work He was doing exclusively to His disciples. He went on teaching in various places (v. 1). Today, there are "pastors" who do no pastoring. They have become CEO's in their enormous congregations. I heard one lecture to a group of men who were trying to become true pastors of small, struggling congregations. He said that he doesn't deal with any of the members of the congregation, only with those who do deal with them. He was insulated from the congregation by a staff who stood in between. Not only was what he advised those pastors inappropriate, but he also disclosed that as a pastor he was a failure. Others who follow such a course claim that they don't need to counsel; they solve their people's problems solely from the pulpit. The implication is that any minister who finds it necessary to counsel his people individually must be a failure as a preacher. That is false. They are saying that they are better preachers than the apostle Paul who found it necessary to do a great deal of counseling (Acts 20:31; see also Colossians 1:28; Acts 20:20). At any rate, Jesus went on ministering as He had at the beginning, even though now He had twelve to help Him. Teach your elders to help you counsel, but stay in contact with your people, pastor. Don't hire some counselor to do all the counseling you ought to do.

Next we come to a section concerning John the Baptist. First John appealed to Jesus, then Jesus assessed John and his work (vv. 2-19). This is a large section, but as such it stands for the importance of John's work in God's scheme of things.

John sent a message to Jesus by means of his **disciples** asking Him if He was **the coming One** or if they were to expect another person. This wasn't inconsistent with all that he had taught about Jesus previously. It was certainly not the result of some "low point" in John's life in which he was losing heart. In reality, it showed that he believed the Bible, but in some ways didn't understand it. Intertestamental writings show that some of the Jews had expected two messianic figures. John most likely was referring to this. Jesus didn't answer directly "yes" or "no." Rather, He

4   Jesus answered them by saying,
        Go tell John what you hear and see—
5   **blind men see again** and lame people walk, lepers are cleansed
     and deaf persons hear, the dead are raised and the **poor have the
     good news announced to them**.
6   Whoever doesn't stumble over Me is happy.
    7 When they left, Jesus began to talk to the crowds about John:
        What did you go out to the desert to see—a reed swayed by the
        wind?
8   If not that, then what did you go out to see—someone dressed in
     soft clothing? Listen, those who wear soft clothing are in kings'
     houses.
9   Well then, what did you go out for—to see a prophet? Yes, I tell
     you; and far more than a prophet.
10   He is the one about whom it is written: **I shall send My messen-
     ger ahead of You, who will prepare Your way before You**.

---

referred to the results of His ministry which accorded with the Old Testament prophecies of the coming Messiah (vv. 5, 6). He added the significant thought, "**Whoever doesn't stumble over Me is happy**" (v. 6). This
was for the sake of the disciples who had come. The same thing is true
today: joy in ministry comes when one has no sinful doubts about Jesus
Christ, but goes on serving Him in simple, undoubting faith.

Following the departure of John's disciples Jesus spoke to the
crowds about John. In verses 7 through 9 He quizzed them about what
sort of person they found John to be when they went out to be baptized by
Him in the wilderness. He asked if he was like those who wear soft clothing, who are dressed in royal finery? The answer, of course, was "Certainly not!" What did they see when they went out then? A prophet? Yes,
but **more than a prophet**. He was about to tell them what He meant by
this. But first, He would show that John's ministry was the fulfillment of
prophecy just as His own was (v. 10). Then, He said that John was the
greatest of the Old Testament saints. But, interestingly, Jesus also asserted
that **one who is least** (or less) **in the** church is **greater than he is** (v. 11).
What did He mean by that? John was still an Old Testament figure. His
knowledge of the new era was deficient (His disciples and he were still
old garments, old wineskins). The one who was a member of the New
Testament church would have knowledge that was greater than his; even if
he was a **lesser** person in his own right. His understanding and privileges
would far exceed those of John.

11 Let Me assure you that among those born of women, a person greater than John the Baptist hasn't arisen; yet one who is least in the empire from the heavens is greater than he is.

12 Now from the days of John the Baptist until now, the empire from the heavens has been vigorously pressing forward and vigorous persons take hold of it.

13 Now all the prophets and the law prophesied until John,

14 and if you are willing to receive it, he is the Elijah who was to come.

15 Whoever has ears, let him hear.

16 Now to what may I compare this generation? It is like children sitting in the marketplace calling to others,

17 "We played the flute for you and you wouldn't dance; we sang a funeral dirge, and you wouldn't mourn."

John's razor edge position is the very apex of the Old Testament order. John ushered in the empire from the heavens, and people (as the result of his preparatory work) were now vigorously pressing into it (v. 12). Yet, while on the brink of the new era, John belonged to the old. All the **law and the prophets** of that old era carried on their activities until John came; he would bring an end to their era (v. 13). He is the one who was like **Elijah**, who would go before the Lord to prepare His way. In verse 15 Jesus used the expression that He used in His letters to the seven churches (Revelation 2, 3). It means that if one has the spiritual ability to understand the somewhat cryptic reference to Elijah in the Old Testament as referring to John, he should make the interpretation.

There is a great deal to convey to your counselees from this section. John was a great man, but they have been far more greatly privileged than he was. Are they aware of that fact? Do they appreciate it? Are they grateful and do they give thanks for all they have? Are they willing to put into practice all that Jesus requires of them? There is too little appreciation of the great privileges that are ours in this era. Try to cultivate a spirit in which those privileges are never taken for granted. Let counselees know that when you turn to the Bible you are handling something precious for which they ought to be eternally grateful. The whole atmosphere of biblical counseling ought to be quite different from any other kind of counseling as a result of this attitude. Let your counselees see in you an appreciation of God's boundless goodness that it may permeate all that they do to please Him.

Jesus then took a look at the last surviving generation before the

101

18   John came neither eating nor drinking and they say, "He has a demon";
19   the Son of Man comes eating and drinking and they say, "See, he is a glutton and a drunkard; he is a friend of tax collectors and sinners." But wisdom is vindicated by her works.

20 Then He began to denounce the cities where most of His miracles had been done, because they didn't repent:

21   Woe to you, Chorazin! Woe to you, Bethsaida! If the miracles that were done in you had been done in Tyre and Sidon, long ago they would have repented in sackcloth and ashes.
22   Let Me say something more to you: It will be more tolerable for Tyre and Sidon on the Judgment Day than for you.
23   And you, Capernaum, weren't you lifted up to heaven? You will be brought down to Hades! If the miracles that took place in you had occurred in Sodom it would have remained till today.

---

holocaust of 70 AD. He appraised them and came up with a generation of people who, no matter what was presented to them, were unmoved. John and He were like **children** at play. John **played** the **funeral dirge** (coming with the message of repentance), but people refused to **mourn** (repent). The people even complained that **he had a demon**. Jesus came eating and drinking (the opposite of John—whose disciples fasted), but there was a similar negative response. They said of Him: **he is a glutton and a drunkard**. Nothing would please them. All legitimate approaches had been tried, but the nation would not turn.

But **wisdom is vindicated** (proven right) **by her works** (v. 19). That is to say, those who rejected both John and Jesus would at the end of the day see that using their distinctive approaches was right and that what they taught was truly God's words. How would this come about? The very works (fruits, results) that would be seen to flow from their ministries would in time validate their ministries. Works, in the Scriptures, are always the means God uses to make a proper judgment, as we have seen previously. Too late, those who rejected John and Jesus would know. Too late, some of your counselees who now refuse to listen (cf. v. 15) will discover that you were right. Jesus is willing to warn that, later, He would have to say, "I told you so." You should be, too. Indeed, the warning is powerful and pertinent.

In verses 20 through 24, Jesus further emphasizes the responsibility that goes with knowledge. Speaking to the cities where He had preached and healed, He compared them to other cities that, had they had the privi-

24   And let Me say something more to you: it will be more tolerable
       for Sodom on the Judgment Day than for you.
   25 At that time Jesus responded to this by saying:
       I thank You, Father, Lord of heaven and earth, because You have
       hidden these things from wise men and intellectuals and have
       revealed them to babies.
26   Yes, Father, for such was Your good pleasure.
   27 Everything has been handed over to Me by My Father; and no one
       fully knows the Son except the Father, and no one fully knows the
       Father except the Son and those to whom the Son chooses to
       reveal Him.
28   Come to Me, all who labor and are heavily burdened, and I will
       refresh you.

---

leges of the cities of Galilee, would have repented (v. 21). And He emphasized the pride that got in the way (**weren't you lifted up to heaven?**)
that will also bring them down into Hades. Again, He makes the point that
He made earlier (v. 24).

In verses 25 through 27 Jesus **responded** to the proud disbelief that
He had seen by speaking to His Father about it. He thanked Him that He
had **hidden** the truth from **wise men and intellectuals** and **revealed** it to
babies. That is an indictment not upon intellectual pursuits *per se*, but
upon those who trust in them. Those who have been able to enjoy education should be humbled by it. If they are not, they either were improperly
educated (a serious problem of our time) or have turned education into an
idol (or both). That is a problem you must address with many counselees.
This verse will provide real help in that regard. You will find, as a rule,
that those who lack education or native wisdom will respond more readily
than those who have them. It is God's pleasure to hide truth from proud
intellectuals and reveal it to humble non-intellectuals[1] (v. 26). So be it!
And Jesus went on to say that all of the Father's authority and knowledge
has been granted to Him. And since They know each Other (as no others),
the Father—in complete accord with His **pleasure**—has given Him (the
Son) the right to reveal the truth about Himself to those that They both
choose.

Then comes the marvelous invitation to those who have the ears to
hear (vv. 28-30), to **come** to Him. Those who have been laboring under
the burden of sin and confusion, harassed without a shepherd, can find

---

1. Cf. I Corinthians 1:26.

29   Put My yoke on you and learn from Me; I am meek and humble in
      heart, and **you will discover refreshment for your souls**.
30   My yoke is easy to wear and My burden is light.

---

refreshment by taking Christ's **yoke** upon them (i.e., by becoming His true disciples). Taking the yoke meant becoming a student (as does the word "disciple").[1] In learning from Him, they would find that their troubled souls were refreshed. If ever there were a passage that encouraged hurting counselees to come to Christ and find the refreshment of soul that they long for in His Word, this is it. Remember, your task is to help counselees come to *Christ* for solutions to their problems. In effect, then, your invitation is the same as His.

And, while a counselee may find some things that Christ requires of him onerous before he discovers their full effects, having done them, he too will be moved to agree that His **yoke is easy to wear and His burden is light** (v. 30). When objections are raised to what Christ asks counselees to do, it is the task of the counselor to do as Christ does—assure them that what Christ is asking from them is to lay down the soul-breaking burdens they presently carry in exchange for the comparatively light and pleasant burdens of the Christian life. Here is where faith—the faith about which Jesus had said so much—comes into the picture. Will the counselee believe Jesus' Word, come to Him, and follow Him? That is the choice that you must put before every would-be counselee.

---

1. See Lamentations 3:27.

CHAPTER 12

1 At that time, Jesus went through the grain fields on the Sabbath. Now His disciples were hungry and began to pick some heads of grain and eat them.

2   But the Pharisees saw it and said to Him: "Look, your disciples are doing something that isn't allowed on the Sabbath."

3   Then He said to them,

Haven't you read what David did when he and those who were with him were hungry—

4   how he went to God's house and ate the bread of the presence, which he, and those with him, weren't allowed to eat, but only the priests?

Controversy! That's what this chapter is about. Doubtless, Jesus brought much of this controversy on Himself by what He had been saying concerning the unbelief of those who heard His message. But He did not cause controversy; His teaching simply exposed the sinful ire of men who would not repent. Counselors will find themselves embroiled in controversy at times, not because they welcome it, but simply because they tell counselees the truth. There is little question about the fact that in this world which is oriented against God, controversy is the order of the day for the Christian minister. The ministry of Jesus was a ministry filled with controversy and the ministries of Stephen, Peter, John, and Paul were similar. Most of the books of the New Testament address error and sinful activity that is controversial. If you are faithful to your calling, counselor, sooner or later you too will become involved in controversy.

The first two incidents have to do with charges that Jesus and His disciples violated the **Sabbath**. The fact is, they did not. They merely transgressed the traditions of the elders that had been added to God's Sabbath commands. The first charge (vv. 1-8) brought forth from Jesus a powerful reply (vv. 3-8). Notice, first, that He appealed to the Scriptures. That is the way to answer false charges—demonstrate that your conduct is scriptural. The interesting thing is that Jesus established the principle that the Sabbath commandment did not even exclude eating food that ordinarily should not be eaten when one was hungry. He demonstrated that God gave a certain flexibility to the command that the rigid Pharisees refused to understand.

Secondly, Jesus mentioned that the **Priests** work on the Sabbath

5   Or, haven't you read the Law that on the Sabbaths the priests in the temple profane the Sabbath and aren't held guilty?
6   I tell you that One Who is greater than the temple is here.
7   Now if you had known what this means, **I want mercy and not sacrifice,** you wouldn't have condemned the guiltless.
8   The Son of Man is Lord of the Sabbath.
   9 Leaving there He went to their synagog,
10   where they saw a man with a crippled hand. So, because they wanted to accuse Him, they asked Him whether it was lawful to heal on the Sabbath.
11   He said to them,
      Which one of you who has a single sheep that falls into a pit on the Sabbath won't take hold of it and lift it out?
12   A man is much more valuable than a sheep! So then, it is lawful to do good on the Sabbath.

(v. 5), and were not considered guilty of breaking the Sabbath. Again, Jesus noted that the commandment has exceptions. Then, He brought in the clincher. "If these things are true, how much more so is it right that I, the **Lord of the Sabbath** (the One Who created, rules over, and regulates it, and thus has the right to say what is or is not to be done on the Sabbath day) and I Who am **greater than the temple** (and all that goes on there) have determined that what I and my disciples do is no violation of the commandment." The principle is that **mercy** overrides the strict observance of a ceremonial law (v. 7). Mercy is the exception God set up over against rigid, pharisaical adherence. The principle is an important one that extends to all ceremonial laws.

The healing of the man with the crippled hand also brought condemnation directly down on Jesus, rather than on His disciples (vv. 9-14). Having been bested before by Jesus' response, this time they asked Him whether it is **lawful to heal on the Sabbath**. His response addressed their own inconsistent activities. If they would rescue a **sheep** on the Sabbath, why not a man who is **more valuable**? The conclusion? **It is lawful to do good on the Sabbath.** Again, this answer circumvents all rigidity attributed to a law that was never intended in the first place to forbid works of mercy and goodness. The counselor will, from time to time, run into counselees who live according to rigid adherence to laws in ways that preclude God's exceptions. They make universal that which God never intended to be so. They may be dealt with powerfully by this section in which Jesus declared that He, the Lord of the Sabbath, has the right to

13 Then He said to the man, "Stretch out your hand." And he stretched it out and it was restored, as healthy as the other.

14 So the Pharisees went out and schemed together against Him about how they might destroy Him.

15 Now since Jesus knew this He left there, and many followed Him, and He healed them all.

16 But He warned them not to make known Who He was,

17 that the prophet Isaiah might be fulfilled:

18   **Here is My Servant Whom I chose,**
        My loved One with Whom I am well pleased.
        I will put My spirit on Him
        and He will announce justice to the Gentiles.

---

interpret the commandment. And, according to Him, the biblical principle of mercy over sacrifice, makes it crystal clear that God never intended the Sabbath commandment to be absolute (with no exceptions or extenuating circumstances).

It is interesting that in verse 13 Jesus asked the crippled man to do what he could not do. That is often His way. One must attempt the seemingly impossible and, in the doing, find that the ability is given. But it is not given before the command is given and before the attempt is made. Counselees who sit around waiting for the ability to perform some difficult task that they think they cannot must be taught this important principle. God blesses *in the doing*. Often He does not give the ability until the very moment when it is needed. It is the counselee's task to obey what God commands; it is His to enable Him to do so. Once more we see the need for faith.

Verse 14 shows the bitter resentment to which the works and the words of Christ led. Those who disagreed did not consider His arguments, but plotted to destroy Him since He disagreed with them and showed how wrong their understanding of the law was. After all, they were the experts. They could not be shown up in the eyes of the people. No way! He threatened their positions, power and other vested interests.

In verses 15 through 23, Jesus justified His preaching and healing ministry by referring to the Old Testament prophecy of Isaiah. He quoted from a prophecy that not only described what He was doing, but also described the coming in of the **Gentiles** in the days to come. This was a two-fold jolt to proud Jewish Pharisees who would not recognize His ministry as a fulfillment of Isaiah 61 and who hated the very word "Gentile." He, then, healed a **blind and dumb demoniac** (v. 22). On top of every-

107

> **19**   **He won't quarrel or shout**
>   **nor will anyone hear His voice in the streets.**
> **20**   **He won't break the bruised reed**
>   **and He won't put out the smoking wick,**
>   **until He causes justice to win.**
> 21   **And the Gentiles will hope in His Name.**
>   **22** Then a blind and dumb demoniac was brought to Him and He healed him, so that the dumb man spoke and saw.
> 23 And all of the crowds were astonished and said, "Could He be David's Son?"
> 24 But when the Pharisees heard this they said, "He can cast out demons only by Beelzebub, the ruler of the demons."
> 25 Now because He knew their thoughts He said to them,
>   Every empire that is divided against itself comes to ruin, and every city or household that is divided against itself won't stand.

thing else, this healing so amazed the people who had been hanging on His every word, that they began to ask, "**Could He be David's Son?**" (i.e., the Messiah; cf. Psalm 2). They were heading down the right track. But the Pharisees became desperate when they heard this sort of talk and charged Jesus with being in league with the devil (v. 24). In response, Jesus delivered a mighty discourse (vv. 25-37) that, in the strongest terms imaginable, exposed the Pharisees for the hypocrites they were. In addition, He declared what their eternal destiny would be.

Incidentally, it may be important to point out to counselees from time to time that Jesus still **knows thoughts** (v. 25). They may deceive others or deceive you, but they can never deceive Him. And since that is true, He will deal with them according to what is in their hearts, not according to what they *say* they believe or think. It is probably true that many counselees fail to find answers to their problems because they are ingenuine.

Jesus strengthened His case by observing that the charge of casting out demons by the power of the devil was absurd. Empires, cities, or households divided against themselves will come to ruin. Why, then, would the devil lend Him the power to destroy his own servants? The charge is senseless (vv. 25, 26). Moreover, they had exorcists; He asked by whose power they attempted to cast out demons (v. 27). The reasoning of unbelievers is often absurd. It is not wrong to punch a hole in such reasoning. But look out for the repercussions.

The true significance of the casting out of demons is that the power of God, resident in Him Who was bringing in the new **empire** of God (the

26	So if Satan is casting out Satan, he is divided against himself. How then will his empire stand?
27	If I cast out demons by Beelzebub, by whom do your sons cast them out? Therefore they will be you judges.
28	But if I cast demons by God's Spirit, then God's empire has come upon you.
29	Or, let Me ask you, how can anyone enter a strong man's house and steal his possessions unless he first binds the strong man? Then he can rob his house.
30	Whoever isn't with Me is against Me, and whoever doesn't gather with Me scatters.

church), was at work. That is what the Jews should have realized. Instead of challenging His work as Satanic they should have accepted it as a verification of His claims. While exposing the foolishness of some of the arguments of unbelievers, it is also right to give the proper, biblical explanation of that which they misinterpret.

Moving a step closer to a full explanation, Jesus draws another analogy. The only one who can enter a **strong man's house** to steal his possessions is the one who is able to **bind** him (v. 29). Jesus had come to do that very thing to the devil (cf. Hebrews 2:14, 15; Revelation 20). Then, in verse 30, He made the statement, "**Whoever isn't with Me is against Me, and whoever doesn't gather with Me scatters**" (v. 30). Jesus is adamant about this matter: you cannot be neutral with reference to Him. Either you work with Him **gathering** the flock or you will **scatter** them. Either you are for His work in a positive and productive way, or what you do is negative. The latter is true even if one thinks he is neutral. It is like going upstream in a boat. You can't stand still. You either row against the current or you drift backwards. Many people, counselees included, will tell you "I didn't do anything wrong." In the light of this verse, your response ought to be, "Exactly; but you didn't do anything good. To do nothing for Christ is to **scatter**." If the sheep are not tended, they will go their own ways. If you do nothing to shepherd the sheep, that will lead to the destruction (scattering) of the flock.

Then, Jesus explained about the seriousness of attributing the work of the Holy Spirit to the devil. To call the *Holy* Spirit an *unclean* Spirit is a **blasphemy** that strikes at the very heart of one's attitude toward God. That one will not be forgiven in this life or in the life to come. These words speak plainly of the two ages: this present one and the eternal **age to come** (v. 32). That means that he will *never* be forgiven.

31   So then I tell you all sorts of sin and blasphemies will be forgiven people, but the blasphemy against the Spirit will not be forgiven.

32   Whoever speaks a word against the Son of Man will be forgiven, but whoever speaks against the Holy Spirit won't be forgiven, either in this age or in the coming one.

33   Either consider the tree fine and its fruit fine, or consider the tree rotten and its fruit rotten; trees are known by their fruit.

34 You brood of vipers! How can you speak good things when you are evil? The mouth speaks from what the heart is filled with.

35   A good person brings out good things from his good treasure, and an evil person brings out evil things from his evil treasure.

36   I tell you that on Judgment Day people will have to give account for every careless word that they speak;

From time to time people who have committed sins of various sorts will come to see you who think that they may have committed the unforgivable sin. Make clear to them what the sin really is. Also make it plain that every other sort of sin is forgivable (v. 31). Point them to this wonderful assurance. Those Christians who show concern over the matter ought to be assured that they could not have committed the unforgivable sin. The Pharisees were not concerned at all; the very presence of concern proves that they are in a different class. Move them to focus on the great assurance that all other sins may be forgiven in Christ (v. 31). Usually, when they deal with whatever sin it is that is bothering them the entire problem disappears.

Jesus then declared that a **tree** is known by its **fruit** (works are the means of judging). If there is **fine** fruit, a fine tree produces it. And the opposite is likewise true (v. 33). The one who is with Christ will make that known by his fruit (which will never include blaspheming the Holy Spirit) and those who are not with Him will also give evidence of their **rotten** condition.

Then, Jesus turned on the Pharisees and called them a **brood of vipers**, making it clear that they could not produce good fruit (**speak good things**) when, like the rotten tree, they were **evil people** (v. 34). Their outer words came from their inner evil **hearts**. That is why they **blasphemed** the Holy Spirit, calling Him **Beelzebub**. The principle is summed up in verse 35. Jesus went on to discuss one's words especially in light of the Judgment Day when every careless word will be taken into account. Again, it is by his outer life (here, words) that one will be judged. The condemnation of those who have committed the sin against the Holy

37   you will be justified by your words, and you will be condemned
        by your words.
  38 Then some of the scribes and Pharisees responded by saying:
"Teacher, we want to see a sign from you."
39 But He replied to them by saying:
        An evil and adulterous generation seeks a sign; so none will be
        given to it except the sign of the prophet Jonah.
40   For just as **Jonah was in the belly of the sea creature for three
        days and three nights** so will the Son of Man be in the heart of
        the earth for three days and three nights.
41   The men of Nineveh will stand up at the judgment with this gener-
        ation and will condemn it; they repented at the preaching of
        Jonah; but now there is something greater than Jonah here!

Spirit will be on the basis of what their words revealed about their hearts
(v. 37).

Having failed in their accusations against Jesus, the religious leaders
took another tack: they asked for a **sign** (v. 38). Jesus responded strongly
by saying that **an evil and adulterous generation seeks a sign** and that
none will be given but **the sign of the prophet Jonah** (v. 39). By that He
meant the **sign** of His resurrection (cf. v. 40). An **adulterous generation**
is one that forsakes Yahweh for something else that it sets up as an idol
and worships. That is precisely what the religious leaders that Jesus was
addressing did.

This is an important point. Many today want signs in order to believe
or before they obey. They ask for revelations, promptings and checks in
the spirit, sensings, feelings, or the like. This is something to watch out
for in your counselees.[1] It is something evil, as Jesus said. It is evil
because they refuse to simply take God's Word for what it says; they want
something more or something else. But as Jesus said in Luke 16, even if
one rises from the dead, they will not believe. He did; they didn't.

Here, Jesus rang the changes on the story of Jonah, saying that people from **Nineveh** (who repented under Jonah's preaching) will stand up
in the judgment of **this generation** and condemn it. After all, people
repented when Jonah came. Here are people who refused to repent even
though Someone greater than Jonah was in their midst preaching to them!
That makes their sin all the greater. Moreover, the **Queen of the South**
will add to the condemnation of this generation. Some strong things will

---

1. For much more on this matter, see my book *A Christian's Guide to Guidance*.

42 The Queen of the South will rise at the judgment with this generation and will condemn it; she came from the ends of the earth to hear Solomon's wisdom; but now there is something greater than Solomon here!

43 When an unclean spirit leaves a person, he passes through dry lands, seeking refreshment, but doesn't find it.

44 Then he says, "I'll return to the place that I left." When he comes he finds it empty, swept and put in order.

45 Then he goes and gets seven other spirits more evil than himself to come with him, and they go in and live there. So the final condition of that person is worse than the first. So too will it be with this generation.

46 While He was still speaking to the crowds, His mother and brothers stood outside trying to speak to Him,

47 [and someone said to Him, "Look, Your mother and Your brothers are standing outside trying to speak to you."][1]

48 But He responded by saying to the one who had spoken to Him: "Who is My mother, and who are My brothers?"

49 Then stretching out His hand toward His disciples, He said,
Here are My mother and My brothers!

1. Vs. 47 is omitted from some MSS.

be said about **this generation** later on in the book, but here is as strong a condemnation as you can find anywhere. There is no question about it; people will be judged by the opportunities that are presented to them. Counselees who reject the teachings of the Bible will be worse off in the long run than if they had never heard what God requires of them. The story of the **unclean spirit** who leaves, and after the house is **swept** clean returns with **seven others more evil than himself** further emphasizes this truth. The one who rejects, after having heard the soul-cleansing message that could have made all the difference in his life, will in the end be much (seven times) worse off than he was before hearing it (vv. 43-45).

The final problem that Jesus encountered came from his family (vv. 46-50). This incident teaches that spirit is thicker than blood. One's spiritual ties are closer than one's physical ties. The deeper family relations are those of brothers and sisters in Christ (v. 50). Many counselees have this backwards too. Because a family member refuses to go God's way doesn't excuse the counselee from doing so. So long as they don't cross the family, they believe all is okay. Well, Jesus countered that in

50   Whoever does the will of My Father in the heavens, he is My
        brother and sister and mother.

---

these verses. To be a disciple of Christ is to be in the family of God. And
it may mean departing from an earthly one. Thankfully, it seems that
Jesus' family eventually came to faith in Him. Teach *spiritual* "family
values" to your counselees.

CHAPTER 13

1 That same day Jesus left the house and sat beside the sea.

2 But such large crowds gathered before Him that He got into a boat and sat down, and the entire crowd stood on the beach.

3 Then He spoke many things to them in parables, saying:
A sower went out to sow seed.

4 And as he sowed, some seeds fell along the road and the birds came and ate them.

The crowds had grown so large that it was impossible to find a place on the shore from which to speak to them, so Jesus **got into a boat and sat down** to teach (v. 2).[1] He spoke largely in **parables**. The versatility of the Lord is apparent here. This is something that wooden, routine-bound counselors need to observe. There was a time when it was necessary, in the early days, for us to counsel in a microbus while waiting for a new building to be made available. The surroundings are not essential. Nice and convenient surroundings help; but they do not determine results. It is the message that counts.

A parable is, literally, a "throwing along side of." It is a story of something that actually happens that illustrates some truth the speaker wishes to convey.[2] The Hebrew word *mashal,* from which we get our term "proverb," may also be translated "parable." Only one Hebrew word covered all sorts of unusual literary devices used to teach truth. That is why the word *parable* describes a variety of expressions. Usually, we think of the longer story as a parable; but that need not be so. G. Campbell Morgan got around the problem of what was a parable and what was not by treating all of them in a book entitled *The Parables and Metaphors of Our Lord.*

The **parable** was useful for various reasons. It made truth memorable (all you need to do is say, "The prodigal son" and the whole story with its teaching comes back to you). It also made it possible to reveal truth to those that were open to it and to conceal truth from those who were not. Many parables take an unexpected turn and make their point by shocking or, at least, surprising the reader.

---

1. Jewish teachers sat down to teach.
2. A fable, on the other hand, relates an incident that couldn't happen (trees talking, etc.).

5   Others fell on the rocky places, where there wasn't much dirt, and they sprouted right away because they didn't have deep ground.

6   But when the sun rose, they were scorched, and because they didn't have roots they dried up.

7   Still others fell on thorns and the thorns came up and choked them.

8   But others fell upon the right sort of ground and gave fruit, one a hundredfold, another sixty and another thirty.

9   Whoever has ears, let him hear.

10 Then the disciples went to Him and asked Him, "Why do You speak to them in parables?"

11   He responded by saying,

Because knowledge about the secrets of the empire from the heavens has been given to you, and it hasn't been given to them.

12   Whoever has will be given more, and he will have more than he needs, but whoever doesn't have it, even what he does have will be taken away from him.

The parable of the **sower** is the standard by which other parables may be interpreted, since the Lord took the time to interpret it for His disciples. The parable is plain. As the Word is preached, there are four responses. The first three are negative, the fourth, positive. But the fourth itself brings three different levels of response.

Some **seed** falls on the hard **road**. It does not take root. **Birds** eat the seed. Some falls on ground with a thin layer of dirt over **rock** so that the roots cannot find purchase and wither away in the sun. Some falls among **thorns** that **choke** the young plant so that it dies. Then, some seed falls on good ground which produces fruit of a hundredfold, sixty-fold and thirty-fold (vv. 3-9).

Now, between the parable of the soils and the explanation of it, there is a section in which Jesus answered the disciples' question about why He speaks in parables. In it He explained what a parable does (vv. 10-17). First, Jesus said, "**knowledge about the empire from the heavens has been given to you, and it has not been given to them**" (that is, it has not been given to those without the **ears to hear**; v. 9). He was speaking about people who "hear" like those depicted by the first three kinds of soil. But those who hear the message with open hearts will receive **more**. Indeed, they will receive **more than they need** (v. 12)! That is a remarkable statement. It should be remembered in counseling. There are those who question the sufficiency of the Bible to meet their spiritual needs. Jesus said it

13   This is the reason why I speak to them in parables, because though they see they don't see, and though they hear they don't hear, nor do they understand.

14   Indeed, Isaiah's prophecy is fulfilled by them:
You will hear, but you certainly won't understand. And you surely will look, but you certainly won't see;

15   **this people's heart has become dull,**
and they have become hard of hearing,
and they have shut their eyes
lest they see with their eyes
and hear with their ears
and understand with their heart
and turn back and I will heal them.

16   But your eyes are blessed, since they see; and your ears, since they hear.

17   Let Me assure you that many prophets and righteous persons desired to see what you see but didn't see it, and to hear what you hear but didn't hear it.

18   Listen then, to the parable of the sower—

---

is not only sufficient, but even more than sufficient.

The one who doesn't have the hearing, understanding, and fruit-bearing capacity of regeneration will lose even what he does have (before long, he will not even remember the parables or messages that he has heard). Jesus spoke in parables, He said, to sort out the two kinds of persons. Those who will not see, hear, or believe (as Isaiah predicted) will wither by the wayside (vv. 13-15). But those who do see and hear will be **blessed** (v. 16). The disciples are doubly blessed: they live in an era in which the Lord has come and has spoken things that the Old Testament **prophets** and **righteous people** would have loved to have heard (v. 17). The blessings of living in the New Testament era ought never to be forgotten. Counselees do forget; counselors must remind them. Tell them. Urge them not to neglect the great privileges that are theirs by failing to produce the quantity of fruit that Jesus desires to see in them (John 15:8).[1]

Jesus then interpreted the parable (vv. 18-23). The parable has to do with how one **hears** the message that Jesus preached (v. 19ff.). Some don't understand, and while they are puzzling over it, the devil, like the

---

1. "Fruit" is not to be limited, as some do, to the winning of converts. It refers to sanctification in general, of which winning others to Christ is but one part.

19 Whenever someone hears the message about the empire and doesn't understand it, the evil one comes along and snatches away what was sown in his heart. This is what was sown along the road.

20 What was sown on the rocky places is the person who hears the message and gladly receives it right away.

21 But it doesn't take root in him, so it is short-lived. When affliction or persecution occurs because of the message, he stumbles right away.

22 What was sown among thorns is the person who hears, but the worries of these modern times and the deceit of riches choke the message and it becomes unfruitful.

23 And what was sown on the right sort of ground is the person who hears the message and understands it; indeed, he bears fruit and yields in one case a hundredfold, in another sixty and in another thirty.

---

birds, **snatches away** the seed (because of confusion, distraction, or whatever). That is the seed on the road. Another person hears and superficially accepts. Perhaps his response is a purely emotional one. But there is no depth. For a time he looks like a Christian, but before long he falls away. His "faith" is not genuine. He is the seed on rocky land. A third person hears and understands; but because other matters (like wealth), about which he is concerned, take over and choke the message, he too is unfruitful. These are three responses to the gospel by those who were never saved. In all three cases, the recipient **hears** but fails to heed the message. Since the parable has to do with how one hears,[1] to hear correctly, then, is crucial. One must understand, he must accept at a level of depth, and he must persevere through trials, pressures, and the like, putting Christ above all else. That is what the fourth kind of person is like (v. 23). He **understands** and **bears fruit**. Some who are saved, however, bear more fruit than others.

Counselors may look for various responses from would-be counselees. Those who are unregenerate (like the first three kinds of soil) will not be able to accept the counsel of the Word, revealing themselves not to be believers. Then there will be Christians who, to a greater or lesser extent, will respond positively. But, as Jesus said, there will be various levels of positive response. Not all will grow as rapidly or as fully as others. Expect this. Do not expect that all believers will respond in the same ways, to the

---

1. For a section on hearing see my book *A Consumer's Guide to Preaching*.

24 He put before them another parable, saying,
The empire from the heavens is like a person sowing fine seed in his field.

25 But while people slept his enemy came and sowed weeds over it among the wheat seeds and left.

26 So when the wheat sprouted and bore grain, the weeds appeared also.

27 Then the household slaves came and said to him, "Lord, didn't you sow fine seed in your field? Where did the weeds come from?"

28 He answered: "Some enemy did this.'" So his slaves asked him, "Do you want us to go and weed them out?"

29 But he replied, "No, otherwise when you are pulling up the weeds you may uproot the wheat along with them.

30 Let both grow together until the harvest; then, at harvest time I will tell the reapers, 'Pull up the weeds first, and bundle them up and burn them. Then gather together the wheat into my barn.'"

31 He put before them another parable, saying,
The empire from the heavens is like a mustard seed that a person sowed in his field.

32 It is the smallest of all the seeds, but when it grows, it is the largest of the plants and becomes a tree, so that the birds of the sky come and roost in its branches.

---

same extent. They will not. The difference will not have to do with your counseling, but with the growth of the plant.

Speaking about the new world-kingdom (the empire from the heavens) which He had come to bring, Jesus told another parable (vv. 24-30). Here it is no longer the message that is in view, but the character of the worldwide kingdom. Within its fold there will be both those who are genuine and those who are not. The **enemy** (Satan) will sow darnel (tares, **weeds** that, until ripe, cannot be distinguished from the **wheat** itself). Separating the two before **harvest** is impossible. The interpretation of this parable is found in verses 36 through 43.

In verses 31 through 33 we encounter two brief parables. The parable of the **mustard seed** tells us that the church would grow from very small beginnings ultimately to reach some from every tribe and kindred and nation. But, as the next parable makes clear, it would do so in an unobtrusive way. It would not be like a great movement heralded on all hands, but would spread quietly from individual to individual, as **yeast** permeates dough bit by bit. The message is spread throughout the world, then, not by

33 He told them another parable:

> The empire from the heavens is like yeast that a woman took and kneaded into three measures of meal until it permeated all of the dough.

34 Jesus spoke all of these things to the crowds in parables; and He didn't speak anything to them without a parable.

35 So what was spoken through the prophet was fulfilled:

> **I will open My mouth in parables;**
>
> **I will tell about things hidden from the world's foundation.**

36 Then He sent the crowds away and went into the house. And His disciples came to Him, saying, "Explain the parable about the weeds of the field to us."

37 He answered them, saying,

> The One Who sows the fine seed is the Son of Man;

38
> the field is the world, the fine seed are the sons of the empire, the weeds are the sons of the evil one,

39
> the one who sowed them is the devil, the harvest is the close of the age and the reapers are the angels.

40
> Just as the weeds are pulled up and burned in the fire, so will it be at the close of the age:

41
> The son of Man will send out His angels and they will weed His empire of all the stumbling blocks and all who act lawlessly,

42
> and they will throw them into the fiery furnace. There people will weep and grind their teeth.

---

human methods, but by God's own impetus, as did the stone cut out of the mountain by God that at length filled the whole earth (Daniel 2:35).

Here Jesus interpreted the parable found in verses 24 through 30. Jesus is the Sower (v. 37). The field is the **world** (the place where the church was to be spread; cf. 28:18-20). The two **seeds** are the two kinds of people (saved and unsaved) who make professions of faith and become part of the visible church. But at the **end of the age,** when Jesus comes at the harvest, He will send His angels to separate the true from the false professors. Likewise in counseling, you will not always know who is genuine. You should consider a member of a Bible-believing church genuine until the facts prove otherwise. The warnings in verses 41 and 42 are important to use with those about whom such facts cause doubts. Don't fail to do so. But the promise of verse 43, in fulfillment of Daniel's prophecy (12:3) is also given. It is a wonderful hope for all true believers. You should often repeat these warnings and promises as Jesus repeated the words about **ears to hear** (v. 43).

43   At that time **the righteous will shine like the sun** in their Father's empire. Whoever has ears, let him hear.

  44   The empire from the heavens is like treasure hidden in the field, that a person found and hid. Then, out of his gladness he went and sold all that he owned, and bought that field.

  45   Again, the empire from the heavens is like a merchant searching for beautiful pearls,

46   who, finding one very valuable pearl, went away and sold all that he had and bought it.

  47   Again, the empire from the heavens is like a net cast into the sea that gathered all types of fish.

48   When it was full they brought it up onto the shore and sat down and collected the worthwhile fish into containers and threw away the worthless ones.

The next parable concerns the value of the empire. It has to do with selling everything else to purchase it. That brief parable (v. 44) teaches that Christ's empire is more important, more essential, and more valuable than anything else one may possess. The next parable, the parable of the **pearl** of great price (v. 46), is similar, with this difference: while the first speaks of losing all in order to gain more, the second seems to go a step beyond by comparing Christ's kingdom with every other religion or substitute. The rest all seem cheap and mean by comparison. Continually stress the superiority of Christ's way to all others. That includes biblical counseling in comparison to other systems.

The parable of the **dragnet** (vv. 47-50), once again emphasizes the mixed nature of the church. Interestingly, it is the righteous who remain and the wicked fish who are thrown away (v. 48). At Christ's coming, the separation that takes place will mean that the wicked are taken away (as in the flood; here as in discarding the inedible fish. Cf. Matthew 24:39-41). Hell is the destination not only of those outside the church, but also of those within its pale who made a false profession.

In verse 51 we are told that Jesus asked the disciples whether they understood the parables. They said "yes." Whenever you have taught your counselees some truth, stop and take the time to be sure that they understand. Ask them, "Did you understand?" If you are not sure they did—even if *they* think they did—you may ask them to tell you in their own words what the truth is.

Jesus revealed in verse 52 that there would be **scribes** in the church. "Scribe" was a name in that day that was given to the official teacher of

49   That is how it will be at the close of the age: the angels will go forth and will separate evil persons from the midst of the righteous,

50   and will throw them into the fiery furnace. There people will weep and will grind their teeth.

     51   Did you understand all of this?

They said to Him, "Yes."

52   So He said to them,

      Therefore, every scribe discipled for the empire from the heavens is like a householder who brings out of his treasure new things and old things.

    53   When Jesus had finished telling these parables, He went away from there,

54   and He came to His home town, and taught them in their synagog, and they were astonished. And they said,

      Where did this man get this wisdom and the power to do miracles?

55   Isn't he the carpenter's son? Isn't his mother's name Mary, and aren't James and Joseph and Simon and Judas his brothers?

56   Don't all of his sisters live here with us? Where did this man get all of this?

57   Then they took offense at Him. But Jesus said to them, "A prophet isn't without honor except in his home town and in his household."

---

the Word. Pastor-teachers are those to whom He is referring (cf. Ephesians 4:11). They, Jesus said, will be able to bring out various sorts of **treasures—new and old**. Doubtless, He was thinking of the parables and other illustrative stories that teachers would use to drive home truth. As the supreme Scribe, that is what He was doing, and that is what He expects you to do. Do you fix truth indelibly by means of illustrations? Do your counselees hear things both new and old from your lips (new biblical truths as well as old ones, presented in new ways as well as old ways)? If they don't, they should.

When Jesus had completed this teaching session, He left for His **home town** and taught in the local **synagog** (vv. 53, 54). The people were responsive not to what He said, but merely to the fact that a carpenter's Son had been able to rise to such a place of prominence (cf. Luke 4). Because this was a form of **unbelief**, Jesus left without doing many miracles there. He said, "**A prophet isn't without honor except in his home town and in his household**" (v. 57). That saying is true today. Don't be surprised if people elsewhere listen to what you say, but those where you

58   So He didn't do many miracles there because of their unbelief.

---

live do not. Someone has said, "An expert is someone who speaks some-where other than where he lives." That is but another way of saying what Jesus said.

CHAPTER 14

1 At that time Herod the tetrarch heard the report about Jesus,
2 and said to his servants, "This is John the Baptist; he has been raised. That is why these miracles are being performed by him."
3 Herod had seized John and bound him and put him in prison because of Herodias, his brother Philip's wife.
4 He did this because John told him, "You aren't allowed to have her."
5 Now though he wanted to kill him, he was afraid of the crowd since they regarded him as a prophet.
6 But when Herod's birthday came Herodias' daughter danced in their midst and pleased Herod.
7 As a result, he agreed with an oath to give her whatever she asked.
8 Under her mother's instructions she said, "Give me John the Baptist's head on a platter."
9 The king was upset, but because of his oaths and those who sat with him at the table, he commanded them to give it to her;
10 and he sent them to behead John in the prison.
11 So his head was brought on a platter and it was given to the girl, and she took it to her mother.
12 Then his disciples came and took his body and buried him; and they went and told Jesus this.

Herod now comes into the picture. He had been hearing about Jesus and was afraid. He imagined that **John the Baptist** had risen from the dead, and Herod attributed Christ's **miracles** to him. Those who have no true interest in serving God *imagine* what facts may be. They fail to consult the Source; had he any true interest in Jesus' miracles, Herod could simply have asked Him. His interest was merely in preserving his own hide. After all, he had put John to death because John preached about his sin. And, though he wanted to kill John, he was afraid of the crowds that regarded John as a prophet from God. So, by explaining the scenario with **Herodias** and her daughter, Matthew gives the background for Herod's present fear (vv. 1-12).

The thing to see here is what desperate measures one may resort to out of fear. A combination of licentiousness, which led to his fateful sin-intoxicated promise to Herodias, and fear of John brought about the terrible scene. Warn against action taken when inflamed with lust, and the fear of man. Counselees frequently find themselves embroiled in difficulties because of this lethal combination of emotions. Whenever one acts purely

123

13 Now when Jesus heard it He left there in a boat privately and went to a desert place. But when the crowds heard it, they followed Him on foot from their cities.

14 So when He left the boat He saw a large crowd, and He was moved emotionally by them and healed their sick.

15 As evening came, His disciples came to Him, saying, "This is a desert, and it is already rather late; send the crowds away so that they may go into the villages and buy food for themselves."

16 But Jesus said to them: "They don't have to go away; you feed them."

17 But they said to Him, "We don't have anything here but five pieces of bread and two fish."

18 So He said, "Bring them here to Me."

19 Then He ordered the crowds to relax on the grass, and taking the five pieces of bread and the two fish, He looked up to heaven and gave thanks and broke the pieces of bread and gave them to the disciples and the disciples gave them to the crowds.

20 So they all ate and were satisfied, and they gathered up twelve baskets full of fragments that were left over.

21 And there were about five thousand men who ate, not including the women and children.

---

on emotion he can expect trouble.

In a flashback, Matthew described what Jesus did upon hearing about John's death. Jesus left the area by boat for a desert place (a quiet, unpopulated region). But the crowds followed on foot. When He left the boat, there they were waiting for Him. Once more, moved by pity, He healed many (vv. 13, 14).

The crowd remained and, as evening came, the disciples mentioned that the people had had nothing to eat. They urged Him to dismiss them so they could go into the towns and get something. But Jesus said, "**you feed them**" (v. 16). In frustration, they explained that there was only five pieces of bread and two fish! He said, "**Bring them here to Me**." Ordering the crowds to relax on the grass, and after a prayer of thanksgiving, Jesus broke enough bread for all as the disciples distributed it. There was more at the end than at the beginning of the miracle (v. 20), even though five thousand men (not including women and children) were fed on that occasion.

Jesus can use that which is small to achieve that which is great. Never is it right to say that one doesn't have the resources to accomplish what He has commanded. He has them and can make them available. Not by miracles, of course. But by the same principle at work in providence is

22 Then immediately He made the disciples get into the boat and go on ahead of Him to the other side, while He sent away the crowds.

23 Now after He sent the crowds away, He went up into the mountain by Himself to pray. And when evening came, He was there alone.

24 Now by this time the boat was about three or four miles out from shore and was being beaten by the waves since the wind was contrary.

25 In the fourth watch of the night, He came toward them, walking on the sea.

26 The disciples saw Him walking on the sea and were terrified and said, "It is a ghost!" And they screamed from fear.

27 But immediately He spoke to them, saying, "Have courage; it is I. Don't be afraid."

28 In response, Peter said, "Lord, if it is You, let me come to You on the water."

29 And He said, "Come." So Peter got down from the ship and walked on the water toward Jesus.

30 But when he looked at the wind, he was afraid, and beginning to sink he shouted, "Lord, save me!"

31 Immediately Jesus stretched out His hand, took hold of him and said to him, "Little-faith, why did you doubt?"

32 And when they climbed up into the boat, the wind stopped blowing.

33 So those who were in the boat worshiped Him, saying, "Truly You are God's Son."

---

the same.

Jesus then sent off the disciples by **boat**, dismissed the crowds, and went **alone** up on a mountain to **pray** (vv. 22-27). The disciples, meanwhile, found themselves in the midst of a windy storm in the middle of the sea. At length, Jesus came to them **walking on the water**. They thought it was a ghost. But Jesus encouraged them, **"It is I. Don't be afraid."** Peter asked Jesus to let him walk on the water too. He said, **"come."** Peter did so, but when he looked at the waves lashed by the wind, he became afraid and began to sink. Immediately, Jesus reached out and lifted him up. Then He said, **"Little-faith, why did you doubt?"** As they both climbed into the boat, the winds ceased. The disciples, seeing all that had happened, said, **"Truly, You are God's Son."**

Peter is like many counselees. They are anxious to please the Lord and will even launch out with energy and enthusiasm to do something for Him, only to fall apart when some danger poses itself. Take heart; look at what Jesus did eventually for the apostle Peter—He turned him into a

34 Now when they had crossed over, they landed at Gennesaret.

35   And when the men of that place recognized Him, they sent into all the neighborhood and brought to Him all those who were sick,

36   and urged Him just to allow them to touch the border of His garment; and all who touched it were healed.

---

rock! Don't give up on them. Fear and doubt can be overcome.

In verses 34 through 36, we see again what we have been encountering throughout—the crowds were waiting with their sick to be healed.

CHAPTER 15

1 Then the Pharisees and scribes from Jerusalem came to Jesus, saying,

2 "Why do your disciples transgress the tradition of the elders? They don't wash their hands before they eat."

3 He responded by saying to them:
   Indeed, why do you transgress God's commandment for the sake of your tradition?

4 God said, **Honor your father and mother,** and **Whoever curses father or mother must surely die,**

5 But you say, "Whoever says to his father or mother, 'What you might have gained from me is designated as an offering,'

6 doesn't have to honor his father [or mother]."[1] Thus you annul God's Word for the sake of your tradition.

---

1. Some MSS omit, *or mother*.

Turning the tables, using the same form and even some of the same words, was a powerful way Jesus put the **Pharisees and the scribes** in their places. It is still a powerful way of responding to unjust criticism (vv. 1-3). The **traditions of the elders** were legalistic additions to God's holy law. The word **transgress** is the pivotal term in the turnabout of which I am speaking. As Jesus pointed out, God's commandments were disobeyed so the elders' traditions would be obeyed. The latter inevitably led to the former. Whenever *anything* is added to the Bible—traditions, lists of do's and don'ts, supposed extra-biblical guidance, psychological practices —it always ends up taking a place superior to God's Word. That is what had happened in the religious leaders' thinking. Point this out to counselees who are tangled in some web of tradition or legalism, that has kept them from doing God's will. It is also a point that may be made with eclectic counselors.

In verses 4 through 6, Jesus illustrates what had happened by referring to the tradition of *corban*. This term meant "a consecrated gift." Jesus contrasts a biblical commandment (Exodus 20:12) with the tradition. They had **annulled God's Word** for the sake of their tradition. How? In consecrating money that should have been used to support his parents in their old age, a son might be able to forego once and for all ever giving it

127

7	Hypocrites! Isaiah prophesied well about you when he said,
8	**This people honors Me with their lips, but their heart is far from Me;**
9	**They worship Me in vain, teaching as doctrines the ordinances of men.**
10	He called the people to Him and said to them:
	Hear and understand:
11	It isn't what enters the mouth that defiles a person, but rather what comes out of his mouth; this defiles a person."

to his parents, even if he reneged on the promise (cf. John Lightfoot). By this consecration of money, then, he could retain for himself what rightfully ought to have gone to help them out. There are "clever" ways of annulling God's law that counselees use today. Expose them as such. Be sure to point out that adopting these ways makes a person who *says* he is obeying God nothing less than a **hypocrite** (v. 7).

Jesus then applies the prophecy from Isaiah that describes such hypocrites. They talk a good game, but down deep inside they have no intention of doing the things they say they will. They are liars! Such **lip worship** is unacceptable to God (v. 9). To teach doctrines other than those found in the Bible is dead wrong—it is no part of Christianity. Yet many today come very close to the same thing when they "integrate"[1] the beliefs of **men** with the Bible.

In order that the people might be able to distinguish the false religion of the Pharisees from the true worship of Yahweh, Jesus called them to come listen to what He had to say (vv. 10, 11). He urged them to listen and to comprehend. Then He delivered this important dictum: "**It isn't what enters the mouth that defiles a person, but rather what comes out of the mouth** [that] **defiles a person**" (v. 11). The Pharisees had objected to the disciples not **washing** their hands before they ate (v. 2). Their concern was about externals. Jesus turned the discussion to the sin of a person's **heart**; that **defiles** him—in a much more serious way than any physical dirt could. Once again, He has turned the tables. Jesus used the words of the Pharisees to make His point, this is something that counselors need to learn to do. A counselee says, "How do you expect me to love a despicable woman like that?" You might respond, "How do you

---

1. As verse 9 implies, such integration cannot be done. The ordinances and doctrines of men are incompatible with the commandments and teachings of God's Word.

12 Then His disciples came to Him and asked Him, "Did You know that the Pharisees were offended when they heard what You said?"

13 He answered, saying,
> Every plant that My heavenly Father didn't plant will be uprooted.

14 > Leave them; they are blind guides of the blind. Now if a blind man leads a blind man, both will fall into a ditch.

15 But Peter said, "Explain the parable to us."

16 So He said,
> Are you also still without understanding?

17 > Don't you know that what goes into the mouth and goes into the stomach passes from the body into the drain?

18 > But those things that come from the mouth come from the heart and they defile a person.

---

expect God to honor despicable talk like that when describing the wife God commands you to love?"

The disciples, who had not yet understood the utter disjunction between Jesus and the Pharisees, seemed to be trying to heal what they could see was a widening breach. They asked Him if He knew that He had **offended** the Pharisees (v. 12). His answer was somewhat enigmatic, but the meaning is plain enough. If God hasn't **planted** a plant, it will be **uprooted**. That is to say, God had not planted the Pharisees; they were not His servants. There needed to be no concern, therefore, about their taking offense. What Jesus said was true; they were every bit as heinous as He said. Indeed, Jesus went on to say, **"they are blind guides of the blind** (v.14) As a result, both they and those they lead will end up in a **ditch**. They do not help the **blind**; they only lead them into greater difficulty."

There are many blind today to the fact that God's Word has all that is needed to solve the problems that have to do with loving God and man. They want to add to His Word, and when they do, they lead many into psychological ditches from which they may never emerge. That is a sad fact about our times, but it is true. Counselor, if you have been among them, let Jesus heal you of your spiritual blindness by the application of biblical truth. Jesus was explicit: **"Leave them,"** He told His disciples (v. 14).

Peter, speaking for the rest (as he often did), asked for an explanation of the **parable** of the defiling heart. Jesus wearily replied, **"Are you also still without understanding?"** (v. 16). Then He patiently went over what He had told them in more detail (vv. 17-20). Physical food, if defiled, only goes through one's system and out into the **drain**. That can't do much

19   From the heart come evil thoughts, murders, adulteries, sexual sins, thefts, false testimonies, blasphemies.

20   These things are what defile a person; but to eat with unwashed hands doesn't defile a person.

21 Then Jesus left there and withdrew to the district of Tyre and Sidon.

22 And there a Canaanite woman from the area came out and called, "Show me mercy, Lord, David's Son! My daughter is suffering severely from demon-possession."

23 But He didn't answer her a word. And His disciples came urging Him: "Get rid of her; she keeps shouting behind us."

24 Answering, He said, "I wasn't sent to anyone but the lost sheep of the house of Israel."

25 But she came and knelt before Him, saying, "Lord, help me."

26 He replied, "It isn't right to take the children's bread and throw it to the pet dogs."

---

harm. The real harm is done by the error, sin, and hypocrisy that is generated in and comes from one's sinful **heart**. Jesus then gave examples of what He was talking about and concluded that it is these things and not unwashed hands that really defile (vv. 19, 20).

This entire section is of great significance to biblical counselors. Pagan counseling cannot reach the heart of man so as to cleanse him. If the heart of man is the heart of man's problem, then the heart must be transformed. But paganism, no matter what it claims, fails utterly to eliminate the sins listed in verse 19. They all have their origin in man's heart. When unbelievers (or believers) say that a problem is "too deep" for a pastor, they have it backwards: man's problems are too deep for anyone other than the one who counsels by the power of the Word and the Spirit. When Bill Goode said, "Every counseling problem is a theological problem," he was uttering a great and important truth. Its corollary is equally true and equally important: *Every counseling solution is a theological solution.* There is no true solution to the problems listed in verse 19[1] apart from the transforming power of Jesus Christ.

Now, we are led out of Galilee into non-Jewish territory: **Tyre** and **Sidon** (for as long as history can remember, a Phoenician district). There He healed the daughter of a **Canaanite woman** that the disciples tried to **get rid of** (vv. 21-28). Jesus' words tested her, but her faith in His ability

---

1. The list is not exhaustive; it contains only samples of what Jesus was referring to.

27 Nevertheless, she said, "Yes, Lord, but even the pet dogs eat the crumbs that fall from their master's table."

28 Then Jesus answered her, "Woman, your faith is great; you will have what you desire." And her daughter was healed at that very hour.

29 Jesus left there and went along the Sea of Galilee. Then He went up into the mountain and sat there.

30 And large crowds came to Him, bringing with them the lame, the maimed, the blind, the dumb and persons with many different sorts of problems, and laid them down at His feet, and He healed them.

31 The crowd was astonished when they saw dumb persons speaking, maimed persons healthy, lame persons walking and blind persons seeing, and they glorified the God of Israel.

32 Then Jesus called His disciples to Him and said,

> I feel sorry for the crowd; they have stayed with Me for three days now, and don't have anything to eat. And I don't want to sent them away without food or they might give out on the road.

---

to heal was so strong that she would not take offense to a seeming rebuke. Instead, out of faith in Him and love for her daughter, she endured the seeming insult about the **dogs** and turned it to her advantage. She developed the image further, distinguishing between the **children's** food and the **crumbs** that the **pet dogs** are allowed to eat. She humbly said, in effect, "I'll settle for crumbs!" You will get somewhere with counselees who want help and will not allow humiliation or any other thing to stand in their way. They believe that God has help for them and will not be satisfied with anything less. When you recognize pride and lack of faith as a hindrance to help, turn to this incident and read it to a counselee. Then ask, "Do you understand why I have read this story?"

Once more we read about the **crowds** that followed (vv. 29, 30). Here they even climbed a mountain to be with Him. That would be difficult for many who had the ailments mentioned in verse 30. It is interesting that Jesus never made things easy. Do you attempt to make them too easy at times? Think about this. The crowds continued to be **astonished** at what they saw Jesus do, and (rightly) they did not praise Him alone, but also the heavenly Father, Whom they realized had empowered Him to do these miracles (v. 31).

Then Jesus, out of compassion, again fed the crowds miraculously (vv. 32-39). That Jesus cares about the physical welfare of your counselees is evident from His words in verse 32. You may turn to this or to the similar passage in the previous chapter to demonstrate this concern. While

33 But His disciples said to Him: "Where are we going to get enough bread to feed such a great crowd in a desert?"

34 Jesus replied: "How many pieces of bread do you have?" And they said, "Seven, and a few fish."

35 So when He had ordered the crowd to relax on the ground,

36 He took the seven pieces of bread and the fish and after He gave thanks He broke them and gave them to the disciples, and the disciples gave them to the crowds.

37 Then they all ate and they were satisfied, and they gathered up seven baskets full of leftover fragments.

38 And there were four thousand men who ate, not including the women and children.

39 Then, after He sent the crowds away, He got into the boat and went to the area of Magadan.

His primary concern was for the spiritual welfare of men, He never forgot the ravages that sin had brought upon their physical bodies. You must not either if you wish to counsel biblically.

CHAPTER 16

1 The Pharisees and Sadducees came testing Him, asking Him to show them a sign from heaven.

2   But He answered them, saying:

>   [When evening comes, you say, "There will be fair weather, since the sky is red,"

3   and in the morning, "There will be a storm today, since the sky is red and overcast." You know how to interpret the face of the sky, but you can't interpret the signs of the times.][1]

4   An evil and adulterous generation seeks a sign, and no sign will be given to it except the sign of Jonah.

So He left them and went away.

---

1. This section is omitted in some MSS.

The religious leaders were not satisfied with the signs that Jesus gave to the people (cf. Acts 2:22). They wanted some special **sign** delivered according to their orders and specifications (v. 1). There are all too many today who are looking for similar indications from the **heavens** in order to discern God's will for their lives.[1] Jesus' reply to the Pharisees and the Sadducees is the one that you should give such counselees today (vv. 2-4). Jesus referred to the fact that they could read the signs of the weather, but that they were unable to interpret the **signs of the times** (that is to say, those that had been performed by the hundreds all around them in the healings and miracles of Christ). No, they were not satisfied with what God gave them; they had to have something special beyond those, signs that were specifically performed for them. Jesus said that **an evil and adulterous generation seeks a sign** and that they would receive no sign other than the resurrection (**the sign of Jonah**). With that, **He left them** (vv. 2-4).

When counselees demand some sign from God, show them that to ask for any other sign than that which God Himself gave them through Christ is **evil and adulterous**. Legitimate signs today are found only in the biblical record. So turn your counselees from looking for signs to the Scriptures in which more than enough **signs of the times** are recorded—

---

1. For data on this matter, see my book *A Christian's Guide to Guidance*.

5 When His disciples arrived at the other side, they realized that they had forgotten to take bread along. So Jesus said to them:

6 "Look out for, and guard against the yeast of the Pharisees and Sadducees."

7 So they discussed this among themselves, saying: "But we didn't bring any bread."

8 Jesus knew this and said,
> Why are you discussing among yourselves the fact that you have no bread? You men of little faith!

9 > Don't you understand yet? Don't you remember the five pieces of bread for the five thousand and how many baskets you gathered up?

10 > Or don't you remember the seven pieces of bread for the four thousand and how many baskets you gathered up?

---

including the greatest sign of all: Christ's resurrection from the dead. (Cf. also Matthew 12:38-40; Deuteronomy 13:1-5.)

A discussion of the lack of **bread** (v. 5) led Jesus to comment to His disciples about the **yeast of the Pharisees and Sadducees** (v. 6). His comment was in the form of a warning: **guard against** it. Evidently, it was possible for them to slip into hypocrisy similar to the hypocrisy and false **teaching** that characterized these blind guides (vv. 5-12; cf. Luke 12:1). These sins are always a possibility, even for the servants of God (here the warning was to the disciples). Counselors should never think that they themselves are immune. The warning should first be taken to heart by counselors and then also sounded for counselees. The discussion among the disciples, who had seen Jesus feed multitudes miraculously continues (v. 7). Jesus points out that He was not concerned about physical bread and yeast, but spiritual bread (should they be concerned about feeding themselves? He could supply all their needs as He had so recently demonstrated in feeding the crowds: vv. 9, 11). Again, the disciples exhibited their lack of **faith** (v. 8).

Yeast starts in one place but soon permeates all the dough. Watch for the beginnings of false teaching, which may, as in this instance, lead to hypocritical thinking and action. Compromise even slightly and before you know it hypocrisy has taken over. Finally, the disciples got the point (v. 12). There is hope. Keep pounding away at something, keep working with those who have difficulty in understanding, and finally something may break through. That counselees at times are dense should be no surprise to those who follow the course of training that Jesus provided for the

11   How is it that you can't understand that I wasn't speaking to you about bread? But be on guard against the yeast of the Pharisees and Sadducees.

12 Then they understood that He wasn't telling them to guard against yeast [in bread],[1] but rather against the teaching of the Pharisees and the Sadducees.

13 Now when Jesus came into the district of Caesarea Philippi, He asked His disciples, "Who do people say that the Son of Man is?"

14 They said, "Some say you are John the baptist, others Elijah, and others Jeremiah or one of the prophets."

15 He said to them: "And who do you say that I am?"

16 Simon Peter answering said,

17 "You are the Christ, the Son of the living God." And Jesus answering said to him:

> You are blessed, Simon, son of Jonah, because flesh and blood didn't reveal this to you, but rather My Father in the heavens.

----

1. These words are omitted in some MSS.

----

disciples. On the one hand, in exasperation He found Himself saying, **"You men of little faith!,"** on the other hand, His patient teachings and explanations eventually paid off. Yours will too. Don't give up. Anyone who possesses the Holy Spirit has the capacity within to understand and obey the Word of God.

Now comes the great section on the founding of the **church** (vv. 13-20). Peter's confession and Jesus' subsequent declaration were the outcome of two questions posed by Jesus, the first of which was, **"Who do people say that the Son of man is?"** (v. 13). The disciples replied by mentioning various wrong guesses that were current (v. 14). Then Jesus asked them who they thought He was (v. 15). Peter said, **"you are the Christ, the Son of the living God"** (v. 17), to which Jesus responded with His great declaration about the church.

This declaration has three parts. First (v. 17) Jesus said that, unlike the peoples' guesses, Peter's answer was a divine revelation, spoken under the special inspiration of the Spirit. The answer didn't come from human thinking or reasoning (**flesh and blood**). That happened during a period when special revelation was still being given; we should not expect such things today since revelation is now complete. Counselees who expect today what could be rightly anticipated then, must be made to see

135

18   I also say to you, you are Peter, and on this rock I will build My church, and gates of the unseen world will not prevail against it.
19   I will give you the keys of the empire from the heavens, and whatever you bind on earth shall have been bound in the heavens, and whatever you loose on earth shall have been loosed in the heavens.

---

that it is not theirs to receive.

Secondly (v. 18), there was the promise to Peter that the **church** would be **built** on **Peter**[1] and that all the strategies that could be cooked up in the city hall (**gates**) of hades (the **unseen world**[2]) would fail to overthrow it. Unlike empires before, it would not be destroyed or given to another (cf. Daniel 2:44). That is a wonderful promise for the church. Counselor, make it clear that in the battle with evil, you and your Christian counselee are on the winning side—no matter how desperate his situation at the moment may appear. These are encouraging words from the lips of Jesus; be sure to use them that way.

Finally, Jesus explained just how the church would be founded by Peter: because of his confession, he would be privileged to use the **keys** to this empire, the church, by becoming the first to preach the gospel to both the Jews (at Pentecost; Acts 2) and the Gentiles (in the house of Cornelius; Acts 10). Which, of course, he did. Through those messages, Peter inserted the key to the church (**the empire from the heavens**), opened the door, and in Christ's Name, invited both Jews and Gentiles into its interior.

The last part of the commission to Peter (v. 19) about **binding and loosing** (cf. Matthew 18:15ff.) has to do with the authority to admit and dismiss persons into and from the church. The power was given to do so, and the encouragement to exercise it was also provided. The essence of this encouragement was that what was determined on earth would be a reflection of what had already been decided in heaven. Counselors should recognize that the church has such authority; decisions about who speaks and acts like a Christian need to be made by the church in relation to those who either accept or fail to accept the teachings of Christ and His authority vested in and exercised by the church. Counselors, as we shall see in Matthew 18:15, are frequently required to deal with such matters.

---

1. The church was founded by Peter, to whom alone was given the keys. There is nothing of a succession of popes.
2. Here, referring to the realm of the evil in that world.

20   Then He strongly warned the disciples not to tell anyone that He is the Christ.

21   From that time, Jesus Christ began to show His disciples that He must go to Jerusalem and suffer many things from the elders and chief priests and scribes, and be killed, and raised on the third day.

22   Then Peter took Him aside and began to rebuke Him, saying, "May God show mercy to You that this shall never be!"

23   But He turned and said to Peter:

> Get behind Me, Satan! You are a stumbling block in My path because you are thinking in a human way, not God's way.

24   Then Jesus said to His disciples,

> If anyone wants to come after Me, he must deny himself and take up his cross and follow Me.

25   Whoever wants to save his life will lose it, but whoever loses his life for My sake will find it.

26   How will it benefit a person if he gains the whole world but loses his life? Or what will a person give in exchange for his life?

27   The Son of Man is going to come with His Father's glory along with His angels, and then He will reward each person according to his actions.

Jesus **strongly warned the disciples** to tell no one **that He is the Christ** (v. 20). Once again, He wanted the full schedule of events to play out over the proper amount of time rather than to rush matters by undue publicity. But the schedule was running. That is what verse 21 is all about. Jesus revealed the next events that would occur. But when Jesus spoke about His coming death at Jerusalem, Peter objected, **rebuking** Him. Then Jesus replied: **"Get behind Me, Satan"** ("adversary"). To suggest such a thing was to put a temptation in Jesus' pathway over which He might **stumble** (v. 23). *Now*, Peter's **thinking** was anything *but* inspired.

Jesus set forth the conditions for discipleship in verses 24 through 26. They would have to **take up the cross, deny themselves, and follow Christ** (v. 24). That is to say, they would have to put their own desires and agendas to death, say "no"[1] to self interests, and say "yes" to Christ's. Verse 25 says the same thing another way: that one must lose his life for Christ which, ultimately, means to save it (and vice versa). To gain everything here and now means nothing when compared to losing life for eternity (v. 26). Which is more valuable—eternal life or what one can obtain

---

1. **Deny** means, literally, "to say no to." To **follow** Jesus rather than one's own agenda is to say "yes" to Him instead.

28   Let Me assure you that there are some of those who stand here who will not taste death before they see the Son of Man coming in His empire.

---

here? That is the kind of question that counselors, from time to time, should put to counselees who are in the throes of decision making. Make them see that they must choose between that which is eternal and that which is temporal, and that no amount of anything here can equal rewards in the life to come. Some day Christ will be manifested in **glory** as He returns with His angels, and will **reward** those disciples who exchanged the temporal for the eternal (v. 27).

Mention of the future of eternal life and the rewards He will give out at His coming suggests the more immediate coming in 70 AD that some of the disciples would live to see occur. That would be the coming of Christ when His empire would take the place of the Jewish state, eventually to be followed by the overthrow of the Roman empire (v. 28). Future certainties are the impetus to live as one should in the here and now. Never hesitate to use them that way in counseling. Jesus certainly did.

CHAPTER 17

1 Now after six days, Jesus took Peter and James and John his brother and led them up a high mountain where they could be alone.
2   And He was transfigured before them: His face shone like the sun and His garments became white as light.
3   Then, before them Moses and Elijah appeared, and they talked with Jesus.

In verses 1 through 13 is the account of the **transfiguration**. Jesus selected the three that He wanted to witness this event (as later He chose the same three to witness the events in the Garden of Gethsemane). One thing that this tells us—a fact about which some counselees wonder—is that it is not wrong to be closer to certain persons than to others. Jesus loved the crowds, but He also selected the twelve to be with Him. Of the twelve there were these three, who seemed even closer, and then there was "the disciple whom Jesus loved" (John).

A description of the transfiguration is given in verse 2: Jesus' **face shone** brilliantly, and His **garments became white** as a bright **light**. The inner person seems to have affected the outer being and His clothing. This event was not like a spotlight playing upon Jesus; it was light that radiated outwardly from within Him. This tells us something of the glory that is His inherently, that He laid aside when He took human nature upon Himself, and which He assumed once more for this brief time in the transfiguration. When Christians rise from the dead, there is a possibility that they too will be radiant since their resurrected bodies are to become like His glorious body (Philippians 3:21).

Moses[1] **and Elijah appeared** (v. 3) and talked with Jesus. Both had something unusual happen to their bodies at their "deaths." Presumably they were also transformed without their bodies experiencing corruption. They also, then, give witness to the condition of believers after the resurrection. They spoke to Jesus about His coming death at Jerusalem. Their appearance does not seem to be for Jesus' sake (as if seeing it might encourage Him for the coming trial) though that is possible. Rather, their presence seems to have been for the sake of the disciples (as was the entire event).

Peter, with his impetuous nature, wanted to remain because things

---

1. At last Moses was admitted to the Holy Land.

4   Peter responded by saying to Jesus, "Lord, it is wonderful for us to be here. If You want me to, I will make three tents, one for You and one for Moses and one for Elijah."
5   While he was still speaking, a bright cloud appeared and overshadowed them, and, then, a voice from the cloud said: "This is My Son Whom I love, with Whom I am well pleased. Listen to Him."
6   When the disciples heard this they fell on their faces and were terrified.
7   But Jesus came and touched them and said, "Get up; don't be afraid."
8   And when they raised their eyes, they saw nobody except Jesus.
    9 Now as they were coming down from the mountain, Jesus charged them: "Don't tell anybody about this vision until the Son of Man has been raised from the dead."
10   So the disciples asked Him, "Why then do the scribes say the Elijah must come first?'

---

were so **good**. So, to prolong things, he offered to make temporary shelters for everyone there on the top of the mountain where it would grow cold at night (v. 4). But, as if to sweep away his foolish misunderstanding of the event, **while he was still speaking** a cloud **overshadowed them**, and the voice of God was heard saying, **"This is My Son Whom I love, with Whom I am well pleased. Listen to Him**." They were not to be interested in or fascinated by Moses and Elijah; this was an event in which Jesus was to be the focus. The appearance of the "dead" meant that even they were interested in Him and His coming sacrifice. So God put the emphasis where it belonged—upon Jesus, and upon no one else! That ought to be true of all that goes on in the counseling room. Never let the counselee focus on you or any other counselee. Constantly say (in one way or another), **"Listen to Him**."

The disciples, in **terror, fell on their faces** (v. 6). While there ought to be no **terror** among true believers (v. 7), there should be a fear of God in them that makes them "fall on their faces" (usually not literally) in humility before God. When what you present to them from the Bible is so plainly presented as the Word of *God*, and not merely your opinion, when counselees are urged to **listen to *Him,*** not you, then the issues in counseling are no longer between the counselor and the counselee, but between the counselee and God—as, indeed they should be. Again, Jesus told them to keep the event quiet for the time being (v. 9).

The disciples were interested in the prophecy of the coming of Elijah that the **scribes** talked about (v. 10). This, doubtless, was occasioned by

11   He answered by saying,

      Elijah, indeed is to come and restore all things;

12   but let Me tell you, Elijah has already come and they didn't recog-
      nize him, but they treated him the way that they wanted to. So too,
      the Son of Man is going to suffer at their hands.

13   Then the disciples understood that He was speaking to them about
John the Baptist.

14   Now when they came to the crowd, a man went up to Him and fell
on his knees before Him and said,

15   Lord, show mercy on my son; he has a very serious case of epi-
      lepsy. Often he falls into the fire, and often into the water.

16   I brought him to Your disciples, but they couldn't heal him.

17   In response Jesus said, "What an unbelieving and twisted generation!
How long do I have to put up with you? Bring him here to Me."

18   So Jesus rebuked the demon and it came out of him, and the boy was
healed from that hour on.

19   Then the disciples came to Jesus privately and asked, "Why couldn't
we cast it out?"

Elijah's appearance on the mountain. Jesus explained that it was John the
Baptist to whom Malachi's prophecy referred (Malachi 4:5, 6). He was
like Elijah (vv. 11-13). They finally understood. Little by little, Jesus
brought the disciples to understand more and more. It is encouraging to
see that constant effort pays off. Jesus' patience with them was amazing.
Learn from this and relate it to your counseling.

    Back among the crowd, a man came to Jesus begging Him to **heal** his
son of **epilepsy**, an infirmity which had serious effects on him (v. 15). The
man told Jesus that the disciples couldn't heal him (v. 16). Once more,
though He had seen some progress in the disciples, Jesus is forced to
speak about the **unbelief and twisted** nature of the generation in which
He was living and of which they were a part (v. 17). **Rebuking** the **demon**
that caused the epilepsy, Jesus healed him (v. 18). How much the world
around permeates the church! Jesus showed His exasperation over that
fact when He exclaimed, "**How long do I have to put up with you?**" All
of us have been affected by the generation in which we live with its particular influences of unbelief and perversion of the truth. So, as counselors,
we too at times become exasperated with it. There will be counselees who
will try your patience. You may become exasperated, as Jesus was, but
you must not give up on them because He didn't.

    The disciples came to Jesus asking why they couldn't cast out the
demon (v. 19). Jesus' answer is clear: because of their small **faith** (vv. 19,

20 And He responded:

> Because of your little faith. Let Me assure you that if you have faith as large as a mustard seed you could say to this mountain, "Move from here to there," and it would move. Indeed, nothing would be impossible for you.

21 [1]

22 As they were strolling about in Galilee, Jesus said to them,

> The Son of Man is going to be delivered into the hands of persons
> 23 who will kill Him, but on the third day He will be raised.

And the disciples became terribly upset.

24 When they came to Capernaum, the collectors of the half shekel tax came to Peter and said, "Doesn't your teacher pay the half shekel tax?"
25 He said, "Yes." So when he came into the house, Jesus spoke first: "What do you think, Simon? From whom do the earth's kings receive toll and tax? From their sons or from strangers?"

---

1. Some MSS add vs. 21: *But this kind won't come out except by prayer and fasting.*

---

20). Faith makes a difference. Because of it, one could do remarkable things, as Jesus indicated by using a favorite image of His (cf. Luke 17:6). Certainly one reason why counselors fail is because of such lack of faith. They don't even attempt to do what the Bible commands at times because they doubt whether the results promised will actually occur. Counselees don't need your doubts added to their own. Prepare for each counseling session with a faith-strengthening study of the Scriptures so that you will enter the session full of faith. Then, let your words and demeanor communicate faith to your counselees.

Jesus had been speaking more and more about His coming **death** and resurrection. But much of what He said was oblique. Here, He came right out and made it the principal topic (vv. 22, 23). The result was that the disciples were **terribly upset**. That is often the way with those who have little faith. They think the worst of what Jesus tells them. They are hesitant to believe that tragedies will really turn out for their good. These men heard about the **death** and it floored them. They failed to focus on what Jesus' said about His **resurrection**, which should have fascinated them. There is never a death apart from a resurrection in Christ's teaching to believers. The good always follows the bad. After the sacrifice comes the crown. Emphasize that.

26 When he said, "From others," Jesus replied,
Then the sons are exempt.
27 But so that we won't offend them, go to the sea and cast out a line,
take the first fish that you catch, and when you open its mouth you
will find a shekel; take it and give it to them for Me and you."

Finally, we come to the teaching about the payment of the **temple tax** (vv. 24-27). Jesus provided the money needed in a miraculous way (through the **fish**). But the important thing to note is how Jesus condescended to others, even when it was unnecessary to do so. There was no need for Him to pay the tax, as He said. He is God's **Son**. Kings don't exact taxes from their sons—only from others. Listen to Jesus' words, **"But so that we won't offend them"** (v. 27). That is why He paid. But the way in which he obtained the tax money evidenced Who He was and that He *was* **exempt**. There are many things you will advise counselees to do that are not strictly necessary, but that they should do simply to avoid unnecessary trouble or controversy. That is a principle to be remembered. This passage should be a great help in making the point. Many counselees want to be quite rigid about everything. Unlike Jesus, they refuse to go the extra mile if not absolutely required to do so. But Jesus here made it plain that it is not always necessary to demand one's rights. So long as one doesn't compromise, for the sake of peace, he may forego a right.

CHAPTER 18

1 At that time, the disciples came to Jesus, saying, "Who is the greatest in the empire from the heavens?"

2 He called a little child and stood him in their midst and said,

3 Let Me assure you, unless you turn around and become like children you won't enter the empire from the heavens.

4 Whoever humbles himself to become like this child is the greatest in the empire from the heavens.

5 And whoever receives one such child because he comes in My Name receives Me.

The unified passage of verses 1 through 14 is informative for a number of reasons. First, notice that the disciples had just been told about Jesus' coming death, but they dismissed this and were talking, instead, about which one of them would be the **greatest** in the **empire from the heavens** (the church). Man's selfishness and pride is not a new development. In order to illustrate their sin Jesus referred to the laws of His kingdom, which are quite different from those of earthly kingdoms; Jesus called **a little child and stood him in their midst** (v. 2). Then He told them that unless they repented (rethought; **turned around**) and became like children they wouldn't even **enter** the **kingdom**. They were to **humble** themselves if they wished to be **greatest**. Of course, He was not setting forth a method for becoming the greatest as some seem to take His words. Rather, He was rebuking them and saying that those who came to the place where they no longer thought in terms of being great, but rather sought to become humble, would in the end find themselves in a greater place as the result (see Luke 18:14). This is difficult for counselees to understand, but quite essential. Learn it—theoretically and experientially—and you will be able to teach them.

Moreover, as counselors, who usually enjoy counseling those with strong intellectual gifts, need to learn, it is the humble who are to be **received** because of Christ. Here, Jesus referred to the disciples themselves who were to be received as Jesus Himself (v. 5). But the opposite is true as well (v. 6). And the consequences to those who reject them may be quite severe.

In mentioning **stumbling blocks** (v. 5), Jesus took the opportunity to discuss the issue of placing temptations in the way of His disciples. Such temptations to stumble (sin) **necessarily** would **come.** Why would these

6   But whoever is an occasion for one of these little ones who
        believe in Me to stumble, it would be better for him to have an
        upper millstone hung around his neck and be drowned in the
        depth of the sea!

7   Woe to the world because of stumbling blocks! Now it is neces-
        sary for stumbling blocks to come, but woe to the person through
        whom the stumbling block comes!

8   So if your hand or your foot is a stumbling block to you, cut it off
        and throw it away from you; it is better for you to enter into life
        maimed or lame than to be thrown into eternal fire with both
        hands and both feet.

9   And if your eye is a stumbling block to you, tear it out and throw
        it away from you; it is better for you to enter into life one-eyed
        than to be thrown into the Gehenna of fire with both eyes.

10   See to it that you don't despise one of these little ones; I tell you
        that in the heavens their angels always look at the face of My
        Father in the heavens.

---

be necessary? From God's perspective, they would be for the strengthen-
ing of the disciples. But from the perspective of the evil one, they were to
bring about their downfall. Counselors must make these facts clear to
counselees who complain about temptation. It cannot be avoided in a
world of sin. Nor did God decree that it would be. But, Jesus said, the one
who tempts His disciples places himself in serious jeopardy (v. 7).

How were the disciples to deal with temptation? They were to do
everything possible through radical amputation to avoid falling over stumbling blocks.[1] Jesus warned the crowds about not **despising** the disciples.
And He informed them that the disciples (all of us as well?) have **angels
in heaven** in close contact with God who watch over them. Presumably,
these angels may help them by inflicting punishment on those who do
despise them. If this is the proper interpretation, and it extends to all
believers so that they can be said to have guardian angels, it also should be
a comforting thought. But whether they do or not, remember it is only one
way of saying that God loves His own and cares for them. Who cares
about angels when he has *God's* promises to care for him (cf. Mt. 6)? The
point to get is this: since believers are under the care of their heavenly
Father, let others beware! And according to the figure of speech in verses
12 through 14, God will care for His own as a shepherd cares for his

---

1. For an explanation of verses 8 and 9 see comments on Matthew 5:27ff.

11 [1]

12   What do you think? If a person has a hundred sheep and one of them wanders off, won't he leave the ninety-nine on the hills and go search for the wandering one?

13   And if he finds it, I assure you, he is happier about that one than about the ninety-nine that didn't wander.

14   In the same way your Father in the heavens doesn't want any of these little ones to perish.

15   If your brother sins against you, go and convict him of his sin privately, with just the two of you present. If he listens to you, you have won your brother.

16   But if he won't listen to you, take with you one or two others so that **by the mouth of two or three witnesses every word may be confirmed.**

17   And if he refuses to listen to them, tell it to the church. And if he refuses to listen to the church, treat him like a Gentile and a tax collector.

18   Let Me assure you that whatever you bind on earth shall have been bound in heaven, and whatever you loose on earth shall have been loosed in heaven.

---

1. Some MSS add vs. 11: *The Son of Man came to save the lost.*

---

sheep. He will not allow even a single one of them to **perish**. The shepherd will deal with predators! There is much comfort to be found in this passage. Don't fail to use it to comfort when it is needed.

Now we come to the powerful passage on church discipline (vv. 15-20). I have discussed fully the implications for counseling that stem from this portion of Scripture in my books *Marriage, Divorce and Remarriage* and *Handbook of Church Discipline.* So I will not deal with these verses in depth. This passage sets forth the vital reconciliation/discipline dynamic by which every difference that separates Christians may be set to rest. It allows for no loose ends. Counselors should instruct counselees in the importance of following these steps whenever anything comes between two brothers that they don't seem to be able to resolve (cf. also 5:23, 24).

Verses 18 through 20 are a powerful incentive to exercise church discipline,[1] even to the extent of exclusion from the church (the place where the **Gentile and the tax collector** found himself). Christ promises to be

---

1. The three verses are wrongly used to encourage small prayer meetings.

19   Again, I tell you that if two of you agree on earth about anything they ask, it will be done for them by My Father in the heavens.
20   Where two or three meet together in My Name, I am there among them.

21 Then Peter came and said to Him, "Lord, when my brother sins against me, how many times should I forgive him? As many as seven times?"

22 Then Jesus said to him,
       I don't tell you seven times but seventy times seven!
   23 Therefore, the empire from the heavens is like a king who wanted to settle accounts with his slaves,
24   and as he began settlement, one was brought to him who owed him ten thousand talents.
25   But since he couldn't repay the debt, the lord commanded that he, his wife, his children, and everything that he owned be sold to repay the debt.
26   The servant fell on his knees and begged him, "Be patient with me and I'll repay you everything."
27   And the lord took pity on his slave and released him and forgave the loan.
28   But when he went out that same slave found one of his fellow slaves who owed him one hundred denarii, and he seized him and throttled him, saying, "Repay whatever you owe."

---

present to guide and bless in the process. And, note, He has already determined the outcome in **heaven** before you declare it on earth. The operative action that moves the disciplinary process forward from step to step is the unwillingness of one or more party to be reconciled. The verb used twice in verse 17 means "to hear without heeding; ignoring." Because these are such vital verses for counselors, if you do not possess the above-mentioned books, I urge you to obtain them. You will have many occasions to use this passage and to refer to the explanations that these books give.

Peter understood that Jesus was talking about **forgiveness**, so he asked how often he should forgive an erring brother (v. 21). Jesus' answer is **seventy times seven**—in other words, every time he repents and seeks it.[1] To emphasize what He said to Peter, Jesus told a parable. This parable

---

1. To understand the ins and outs of forgiveness (another vital interest in Christian counseling), and in particular the fact that one does not forgive another until he is repentant, see my book *From Forgiven to Forgiving*. If one forgave apart from repentance, he could not obey verses 15-20.

29 So his fellow slave fell down and begged him, "Be patient with me and I'll repay you."

30 But he wouldn't. Instead, he went and threw him into prison until he paid the debt.

31 When his other fellow slaves saw what had happened, they were greatly upset and went and told their lord all about what had taken place.

32 Then his lord called him and said to him: "You wicked slave, I forgave you your entire debt because you begged me.

33 Shouldn't you also have shown mercy to your fellow slave as I showed mercy to you?"

34 And his lord became angry, and handed him over to the torturers until he paid his entire debt.

35 So also will My heavenly Father do to you unless each of you forgives his brother from his heart.

---

shows how people in **the empire from the heavens** (church) should deal with one another. Showing compassion on him, the **king forgave** the huge debt of a servant that was far beyond his means to repay. But the very same **servant** refused to do the same for a **fellow slave** who owed a paltry debt. When other servants saw this, they told the king who handed him over to the **torturers**. God says they will not be forgiven unless they treat others as He has treated them (cf. Matthew 6:15, and comments there). These matters are of great significance to counselors. Acquaint yourself thoroughly with them; you will use the chapter frequently in counseling.

CHAPTER 19

1 So it happened that when Jesus finished speaking these words, He left Galilee and went into the district of Judea across the Jordan,

2   and large crowds followed Him and He healed them there.

3 Then Pharisees came to Him to test Him. They asked, "Is it lawful for someone to divorce his wife on any ground?"

4   And He replied:
      Haven't you read that the Creator at the beginning **made them male and female**

5   and said, **For this reason a man must leave his father and his mother and must cleave to his wife and they will be one flesh?**

6   Thus they are no longer two but one flesh. So then, what God has yoked together, a human being must not separate.

We do not know how long Jesus remained in transjordan Judea (v. 1). But He drew crowds as He had in Galilee (v. 2). He continued to heal the sick. **Then Pharisees came to test Him**. They wanted Him to tell them if it was lawful to divorce one's wife on **any** grounds (v. 3). There will be "counselees" who will also test you. Their motives may be different, but if you counsel for any length of time you will run into such people. From Jesus' replies, you will know how to answer them—by means of the Scriptures.[1]

The question asked was a live issue between the followers of Hillel and those of Shammai. The question was frequently asked and discussed. The issue arose over the words about divorce in Deuteronomy 24. Jesus rebuked them for not being able to reason from the Bible to a solid answer (v. 4): **Haven't you read. . .** Rather than getting into the intricacies of the Deuteronomy passage which they were grossly misinterpreting, Jesus went back to creation and noted how God set things up originally. There was no polygamy and there was no divorce. This He does to counter the wrong use of Deuteronomy. He mentioned the male/female orientation of marriage.[2] Then shows how the two were linked by God in a **one flesh** relationship that was to be indissoluble (vv. 5, 6). And finally, He added, **what God has yoked together, a human being must not separate.** That

---

1. Some would call Jesus' method of using the Bible "prooftexting." If so, then it is legitimate.
2. There is no place for same sex "marriage."

7   They asked Him: "Why then did Moses command him to give a certificate of divorce and send her away?"

8   He said to them,

> Moses, because of the hardness of your hearts, allowed you to
> divorce your wives; but from the beginning this was not the way
> that it was.

9   Now I say to you that whoever divorces his wife except because of
sexual sin and marries another commits adultery.

10 The disciples said to Him, "If that is the way that it must be between
a man and his wife, it would be better not to marry."

11   And He said to them,

> Not everybody has the capacity for that, but only those to whom it
> has been given.

---

needs to be taught to counselees who feel free to leave a marriage partner.

The Pharisees then referred directly to Deuteronomy 24 asking why
Moses **commanded** that a **certificate of divorce** be given. This was a
misquotation. There was no such command. Moses referred to the practice of divorce through the giving of such a certificate and taught that
when it took place, the divorced persons were not to remarry one another
if either had subsequently married and divorced another. Moses was regulating a bad situation. Note the contrast of verbs in verse 7 (**commanded**)
and in verse 8 (**allowed**). Moses allowed divorce, Jesus said, because of
the low moral conditions of things represented by the **hardness of hearts**
of husbands and wives. But this was not the way God had originally set
marriage up (v. 8). Jesus then stiffened current, man-made rules, saying
that for covenant people, there was only one legitimate cause of divorce—
sexual sin (v. 9). Divorce for any other reason is adultery and causes those
who remarry such divorced persons to become adulterers also.[1]

The disciples' response is interesting. They said, **If that is the way
that it must be between a man and his wife, it would be better not to
marry** (v. 10). But, as Jesus remarked (vv. 11, 12), celibacy is not for all.[2]
It is only for those whom God has singled out and gifted to live the single
life. Some **eunuchs** are that way naturally (by birth), others unnaturally
(by castration) and some supernaturally (by a special gift from God). For

---

1. For further help concerning divorce see my *Marriage, Divorce and Remarriage in the Bible.*

2. Indeed, in time, all the disciples did marry (cf. I Corinthians 9:5).

12   There are eunuchs who were born that way, there are eunuchs who
        were made eunuchs by men, and there are eunuchs who make
        themselves eunuchs for the sake of the empire from the heavens.
        Whoever has the capacity must exercise it.

13 Then they brought children to Him that He might lay His hands on
them and pray. But the disciples rebuked them.

14 So Jesus said, "Let the children come to Me and don't stop them, for
of such is the empire from the heavens."

15 And He laid His hands on them and left there.

---

those with the gift of celibacy to marry would be a sin: if they have the
capacity they **must exercise it** (v. 12). Single Christians should devote
the extra time they have to service in the **empire from the heavens**. They
ought not to selfishly indulge themselves by using it for their own interests. They have been **gifted** especially for this purpose. If someone isn't
certain about his/her gift, let him spend his time in service and see what
happens. If not gifted, he is likely to find a marriage partner somehow in
connection with that service. And, on the other hand, to find the right marriage partner, it is wise to look for someone who likewise is involved in
Christian activity. Positioning himself in Christ's service, therefore,
places him precisely where he ought to be from either aspect. Teach counselees this.

Moving on, we turn now to three verses (13-15) in which we see
Jesus' attitude toward **children**. The disciples had the idea that children
would interrupt Jesus' activities, so they **rebuked** people who brought
children to Him. But Jesus straightened them out. "**Let them come, and
don't stop them**," He said. Then, He declared that **the empire from the
heavens** is composed of such childlike persons (v. 14). So, in harmony
with the Abrahamic covenant, in which children were included as a part
of the covenant community (cf. Genesis 17) and thus entitled to all the
blessings of it, Jesus **laid hands on** them and **prayed** for them. Counselors should not discount children in counseling. If they are very young,
then a counselor will most likely deal with their parents. But when they
become old enough to understand what you are saying (presuming that
you have learned how to speak in children's language[1]), a counselor
should make every attempt to help them too. However, he should be careful not to allow the child to think that he is a "case."

The rich young ruler came to Jesus, Who challenged his understand-

---

1. Often by drawing pictures and telling stories.

16 Then, someone came to Him and said, "Teacher, what good deed must I do to have eternal life?" And He responded by saying:

17 "Why do you ask Me about what is good? If you want to enter into life, keep the commandments."

18 He said, "Which?" And Jesus replied,

> **Don't kill, Don't commit adultery, Don't steal, Don't give false testimony.**

19   **Honor your father and your mother**, and **You must love your neighbor as yourself.**

20 The young man said to Him, "I have kept all of these; what do I still lack?"

21 Jesus said to him,

> If you want to be complete, go sell your possessions and give to the poor, and you will have treasure in the heavens, and come follow Me.

22 But on hearing that statement, the young man left sadly, because he had many possessions.

23 So Jesus said to His disciples,

> Let Me assure you that it will be hard for a rich man to enter the empire from the heavens.

---

ing of what was **good** and exposed his utter lack of goodness as God views goodness (vv. 16-22). In telling him that the way to **eternal life** is in keeping the **commandments**, Jesus was helping him to understand that he had failed completely to do so and therefore needed a Savior. This man, as the story unfolds, thought that he had kept the commandments because he had not breached them outwardly. In order to make it clear that there was a more important, inner obedience, Jesus concentrated on the summary of the commandments (to love God and to love one's neighbor). He told him to sell everything, give his money to the poor and follow Him. The man **left, sadly, because he had many possessions.** To sell and give the proceeds to the poor would relate to the second great command, while following Jesus (rather than his own plans) would relate to the first. Never allow any counselee to think that he has kept any commandment (let alone all) by outwardly obeying it. The homework assignment Jesus gave this young man clearly exposed his inner problem, as homework assignments left undone by counselees so often do. Look for such evidence.

This event with the rich young man led to a discussion about money and possessions (vv. 23-26), which subsequently led to a discussion of the rewards to be given to the disciples who *had* left all for Christ's service (vv. 27-30). Jesus' comments about **rich** persons have held true down

24 Again I tell you, it is easier for a camel to go through the eye of a needle than for a rich man to enter into God's empire.

25 When the disciples heard this, they were astounded and said, "Who then can be saved?"

26 But Jesus looked at them and said, "With human beings this is impossible, but with God everything is possible."

27 Then Peter responded by saying, "Consider us—we have left everything and followed You; what will we have?"

28 Jesus said to them:

Let Me assure you that in the regeneration, when the Son of Man sits on His glorious throne, you who have followed Me will also sit on twelve thrones, judging the twelve tribes of Israel.

29 And everyone who has left houses or brothers or sisters or father or mother or children or farms for the sake of My Name, will receive many times as much and will inherit eternal life.

---

through the ages. Riches tend to give people a false sense of security. They often come to depend on their riches rather than on God. Moreover, they love the things that riches can buy, so they find it hard to part with them. These things being true, it is difficult for rich persons to follow the commands of Christ and find their way into God's empire. They don't think they need what it offers, and they are afraid it will mean sacrificing some of their riches if they do enter it.

In answer to the disciples' question, **"Who then can be saved?"** Jesus said that it was impossible for men, but with God it was possible (v. 26). On this occasion, He also uttered His memorable parable about a **camel's** passing through **the eye of a needle** being easier than a rich man's becoming a believer. Here, through hyperbole, Jesus stressed an impossibility. Apart from God's transforming him, no rich man will place Christ above his riches. It is only when God intervenes, as He did in the instance of Moses,[1] that what is impossible with man actually occurs.

In answer to Peter's question about the future reward of the disciples, who had **left everything** and followed Jesus, He gave them a glimpse of the situation in the new heavens and the new earth (**the regeneration**) when they would rule with Him (v. 28); He also explained that in this life others would take the place of their earthly families (v. 29). As things appear now, many who are **first** will be **last** in the regeneration, and vice versa. The way God reckons service, as Jesus had just demonstrated, has

---

1. Cf. Hebrews 11:24-26.

30   But many who are first will be last, and many who are last will be
        first.

---

to do with the inner person, and not with the outer person alone. That would mean that even among those who were saved, when it comes to judgment there will be many surprises. Continue to make it clear to counselees that outer conformity (though good) is not acceptable if it stands alone. That is the essence of hypocrisy which Jesus described so aptly when He spoke of those who were like cups, which were clean on the outside, but filthy on the inside. Too often counselees, like the rich young man, are ready to settle for outward conformity.

CHAPTER 20

1	This is true because the empire from the heavens is like the owner of an estate who went out early in the morning to hire workers to labor in his vineyard.
2	And when he and the workers had agreed that he pay a denarius for the day, he sent them to the vineyard.
3	But when he went out about the third hour, he saw others standing idle in the market place,
4	and said to them, "You go to the vineyard too, and whatever is right I will give you." So they went.
5	Again, he went out about the sixth hour and the ninth hour and did the same thing.
6	Then about the eleventh hour he found some others standing and said to them, "Why are you standing here idle all day long?"
7	They said to him, "Because no one has hired us." And he said to them, "You too go to the vineyard."
8	Now when evening came, the lord of the vineyard said to his steward, "Call the workers and pay them their wages, starting with those hired last and ending with those hired first."
9	And those who went at the eleventh hour received a denarius,
10	so when the first came, they thought they would receive more, but they too each received a denarius.

From this chapter through the twenty-fifth we increasingly encounter eschatological material. Some of it is parabolic, some straightforward, and some apocalyptic. Probably, the nineteenth chapter should not be divided from the twentieth. The last verse of chapter nineteen and the last verse of the parable with which the twentieth begins say the same thing (v. 16). They both tell us that many reversals in our judgments about people will take place in the Judgment. The parable illustrates the principle.

The vineyard parable is certainly foreign to our culture. Business practices are quite different today when the government regulates the way in which businessmen hire their workers. Verse 15^a states a principle that no longer holds in modern America (that an owner of a vineyard is allowed to **do as he wants with his own money**). So, in using the parable, you will probably have to explain that conditions in our culture have changed matters and that the point of the parable will be lost if a counselee becomes entangled in the contrasts between today and biblical times.

11   Now when they received it they complained against the owner of the estate, saying,

12   "Those who were hired last worked one hour, and you have made them equal to us who have borne the burden of the day's work and the heat."

13   But he answered one of them and said, "Fellow, I wasn't unfair to you; didn't you and I agree on a denarius?

14   Take what is yours and go. I want to give the last as much as you.

15   I'm allowed to do as I want with my own money, am I not? Or do you have an envious eye because I am generous?"

16   Thus, the last will be first and the first will be last.

What is the point of the parable? Verse 11 tells us that the day laborers who worked all day for what they got and received the same amount as those who worked only from the eleventh hour on **complained against the owner of the estate**. But the owner said several things in response. First, that he paid them exactly what they had agreed upon (they had been happy enough at the first to work for that amount; v. 13). Secondly, he told them that he had a right to pay whatever he wished, since the money was his to do with as he pleased. Lastly, he said he also had the right to show **generosity** to those whom he wished, and that others had no reason to envy them (v. 15). Jesus then commented that the **last will be first and the first will be last**.

God is sovereign. Some will come into the empire from the heavens early in their lives and receive rewards for what they have done. Others, having wasted many years, will come to Christ later on but, because of God's generosity, will be accorded similar rewards. That this is **unfair**, as some complained (v. 13), is not in the picture since, in His sovereign mercy, God may be generous to the latter if He pleases. That is His business and it is up to us to praise Him for whatever He does—especially if in His grace He saves people like the thief on the cross in the last moments of their lives. God, Himself, is the One Who determines the standard of what is fair and unfair. By definition, whatever He does is fair. We must adjust our thinking to His ways; He will not adjust to ours.

There are counselees who, instead of rejoicing about their salvation, complain about others who are saved late in life and who are given responsibilities they have never been accorded (they may become elders or deacons, for instance). This is wrong. If God has given them the gifts and they are rightly exercising them, they have a right to be placed in those positions. If others, who have been Christians for a much longer

17 Now as Jesus was going up to Jerusalem, He took the twelve aside privately and on the road He said to them:

18   Listen carefully; we are going up to Jerusalem, and the Son of Man will be handed over to the chief priests and scribes and they will condemn Him to death,

19   and they will hand Him over to the Gentiles to be mocked and scourged and crucified. But on the third day He will be raised.

20 Then the mother of the sons of Zebedee came to Him with her sons, and she kneeled and asked Him if He would do something for her.

21 He said to her: "What do you want?" She said to Him, "Promise that these two sons of mine will sit, one at Your right and one at Your left in Your empire."

22 But Jesus responded by saying, "You don't know what you are asking! Can you drink the cup that I am going to drink?" They replied, "We can."

---

time, are not raised to positions in the church because they didn't have the gifts (or, having them, failed to exercise them) that is perfectly okay. They have no reason to complain about "Johnny-come-latelys." God is running His church, and it is our task to rejoice in the salvation and subsequent ministries of all who come to Christ at any time in their lives. You will run into the problem expressed in this parable in counseling. Pride, envy, and general discontent are all brought to the surface by the generosity of God. Point out that there is no place for any such thing among God's children in His kingdom, since we are all there by grace, and grace alone, anyway. No one *deserves* anything.

In verses 17 through 19, we read that once more Jesus predicted His death and resurrection to the disciples who, it seems, didn't want to hear about it. Like many counselees, they preferred to hide their heads in the sand. Jesus, then, had to repeat the facts about what lay ahead again and again to get them through their hard heads. You may find yourself saying the same thing again and again to counselees who don't want to hear some hard truth. Keep at it until you finally get through.

Verses 20 through 28 have to do with who will be **first** in the kingdom (cf. v. 27). The **mother of the sons of Zebedee**, like many mothers, wanted the best for her sons. So she asked Jesus to place her boys at His **right** and **left** in the new **empire** (v. 21). Turning to the boys, He asked if they were **ready to drink the cup** (of death) **that He would drink**. They said, "**We can**." But they had no realization of what would come—even though He had just told them (vv. 17-19). He then said that they would drink the cup, but that He would make them no such promise as their

23 He said to them,

> Indeed, you will drink of My cup, but to sit at My right and at My left is not Mine to give, but it is for those for whom it has been prepared by My Father.

24 Now when the ten heard this, they were infuriated about the two brothers.

25 So Jesus called them to Him and said,

> You know that the rulers of the Gentiles lord it over them and their superiors show their authority over them.

26   This isn't the way it is with you. Instead, whoever among you wants to become great must be your servant;

27   and whoever wants to be first must be your slave;

28   just as the Son of Man did not come to be served, but to serve and to give His life a ransom for many.

---

mother has requested because, in His sovereignty, God had already **prepared** those places for particular persons (whose names He did not reveal). Once more, Jesus was setting forth the fact that God sovereignly rules over and directs the affairs of His people in His church. We have no right to tell Him how to do so or to complain about what He does. This is a very important principle to get across to counselees who live in a society in which pressure tactics like those that this mother tried to exert upon Jesus are often the norm rather than the exception. The great point is that God is in charge, and He will do as He sees fit. You can't successfully lobby for anything with God.

The ten other disciples who heard what had happened were incensed (v. 24). Jesus talked to them about the incident. He contrasted God's rule with that of pagan nations. The superiors of these nations **lord it over** their subjects and *make themselves great*. However, in Christ's kingdom, it is not those who are at the forefront who have the right to claim these positions for themselves. They are sovereignly given by God. Indeed, they must learn to take a back seat, humbling themselves if they would have a place of importance in the future (v. 26). Just because they were disciples that did not give them authority to put themselves forward. Those who will find a first place in the kingdom must be like Christ Himself Who, when He came, **did not come to be served, but to serve and give His life a ransom for many** (v. 28). The law of the kingdom, tell counselees, is that God exalts those who humble themselves, not those who exalt themselves as the Gentiles (unsaved) do. This is a difficult lesson for sinners to learn. But when counselees learn and practice it, it will make a great dif-

29 As they were leaving Jericho a large crowd followed Him.

30 And there, sitting beside the road, were two blind men who, when they heard that Jesus was passing by, shouted, saying, "Lord, show mercy to us, Son of David!"

31 But the crowd rebuked them, telling them to be quiet; but they shouted all the more, saying, "Lord, show mercy to us, Son of David!"

32 Jesus stood still and called them and said, "What do you want Me to do for you?"

33 They said to Him, "Lord, we want our eyes opened."

34 And Jesus, emotionally moved, touched their eyes and instantly they saw again and followed Him.

---

ference in their lives—especially in their relationships with others.

The final incident in the chapter has to do with two blind men whom Jesus healed (vv. 29-34). Christ's compassion is evidenced in this healing (cf. v. 34). These men recognized Christ as the Messiah (the **Son of David**; cf. v. 31). That was more than the Pharisees and Sadducees did. How often this is true. The ones you would expect to believe don't and those you expect not to believe do. Again, this seems to be a manifestation of the first/last principle that we have been noting throughout the section. Notice that the crowd told these men to be quiet, but Jesus called them to come to Him. His will is rarely in sync with that of the crowd, or even the disciples in the matter of who may come to him—remember the children (19:13)? As counselors, we should be careful who we turn down; they may be the very ones whom Jesus is sending to us. Humble yourself to help even the lowliest. They may turn out to be those that in time God puts first, while others you thought would be found at the front of the line will be found at the end.

CHAPTER 21

1 At the point when they drew near to Jerusalem and came to Beth-phage, at the Mount of Olives, Jesus sent two disciples,

2 telling them,

Go into the village opposite you, and the first thing that you will find is a donkey tied up, together with a colt. Untie them and bring them to Me.

3 And if anyone says anything to you, tell him, "The Lord needs them," and he will send them immediately.

4 Now this happened to fulfill what the prophet spoke when he said,

5 **Tell Zion's daughter, "Look, your King is coming to you, meek and riding on a donkey, on a colt, the foal of a donkey."**

6 The disciples went and did as Jesus directed them;

7 they brought the donkey and the colt and put their clothes on them, and He sat on them.

8 A large crowd of people spread their clothes in the road, and others cut branches from the trees and spread them in the road.

9 And the crowds that went before Him and those that followed Him shouted, saying, "Hosanna to David's Son! **Blessed is the One Who comes in the Lord's Name**; Hosanna in the highest!"

Presumably according to previously made arrangements, Jesus sent **two of His disciples** to **Bethphage** on **the Mount of Olives** where they had arrived, to take care of transportation into the city of Jerusalem. The **donkey**, which was obtained, as the quotation from Zechariah 9:9 makes clear, was the symbol of peace. A horse, in contrast, was the symbol of war. A large crowd followed and went before Him, as He rode into the city. Jesus and the disciples could have walked the short distance down into the ravine and then up into the city. But according to prophecy, Jesus was making an "entrance" (as it has been called) into the city of God over which, by all rights, He ruled as **King**.

Until now we see Jesus, again and again, trying to allay undue publicity. But, the time now came for Him to reveal Himself as the Messiah Who had come in order to redeem a people for God. So He "pulls out all the stops." And, in God's providence, His raising of Lazarus together with the multitude of His past healings and miracles, He had performed, brought forth a large **crowd** to welcome and escort Him into Jerusalem.

There is a time to back off, and there is a time to come forth. That is true of most activities in life. Counselors must learn to recognize these

10   When He entered Jerusalem the whole city was stirred up, saying, "Who is this?"

11   And the crowds said, "This is the prophet Jesus from Nazareth of Galilee."

12   Jesus went into the temple and threw out all those who were selling and buying in it. He overturned the moneychangers' tables and the seats of those who sold doves,

13   and said to them, "It is written: **My house will be called a house of prayer**, but you are making it a robber's den."

---

times in their approaches to counseling problems and make adjustments accordingly. Many counselees have never learned the difference. It is important to teach them.

The crowds, thinking of Jesus as a coming conqueror who would enable them to prevail over Rome, thronged the streets crying **Hosanna** (which means "save now"). He had come to save, and He was about to consummate the saving act at Calvary. Yet He had come to save His own not from Rome's military power, but from the grip and hold of sin on their lives. Ironically, God's providence called forth the right words (even though misapplied) from the crowd to announce His epiphany at Jerusalem. God's ways are interesting, and counselors ought to be aware of such providential "coincidences" that they can use to teach counselees.

Attributing Jesus' miraculous powers to the fact that He was a **prophet** was only partially correct. He had come as Prophet (to teach), Priest (to sacrifice Himself), and King (to rule over His church). People almost always understand in part and must be further instructed. This is what the apostles would do after the resurrection. Though Jesus had informed them adequately at this time, they themselves were confused as to His mission and would only understand later on.

Verses 12 and 13, which follow the entrance into Jerusalem, show how Jesus cleansed the temple once again, thus declaring His authority over what was done there. He refused to allow His **Father's house** to be made a **robber's den**, into which the priests had transformed the temple grounds. They charged high prices for allowing traders in goods and money the privilege of setting up booths there. Selling there had become a business and profit-making enterprise rather than a worship convenience. There are counselors today who border on this same approach by what they do. In the name of "Christian counseling," they charge enormous sums for counsel that, in many cases, is no more Christian than what is offered up the street by a non-Christian. Indeed, considering the effects on

14 Blind persons and lame persons came to Him in the temple and He healed them.

15 But when the chief priests and the scribes saw the amazing things that He did and the children shouting in the temple, saying, "Hosanna to David's Son," they were infuriated.

16 So they said to Him, "Do you hear what they are saying?" And Jesus said to them: "Yes. Haven't you ever read, **Out of the mouths of babies and nursing children You have prepared praise for Yourself?**"

17 And He left them and went out of the city to Bethany and spent the night there.

---

counselees, what they do is more harmful than what the temple merchants did. Of course, finally what was being done to Christ's Father's house was the basic problem. The merchants were, in His Name, turning His **house** (the temple) into a place for **robbing** the worshippers. Every counselor must be clear about this matter and be blameless financially before the Lord.

Jesus' healings and acclaim **infuriated the chief priests and scribes**. This time Jesus was allowing everything to become public, because "His hour had come." They asked Him whether He had heard what the crowds were saying. The implication was that they wanted Him to stop them; such things they considered blasphemy. But Jesus accepted the acclaim and quoted the proverb that indicated the wise would not know, but the innocent and simple would (vv. 14-16). Then He left.

In these events you encounter two instances of anger, the first by Jesus, which was righteous anger over what was happening at the temple, and the second by the religious leaders over their views of the events surrounding Jesus' entrance. Anger is not wrong in itself. It is what occasions it and how it is expressed that determines whether it is correct or not. In one case, the anger was righteous because it was directed at those insulting the Name of God; in the other it was the result of unbelief and envy.

Some counselors speak about "negative emotions," as if some emotions are right and some are wrong. Of course, there is no such thing as a negative emotion. All emotions were built into the human being by God and reflect something of God Himself (Psalm 7:11). All emotions have a proper place in the Christian's life when they are properly aroused and properly exercised. At times, every emotion is wrongly aroused and wrongly manifested by sinners. What counselors need to emphasize is not the rightness or wrongness of an emotion but the rightness or wrongness

18 Early the next day, as He was going up to the city, He grew hungry.
19 Seeing a lone fig tree along the road, He went over to it, but He found nothing but leaves on it. So He said to it, "May you never bear fruit again!" And the fig tree dried up at once.
20 When the disciples saw this they were astonished and said, "How did the fig tree dry up all at once?"
21 Jesus responded:

> Let Me assure you that if you have faith and don't doubt, you won't only be able to do what was done to the fig tree but even if you were to say to this mountain, "Be lifted up and thrown into the sea," it would happen.

22   Everything that you ask for in prayer you will receive if you believe.

---

of what arouses it in counselees and how they exhibit it.

In verses 18 through 22 Matthew recorded the story of Jesus' withering of the **fig tree**. Because a fig tree produces fruit before the leaves, which afterward accompany the fruit, this tree was (in effect) "boasting" that it was bearing fruit, when there was none. Jesus then took the occasion to turn the event into a parable for His disciples. He cursed the tree[1] (v. 19). The parable He thus construed from the incident concerned the Jewish nation. This nation boasted about being God's own, but didn't bear fruit as the people of God. The disciples, however, were interested in the miracle, rather than its meaning (which Jesus would soon explicate in other parables). They wanted to know how a fig tree could **dry up at once** (v. 19). So Jesus spoke to them about the power of faith, using one of His favorite figures of speech (cf. Mt. 17). Then He made it clear that as apostles they would have the same power to perform such works if they believed (vv. 21, 22).

Faith, though not able to accomplish all that a specially endued apostle who was receiving and writing revelation, can accomplish much for believers today. It is certain from the many passages that speak to all Christians about how God blesses faith that there are counselees (and counselors) who miss out on blessings for lack of faith. Understand, however, that it is not faith *per se* that accomplishes anything. Contrary to the saying that you frequently hear, that **"prayer** changes things," prayer itself does nothing. It is God Who brings about change, when asked by faith in prayer. The counselor must make this clear. Otherwise, he may

---

1. This curse, that it would **never bear fruit again**, meant total rejection.

23 When He went into the temple, the chief priests and the elders of the people came to Him as He was teaching and asked, "By what authority are you doing these things, and who gave you this authority?"

24 Jesus responded by saying to them:

I will also ask you one question, and if you answer Me I will tell you by what authority I am doing these things:

25 John's baptism—where did it come from: from heaven or from men?

And they argued with one another, saying,

If we say "from heaven," he will ask us, "Why then didn't you believe in him?"

26 But if we say "from men," we will have to watch out for the crowd (since everybody held that John was a prophet).

27 So they answered Jesus by saying, "We don't know." And He said to them:

Neither will I tell by what authority I am doing these things.

---

misplace his faith in faith itself, or in prayer.

Verses 23 through 27 deal with the matter of Jesus' authority. The religious leaders wanted to know the **authority** behind Jesus' words and actions (v. 23). That they considered what He had been doing—even raising the dead—was not itself a sign of His authority from God seems strange. Yet, it was not enough for them. As we saw, they wanted a sign specially calculated to show them that He was authorized by God. Jesus would not give it to them since He was in no sense under their authority. So, once more, Jesus answered with a question of His own (a favorite method of dealing with hostility, as we have seen). He asked them to tell Him if John came from **heaven** or merely from some human source before He would tell them the source of His authority. They thought that they would put Jesus on the spot; it turns out instead they were the ones who were put on the defensive. Jesus put His finger on a sensitive spot. The religious leaders had failed to believe John and be baptized by Him. But they knew how the people regarded John (**everybody held that John was a prophet**; v. 26). They actually feared what the crowd might do if they said they didn't believe that John came from God, so they said "We don't know." Since they refused to give a straight answer, Jesus also refused to do so (v. 27).

The interesting thing to note here is that these men lied out of fear. They knew full well that they had rejected John and his claims. But they

28 Now, what do you think? A man had two children. And he went to the first and said, "Child, go to work today in the vineyard."

29 And he replied, "I am going, sir," but he didn't go.

30 Then he went to the second and said the same thing. And he replied, "I don't want to," but later he regretted this and went.

31 Which of the two did his father's will?
They answered, "The latter." Jesus said to them,
Let Me assure you that the tax collectors and the prostitutes are going into God's empire before you.

32 John came to you with the way of righteousness and you didn't believe in him. But the tax collectors and the prostitutes believed in him; and even when you saw this you didn't have any regrets later on and believe in him.

---

lied about this since they feared the **crowds**. It is plain that many counselees will lie to others out of fear. This habit that many resort to when they find themselves under pressure is one that every counselor deals with again and again. He can use Ephesians 4 and other passages to help point out God's solution to the problem by replacing it with the biblical alternative of truth telling. He can help his counselees to develop such new habits by staying with them until the new pattern is formed. But he must emphasize that such a change in living patterns is possible only for those who repent of the sin of lying and who sincerely pray in faith for the help needed to make the change.

Jesus then told them a parable (vv. 28-32). Two sons were the opposite of one another. When asked to serve, one said to His father, "**I am going, sir.**" He was polite, and immediately responsive, and all looked good. But he didn't go. The other said, "**I don't want to.**" Later, he repented and went. Jesus asked, "**Which of the two did his father's will?**" The religious leaders were forced to answer, "**the latter.**" Then Jesus applied the parable to them. The despised outcasts of society, prostitutes, and tax collectors, who repented of their sin under the preaching of John, would enter the **empire** before they would. They were hypocrites who, like the first son, talked a good game, but were ingenuine. The outcasts were like the second son. There are, of course, many counselees who talk rightly but fail to follow through. This passage is a powerful one to use with them. Warn them by means of it, and encourage them to repent. Jesus was giving these leaders a final opportunity to repent, but their hearts were hardened against God and His Son. Repentance by others ought to have brought them to repentance (v. 32^c). The fact is, it did the

> **33** Listen to another parable. There was an owner of an estate who **planted a vineyard, and put a hedge around it, and dug a wine press in it, and built a tower**, and rented it to tenant farmers and took a trip to another country.
> **34** Now when the time came to harvest the grapes, he sent his slaves to the farmers to receive the fruit.
> **35** But the farmers grabbed his slaves, beating one, killing another and stoning a third.
> **36** Again, he sent other slaves—more than in the first group—and they did the same thing to them.
> **37** At last he sent his son to them, saying, "They will respect my son."
> **38** But when the farmers saw his son they said to each other, "This is the heir; come on, let's kill him and get hold of his inheritance."
> **39** So they grabbed him and threw him outside of the vineyard, where they killed him.
> **40** Now, when the lord of the vineyard comes, what will he do to those farmers?

opposite. They thought that they were too good to be classed with tax collectors and prostitutes! When you hear this attitude among counselees, be sure to show them the dire consequences of that sort of thinking. All are wretched sinners. No one is good.

The parable of the two sons is followed by another (vv. 33-46). Once He had begun, Jesus refused to let go. Instead He drove home His message.[1] This time Jesus told the parable of a vineyard in which the farmers who sharecropped the vineyard with the owner refused to give him his share. The Owner, representing God, sent messenger after messenger with no positive results. Indeed, things went from bad to worse (just as Israel would not listen to the prophets). Finally, He sent His Son (Jesus). Instead of listening to Him, in an attempt to take over the vineyard, they killed Him. The cup was full. Then came the final indignity at which it overflowed.

Jesus put the question to the religious leaders (v. 40): "**Now when the lord of the vineyard comes, what will he do to those farmers?**" They answered, pronouncing their own sentence (one of the ironies of their dealings with Christ). The answer was twofold (v. 41): He would put the farmers to a **miserable death** (70 AD) and he would rent the vineyard

---

1. Too many counselors speak weakly rather than driving the message home!

41 They replied, "He will put those miserable farmers to a miserable death, and he will rent the vineyard to other farmers who will give him fruit whenever it is ripe."

42 Jesus said to them,

> Didn't you ever read in the Scriptures: **The same Stone that the builders rejected has become the Head of the corner; this has happened because of the Lord and it is astonishing in our eyes**?

43 So then I tell you that God's empire will be taken away from you and will be given to a nation who will produce its fruit.

44 [Whoever trips on this Stone will be broken to pieces, and whoever it falls on will be pulverized.][1]

45 When the chief priests and the Pharisees heard Jesus' parables, they knew He was talking about them.

---

1. Vs. 44 is omitted from some MSS.

---

to **other farmers** who would produce fruit (Gentiles and believing Jews of the church). This was the fulfillment of the prophecies of Deuteronomy 28:25, 49-57. Now there is a new Israel who have become a chosen race (cf. I Peter 2:10). The prophecy of the stumbling-crushing **Stone** has also been fulfilled (vv. 42-44).

This was powerful preaching. It was like sticking a knife into the religious leaders and twisting it. They finally caught on that He was speaking of them (v. 45), and they didn't like it. They would have **arrested** Him if they had not feared the reaction of the **crowd** (v. 46).

There comes a time when it is so late that nothing short of the most severe warning can be issued. That was true here. It will be true (in a lesser sense) of believing counselees from time to time. If they have determined to persist in an unrighteous course of disobedience, and refuse to hear warning after warning, it may be time to level the big guns at them—as Jesus did.

Today, every counselee is one of God's new sharecroppers. That is both a privilege and a fearful position to be in. God is good, kind and helpful. But He still expects fruit. Make that clear. Even if the counselee hasn't stoned God's prophets or killed His Son, ask him if he has handed over the fruit due God. Ask, "Do you take the credit for all you do, rather than give God the glory? That's stealing His fruit. Do you give the cup of cold water *in His Name*?" This doesn't always mean making a point of your piety. But it does mean in your heart as well as from your mouth to

46   They looked for a way to arrest Him, but they were afraid of the crowd because the people held that He was a prophet.

---

avoid all pride and boasting. There is more than enough fruit-stealing going on among Christians. The parable is a useful one to make this plain.

CHAPTER 22

1 Now Jesus responded by speaking to them again in parables, saying,
2   The empire from the heavens is like a king who gave a marriage feast for his son.
3   He sent his slaves to call those who had been invited to the marriage feast, and they didn't want to come.
4   Once again he sent other slaves, saying, "Tell those who have been invited, 'Listen, I have prepared the supper, my oxen and fattened calves have been butchered, and everything is ready; come to the marriage feast.'"
5   But they didn't care and went off, one to his farm, another to his business,
6   and the rest seized his slaves and insulted and killed them.
7   So the king was furious and sent his armies and destroyed those murderers and burned their city.
8   Then he said to his slaves, "The marriage feast is ready; but those who were invited weren't worthy of it.
9   Go, then, out on the street corners and whoever you find invite to the marriage feast."
10   So his slaves went out and gathered together all they could find, bad and good, and the wedding hall was filled with guests seated at the table.

The twenty second chapter is a continuation of the previous one. In it Jesus hammered home His message with another parable (vv. 1-14). This is the parable of the king's wedding feast. It is not enough that those who were invited refused to come, but the special point is made that this was an exceptional feast—the feast that a *king* made for his son's wedding! To ignore the invitation of a king was unheard of. It was not bad enough that some ignored the invitation, making light of it, but it is said that **the rest seized his slaves and insulted and killed them** (v. 6). Again, the fury of God against the Jews in the destruction of Jerusalem is predicted as it was in the last chapter (v. 7). And the coming in of the Gentiles is prefigured as well (vv. 8-10). This "gathering" of the elect from hither and yon will be repeated in other terms in Matthew 24:31. The interesting thing is that those gathered were good and bad (a thing abhorrent to the religious leaders). There is little to apply here that we have not mentioned already under other topics. But there is an additional section to this parable that adds something new (vv. 11-14).

> **11** But when the king came in to look over the guests seated at the table, he noticed a person there who wasn't wearing wedding clothes.
>
> 12   So he said, "Fellow, how did you get in here without wedding clothes?" But he had nothing to say.
>
> 13   Then the king said to his servants, "Tie him hand and foot and throw him outside into the darkness; there people will weep and grind their teeth.

Why did Jesus add the words about a man without a **wedding garment** to the parable? To allow the first part of the parable to stand alone was to leave it open it to misunderstanding. It would seem from what was said that anyone could enter the kingdom on almost any basis. That, of course, was not true. God was not lowering His standards simply because the Jews had refused to respond to His invitation. To enter the kingdom a person *had to be perfect*. But no one is. Perfection comes only by putting on the robe of Christ's righteousness. The king looked over his guests and saw that all but one had donned the robes graciously provided for and given to them by the king. We are not told why this gate crashing, nonconformist refused to wear the robe (whether from a false humility, which is pride, whether he liked his own better—or what). But one thing is clear: he wanted to be there *on his own terms*.

That is a profound danger in counseling. Counselees may not receive the answers to their problems on their own terms. Yet many think they can. They must accept God's terms. This attitude seems widespread among counselees. It is, naturally, one reason they are in need of counsel. They have ignored God's way of sanctification and seek to become righteous by their own efforts, apart from the work of the Spirit in their lives. Whenever you encounter such pride and unwillingness, use this parable to counter it.

Jesus' singling out of one person made it clear that entering the kingdom was an individual matter. One does not come to Christ as a member of a class, race, nation, or any other group. He is responsible to come in faith on his own to be clothed with Christ's righteousness.

This improperly clothed person was thrust outside. He was not fit for the kingdom because he came in his own righteousness. Some of those who stick by their own efforts, like this guest, may not really belong to the kingdom. They may be unbelievers, and may reveal themselves to be such by their very unwillingness to conform to God's way of righteousness through His Son. They must be excluded by church discipline now, or in

14   Many are called but few are chosen."

15 Then the Pharisees met to counsel together about how they might trap Him by a discussion.

16 And they sent their disciples to Him, together with the Herodians, saying,

> Teacher, we know that you are truthful and teach God's way truthfully, and you aren't influenced by anybody, and you aren't concerned about what they think of you.

17   Tell us, then, what do you think—is it right or wrong to pay taxes to Caesar?

18 But Jesus knew their evil intentions and replied: "Why are you testing Me, you hypocrites?

19 Show Me the money for the tax." So they brought Him a denarius.

20 Then He said to them, "Whose picture and name is this?"

21 They said, "Caesar's." Then He said to them: "Well, then, pay Caesar what belongs to Caesar, and God what belongs to God."

22 When they heard this, they were astonished and left Him and went away.

---

the end God Himself will exclude them. Jesus made the point once more that **many are called but few are chosen** (v. 14). That is to say, only a limited number of Jews who heard the preaching of the gospel would respond in faith.

In verses 15 through 22 we read of a plot by the **Pharisees** to entrap Jesus. They, together with the **Herodians** (each group held opposite political views), sent disciples of theirs to Jesus. They spoke as with butter melting in their mouths, but their hearts were cold as stone (v. 15). They applauded Jesus' lack of kowtowing (v. 16) and ask His opinion of paying taxed to Caesar (v. 17). The Pharisees opposed paying; the Herodians were all in favor of it. Either answer Jesus gave, they thought, would land Him in disfavor with one party or the other. Jesus knew what they were up to (v. 18), so He asked for a coin, which they brought (v. 19). Then He asked whose picture was on the obverse. They answered Caesar's. He replied, "**pay Caesar what belongs to Caesar, and God what belongs to God**" (vv. 20-21).[1] They were amazed at this answer by means of which Jesus avoided their trap.

The answer to a counselee's question may be one in which you surprise him. Often this will be true since he may know so little of the Word of God. Whenever you can, use such an illustration or visual aid; it will be

---

1. On the reverse was the image of a false deity who could not replace Yahweh.

23 On the same day the Sadducees came to Him (they are the ones who say that there won't be a resurrection) and questioned Him:

24   Teacher, **Moses said that if a man who doesn't have any children dies, his brother must raise up children for him**.

25   Now there were seven brothers among us. The first one married and died, and since he didn't have any children, he left his wife to his brother.

26   The same thing happened to the second, then to the third, and all the way down to the seventh.

27   Last of all, the woman died.

28   Now, in the resurrection whose wife will she be of the seven? They were all married to her.

29 Jesus responded by saying to them:

     You are mistaken because you don't know either the Scripture or God's power.

30   In the resurrection people won't marry or get married. Instead, they will be like the angels in heaven.

31   And, concerning the resurrection of the dead, haven't you read what God said to you:

32   **I am the God of Abraham, and the God of Isaac and the God of Jacob**? He isn't the God of dead persons but of living ones.

33 Now when the crowds heard this they were astounded by His teaching.

---

impressive enough to be remembered, as this incident is remembered by all who hear it. Counselees, like those in Jesus' day, need mnemonic devices.

Since the **Pharisees** failed, the **Sadducees** had a try at besting Jesus (vv. 23-33). They posed a theoretical question that must have gone the rounds for some time. It was one they used to stump the Pharisees who believed in a resurrection of the dead (the Sadducees, did not). Seven brothers married the same woman because of the Levirate marriage law which provided for their raising up of children to a deceased brother.[1] The question was this: **in the resurrection whose wife will she be of the seven**? Jesus responded by telling them that they knew neither the Scriptures nor the power of God (v. 29). People won't marry in the resurrection, but will be like the angels (unmarried; v. 30). And since the Bible says that God is the God of Abraham, Isaac and Jacob, these patriarchs are still alive. God isn't the God of persons who do not exist (vv. 31, 32). Again, the crowds were astounded (v. 33).

---

1. Deuteronomy 25:5-10.

34 But when the Pharisees heard that He had silenced the Sadducees, they came together,

35 and one of them—an expert in the law—asked Him a question to test Him:

36 "Teacher, which is the greatest commandment in the law?"

37 And He replied,

> **You must love the Lord your God with all your heart and with all your soul and with all your mind.**

38 This is the great and first commandment.

39 The second is just like it: You must **love your neighbor as yourself.**

40 On those two commandments hang all the Law and the Prophets.

The crazy binds that people get themselves into (or imagine that they will get into) exist because they, too, fail to understand the Bible or the power of God. God's Word has answers. Many who do not think the Bible is sufficient to deal with the problems of living are simply ignorant of what it says or how to use it in determining the answers to their questions. Moreover, they think that human tangles into which sinners twist themselves are too great for remedy. They think this way because they fail to understand God's power to extricate repentant sinners from the cords of their sin. Counselees need to recognize the power of God and not give up on themselves or others with whom they are associated. God's grace is greater than all our sin.

The Pharisees wanted another shot at Jesus since their rivals, the Sadducees, had lost their battle (v. 34). A Bible lawyer asked Jesus which was the greatest commandment. Any one He chose would then give them reason to contradict Him with their own views of which was the greatest. But Jesus reached back into the Old Testament for the two great summaries of the law that encompassed all the rest: love God and love your neighbor. Some modern day integrationists have distorted the meaning of the second great commandment. They teach that one must love himself first before he can love another. Neither Jesus nor the commandment teaches any such thing. The commandment tells us we need to love others with the same intensity with which we already love ourselves.[1] Jesus then made it clear that by those two commandments all the Bible is summed up (v. 40). If a counselee suggests anything that is contrary to one or the

---

1. For more on this see my book *The Biblical View of Self Love, Self Esteem & Self Image.*

41 Now while the Pharisees were gathered together Jesus asked them a question:

42 "What do you think about the Christ? Whose Son is He?" They said to Him: "David's"

43 How then is it that David, by the Spirit, called Him "Lord," saying,

44 **The Lord said to my Lord, sit at My right hand until I put Your enemies beneath Your feet?**

45 If David calls Him "Lord," how, then, can He be his Son?

46 No one could answer Him a word; and from that day nobody dared to question Him again.

---

other of these commandments, it is wrong. If there is any seeming counseling issue that cannot be dealt with under one or the other of the two rubrics, it isn't really a counseling issue. The Bible is sufficient; these two commandments sufficiently sum up all that man must believe and do to please God.

Jesus asked the Pharisees a question: "Whose Son is the Christ?" They said, "**David's**." Then, He posed a question they could not answer; "**How then is it that David, by the Spirit, called Him Lord?**" (and then He quoted Psalm 110:1). The word **lord** was used by a son referring to his father, but never of a father referring to a son. Unless there was one greater than David referred to in the expression, there was something wrong. Of course, that is precisely the point.

People were silenced by the way Jesus answered and asked questions (v. 46). If you, as a counselor, do not learn to be adept at these two things, you will find yourself in trouble. You must learn to deal with every aspect of questions. You are not Jesus; you will often fail. But you must keep at it. After all, when He was twelve, He was asking questions among the doctors in the temple (Luke 2:46, 47).

CHAPTER 23

1 Then Jesus spoke to the crowds and to His disciples, saying:
2   The scribes and the Pharisees sit in Moses' seat,
3   so do and observe the things they tell you, but don't do the same
       deeds that they do, since they don't practice what they preach.

This chapter is about **the scribes and the Pharisees.** First (vv. 1-12) Jesus spoke to the crowds about them. Then, in the verses following, He spoke directly to them. It is a fearful chapter that speaks of an encounter that had to occur. When people oppose the Lord Jesus Christ and the truth of God, the church must be warned about them. There is a tendency in the church today to sweep error and hypocrisy under the rug. Jesus did nothing of the sort. He called a spade a spade. He exposed errorists for what they were. But then, out of concern for them, He made one last very powerful appeal to them to repent. He unveiled His loving heart to their wicked hearts, showing them their fearful future unless they repented. When it is the last hope for those who are otherwise doomed, there is a time to let it all hang out; this is what Jesus did.

Addressing the **crowds** and the **disciples**, Jesus distinguished between a teacher and his teaching. The two may not be in sync as, indeed, they were not in the case of the scribes and the Pharisees. These were men who taught one thing, but practiced another (v. 3). To be **in Moses' seat** was to be an official expounder of the law of Moses. As such, they often were correct in their expositions. For instance, unlike the Sadducees, they rightly taught the resurrection of the body. But their lives belied all that they taught. And, when they overlaid the **law** with their traditions, it was then that they perniciously made the law of no effect. Jesus had made this clear in the Sermon on the Mount. So the words of verse 3 are not to be taken absolutely.

Today, there is a similar situation. There are many preachers and theologians (and counselors) who teach truth but fail to live by it. The average counselee may learn from them if he is careful to separate the life of the teacher from his exposition. Yet, it seems almost impossible for some to do so. If they see inconsistency many throw over everything. But God's truth and man's faulty living are distinct. It will always be so, even for the best of us. While counselors may never use this passage as an excuse for their own failures in Christian living, if they had to wait to counsel others until every truth was resplendent in their own lives, no one

4	They tie together heavy loads and put them on people's shoulders, but they don't want to lift a finger to budge them.
5	All the deeds that they do they do to be seen by people. They broaden their phylacteries, and lengthen their fringes;
6	they like the chief seat at dinners and the chief seats in the synagogs,
7	and acknowledgments in the marketplaces and having people call them "Rabbi."

would counsel. There is a way of distinguishing truth from life. This is possible because the truth is God's truth, and the life is only in part the reflection of that truth.

In verse 4 Jesus mentioned the traditions that were added to Moses' law. These became very burdensome for the people. To learn all of them, let alone observe them, was nearly impossible for the average Joe. And the interesting thing is that the religious leaders unmercifully enacted these legalistic strictures; there was no attempt to help people learn how to obey God. Many today in legalistic churches and institutions teach only the "what to"; people are never taught the "how to". Moreover, the Pharisees showed no mercy on those who violated the minutest of their traditions. And while they loaded down the people with traditions, they invented ways around their own laws and customs in order to exempt themselves. This sort of hypocrisy is, to some extent, in all of us. But it is preeminent in those who set up legalistic customs alongside the Bible. Point these facts out to counselees who come enmeshed in legalism and who are in trouble because of their failure to please some leader. Their consciences often need to be reeducated. In many cases, the only solution is to encourage them to leave such environments if there is no hope of reforming them. If they leave and unite with a non-legalistic body, they will need help to make the transition. Usually, their ill-informed consciences will continue to accuse them until they have been reeducated in the freedom of truth as it is presented in the Bible. Be patient with them (reread Romans 14).

In verses 5 through 10, Jesus gave three indications of how the Pharisees did their acts **to be seen by people**. This was their motive. They wore broader phylacteries[1] on their hands and foreheads and lengthened the fringes on their garments. So, in their ordinary attire, they called attention to themselves (this reminds one of certain contemporary religious

---

1. Small containers in which Scripture was inserted. This was their misinterpreta-

8	Don't be called "Rabbi;" you have one Teacher, and you are all brothers.
9	And don't call anyone on earth "Father;" you have one heavenly Father.
10	Moreover, don't be called "Leaders;" you have one Leader, the Christ.
11	Now the one among you who is greatest will be your servant,
12	and the one who exalts himself will be humbled, and the one who humbles himself will be exalted.

orders that require clothing of a particular sort that makes them stand out among others). When you can identify a preacher simply by the outfit he wears there is something wrong. Then there are those who flaunt their importance by pushing themselves forward. Like the religious leaders of Jesus' time, they like to have the chief place. Finally (and Jesus dwells on this), they like titles that set them apart from the crowd. There are those today who love to be called "Doctor" so-and-so just as the scribes loved to be called **Rabbi** or **Father** or **Leader**. Christ alone is the "Doctor" ("Teacher"). Beware of those who love to have a principal place above others in whatever way that they manifest this tendency (as Jesus indicates, there are varieties of ways in which this happens).

Jesus rang the changes on this point summing it up with the important words, **the one among you who is greatest will be your servant** (v. 11). And in verse 12, He stated the corollary as well. These are the conditions for greatness—in effect, they say that one must not even strive for greatness. But if and when it comes it will be a by-product of seeking the opposite. That is one of the seeming paradoxes of the empire from the heavens. Many counselees, who are offended by others who have not recognized them as superior in some fashion, need to hear precisely what Jesus had to say in this discourse. There are "scholars" and preachers who also need to be brought down a peg or two, as Jesus did here. They are proud of their attainments and the praise they are accorded for their degrees and titles. Help them, if you have a chance, to repent of this and to recognize that among Christians, we **are all brothers** (v. 8).

We come now to the denunciation of the scribes and the Pharisees (vv. 13-36). Remember, these hard words are spoken in a final attempt to bring them to repentance. This is a denunciation in grief over the coming

---

tion of Exodus 13:16; Deuteronomy 6:8; 11:18. Numbers 15:38, 39 was the ground for the fringes.

13 Woe to you scribes and Pharisees—you hypocrites—because you shut up the empire from the heavens in people's faces! You don't enter and you won't let others who are trying to enter do so either.

14 [1]

1. Verse 14 is omitted by the best MSS.

calamity. All else had failed; it was now time to expose them before the people for what they were (contrary to all the admiration in which they were held) while giving them one last opportunity to repent of their sins. The word **woe** which permeates the following verses is a term used by the prophets to pronounce judgment on cities, nations, and leaders who had resisted God. It is not a word of triumph but one that is evoked from a prophetic vision of tragedy to come. The mix of judgment, sorrow and pathos in the word should not be missed. Similarly, counselors ought to deeply regret it whenever they see counselees refuse to accept God's Word—whether they are those who are disciplined out of the church for continually rejecting the authority of Christ, or those believers who temporarily do so.[1]

In verse 13 Jesus pronounced woe on the **scribes and Pharisees.** By their traditions that overlaid God's commandments, and by the works' righteousness that they taught, both their doctrines and their examples made it impossible for those who accepted them to find salvation. Jesus graphically described them as slamming the door to entrance into God's empire **in people's faces**. They themselves didn't enter, and tried to keep others from doing so, even when they were attempting to find the true way. They smeared the names of John the Baptist and Jesus before the people and tried in every way to convince them that they were false prophets. This is dangerous to do. Those who in our day have kept potential counselees from coming to those who could help them by the ministry of God's Word place themselves in a dangerous position. They "pooh pooh" biblical counseling and say that it is superficial—as if the ministry of the Word could be! Surely, while they may not keep people out of the kingdom of God, they do confuse many and keep Christians from receiving the very help that would enhance their lives and make them more useful for Christ.

Evidently the religious leaders worked zealously at making **prose-**

1. Away with sayings like, "Back door revival" and "Good riddance."

15 Woe to you scribes and Pharisees—you hypocrites—because you go about on sea and land to make one proselyte; and when he becomes one, you make him twice as much a son of Gehenna as yourselves.

16 Woe to you blind guides who say, "If anyone swears by the temple, that doesn't count; but if he swears by the temple gold, he is bound by his oath."

17 You blind fools! Which is greater, the gold or the temple that makes the gold holy?

---

lytes (v. 15). Their doctrines—adding to the truth of God, and thus nullifying it—made an already unsaved person doubly unsaved. Not that there is such a thing as double loss of eternal life, but Jesus means that they are twice as far from the kingdom. They were unsaved because of the various barriers their sin raised between them and God. But then, having left that behind, they thought they were coming to the true God; but they were sidetracked on legalistic, self-righteous Pharisaic rails and were twice as far from the truth as before. Before, they may have known that the pagan gods they worshipped were false. But now that they learned about the true God, yet were being taught a false way of access to Him, they would be harder to convince of their lostness.

A similar thing takes place when counselors present the wrong way of help to would-be counselees. This happens, for instance, when they try to counsel unregenerate people. An unregenerate person can do nothing to please God (Romans 8:8). An unregenerate person, therefore, cannot be counseled into a relationship to God that is correct (counseling is an aspect of sanctification). So, to help him change his lifestyle from one that displeases God, the counselor can only assist him in changing to another lifestyle that displeases God. That is sure to remove him a step further from God than he was before. He is twice the child of **Gehenna**. He now thinks that he has changed to God's way, when all that has happened is that he has put on a different way of life that displeases God.

The true believer who is counseled in such a way that he changes outwardly, but not inwardly, also is deceived. While he is not destined for hell, he is driven farther from the truth and from pleasing God because he too is guided into hypocrisy. The inner and the outer person are not in sync. They are at odds with one another. That is the essence of hypocrisy—looking good on the outside while not changing for the better on the inside.

In verses 16 through 22 Jesus called the religious leaders **blind**

18   Now (you say), "If anyone swears by the altar, that doesn't count; but if anyone swears by the gift that is on the altar, he is bound by his oath."

19   You are blind! Which is greater, the gift or the altar that makes the gift holy?

20   So then, whoever swears by the altar swears by it and by everything that is on it;

21   and whoever swears by the temple swears by it and by the One Who dwells in it;

22   and whoever swears by heaven swears by God's throne and by the One Who sits on it.

23   Woe to you scribes and Pharisees—you hypocrites—because you tithe mint and dill and cumin, but you have neglected the weightier matters of the law: justice and mercy and faith. You ought to have practiced these without neglecting the others.

---

guides and **blind fools** (vv. 16, 17). They lead others astray while deceiving themselves. How often is this duplicity seen in sinners! The Pharisees made distinctions that were not valid. These they made in order to get around keeping the commandments of God. The examples that Jesus gave are from the practice of oath taking and tithing (vv. 23, 24). In oath taking, they allowed one to break his oath (it **didn't count**) if he swore by the temple, but not if he swore by its gold. As all casuistic legalists do, it seems, they got things backwards. Which was greater, the temple or the temple gold? Jesus asked. It was its presence in the temple that sanctified the gold in it. The same point is made about the altar and the gift on it. Whenever one swears, he swears by God (see earlier comments on this fact in the discussion of oath-taking in the Sermon on the Mount). To swear at all is to bring God into the picture as a third party witness. It really doesn't matter if what you swear by is connected to God; swearing makes Him a party to the transaction. That is what is important. Watch out for the legalistic streak in some counselees who will justify sin (i.e. breaking their word) by some turn of a phrase that is supposed to make all the difference. As Jesus said, in effect, to make such distinctions is wrong (vv. 20-22). They are false distinctions designed to deceive rather than to bless others. The distinctions are worse than worthless.

To salve their consciences, the Pharisees tithed mint and anise—minute amounts of garden herbs. By this they were saying, "Look how carefully I keep the law!" Actually, by these minuscule applications of the law they were drawing attention away from their gross failure to keep the

24   You blind guides, you strain out a gnat and swallow a camel!
   25 Woe to you scribes and Pharisees—you hypocrites—because you clean the outside of the cup and saucer, but inside they are full of robbery and dissipation.
26   You blind Pharisee! First clean the inside of the cup so that its outside may be clean.
   27 Woe to you scribes and Pharisees—you hypocrites—because you resemble whitewashed graves that outwardly look attractive but within are full of dead men's bones and all sorts of uncleanness.
28   Just so you also outwardly appear righteous to people but within you are full of hypocrisy and lawlessness.
   29 Woe to you scribes and Pharisees—you hypocrites—because you build tombs for the prophets and adorn the monuments to the righteous
30   and say, "If we had been alive in the days of our fathers, we wouldn't have taken part in shedding the prophets' blood."
31   Thus you testify against yourselves that you are the sons of those who murdered the prophets.

---

weightier matters of the law. They may have satisfied their own consciences by performing such minute duties, but they didn't satisfy God. Their lives were as hypocritical as they could be. Legalists today think they satisfy God by keeping a list of dos and don'ts, but often they fail to show love and mercy. Here we encounter that very problem (cf. v. 4). There will be counselees who have gotten themselves into trouble with God and others who point to how very carefully they have observed some duty or other in order to justify themselves and draw attention away from their large failures to keep the weightier commands of the Bible.

Jesus' summary comment is that they **strain out a gnat and swallow a camel** (the correct word is "out," not "at;" the King James has a typo at this point). The picture here is of a tiny gnat landing in one's drink which the listener would carefully strain out before drinking, while the very same person would swallow something as large as a camel! He is all caught up in minutiae while ignoring large issues. There are many like that in counseling. Watch out for them and use this passage to point out their error when they emphasize minute things.

Verses 25 through 28 expose hypocrisy at its core in two striking illustrations. Jesus spoke of the **outside of the cup** and the **grave** as opposed to the **inside** of each. The Pharisees appeared good and righteous, but within were corrupt. Their hearts were filled with dissolute thinking and lawlessness (vv. 25, 28).

32 Fill up the measure of your fathers.

33 You snakes! You brood of vipers! How will you escape from the judgment of Gehenna?

34 That's why I am sending prophets and wise men and scribes to you. But you will kill and crucify some of them, and you will scourge some in your synagogs and you will persecute them from city to city,

35 so that all the righteous blood that has been shed on earth, from the blood of righteous Abel to the blood of Zacharias, son of Barachias, whom you murdered between the temple and the altar, will come upon you.

36 Let Me assure you that all these things will come upon this generation.

37 Jerusalem, Jerusalem, who kills the prophets and stones those who are sent to her! How often I have wanted to gather together your children as a hen gathers her young under her wings! But you didn't want Me to!

38 See, your house is left desolate for you.

Verses 29 through 36 hang together. It was easy to laud prophets who were dead and gone. No one had to deal with them. But what of those in their midst in Jesus' time? They persecuted them just as the **fathers** did in days gone by when they persecuted those who were honored by the Pharisees. It is one thing to deal with the dead, and another to deal with the living! Today, all sorts of people praise Luther and Calvin and others who would have opposed them had they lived in their day. Counselors will run up against this tendency in counselees who strongly claim that they would never have acted as others did in the past, yet, in their own lives, are doing the very same thing in relation to those whom they disapprove of. Hypocrisy takes many forms. What Christ thinks of hypocrisy of this sort is clear from His words: "**You snakes! You brood of vipers!**"

Two important prophetic words are nestled among the rest in verses 32, 34 and 35. According to these verses, over the years the Jews had been **filling** up the cup of God's wrath. Now, with the death of His Son and the persecution and murder of the apostles, the present **generation** would fill the cup to overflowing. God's wrath, which had been pending for sometime, would now be poured forth in great fury upon the generation alive in 70 AD. The punishment of the guilt of the fathers and Christ's contemporaries would **come upon this generation**.

Taking this thought one step further, in great sorrow and grief, Jesus poured out His heart for **Jerusalem** (vv. 37, 38). The compassion in

39   I tell you that you will never see Me again until you say, **Blessed is the One Who comes in the Lord's Name**.

---

verse 37 is striking. His heart was for them; their heart was against Him. Yet, this compassion would not cause Him to deviate from His righteous judgment. He declared that God had left the **temple**: "Ichabod" (the glory has departed; v. 38). And then Jesus said that He, Who is this divine glory in fleshly form, was leaving. The people of Jerusalem would not see Him again unless they would see Him for the One Who He is. They must come to Him in faith, declaring that He did, indeed, come in the Lord's Name as the children and others claimed on the day of the triumphal entry into the city.

There are those who think that they can presume upon the Lord's compassion: they think He is like an indulgent grandfather who will let them get away with most anything and still give them what they want. Jesus shows compassion; but He refuses to lower the standards. One must repent, believe, and come to Him for Who He is. Nothing less than that will be accepted. Out of compassion counselors must not abandon the Word of God. That is not true compassion at all, as Jesus showed us. Keep that in mind when counselees try to get you to settle for something less than what the Bible teaches.

CHAPTER 24

1 Jesus left the temple and was going away when His disciples came to call His attention to the buildings of the temple.

2 He responded by saying,

> You see all of these, don't you? Well, let Me assure you that there isn't going to be left here one stone on another; they are all going to be thrown down!

3 And as He sat on the Mount of Olives, the disciples came to Him privately, saying, "Tell us when this will take place and what the sign of your coming and of the close of the age will be."

The apocalyptic material in Chapter Twenty four naturally follows the predictions of the destruction of Jerusalem in the previous Chapter. The present Chapter details the destruction in relationship to the disciples and those who would follow them. As Jesus had predicted the effects of that event upon the unsaved religious leaders and those who followed them, so here He would talk about what it would mean to His own. That is understandable since the disciples would want to know what would happen to the church.

The **disciples came to call His attention to the buildings of the temple** which occasioned this discussion (v. 1). Jesus, as He so often did, took the opportunity to instruct them. He detailed what would happen and how they should relate to it. Jesus pointed out that in the destruction all of the stones in the temple would be thrown down (v. 2). This of course happened as the soldiers of Titus pushed them off from one another. He then **sat down on the Mount of Olives,** overlooking the city, indicating to His disciples that He was about to teach them (v. 3). Recognizing this, they asked Him to tell them two things: *when* the destruction would take place and *what* would be the sign of His coming at the close of the Old Testament age. Jesus then responded to these questions, using them as the springboard to drive home their duties.

How frequently an event, a question or a comment (all of which here are combined) affords a counselor the opportunity to say many things that he would probably not be able to say so pertinently at another time. He should look for these opportunities and seize upon them when they come. It is often easy enough to move from one thing to something else one wants to say, if only he will learn how to do this. This was one of Jesus' common means of teaching. This way, the interest of the counselee meets

4   In response, Jesus said to them:
         Watch out that nobody misleads you,
5   For many will come in My Name, saying, "I am the Christ," and
         they will mislead many.
6   You will hear of wars and rumors of wars; be sure that you aren't
         alarmed by them; these must take place, but they are not the end.
7   Nation will rise against nation and kingdom against kingdom, and
         there will be famines and earthquakes in various places,
8   but all these things are but the beginning of labor pains.
    9 Then they will hand you over for affliction, and they will kill you,
         and you will be hated by all nations for My Name's sake,
10   and then many will stumble and will betray one another and hate
         one another,
11   and many false prophets will arise and will mislead many,

---

and combines with the interest of the counselor in a serendipitous fashion. Politicians use this technique all the time. Asked about something or other, they answer by saying something they have intended to say from the beginning.

Jesus takes up the second question first: the *sign*. There would be the possibility of mistaking it (v. 4). Others might deliberately try to mislead believers. So Jesus warned against this possibility. There will be **many** false Christs **who come in His Name** who will do just that (v. 5). There will be civil unrest—**wars and rumors of wars**. The commentators have accumulated the data of the fulfillment of both of these misleading "signs". There will be war (v. 7) and **famines and earthquakes**. These things won't be signs of His coming to judgment; but they will be only the **beginning** of the trials (**labor pains**) that would issue in the destruction, but not the birth (actual happening) itself. Even today, those who think that this is speaking of the second coming will refer to these predicted happenings as signs of the second advent, when Jesus clearly says that they are not signs at all. The way in which people miss the clues that Jesus gave in His discourses is phenomenal; watch out for such lapses in counselees who are attempting to find answers in the Bible.

Before the destruction, the disciples would be **persecuted** and some **killed** because of their witness for Christ (v. 9). And there will be desertions from among the ranks of those who have professed faith in Christ, along with serious betrayals even of family members. False prophets, who must not be followed, will arise. **Many** will be led astray by them (v. 11).

Because of the influence of the **lawless** times in which they will be

12   and because lawlessness will increase, the love of many will grow cold.

13   But whoever endures to the end will be saved.

14   And this good news about the empire will be preached in the whole civilized world for a testimony to all the nations, and then the end will come.

  15 So then, when you see the **abomination that leads to the desolation** of which the prophet Daniel spoke, standing in the holy place (let the reader understand),

---

living many will defect from their first **love**. Here is an important fact: people more readily tend to go astray when the times are unsettled and values are up for grabs. The times encourage it. This has been apparent in our day. We too live in a time of transition. The 60s upset generations of values that had been building in this country. We now live in a society in which anything goes if one can get away with it. This attitude will become apparent in the discussions that you have with counselees. The **lawlessness** that prevails seeps down even into the hearts of many of the best Christians and adversely affects their lives. You will have to contend with twisted values, many which believers have unwittingly accepted because they prevail.

"**But,**" said Jesus, "**whoever endures to the end will be saved**." He was saying that true Christians will persevere to the end. This biblical doctrine—the perseverance of the saints—is one with which every counselor should be familiar. Jesus stated here that at the end of the day after all the smoke has cleared, many may be wounded and weary, but true believers will still be standing.

The **gospel** would be preached throughout the Roman empire (**the civilized world**), according to Jesus (v. 14). This too happened in His day. Paul, writing prior to the Destruction of Jerusalem (see Colossians 1:6, 23), clearly said so. Only then, when all of these things have occurred, will the **end** of the age come (v. 14). The end of the age officially was brought to a close when the forty year period of grace was over in 70 AD. The events mentioned in the verses we have just been studying would take place during that period. That is what Jesus was teaching. Then with the destruction, the **end** of the old era would be brought to a close in a definitive way. During the forty years there was an overlap of the New and the Old testament periods.

The sign for which the believers in Jerusalem were to look was **the abomination that leads to the desolation of which the prophet Daniel**

16	then let those who are in Judea flee to the mountains,
17	let the one who is on the housetop not come down to take anything out of his house,
18	and let the one who is in the field not turn back to get his coat.
19	Woe to the pregnant women and to nursing mothers in those days!
20	Pray that your flight won't take place in winter or on a Sabbath,
21	because there will be great affliction, such as has not happened since the beginning of the world until now, and will never happen again.
22	If those days had not been shortened, nobody would survive; but for the sake of the chosen ones, those days will be shortened.

spoke (v. 15). This was the surrounding of the city by the Roman armies who had brought religious symbols into the land (that were an **abomination**). This event would lead to the **desolation** about which Jesus spoke at the conclusion of the previous chapter when He told the disciples that their **house** would be left to them desolate (v. 38). He, the Lord Who came to His temple (Malachi 3:1), would now leave it, thereby declaring it abandoned. The actual destruction of the temple and the city occurred in 70AD after the forty year grace period during which the disciples preached the gospel to people in the land and in the nations.

That God warns of coming judgment, and that He often gives such periods of grace, is a remarkable fact. It is not necessary for Him to do so. But every counselee who reflects carefully upon his situation will have to agree that God has been gracious to him in such ways. No one ever has a legitimate reason to complain about the way in which the Lord treats him. Here, the religious leaders, the people of the city, and all the believers who were involved with them, had ample warning. In addition, believers were provided a divinely given sign that signaled the end. It was, as Luke explained, that pagan armies would surround the city. This would be the sign to **flee** immediately to safety in the **mountains** (vv. 16-20). They were to get out instantly and not attempt to take anything with them (v. 17).

What happened, as Josephus (the Jewish historian who lived through the siege) tells us, is this: for some unknown reason after surrounding the city in order to lay siege to it, the armies withdrew for a time. Then, when they resumed the siege, it was continued unabated until the city fell. It was during that brief period that, in God's good providence, His elect believers got out of the city and fled to Pella, a free city in the mountains. Thus were the believing Jews preserved from the terrible tribulation that fol-

23   At that time if anybody tells you, "Look, here is the Christ," or, "There He is," don't believe it.

24   False Christs and false prophets will arise and they will perform great signs and wonders, so that (if it were possible) they would mislead even the chosen ones.

25   See I have told you beforehand.

26   So then, if they tell you, "See, He is in the desert," don't go there; "See, He is in the inner rooms," don't believe it.

27   As the lightning comes from the east and shines as far as the west, so will be the coming of the Son of Man.

28   Wherever the carcass is, there the vultures will gather.

---

lowed (cf. v. 21).[1] This event triggered on the part of those who wanted to take advantage of the situation a spate of claims that Jesus had returned (vv. 23-25). But Jesus was clear—there is no reason to be **misled**—He had told them **beforehand** (v. 25). They should learn and apply all that He said by way of forewarning. So, too, should counselees today heed biblical warnings. If they don't, and are misled, as Jesus intimated that they might be, there is no one to blame but themselves. Again, Jesus made it plain that He would not return in any visible way—regardless of what people may say (vv. 26, 27).

During this time of chaos, there would even be people who would perform false **signs and wonders** to gain a following—supposed miracles are never the reason for one to follow a could-be leader (cf. Deuteronomy 13)—and people would be deceived. Times have not changed in this regard; there are all too many who gather followers because of their supposed miracles. Counselors must warn against these charlatans.

Jesus made it plain that when He **comes** in judgment upon the city,[2] it will be as apparent as **lightning** that lights up the entire sky (v. 27). He was still speaking of the destruction of Jerusalem which is clear from His next reference: **Wherever the carcass is, there the vultures will gather.** Jerusalem, in all of its sin and rejection of God and His Son, was like a rotting **carcass.** The Roman armies were like the **vultures** that would

---

1. Josephus should be read for an account of the tragic events that took place during the siege. Women, from starvation, even boiled and ate their children! These days would be so severe and hardships so great that if they hadn't been shortened for the elect's sake, **nobody would survive** (v. 22).

2. The **coming** referred to here is the coming in His empire that replaced the old order.

29 Right after the affliction of those days,
  The sun will grow dark
  and the moon will not give her light;
  the stars will fall from the sky
  and the powers of the heavens will be shaken.
30   At that time the sign of the Son of Man will appear in heaven and
     at that time all the tribes of the land will mourn, and they will see
     the **Son of Man coming on the clouds of heaven** with power and
     much glory.

---

descend upon this carcass to dismember and devour it. The continual
warnings of Christ about false teachers, as well as continued warnings
from the apostles, ought to alert believers today to the problem. Yet, every
counselor encounters counselees whose lives have been ruined by such
false teachers. Regardless of the problem that a counselee has, find the
right moment and take the opportunity to warn him as Jesus did.

Verse 29 is but a symbolic way of saying that seemingly unshakable
things would be shaken. This sort of imagery was used throughout the Old
Testament by prophets to predict the downfall of nations or political systems that it seemed would remain forever. Here, it is used similarly to predict the passing of the old order of Judaism and the coming of the new
order, the kingdom of Christ (see the next three verses).

The **sign** mentioned in verse 30 is **the Son of Man appearing in
heaven** as Daniel predicted He would when He would appear before the
heavenly throne to receive the rule and authority of the new kingdom that
would never be handed over to another (Daniel 7:13, 14). This heavenly
event would be made known by the 70 AD event. In Daniel it was said
that Jesus (at His ascension) would come to the Father **with clouds** and
receive the rule. The **coming on the clouds of heaven** mentioned in Matthew 24:30 and the **power and the glory** that is attributed to Him is but
the fulfillment of these verses in Daniel. The unfaithful Jews who rejected
Him would then have cause to **mourn** over *their* rejection by *Him*. Obviously, there are times when it is too late. That is the import of verse 30.

Daniel 7:14 states that Christ's empire would be worldwide with
people from every nation and language serving Him. Verse 31 strikes the
same note: Jesus will summon (as by a trumpet call to action) and send
out His **messengers** (the word **angels** means "messengers"), the disciples,
to preach the gospel in all parts of the known world, thereby gathering
God's **chosen ones** into the empire. The themes, the sequences, and the
import of Daniel and Matthew are identical. What God said would hap-

31   He will send out His messengers with **a loud blast of the trumpet, and they will gather** His chosen ones from the four winds, from one end of the heavens to the other.

32 Now, learn a parable from the fig tree: when its branch becomes tender and shoots forth leaves, you know that summer is near.

33   So too, when you see all of these things, know that He is near, at the door.

34   Let Me assure you that this generation surely will not pass away until all these things take place.

35   Heaven and earth will pass away, but My words will never pass away.

---

pen, did. Whenever counselees doubt the promises of God, take them to fulfilled prophecy. This is an unanswerable argument that should move them from unbelief or doubt to strong faith. And as we have seen in several places earlier in this book, it is impossible to effect true, lasting, God-honoring change without faith.

Jesus now added a **parable** to help His followers understand—the parable of the **fig tree**. He said, "When you see that a fig tree **shoots forth leaves, you know that summer is near**. So, when **all these things** happen, you know that this judgment coming and the full realization of the coming empire of the Lord is **near**" (vv. 32, 33).[1] He was here answering the disciples' other question. Jesus then added (what He had affirmed already in the previous chapter) that the present **generation** would not pass away until the judgment on Jerusalem, the fall of the old order, and the coming of Jesus into His predicted empire would take place (v. 34). And then He added, when speaking of things not passing away, that His **words** would not do so either (v. 35). The promises, the warnings, and the prophecies of Christ are like prewritten history; they are as certain as if they had already happened. Counselees need to see that kind of certainty in the words of their counselors. They will take heart when they recognize that a counselor believes with all *his* heart exactly what Jesus said in verse 35.

As man, Jesus didn't know the exact time of these events (He did know they would happen in the lifetime of some who were listening to

---

1. The emphatic, repetitive **all these things** (vv. 33, 34) refers to everything mentioned thus far in the chapter, including vv. 30, 31. They would occur before the present **generation** would pass away. The idea that generation refers to "race" has been shown to be utterly untenable.

36 Now nobody knows when that day and hour will be, not the angels of the heavens, nor even the Son; only the Father knows.

37 As the days of Noah were, so will the coming of the Son of Man be.

38 As in those days, before the flood, they were eating and drinking, marrying and being given in marriage until the day Noah entered the ark,

39 and they didn't know about it until the flood came and took them all away; so too will it be at the coming of the Son of Man.

40 At that time two men will be in the field; one will be taken away and one left.

41 Two women will grinding at the mill; one will be taken away and one left.

42 So then watch, because you don't know on what day your Lord is coming.

43 You can be sure of this: if the house-holder had known in what watch the thief was coming, he would have watched and wouldn't have let his house be broken into.

Him (cf. Matthew 16:28)). But only God Himself knew **the day and the hour**. To not reveal this was part of God's wisdom. It kept those who heard on their toes. There was no way they could know that it would be possible to wait until some distant date. It could happen any time in their lifetime. God does much that way. He doesn't reveal the personal future of any of us beforehand. This ought to have a salutary effect on us. We should be ready for Christ's second coming during our lifetime, if He so chooses to come. We should be ready to die and go to be with Him at any time. We always should be ready to meet great trial and temptation, or prepared to handle great blessing and prosperity. To live the Christian life is to venture into the future with God. That ought to be exciting. Help counselees to see things that way.

When the destruction came, there would be a division between those who believe and those who are lost (vv. 37-42). Like the **flood** that suddenly swept some away and left others safe in the ark, so in the day of judgment upon Jerusalem some would be **taken away** and others left.[1]

---

1. There is nothing here about being taken away to heaven. The picture is of the unsaved being taken away by the flood, and the unrighteous being taken away by the judgment on Jerusalem. Notice, plainly, who it is that is taken—the lost; not the saved.

44	That's why you too must be ready; because the Son of Man is coming at an hour that you won't expect.
45	Who then is the faithful and sensible slave whom his lord has appointed to be over his household to give them food at the proper time?
46	The slave that his lord finds doing so when he comes will be happy.
47	Let Me assure you that he will appoint him to be over all his possessions.
48	But if that wicked slave says in his heart, "My lord is delaying his return,"
49	and begins to beat his fellow slaves, and eats and drinks with drunkards,
50	his lord will come on a day that he doesn't expect and at an hour that he doesn't anticipate,

The separation[1] of the saved and the lost would occur at this destruction; as we shall see, it will also occur at the final judgment (ch. 25). So a believer, not knowing the time of the Lord's judgment, must continually **watch.** The illustration and the exhortation found in verses 43 and 44, further strengthen Jesus' words about watching.

Why would believers need to be concerned about the time of Christ's coming and so be careful to watch? Because they were to be faithful **slaves,** doing what their Lord commanded them to do when He came (vv. 45-51). A **wicked** slave (there were unbelievers among the members of the church) would be careless and try to get away with his evil actions (v. 49) should he think that the Lord was not coming for a long time. A sinner illogically thinks that if an event is off in the future, what he does today won't matter so much. Perhaps he hopes that what he has pushed to the back of his mind, others will also forget. But God doesn't forget. In the *eternal* future, Jesus said, such persons will be classed and punished along with the other **hypocrites** (see chapter 23: especially v. 15) in Gehenna. Always warn counselees who manifest such tendencies as those mentioned in this section about the danger of hypocritical faith. Verses 1 through 30 of the next chapter continue this theme, thereby revealing how important it is. The division of chapters at this point is unfortunate. In your reading, mentally erase the chapter heading from this place. We shall see that these eternal consequences mentioned in each of the parables lead

---

1. The word judgment means "separation" or "division between."

51   and will cut him to pieces and appoint him a place with hypo-
        crites; there people w.ll weep and grind their teeth.

Jesus to describe the scene in which that final judgment will take place
(25:31-46).

CHAPTER 25

1 At that time the empire from the heavens will be likened to ten virgins who took their lamps and went out to meet and escort the bridegroom.

2 Now five of them were foolish and five were sensible.

3 The foolish ones took their lamps and they didn't take oil with them,

4 but the sensible ones took containers of oil with their lamps.

5 Now while the bridegroom delayed in coming, all of them became sleepy and went to sleep.

6 At midnight there was a shout, "Here comes the bridegroom; go out and escort him back!"

7 Then all the virgins awoke and trimmed their lamps.

8 Now, the foolish ones said to the sensible ones: "Give us some of your oil; our lamps are going out."

9 But the sensible ones said, "No; there may not be enough for us and you too. Go to the shopkeepers and buy your own."

10 Now as they were going their way to buy it, the bridegroom came and those who were ready went in with him to the marriage feast, and the door was shut.

11 Later, the rest of the virgins came too, saying, "Lord, lord, open the door for us."

Two parables follow. One has to do with the wisdom of those who are prepared for the coming of the Lord over against the foolishness of those who are not. The other has to do with faithfulness and industry. Thus the themes of watchfulness, preparation, and readiness are continued.

The parable of the **ten virgins** stresses wisdom (vv. 1-13). All had the same time to prepare. Some took advantage of the time and were ready when the **bridegroom** appeared. Others were not. The former went out to escort him back at his coming; the latter could not. When it came time to go in to the marriage feast, the former did, the latter were shut out. When they tried to enter, they were refused (v. 12). To **watch**, then (v. 13) meant more than simply to "be alert;" it meant to be ready for the event, and on the alert for it. When the bridegroom came, it became clear that some were members of the church who were saved (had **oil**) and some were not. Their eternal destiny was exclusion from the **empire from the heavens** (vv. 1, 12). Hypocrisy, once more, underlies the story. Some

12   But he answered, "I tell you—and I mean it—I don't know you!"

13   Watch, then, since you don't know the day or hour.

14   It is as if a man, when he was going on a trip, called his slaves and entrusted his possessions to them.

15   To one he gave a sum of five talents, to another two and to another one, according to the ability of each, and went away.

16   At once the one who received five talents traded with them and gained another five talents.

17   Similarly, the one who received two gained two more.

18   But the one who received one went and dug a hole in the ground and hid his lord's money.

19   After a long while, the lord of those slaves came and settled accounts with them.

20   So the one who had received five talents brought five more talents and said, "Lord, you entrusted five talents to me; here, I have gained five more talents."

21   Then his lord said to him, "Well done, you good and faithful slave. You have been faithful over a little, I will appoint you over much. Come on, share your lord's gladness with him!"

22   And the slave who had received two talents came to him also and said, "Lord, you entrusted two talents to me; here I have gained two more talents."

---

foolishly put off exercising faith in Christ, though they claimed to be saved (they too were classed among the virgins); others genuinely had faith. The truth of who was genuine and who was not was made clear in the end.

The second parable (vv. 14-30) has to do with three servants who were given talents by their lord before he went to obtain a kingdom from Rome. One received five talents, one two, and the other only one, according to the ability of each. The two with multiple talents traded and doubled their money. The one with one buried his talent in the ground, because he was fearful about making a bad trade. His worry thus ruined him. When the lord returned he commended the first two, appointed them a higher place in his service and invited them to enjoy his gladness with him (vv. 21, 23). But to the one who buried his talent, who pleaded fear and worry (vv. 24, 25), he declared, "**You** are a **wicked, lazy servant**"[1] (v.

---

1. Notice, fear leads to laziness (one cannot do anything about the future that he fears because it is not yet present). He becomes lazy because he focuses on tomorrow rather than on today's work. Thus, his service is wicked rather than faithful.

23   His lord said to him, "Well done, you good and faithful slave. You have been faithful over little, I will appoint you over much; come on, share your lord's gladness with him!"

24   Then the one who had received one talent came to him and said, "Lord, I knew that you are a hard man, reaping where you didn't sow and gathering where you didn't scatter seed,

25   so because I was afraid, I hid your talent in the ground. Here, take what is yours."

26   But his lord answered him and said, "You wicked and lazy slave! You knew that I reap where I didn't sow and that I gather where I didn't scatter seed, didn't you?

27   Then you should have invested my money with bankers, and upon my coming I would have received what is mine with interest.

28   Take the talent from him and give it to the one who has ten talents;

29   to everybody who has much, more will be given, but from everybody who doesn't have anything, even what he has will be taken away.

30   And throw the useless slave outside into the darkness, where there will be weeping and grinding of teeth."

31   Now, when the Son of Man comes in His glory together with all of His angels, at that time He will sit on His glorious throne,

32   and all the nations will be assembled before Him, and He will separate them, one from another, as a shepherd separates the sheep from the goats.

---

26), took away his one talent, and threw him outside into **darkness, where**, because of agony from his punishment, **there** [was] **weeping and grinding of teeth** (v. 30). Once again, the parable leads up to the eternal state of an unfaithful servant. He is revealed as ingenuine from his failure to do works that grow out of faith.[1]

In various ways, it is clear, those who truly believe will be separated from those who don't, and this separation will take place according to their works. Works of wisdom and of faithfulness grow out of faith and characterize and identify true Christians. Those false professors who are foolish and unfaithful to the Lord will, at length, be exposed by their lack of the same. And their end is sure—hell.

After Jesus stressed the eternal destiny of those who were not true over and over again,[2] He then more fully developed the facts about that

---

1. Salvation is by grace through faith; not by works. But works are evidence of salvation.
2. Cf. 18:23-34; 20:1-16; 21:33-41; 22:1-14; 24:45-51, and the two parables in this chapter.

33   He will set the sheep at His right side and the goats at His left.

34   Then the King will say to those on His right, "Come, you who are blessed by My Father, inherit the empire prepared for you from the foundation of the world.

35   I was hungry and you gave Me something to eat; I was thirsty and you gave Me something to drink. I was a Stranger and you showed hospitality to Me.

36   I was naked and you clothed Me, I was sick and you took care of Me, I was in prison and you came to Me."

37   Then the righteous will answer Him, saying, "Lord, when did we see You hungry and give You something to eat, or thirsty and give You something to drink?

38   When did we see You as a Stranger and show You hospitality, or naked and clothe You?

39   When did we see You sick or in prison and come to You?"

40   And the King will respond by saying to them: "Let Me assure you that insofar as you did it to one of the least of these, My brothers, you did it to Me."

41 Then too He will say to those on the left, "Depart from Me, you cursed ones, into eternal fire prepared for the devil and his angels!

42   I was hungry and you didn't give Me something to eat; I was thirsty and you didn't give Me something to drink.

---

final judgment. Thus, the rest of chapter 25 is devoted to a description of it (vv. 31-46). Readiness for 70 AD would reveal readiness for the final judgment.

In the final judgment of those in all the nations the interesting fact is the utter unconsciousness of both groups. In a total lack of understanding, both ask, "**When**" (vv. 35-39; 44)? The believer, because he is changed in both motive and life, is oblivious of how greatly he has been changed by the Spirit. He naturally leads a life of faith and works. The unbeliever is oblivious of his sin. He naturally does the opposite. Both live in the spirit and ethos of their separate natures. They cannot do otherwise. The fruit is evidence of what sort of tree it comes from. It is these characteristics that distinguish them as **sheep** or as **goats**. Final judgment, then, will be made according to what saving faith (or its lack) has produced in the lives of human beings. What God sees in their hearts will be made visible to all by their works (since men can't read other men's hearts).

The punishment of unbelievers is described by the same terms as the blessedness for believers, it is **eternal**. Those who try to shorten or lessen the nature of the punishment, to be consistent, must do the same with the

43   I was a Stranger and you didn't show Me hospitality, I was naked and you didn't clothe Me, I was sick and in prison and you didn't take care of Me."

44   Then they also will answer, saying, "Lord, when did we see You hungry or thirsty or a Stranger or naked or sick or in prison and didn't serve You?"

45   Then He will answer them, saying, "Let Me assure you that insofar as you didn't do it for one of the least of these, you didn't do it for Me."

46   They will go away into eternal punishment, but the righteous into eternal life.

---

blessedness of the redeemed. Given all the scriptural data, such a thought is utterly unthinkable!

Counselors may wish to make a preliminary, tentative judgment of their counselees. As they hear how they treat Jesus' brothers and sisters in the church, they may ask, "Do you think that sort of attitude and action will pass muster in the judgment? Are you sure that your faith is genuine? Do you realize, as I John tells us again and again, love for the brothers is a reason for assurance—and the lack of it for the opposite? Where is there any evidence of that love?" These sorts of questions Jesus certainly wanted His listeners to ask themselves in preparation for that time when the door would be shut and it would be too late to do otherwise. Counselors who fail to see loving concern for other Christians in the lives of counselees would be sorely remiss not to point out the possibility of the precarious position in which their counselees may find themselves. This sort of probing on their part may change a counseling session into a pre-counseling (evangelistic) one.

CHAPTER 26

1 Now, when Jesus had finished speaking all these words He said to His disciples,

2 "You know that the Passover takes place in two days, and the Son of Man will be handed over and crucified."

3 Then the chief priests and elders of the people came together in the courtyard of Caiaphas, the high priest.

4 They plotted about what sort of stratagem they might use to seize and kill Him.

5 But they said, "Not during the feast, or there will be a riot among the people."

6 Now when Jesus was in Bethany at the house of Simon the leper,

7 a woman came to Him, carrying an alabaster jar of very expensive perfumed ointment, and poured it on His head as He sat at the table.

8 But when the disciples saw this they were angry and said, "Why has this been wasted?

9 This could have been sold for a lot of money that might have been given to the poor."

Jesus had now **finished** His discourse about the destruction of Jerusalem (a colossal event in the history of the world). In parable after parable He had alluded to the final judgment. His basic teaching to the disciples and crowds was complete. He then headed into the final hours that would prepare Him and them for the great sacrifice for sins that would take place on Calvary. Once more Jesus explained what would happen to Him. He then made it clear that the cross was but two days away (v. 2). Though the religious leaders wanted to postpone His arrest and death until after the Passover, God's timetable would prevail (vv. 3-5).[1]

Jesus interpreted the **anointing** as an act that would prepare Him for His **burial.** Of course the woman who performed the act out of gratitude had nothing of the sort in mind. Again, we see the providence of God at work. God may have ends in view that are quite different from those who bring them to pass. That is often true in the lives of counselees. They should be taught to look for a larger picture than the one that they are focusing on. Teach them to wait and see the outcomes God has in mind

---

1. The opportunity to accept Judas' proposal moved up their action to conform to God's timetable. In His providence God uses even men's sin to achieve His purposes.

10   So Jesus, knowing what they said, responded:
Why are you making trouble for this woman? She has done a fine thing for Me.

11   You will always have the poor with you, but you won't always have Me.

12   By pouring this ointment on My body she has prepared Me for burial.

13   Let Me assure you of this: wherever this good news is preached in the whole world, what she did also will be told as a memorial to her.

14   Then one of the Twelve, the one who was called Judas Iscariot, went to the chief priests and said:

15   "What will you give me if I betray him to you?" And they paid him thirty pieces of silver.

16   From that time he looked for an opportunity to betray Him.

(these cannot be known until after the facts themselves—and even then, only in part).

The disciples were angry about the "**waste**" of the **perfume** (v. 8). Jesus would have none of this talk (v. 10). Gratitude may at times be extravagant; unlike many believers today, the Lord is not One to always sanction thrift. There are times and situations in which people do things for Him that may in other circumstances be bad stewardship. There is stewardship and stewardship. We must not be too quick to judge. Caution counselees about this issue with this passage.

Verse 11 indicates two things. We will never be able to remove poverty absolutely. Poor people, of their own making as well as out of circumstances external to them, will always be with us. Opportunities to help the poor will continue to afford themselves after such acts of extravagance are finished. This is not the only opportunity available. Indeed, Jesus so commended her act that He said, along with the preaching of the gospel, a report of this woman's act would also be mentioned. He knew that throughout the centuries people would read, write, and preach about it, because He knew that it would be recorded in the Bible. Jesus appreciated what His disciples did not. Often it is that way. That is why counselees of a very practical bent must often be brought up short when they criticize the actions of others.

Judas' treachery is now described (vv. 14-16). His initiative altered the decision of the religious leaders to wait until after the feast of Passover to kill Jesus. Jesus, the true Passover Lamb, would have to be killed at the

17 Now on the first day of the feast of Unleavened Bread, the disciples came to Jesus and said, "Where do You want us to prepare a place for You to eat the Passover?"

18 He replied,

> Go to the city to a certain man and say to him, "The Teacher says, 'My time is at hand; together with My disciples I will keep the Passover at your house.'"

19 Then the disciples did as He directed them and prepared the Passover.

20 When evening had come, He was reclining at the table with the Twelve.

21 Now as they were eating, He said, "I want to tell you for a certainty that one of you will betray Me."

22 They became terribly upset and each one began to say to Him, "It isn't I, is it, Lord?"

---

time of the Passover.[1] He sold out Jesus for **thirty pieces of silver** (the price of a slave!). This act indicated Judas' utter lack of love and concern for the Lord Jesus. There will be people among the flock who will **betray** you, betray pastors, and betray others; this should not be surprising to those who know about Judas. That they will sell out for so little in return, showing utter contempt, in the light of his act, is understandable. If Jesus experienced this, why not His followers? Point this out to those who act as if their faith depends on not being betrayed.

Now comes the **preparation** for observing the **Passover** (vv. 17-19). Jesus wanted very much to observe this feast with His disciples. He had made arrangements which were otherwise unknown until He revealed them to the disciples. Presumably, these were kept secret so that Judas would not be able to lead the religious leaders to the place where they would observe the feast, thus interrupting their time together. All had been set.

The events of the Passover meal now follow (vv. 20-30). It was a solemn gathering. In two days, Jesus had revealed, He would be crucified. Apprehension, like a thick cloud, hung over the event. This was even heightened by Jesus' prediction that one of them would betray Him (vv. 21, 22). While Judas knew he was the one, the others did not. Indeed, they shared their basic insecurity by their condition and their question in verse 22. Counselees may also be uncertain about themselves. This is because as sinners, like these disciples, they know that they have failed so

---

1. Passover was a seven day feast.

23 He answered and said to them,
> The one who dipped his hand into the dish with Me is the one who will betray Me.
24 The Son of Man is going just as it has been written about Him, but woe to that person by whom the Son of Man is betrayed. It would have been better for him if he had never been born.
25 Then Judas (the one who was betraying Him) responded, "It isn't I, is it, Rabbi?" And He answered, "You said it yourself."
26 As they were eating Jesus took bread, gave thanks and broke it, and gave it to His disciples and said, "Take it and eat it. This is My body."
27 Then He took a cup and gave thanks and gave it to them, saying,
> All of you, drink some of it;
28 this is My blood of the covenant that is poured out for many for the forgiveness of sins.
29 I tell you I will not drink of this fruit of the vine again until the day when I drink the new wine with you in My Father's empire.

---

often. This must be dealt with through repentance, confession of sin, and learning to live as one ought.

Jesus revealed that Judas, who dipped into the bowl with Him, was the betrayer (v. 23). Then He made it clear that what was going to happen would be no mistake; it was precisely what had been written about Him in Old Testament prophecy. But, notice, although it was certain (God's prophecy never fails), Judas was still held responsible. No one can ever plead innocence—that he couldn't help his actions because of God's pre-destination.[1]

As a ploy to throw others off, Judas also asked the same question of Jesus (v. 25). Jesus' reply indicated that by saying it, he had condemned himself. People will ask you questions to which they know the answer for other than informational reasons. Likewise, they may wish to feign innocence. They may also ask in order to seem humble or teachable. Many other reasons may be imagined. But always be aware that questions that *seem* to be genuine may not be.

In verses 26 through 30 Jesus instituted and celebrated the Lord's Supper. It grew out of and replaced the Passover for the New Testament church.[2] He commanded His followers to observe this as a means of

---

1. For a detailed discussion on predestination and responsibility see my book *The Grand Demonstration.*
2. That it ought to be celebrated yearly, as Passover was, is a good possibility. The eating together weekly mentioned in Acts was probably an *agape* feast,

30   And when they finished singing a hymn they went out to the Mount of Olives.

31   Then Jesus said to them,

Every one of you will stumble because of Me this very night; it is written, **I will strike the Shepherd and the sheep of the flock will be scattered.**

32   But after I am raised, I will go before you into Galilee.

33   But Peter answered and said to Him, "If everyone stumbles because of You, I will never stumble."

34   Jesus said to him, "Let Me tell you without doubt that this very night, before a cock crows, you will deny Me three times."

35   But Peter replied, "Even if I must die with You, I won't deny You." And all of the disciples said the same thing.

36   Then Jesus went with them to a place called Gethsemane, and He said to the disciples, "Sit here while I go over there and pray."

---

showing forth His death until He would come again. After His death and resurrection Jesus did return to eat and drink with them in the newly-established dispensation (Acts 10:41). This, He indicated, was the last time they would eat together until then. They finished the meal with the singing of a Psalm and went out to the Mount of Olives (v. 30).

On the way, Jesus gave another ominous prediction: every disciple would **stumble** (sin) because of Him (v. 31). And, He made clear, this would happen that very **night**. To bolster His word, He quoted an appropriate biblical passage. By this they should have understood that all was being orchestrated by God to fulfill His Word. He also told them He would rise from the dead and expected to meet them in **Galilee**.

Now Peter said (too quickly) that he would never stumble because of Jesus. His heart was right, but his understanding of his own sin and fear was not. Many counselees make rash promises they later regret. Jesus predicted that he would stumble, and even tells him when: **before a cock crows** (v. 34). Peter said no, that he was willing to **die** with Him if necessary. And all the disciples assured Him they were in complete agreement with Peter's sentiments. The fact is, He had said the **flock** would be **scattered**. They did not believe Him or the Scripture He quoted. Counselees also always go wrong when they refuse to believe His words.

Then He led them to the **Garden of Gethsemane**, singling out Peter, James, and John to accompany Him farther into the garden while He

---

and, in itself, may have had nothing to do with the Lord's Supper. Quarterly observance has no biblical basis whatsoever.

37 He took Peter and the two sons of Zebedee and He became sad and distressed.
38 Then He said to them, "My soul is deeply grieved, even to the point of death. Stay here and watch with Me."
39 Going ahead a little, He fell on His face, praying and saying, "My Father, take this cup away from Me if it is possible; yet don't do what I want but what You want."
40 Then He came to the disciples and found them sleeping, and He said to Peter,
    So, you couldn't watch with Me for one hour!
41   Watch and pray or you will enter into temptation. The spirit is willing but the flesh is weak.
42   Again, for the second time He went off and prayed, saying: "My Father, if it isn't possible for this to be taken away unless I drink it, may Your will be done."
43 When He came again, He found them sleeping, because their eyes were heavy.
44 So He left them again and went off and prayed a third time, saying the same words again.
45 Then He came to the disciples and said to them,
    Are you still sleeping and resting? The hour is at hand and the Son of Man is being betrayed into the hands of sinners.
46   Get up, let's go; the one who is betraying Me is nearby.

---

prayed. Here, Jesus began to feel the full weight of what was to happen. It was evident in His physical appearance that bearing the sins of His own would be a horrible trial for the sinless Son of God (vv. 37, 38). He even commented to the three disciples about His agony (v. 38). He asked them to stay where they were, and watch and pray. He went a little farther, **fell on His face**, and in agony of soul asked the Father to relieve Him of the **cup**. This was the cup of God's wrath that those He was dying for should have experienced. He, instead, would do so as He would be counted a sinner by God. But He realized that it was not possible to avoid that wrath; there was no "ram caught in the thicket" that would take His place. He, Himself, was the sacrificial substitute!

He then came and found the disciples **sleeping**. His word in verse 41 was pertinent to their later stumbling of which He had spoken previously. If, like Him, they had prepared for the cross by prayer, they might have faced successfully the **temptation**. But because they did not, they would fail in that hour. Jesus' ultimate statement in verse 42 is the one that ought to characterize the prayer of every counselee: **may Your will be done**. Counselees who honestly pray this prayer should be easy to counsel.

47 While He was still speaking, Judas (one of the Twelve) came, and with him a large group from the chief priests and elders of the people with swords and clubs.

48 Now the betrayer had given them a sign, saying, "The one I kiss is the one you want; arrest him."

49 And he came up to Jesus at once and said, "Hello, Rabbi," and kissed Him with great display.

50 But Jesus said to him, "Fellow, do what you came for." Then they came and grabbed Jesus and arrested Him.

51 One of those who were with Jesus stretched out his hand and drew his sword, and struck the high priest's slave, cutting off his ear.

52 Then Jesus said to him,

> Put your sword back into its place; everyone who takes a sword will die by a sword.

53   Don't you think that I could ask My Father and He would send Me more than twelve legions of angels at this very moment?

54   How then would the Scriptures be fulfilled that say that this is to take place?

55 At that time, Jesus said to the group,

> Have you come out as if you were after a robber to take Me with swords and clubs? Day after day I sat teaching in the temple and you didn't arrest Me.

After the third season of prayer, Jesus awakened the disciples and led them forth to His betrayal (vv. 44-46). As Jesus was telling them that the time had come for the betrayal, Judas came accompanied by the religious leaders and a band of thugs who were armed with **swords and clubs**. Judas' ultimate betrayal was the use of a **kiss** as a sign. He kissed Jesus with **great display**. The heinousness of this act is emphasized by these words. People who sin often attempt to cover it over with insincere displays that might indicate to others that they are doing just the opposite. Don't be taken in by such ploys. Especially beware of those who are making too much of what they purport to be doing, as Judas did. Then Jesus was arrested (vv. 47-50).

In verses 51 through 54 the account of Peter's cutting off the **ear** of the high priest's slave is recorded. Jesus made it plain that He would have nothing to do with such action in the propagation of His empire. If they attempted to use force to do so, force would be used in return. Jesus also indicated that if He wanted to, He could call for all the aid He needed to stop what was happening (v. 53). But if He did, the **Scripture** would not have been fulfilled.

56   But all this has happened so that the prophet's writings might be
          fulfilled.
Then all of His disciples left Him and fled.

57   Then those who arrested Jesus led Him away to Caiaphas the high
priest, where the scribes and the elders had come together.

58   And Peter followed Him at a distance all the way to the high priest's
courtyard. Going in he sat with the guards to see how it would end.

59   Now the chief priests and the whole Sanhedrin were looking for false
witnesses against Jesus so that they could put Him to death.

60   But they couldn't find any, even though many false witnesses came
forward. At last two came forward and said,

61   "This man said, 'I can destroy God's temple and rebuild it in three
days.'"

62   Then the high priest stood up and said to Him: "Don't you want to
respond? What is this testimony that these men have given against you?"

63   But Jesus remained silent. So the high priest said to Him, "I ask you
under oath before the living God, tell us if you are the Christ, God's Son."

64   Jesus replied,
          You said it. And what is more, I tell you all that you are going to
          see **the Son of Man sitting at the right hand of power and com-
          ing on the clouds of heaven**.

65   At that the high priest tore his clothes apart, saying, "He has blasphemed!

In verse 55, Jesus rebuked them for the manner in which they were
handling Him. There was no need for them to come after Him like a common criminal who was hiding out. He had been **teaching** in the open **day
after day** but they didn't arrest Him (because they feared the crowds). But
the way in which everything was taking place had to be exactly that was
so that the Bible prophecies would be fulfilled (v. 56). Then, as He had
predicted, fear took hold of the disciples and they all **fled**.

Next, the mock trials took place (none of them was legally or fairly
conducted). First, He was taken before **Caiaphas** and the Sanhedrin
(v. 57). Peter followed **at a distance** (v. 58). Jesus' accusers were searching for **false witnesses** to enable them to trump up charges to bring before
Pilate. They needed these because they didn't have the right to exercise
the death penalty. He would have to be charged before a Roman represen-
tative and be ordered by him to die. At first, they couldn't find any
(vv. 59-60). Finally, they found a couple whose charges seemed as if they
might be used to establish probable guilt. They had heard Jesus speak
about His body as a **temple**, but they distorted His word, saying that He
had said He would destroy the edifice at Jerusalem (v. 61).

66 What do you think?" And they responded: "He deserves death!"

67 Then they spit in His face and hit Him; and they slapped Him, saying,

68 "Prophesy to us, Christ, who is it that hit you?"

69 Now Peter sat outside in the courtyard. And a single servant girl came to him saying, "You also were with Jesus the Galilean."

70 But in front of them all he denied it, saying, "I don't know what you are talking about."

71 And when he went out to the porch another girl saw him and said to those who were there, "He was with Jesus of Nazareth."

72 But he denied it again with an oath: "I don't know the man!"

73 After a short time, those who were standing there said to Peter, "Certainly you too are one of them; your accent makes that clear."

74 Then he began to take a curse upon himself and swear, "I don't know the man." And just then a cock crowed.

75 And Peter remembered Jesus' words, "Before a cock crows you will deny Me three times." And he went out and wept bitterly.

The high priest asked Jesus to respond, but Jesus remained **silent** (vv. 62, 63). Then, He asked Him, under oath, if He was the **Christ**. Jesus agreed that the high priest had spoken accurately—He was the Messiah. And, to confirm it, He repeated the fact that He had often mentioned to the disciples that the day would come when they would see Him fulfill Daniel's prophecy (cf. Daniel 7, Acts 7:56 and previous comments). At this, the high priest **tore his garments** (a sign of shock at another's words or actions) and declared that Christ had **blasphemed** by His reference to Daniel 7. The entire Sanhedrin then agreed that Jesus should be put to death (vv. 62-66).

Consequently, they **spit in His face, hit and slapped Him**, and mockingly told Him to **prophesy** each time who it was that slapped Him (vv. 67, 68). These indignities were not only allowed but encouraged by this kangaroo court, contrary to all Jewish law.

The narrative now returns to **Peter** and his three denials. Fear is a terrible thing when it controls a person. Many with good intentions fail to realize them because of fear. When the fear of man gets hold of him, a counselee will lose hold on the fear of God. Peter even denied his Lord with an oath. When the cock crowed, Peter **remembered**. And **he went out and wept bitterly.** Such memories haunt some counselees. John tells us Jesus restored Peter three times (John 21). Let them know that restoration is possible for them as well if they are true believers.

CHAPTER 27

1 Early, when morning came, all the chief priests and elders of the people determined to put Jesus to death.

2   So they bound Him, led Him away and turned Him over to Pilate the governor.

3 When Judas (the one who betrayed Him) saw that He was condemned, he regretted it and returned the thirty pieces of silver to the chief priests and elders, saying,

4   "I have sinned by betraying innocent blood." But they said, "So what? That's your problem!"

5   Then he threw the pieces of silver into the temple and left and went off and hanged himself.

6   But the chief priests took the pieces of silver and said, "It isn't lawful to put them into the treasury since they are blood money."

7   So they decided to buy the potter's field with them as a cemetery for strangers.

8   That's why that field has been called the "Bloody field" to this very day.

9   Then that which was spoken by the prophet Jeremiah was fulfilled when he said,

> **And they took the thirty pieces of silver, the price set for Him on Whom** some of the sons of Israel **set a price**,

---

In this extensive chapter we read about Jesus' final hours before the crucifixion and about the crucifixion itself. This is holy ground, and we shall not spend much time making applications. When people are **determined** to sin, as the religious leaders were (v. 1), truth, reason and argument are of no avail. They will push forward to obtain their desires regardless of what is presented to them. They will use lies, subterfuge, rationalization, and the like to further their nefarious designs. This will be found to be true of counselees and their associates.

Jesus was then brought to Pilate for a civil trial, the religious farce before the Sanhedrin having ended. Judas' remorse could not be relieved by returning the money he had received (vv. 3, 4), so he **threw** it into the **temple, went off and hanged himself** (vv. 4, 5). Judas did not repent. Many today, like him, see suicide as the only escape from guilt. It clearly isn't. Indeed, it means going to face God—having cut off all opportunity for repentance before death—and finalizes their state. Since it was recognized that this was **blood money**, it was used for other than holy pur-

10   **and they used them to buy the potter's field, as the Lord directed me**.

11   Then Jesus stood before the governor, and the governor questioned Him saying, "Are you the King of the Jews?" And Jesus replied, "You said it."

12   But when He was accused by the chief priests and elders, He didn't answer.

13   Then Pilate said to Him, "Don't you hear the testimony that they are giving against you?"

14   But He didn't respond with a single word—to the governor's great surprise.

15   Now at the feast the governor followed the custom of releasing to the crowd any one prisoner that they wanted.

16   At that time they had a notorious prisoner named Barabbas.

17   So, when they assembled, Pilate asked them, "Whom do you want me to turn loose for you, Barabbas or Jesus who is called Christ?"

18   (He knew that it was out of envy that they had delivered Him.)

19   Now as he sat on his judgment seat, his wife sent a message to him that said, "Don't get involved with that innocent man; I have had a terrible dream about him today."

20   But the chief priests and the elders persuaded the crowds that they should ask for Barabbas, and thus destroy Jesus.

21   So the governor said to them in response, "Which one of the two do you want me to turn over to you?" And they said, "Barabbas."

---

poses—to buy a field as **a cemetery for strangers** (vv. 5, 7). In God's providence, even blood money can be used for benevolent purposes. This all fulfilled Old Testament prophecy (vv. 8-10).

Jesus was questioned by Pilate as to whether He was the King of the Jews. Once more, Jesus answered "yes" by saying that Pilate had spoken the truth (v. 11). He answered Pilate, but He refused to reply to the accusations of men like those mentioned in verse 1. Pilate then prompted Him to reply to them, but He refused to even acknowledge them with a reply. Pilate was amazed. (vv. 12-14). There are times to take up an issue and people with whom one ought to contend for the truth. There also are times to refuse to do so, as Jesus illustrated here so vividly.

By the custom of releasing a prisoner at the feast (vv. 15-26) Pilate attempted to obtain Jesus' release. He asked, "do you want me to release Jesus or Barabbas?" (a very undesirable criminal). Egged on by the religious leaders, the crowds shouted, **Barabbas**. In response to the question of what to do with Jesus, they yelled, **"Crucify Him!"** Pilate's wife urged

22 Pilate said to them, "What then should I do with Jesus who is called the Christ?" And they all said, "Crucify Him!"

23 But he replied, "Why? What wrong has he done?" But they shouted all the more, "Crucify him!"

24 So when Pilate saw that he was accomplishing nothing except to stir up a riot, he took water and washed his hands in front of the crowd, saying, "I am innocent of this man's blood. You see to it yourselves."

25 And all the people said in response, "His blood will be on us and on our children!"

26 Then he turned over Barabbas to them, and after scourging Jesus he handed Him over to be crucified.

27 Then the governor's soldiers took Jesus into the Praetorium and the entire cohort gathered before Him.

28 They stripped Him and put a scarlet robe on Him.

29 And they plaited a crown of thorns and placed it on His head and put a reed in His right hand. And kneeling in front of Him they mocked Him, saying, "Hail, King of the Jews!"

30 And they spit on Him and took the reed and struck Him on the head.

31 After they finished mocking Him, they took off the robe and put His clothes on Him and led Him off to crucify Him.

32 As they went out, they found a man from Cyrene, who was named Simon, and they forced him to carry His cross.

33 When they came to a place called Golgotha (which means "The Skull-like Place"),

---

him to have nothing to do the with condemning of Jesus because of a dream she had, but Pilate wanted to please the Jews, so he continued his charade of meting out "justice." **Washing his hands**, Pilate claimed he was **innocent** of Christ's blood. But removing guilt is not as easy as all that. The guilt of injustice cannot be washed away by anything but Christ's blood. It couldn't then; it can't be now. The **people** uttered a terrible oath: "**His blood will be on us and on our children**" (v. 25). As they wished it, so it has been! Jesus was **scourged** and handed over to soldiers to **crucify** (v. 26). The soldiers **stripped** Jesus and put a **scarlet robe** on Him. Then they pressed a **crown of thorns** into the flesh of His head, **spit** on Him, and **struck** Him with a reed. They insulted Him, making mockery of His kingship. Then, in that condition, they led Him away to be crucified (vv. 27-31).

Simon was pressed into service to carry Jesus' cross to the place of the Skull. Jesus refused the stupifying **drink** offered to Him, and then He was crucified. They cast **lots** for His clothes, sat down, and waited for

34   they gave Him wine mixed with gall to drink, but when He tasted it He refused to drink it.

35   And they crucified Him and divided His clothes among them by casting lots.

36   Then they sat down there to guard Him.

37   And they placed over His head the written charge against Him: THIS IS THE KING OF THE JEWS.

38   At the same time there were two robbers who were crucified with Him, one on His right and the other on His left.

39   Those who passed by blasphemed Him, wagging their heads and saying,

40   "You who were going to destroy the temple and rebuild it in three days—save yourself! If you are God's Son, come down from the cross!"

41   In the same way the chief priests, together with the scribes and elders, mocked Him, saying,

42   "He saved others, but he can't save himself! So he's the King of Israel, is he? Well now, let him come down from the cross and we will believe in him.

43   **He depended on God, did he? Then let Him rescue** him **if He wants him**; he said, 'I am God's Son.'"

44   And the robbers who were crucified with Him abused Him, saying the same sort of things.

45   Now from twelve noon to three o'clock darkness descended on the whole land.

46   At about three o'clock Jesus cried out in a loud voice: "Eli, Eli, lama sabachthani!" (that is, **"My God, My God, why have You forsaken Me?"**).

47   Some of those who stood there, hearing Him, said, "He is calling Elijah."

48   At once one of them ran and got a sponge and filled it with vinegar and put it on a reed and gave it to Him to drink.

Him to die (vv. 32-36).

Over Jesus' head the charge against Him was framed this way: **THIS IS JESUS THE KING OF THE JEWS**. Bypassers mocked Him, taunting Him to come down from the cross (vv. 37-40). Verses 41 through 44 record some of the other insults thrown at Jesus. **Three hours of darkness then came upon the whole land** during the period of Jesus' bearing the wrath of God (v. 45); at the conclusion Jesus cried out in the agony of having been judicially **forsaken** by God so that His people would never be forsaken (v. 46). His words were misinterpreted (v. 47). The end was at hand. Jesus died (vv. 47-50).

49 But the rest said, "Stop; let's see if Elijah comes to save him."

50 Then Jesus shouted in a loud voice once more and gave up His spirit.

51 At that point the temple curtain was ripped in two from the top to the bottom and the earth shook and the rocks split.

52 The graves opened up and many bodies of those who had fallen asleep were raised,

53 they came out of their graves, and after His resurrection they went into the holy city and appeared to many.

54 When the centurion and those who were guarding Jesus saw the earthquake and what happened, they were terrified and said, "Truly this was God's Son!"

55 Now there were many women watching from a distance, who had followed Jesus from Galilee to help Him.

56 Among them were Mary Magdalene, Mary the mother of James and Joseph, and the mother of the sons of Zebedee.

57 When evening had come, a rich man from Arimathea, named Joseph, who was a disciple of Jesus, came.

58 He went to Pilate and asked for the body of Jesus. Then Pilate ordered that it be given to him.

59 Joseph took the body and wrapped it in a clean sheet,

60 and laid it in his new grave that he had cut into the rock, and rolled a large stone over the entrance of the grave and left.

61 Mary Magdalene and the other Mary were sitting opposite the grave.

At the moment of Jesus' death, the **temple curtain was ripped in two from top to bottom,** indicating that it was God Who ripped it as a sign that the temple was no longer valid or needed since Jesus had made atonement once for all for His people's sins. An **earthquake** rumbled through the land, **rocks were split,** and some persons (who they were we don't know) were **raised** from the dead (vv. 51-53). The **centurion** and his soldiers guarding the cross saw and heard this and declared, **"Truly this was God's Son!"** (v. 54). Though the disciples fled, the **women** who had followed them remained at the scene (vv. 55, 56). This was important; they actually saw Him die. Their reports later on, then, were not hysterical ravings, but the sober statements of people who had witnessed both Jesus' death and resurrection.

Joseph collected the body of Jesus and laid it in his **new grave.** They **rolled a large stone** across the mouth of the grave (vv. 57-61). The religious leaders, remembering His predictions of a resurrection and thinking that there might be some fraud committed, (His enemies remembered; it seems that His friends forgot), had the tomb secured, sealed and guarded

62 On the next day, which is the day following the Preparation, the chief priests and Pharisees gathered before Pilate and said,

63   Lord, we remember how that deceiver said while he was still alive, "After three days I will rise again."

64   So then order the tomb to be secured until the third day; otherwise his disciples may come and steal him and tell the people that he was raised from the dead, and the last deception will be worse than the first.

65 Pilate said to them, "You have a guard; go secure it the best way you know how."

66 So they went and secured the tomb by sealing the stone and setting a guard.

(vv. 62-66). That ends the scene.

In all of this, the hand of God is visibly at work. Men crucified Jesus—as the plan of God was carried out by them. Thank God that He died for guilty sinners like us! Never forget the death of Christ in counseling; keep the fact of His death up front at all times.

CHAPTER 28

1   But after the Sabbath, at dawn on the first day of the week, Mary Magdalene and the other Mary went to look at the tomb.

2   As they arrived there was a great earthquake; an angel of the Lord came down from heaven, went to the stone, rolled it away and sat on it.

3   His appearance was like lightning, and his dress was white as snow.

4   And out of fear of him the guards became like dead men.

5   Then the angel responded by saying to the women,
       Don't be afraid. I know that you seek Jesus Who was crucified.

6   He is not here; He has risen, as He said. Come see the place where He was laid.

7   Now go quickly and tell His disciples that He has been raised from the dead, and now He is going to Galilee before you. You will see Him there. See, I have told you.

8   So they left the grave quickly with fear and great joy and they ran to tell this to His disciples.

9   And suddenly Jesus met them, saying, "Hello!" And they went to Him and held His feet and worshiped Him.

10   Then Jesus said to them, "Don't be afraid. Go tell My brothers that they may go off to Galilee, and there they will see Me."

11   Now while they were going some of the guards went into the city and told the chief priests everything that took place.

The last chapter of Matthew's Gospel is brief but full of cheer. There is much to be cheerful about. The **women** at the tomb met an **angel** who rolled away the stone from the tomb (not to let Jesus out, but to let the women in). The **guards** were frozen as corpses. And the angel declared, **"Don't be afraid. . . He is not here; He was raised, as He said."** That "I told you so" note in the angel's speech was a mild rebuke. The enemies remembered Jesus' prediction; His friends failed to. How often this is so. The women were sent to inform the disciples so that they could meet Him in **Galilee** (vv. 1-7). There was no time to lose; they were to go **quickly**. Jesus had been raised and He was on the move! They left, **fearful** over the event but **rejoicing**, and **ran** to tell the disciples (v. 8). Jesus **suddenly met** them as they went. They sought to hold on to Him, **worshipping** at His feet. He repeated the angel's message (vv. 9, 10).

The **guards** went back and told the **chief priests** what had happened. They were bribed to lie about the event, and their lies continued until the writing of the Gospel (vv. 11-15).

12 When they had gathered together with the elders, they decided what to
do: They bribed the soldiers with whatever money it took to do so, telling
them,

13 Say that his disciples came and stole him at night while you were
asleep.

14 And if the governor hears about this we will take care of that, and
you won't have to worry about it.

15 Then they took the money and did as they were instructed. And this
explanation has been spread about by the Jews to this day.

16 So the eleven disciples went to Galilee to the mountain where Jesus
had directed,

17 and they saw Him and worshiped, but some doubted.

18 Now Jesus came to them and said to them,
All authority in heaven and on earth has been given to Me.

19 Go, therefore, and disciple all nations, baptizing them into the
Name of the Father and of the Son and of the Holy Spirit,

20 teaching them to observe all that I have commanded you; and
remember, I will be with you always, to the close of the age.

The eleven then went to the **mountain** where Jesus had directed
them to meet with Him, saw Him, and **worshipped** Him (vv. 16, 17). But
some doubted (there will always be some who do). Then Jesus gave them
what has been called "The Great Commission." Interestingly this call to
evangelize is an educational call. Because He had been **given all authority in heaven and earth** (Daniel's predictions referred to before had
finally been fulfilled), they were to go and **make disciples** (learners,
pupils) from **all nations**. They were to be **baptized** into the church by
being connected to the **Name** of the members of the Trinity. Then, they
were to be **taught** to **observe** all that He **commanded** them to do.[1] That is
the work of the preacher in preaching and in counseling as He ministers
the Word. And Jesus promised to be **with them** until the **end of the age** as
they would preach throughout the known world (the end of the Old Testament age, as we have seen, drew to a close in 70 AD). Jesus is, of course,
still with His church and those who preach today. But this promise was a
special one that meant that He would infallibly direct the disciples in all
their preaching and in the writing of the Scriptures.[2]

Well, there you have it. Matthew, the Gospel to the Jews, is full of

1. See my book *Teaching to Observe* for more information.
2. For more about infallible, inerrant apostolic preaching, see the volume on Acts
in this series.

insights for counselors. Those who fail to make full use of it (especially of the Sermon on the Mount, of the 18th chapter and of the many parables) to the extent that they fail will have an insipid counseling ministry. Don't let that happen to you. Matthew can make a vast difference in your counseling; shouldn't it?

Introduction to
The Gospel of Mark

Mark is the shortest of the four Gospels. With its repetitious use of **straightway** ("immediately, at once") it presents a Savior Who, not frantically but urgently, moves from one event to another, never wasting time, always buying up the opportunities. The Busy Servant heralds, heals, helps. And He gets it done forthwith. That is the mood one senses when he studies this gem from the mouth of Peter (transcribed by Mark as his amanuensis—or so the fathers tell us). It is like Peter, rushing forth to disclose all he can of the loving Lord's ministry in as short a time and space as possible. We can learn even from this as counselors. There is much to do; there are many to help. We cannot afford to spend time dallying. Like our Lord, we must be about His work.

Whether Mark was the first gospel written is uncertain; much time and effort has been expended on this matter—much of it fruitless. There are, of course, harmonization problems between the gospels; but in these commentaries we shall make no effort along those lines. There is plenty already written on the subject. It will be our concern simply to take the words of the gospel as they appear and comment on them from the book itself.

Like the writer, we shall be concerned with brevity. We shall also endeavor to be careful not to neglect that which is important to understand and profit from what is written. The goal inspired by the book, then, is for concise completeness. That is a goal that every counselor ought to have for each counseling session.

With some exceptions, Mark's desire to demonstrate the authority of Christ is fulfilled through his use of samples. There are samples of healings, speeches, the casting out of demons, control over nature, and His Lordship over rites and ceremonies. Mark presents a Savior Who is in charge. That, of course, is precisely what every counselee needs, and it is the privilege of every biblical counselor to offer the counsel and help from just such a Lord. The loving concern of the Lord Jesus, Who out of compassion heals even when pressed from every side, is a worthwhile example for every counselor.

CHAPTER 1

1 The beginning of the good news about Jesus Christ, God's Son.

Mark announces that he will disclose how the **good news** that he preached and that Christians believe came about. He also will tell what this **good news** is all about. That is a sensible, logical and straightforward way to open his Gospel—by telling us about the **beginning** of the faith that he will set forth. We should be grateful to him (and to the Spirit of God) for such a simple, clear approach to the matter.

Counselors are not always as straightforward as Peter/Mark[1] are in this book. They can take a leaf from this gospel about how to eliminate unnecessary verbiage. Too often counselors like to hear themselves talk. The author of this book had learned to do otherwise. Notice: the message is about **news**. The faith is set forth not as works to be performed but as a message about something that has already taken place, that is to be believed. Unlike **news** in our day, in which the writer may be likely to invent aspects of the story about which he writes in order to bias the argument, make it more interesting or sensational, **news**—in a Holy Spirit inspired writing—was factually accurate. It relayed that which actually transpired.

This **news**, however, is unique: it pertains to **Jesus Christ, God's Son**. There is much in this first verse of Mark. In a sense, everything. The message concerns **Jesus Christ** (the Messiah-Savior, as those two words in reverse order mean) Who is **God** manifest in the flesh. Biblical counselors bring **news** to their counselees. Defeated and torn sheep who have wandered from the Shepherd need the very same news: the good Shepherd has been seeking them and will heal and restore them. That is your message to the Christian counselees who seek your help. Never allow the focus to be on you but always on the Good Shepherd Who, in the Person of the **other Counselor** Whom He sent to take His place, is the true Counselor in every counseling session. Of course, if the would-be counselee is not a believer, he must first be introduced to the Lord Jesus Christ

---

1. There is widespread consensus from the earliest times on that Peter wrote and Mark transcribed. Though we shall refer to the author as Mark, please keep in mind the thought that this was probably a joint production.

2   As it is written in the prophet Isaiah:
     See, I send My messenger before You who will prepare Your
     way;
3   **A voice of someone shouting in the desert:**
     "Get the Lord's road ready,
     Make His paths straight!"
4   So John appeared in the desert, preaching a baptism of repentance for
the forgiveness of sins.

---

as Savior through the good news that tells of His death and resurrection
that leads to the forgiveness of guilty sinners who come to Him in faith.

Like all that follows, Mark now quickly gets down to business. This
news is unusual: it was announced before it occurred. It had been predicted in **Isaiah** and the prophets, and it was heralded by **John the Baptist** who, as the forerunner of Jesus Christ, was also a subject of prophecy.
John was to **prepare** Christ's way. He was to be but a **voice shouting in
the desert**. By that shout he declared his work—he was a one-man pick-
and-shovel crew preparing the highway by which the Savior was to come.
He was to **make His paths straight**. Of course this description is figura-
tive. When Emperors rode into a community, crews literally went before
them to prepare the road on which they would travel. Bumps were leveled
off and gullies were filled. Where roads were crooked or inconvenient,
they were made **straighter** for the important person who would travel
them. Thus John announced that the world's most important Person was
coming and that it was his task to **prepare** a people whose hearts were
ready for the Son of God to ride smoothly into them.

Counseling is much the same. Counselors are in the business of
introducing people to the One Who can change their lives. That is why
they do not put *themselves* forward but, rather, the Lord Jesus. It is He
Who is coming into their lives to make them different; a human counselor
cannot do that. His task, like John's, is to prepare the counselee for that
coming by the timely application of truth from God's Word. His message
and method are similar to John's.

How would John do it? By **preaching repentance** (v. 4) and **baptizing** people as a sign of that repentance. There are two things here:
preaching and **baptism**. Both were important. John believed in **preaching** and effected tremendous results by it (hordes of people came to hear
and be **baptized**; cf. v. 5). Preaching has fallen on hard times. Many ministers think that it is outmoded. There are whole congregations that agree
with them. But God has used, and continues to use, the preaching that is

5   All the people of Judea and all Jerusalem went out to him, and were baptized by him at the Jordan River, confessing their sins.

---

properly oriented to bring men to repentance. Counseling is not all that different from preaching. One is public; the other is private. One conveys God's message to crowds, the other to a few. Yet the message is the same.

These two means constitute the substance of John's method. Its purpose was to bring about **the forgiveness of sins** (v. 4). **Repentance** brought about the **forgiveness of sins**, whereas **baptism** was the sign that one had **repented** of his sins. **Baptism** itself was not part of the gospel (cf. I Corinthians 1:17 where the two are clearly distinguished). It was a visible sign that one had believed the gospel.

How important it is that counselors, like John, proclaim exactly the same message and follow the method that the Scriptures set forth. What was said prophetically took place as John carefully did what the Scriptures required of him. Counselors dare not introduce non-biblical thoughts, ideas and methods into their counseling lest they dishonor the Lord and lead people astray. Many of your counselees need to come to repentance. **Repentance** is not regret (feeling sorry for the consequences of sin). It is, rather, a "rethinking" (as the Greek term *metanoia* signifies) that leads to a "turning" from sin (as the Hebrew term *shub* indicates). In **repentance** one **confesses** his **sins** before God (v. 5). Many counselees must be brought to repentance before God so that they may be prepared for the changes that the Lord Jesus will make in their lives—both in their thinking and in their behavior. Too often counseling fails because the preparatory work of repentance has been neglected. Does your counsel lack this essential ingredient?

In our modern times, when there is so little teaching about **sin**—even in so-called evangelical churches—be sure to emphasize the fact that all **sin** is against God. It is not merely an act of transgression against another human being, moreover, it is *disobedience* to God. **Sin** occurs whenever one does what God forbids or when he fails to do what God requires. It is not mere alienation from God—that is one *effect* of **sin**. **Confession** means, literally, "saying the same thing." It therefore refers to *agreement* with God's assessment of one's sinful standing and deeds. People who were willing to confess that they were sinners and demonstrate this by baptism were prepared to meet the Lord Who came to die for the iniquities of those sinners who would do so. Often, when dealing with counselees, you will find it necessary to show them that when they hedge

> **6** Now John was clothed in camel's hair and had a leather belt around his waist, and he ate locusts and wild honey.
> 7 This is what he preached:
> One Who is mightier than I will follow, the thongs of Whose sandals I am not worthy to stoop down to untie.
> 8 I baptize you with water, but this Man will baptize you with the Holy Spirit.

---

regarding their sin—calling it something less or excusing themselves for it—they will not be prepared for Him to change them by His Spirit. Particularly, point out that sin is *sin*, not sickness or some genetic flaw. Today, people are excusing their sin on the strength of those fallacious ideas. If one is a "patient," he must patiently await its passing, and we should be patient with him. If, on the other hand, he has been sinning, he must become so *im*patient with himself that he will **repent** of his sin. And counselors, who are anxious to help him be forgiven of his sin, must become impatient with the sin as well.

Verse 6 describes John's austere dress and his meager diet. These things fit in with his appearance in the **desert** (v. 4). The country long since had lost its spiritual vitality. Apart from an insignificant remnant, over the 400 years of silence during the intertestamental period the Jewish nation had become apostate. John's was the very first word from heaven to a Word-starved people. The **desert**, therefore, was an appropriate place for John's ministry; it spoke of the arid spiritual condition of the people. His raiment and food likewise depicted these conditions and the hard message of repentance that he preached.

While I certainly don't advise counselors to attire themselves in like manner (they have no such command to do so), it is important for them to assume a very serious attitude about what they are doing. Certainly there is room for a smile, for humor and even, at times, for levity. But the overall attitude of the counselor and of the sessions in which he deals with sin and the Word ought to be serious. That does not mean there will be an absence of hope. Indeed, just the opposite. John's appearance to a desolate people was just that—a shining light of hope at last. The biblical counselor ought to be the same as he deals with the lives of Christians who are in trouble.

John's message that brought people to **repentance** and **confession** is summarized in verses 7 and 8. John, you note, preached not only about judgment to come, but also about the One Whose way he was preparing. He compared himself to a slave (**untying sandals**) in relation to the com-

9 And so it happened that in those days Jesus came from Nazareth in Galilee and was baptized by John at the Jordan.
10 Then, as soon as He came up from the water He saw the Heavens split apart, and the Spirit coming down upon Him like a dove.
11 And there was a voice from the heavens: "You are My dear Son, I am well pleased with You."

---

ing Lord. He carefully contrasted his message and work to that of Jesus. John's **baptism** was negative—it was an outer **baptism** with **water** that signified **repentance** (v. 4). In addition to the negative, Jesus' baptism also struck a new, positive note. He was coming to baptize His people into His church by the inner **baptism** of the **Holy Spirit** (I Corinthians 12:13). Our counseling message has two dimensions as well—the put off and the put on. John represents the first, Jesus the second. The first exists for the second, not the other way around. John came to point men to Jesus; Jesus didn't point men to John. There are too many who want to emphasize repentance and the forgiveness of sins apart from the positive elements involved in becoming part of the body of Christ. Too many people want to talk about the remnants of sin in us; not enough want to talk about what Christ can do to make us more like Himself. Sin abounds, but grace far more abounds (Romans 5:20). Light is more powerful than darkness: whenever light appears darkness is driven out. What Jesus can do for poor, guilty, sinning counselees to bring about righteousness is so stupendous that it should by all means supersede everything that is done to bring them to repentance. Keep the right emphasis in your counseling.

Jesus identified Himself with the people (v. 9) by being **baptized by John** at the Jordan river. When He left the river and stood on the bank the heavens **split apart** and the **Spirit** came down on Him in a **dove**-like manner. And then the voice of the Father sounded from the heavens, affirming that Jesus was His **dear Son** and that He was **well-pleased** with Him because of what He was doing. The Spirit, Whom Jesus as the God-man received by this anointing, was the Source of His power throughout the three and one-half year ministry that followed. There can be no other legitimate Source from which counselors draw their effectiveness today. That is why biblical counseling is unlike any other. It draws upon the Spirit's wisdom found in His Book, the Bible. And it elicits His power to enable counselees to do what the Book requires. No other kind of counseling even begins to approximate *biblical* counseling. Counselor, you have something unique, wonderful, to offer suffering, sinning, confused

223

12 Next, the Spirit led Him out into the desert,

13 and He was in the desert forty days being tested by Satan; and He was with the wild animals, and angels took care of Him.

14 Now after John had been arrested, Jesus went to Galilee, preaching the good news from God,

---

Christians. Don't let others denigrate it by placing it alongside other systems as merely one option among many.

In verses 12 and 13, Mark tells us that Jesus was **led** by the **Spirit** into the **desert** where during a **forty-**day period of fasting, He was **tempted by Satan**. The time when we are most vulnerable to **temptation** by the evil one is when we are in an unusual place (here, the **desert**) doing some unusual thing (here fasting for **forty** days). Warn counselees about this fact. He was in a weakened condition from the fasting, and there was no human help for Him to call upon in this situation. However, *angels took care of Him*, protecting Him from the **wild animals** which lurked on every side. This additional fact, not mentioned elsewhere, makes it clear that Mark's focus was on the temptation from the adversary (the meaning of the word **Satan**). There was no angelic protection from him. That is what was central; nothing else could interfere with it—not even wild beasts.

There are times when the Spirit will lead your counselee into a desert (some unusual place, perhaps where there is little to sustain or help him). But He will protect him from all harm beyond the temptation in which He places him. Counselees should be taught that "**temptation**" is but one of the ways to translate the Greek word. The other equally acceptable translation is "trial or test." The word itself is colorless, taking its peculiar meaning from the context. However, whatever the emphasis in any given passage, it is well to remember that every incident of **temptation** is a **test**; every **test** is a **temptation**. If one successfully passes the **test** (endures the trial) he will grow spiritually. If he falls under **testing** (**temptation**) then his spiritual life will suffer. Satan intends the trial to become a temptation to sin; God sends temptations in order to test His children.

Verse 14 tells us about **John's arrest**. That he was arrested for fearless preaching we learn elsewhere. When a counselor tells counselees the truth (as John told it to Herod) it is likely to anger them. While it is unlikely that they will have you **arrested**, angry counselees can make life miserable. Nevertheless, you must be as fearless as John was to speak the truth. A counselee has asked you to become personal; you dare not fail to

15   saying, "The time is completed and God's empire is at hand; repent and believe the good news."

---

tell it like it is. Probably, you will be the one person who has the courage to confront him with the truth about his life. Very few persons give others an accurate reading of themselves. Part of your task is to do so. If you fail to do it, he may never hear the truth about himself from anyone else.

John's arrest is mentioned here in order to note how at that time the preaching of Jesus succeeded it (v. 14). Notice, **Jesus preached** the same message that John preached: the **good news**. He began to preach in **Galilee**, away from the area where John had preached. His message also included an emphasis on **repentance** (v. 15). From the beginning there was the two-sided message: first, **repent**; second, **believe the gospel** (good news). Once more, remember, *your counseling* must be twofold also: first there must be the clearing of the rubble by repentance; then the building by faith and the works that flow from it. You cannot build for the future until you clear away the rubble of the past. But clearing rubble is useless unless you build something worthwhile in its place. Counseling requires both demolition and construction.

When Jesus preached that **the time is completed and God's empire is at hand** He was referring to Daniel's prediction of the fifth world **empire** that, unlike the previous four, would not pass away. It was the empire from the heavens which the God of heaven would set up; This "kingdom of God," as it is usually called, is the same as the New Testament church. Truly, Jesus had come to build His church (Matthew 16:18). People entered it by repenting and believing the good news. The continuity of the message from John to Jesus (and later to the apostles) is clear. Counselors today do not need to innovate. They, too, have the same saving and sanctifying message to deliver to needy counselees. It is important to realize that one is in a line of continuity that God Himself set up. Those who buy into the psychological theories of sinful men deviate radically from that line. That is serious. It should not happen in the church. It jeopardizes all who become ensnared in it. It is coherent with a line of thinking that the Bible calls the "counsel of the ungodly." It is my hope that after the battle for the sufficiency of the Bible in counseling has been successfully fought and won (probably after my demise) creedal statements of faith will be adopted (as there have been throughout the history of doctrine) that exclude all counseling that is out of line with that of John, Jesus and the apostles. It is time that the church pronounced all counseling from

16 As He was walking along beside the Sea of Galilee, He saw Simon and Andrew, Simon's brother, throwing a net into the sea (they were fishermen).
17 And Jesus said to them, "Follow Me, and I will make you fishers of men."
18 So then and there they left their nets and followed Him.
19 Then, going on a little farther He saw James, Zebedee's son, and John, his brother, mending their nets in a boat.
20 Immediately He called them, and they left their father Zebedee in the boat with his hired men and followed Him.

---

the ungodly as part of the line of the ungodly that has opposed itself to God's Word of truth since the Garden of Eden.

Verses 16 through 20 record the call of some of the disciples. These men were at work when the Savior called them. Those are the sorts of persons He ordinarily uses for ministry—busy, hard working individuals. He took the occasion to call them in terms of their livelihood: **"Follow Me and I will make you fishers of men."** Here is a technique important for every counselor to develop. Learn how to use something in the conversation, the background of the counselee, etc., to emphasize points that you wish to make. That way the counselee will understand and be able to more easily relate to what it is you are after. With a person in construction, for instance, you may be able to use with profit the imagery I have employed about the impossibility of building on the rubble of the past. With a truck driver, you may wish to speak of getting things into gear.

The willingness of the disciples to follow Jesus and leave their nets is useful in pointing out how counselees ought to obey (vv. 18, 20). They should neither make up all sorts of excuses why they cannot do so nor delay in responding. When Jesus tells them to do something, they must do it NOW.

The Jews brought **synagog** worship back with them from the captivity in Babylon. It continued up until Jesus' time. Even in Palestine, where there was a temple, they continued to sing, pray and teach in the synagog service. These services provided a great opportunity for Jesus to teach the people (as they did for the apostles throughout the dispersion later on). In verses 21 and 22 we read of Jesus preaching in the synagog at **Capernaum** (a city which became the headquarters for His ministry). Here we are given a description of the effect of that teaching on the people: **He taught as an authority, and not as the scribes**. The **scribes** handed out

21 Then they went on to Capernaum, and on the very next Sabbath He went to the synagog and taught.

22 They were astonished at His teaching, because He taught them as an authority, and not as the scribes.

23 On that same occasion there was a man in their synagog with an unclean spirit who called out, saying,

24   What do You want with us, Jesus of Nazareth? Did You come to destroy us? I know Who You are—God's holy One!

25 Jesus rebuked him, saying, "Be quiet, and come out of him."

---

opinions of various rabbis ("Hillel taught this, but Shammai taught that"). There was no sound **authority** behind this Hebrew scholasticism. The same is true of much teaching in the modern church. You may read Christian magazines where all views are taught (e.g. biblical or eclectic counseling) and you can take your pick. Books are published giving "Five views of this or that." At least four of these are false! Jesus did no such thing. He **authoritatively** taught the truth, and taught it as such. You had no choices except to believe it or not. That is the way biblical counselors should teach (as *we* say, "dogmatically"). When I am accused of being too dogmatic, I usually respond by saying, "Yes, I am dogmatic; but not *too* dogmatic. If you knew all that I didn't understand about the Bible, you wouldn't think that. You see, I only speak about that which I am sure of. I want to teach as Jesus did—with authority." Too few speak **authoritatively** today. They are wishy-washy. Instead of proclaiming or declaring, they "share." They present their own ideas, or those of some other *human* authority. A counselee in doubt doesn't need that. He has enough uncertainties of his own. He needs to hear true, biblical dogmatism—an authoritative presentation of biblical truth. But every counselor must be fully persuaded in his own mind that what he says *is indeed* the very truth of God. Otherwise dogmatism can be dangerous.

Jesus took this occasion to **heal** a man with an **unclean spirit** who happened to be attending the synagog service. Using the man's voice, the demon identified **Jesus**, His home town and the fact that he knew the time was coming when he was to be **destroyed**. He also knew that Jesus was **God's holy One**. Where demons obtain their information we do not know. Whether they obtain it from an unrecorded judgment that God pronounced against them, from Scripture or by observation, they seem to be privy to much truth. One thing is clear from this healing—Jesus told him to **be quiet** and to leave the man. The command to **be quiet** was in line with the fact that we shall observe presently—crowds of people were

26 And the unclean spirit threw him into a convulsion and shouted with a loud voice and left him.

27 The people were all so dumbfounded that they began to ask each other, "What is this? This is brand new teaching with authority! He even orders the unclean spirits around, and they obey Him!"

28 And right away this began to be reported about Him in the whole region of Galilee.

29 Just after they left the synagog, they went with James and John to the house of Simon and Andrew.

30 Now Simon's mother-in-law was in bed with a fever, and they told Him about her right away.

31 So He went to her and, taking her by the hand, raised her up, and the fever left her, so that she was able to serve them.

---

beginning to throng Him. He wanted no more publicity than He already had. Upon leaving, the demon used the occasion to display his presence by **shouting** loudly and throwing the man into a **convulsion** (v. 26). Seeing and hearing what had taken place, the people were even more amazed at Jesus' **authority**—an **authority** over demons who were forced to **obey Him** (v. 27). There was consternation; people asked, "**What is this?**" They were confused. And the word spread rapidly throughout northern Palestine about what He was saying and doing (v. 28).

Here the **authority** of Jesus' word was buttressed by the authority He possessed over demons. Christian counselors depend wholly on the Word and the results that it reaps. The fact is, however, they have the very same authority. They ought not hesitate, therefore, to assert the truths of the Bible (so long as they thoroughly understand them) with vigor and certainty. Counselors, like Jesus, need to stress the fact that God stands behind His Word. That Word will produce results that nothing else will. Hardened criminals will be softened and turned into model citizens, child abusers will be transformed and broken homes will be mended. Let the authority of Christ in His Word, then, astound people today when they see the changes that His Spirit effects.

The next three verses tell of the Savior's authority over disease (vv. 29-31). The healing was immediate and it was complete (she began to **serve** them). Jesus can change lives of counselees instantaneously. He does not always deign to do so, but He is still capable of it. It is not always necessary to spend sustained periods of time counseling. There are many situations in which one visit is sufficient. Learn to discern when this is the situation.

32 Now in the evening, when the sun had set, they brought to Him all those who were sick and those who were demoniacs;

33 and the whole town gathered together at the door.

34 He healed many who were sick with various diseases, and He cast many demons, but He didn't allow the demons to speak, because they knew Who He was.

35 And He got up very early, before it was light, left and went off to a lonely place and prayed there.

36 Simon, and those who accompanied him, hunted for Him,

37 and found Him and said to Him: "Everybody is looking for You."

38 But He responded, "Let's go elsewhere to the nearby towns so I may preach there too. That's why I came."

39 So He went through all of Galilee, preaching in their synagogs and casting out demons.

40 Then a leper came to Him, begging Him on his knees, saying, "If you want to, you can make me clean."

41 And He was moved with pity and stretched out His hand and touched him and said to him, "I do want to; be clean."

In verses 32 through 39 Mark tells us how Jesus handled **crowds**. Jesus did what He could, but it was impossible to heal and help all who came. One thing they all could benefit from, however, was His **teaching** (indeed, He said it was more important than the healings: cf. v. 38). It is not always wrong to leave the crowds behind—even with cases untouched. Jesus did in order to **pray** (v. 35), to rest, and to preach elsewhere (v. 38). This, note, was in the midst of a healing revival (v. 34). It is not necessary to help all who want help, though it seems that you must help all you reasonably can be expected to help. Note, however, how Jesus kept the purpose for His coming in view; He would not subordinate it to anything else (v. 38[b]). Likewise, you must not allow the demands for counseling to crowd out other legitimate purposes you may have. Eventually, Jesus enlisted the disciples and the seventy to assist Him in both activities. You must train and enlist your elders, pastor. You cannot do it all yourself.

Even **leprosy** was healed (vv. 40-45). Note the compassion that drove Him to heal the leper (v. 41). **Compassion** must never be far from any counselor. If and when he loses that he will cease to be a *biblical* counselor. Many think that biblical counselors are not compassionate because they often speak of sin and ask people to follow difficult biblical courses of action. But it is precisely out of compassion that they do so. One cannot be more compassionate than God Whose directions we follow

42 Immediately the leprosy left him and he was clean.

43 And He sent him off at once and sternly warned him,

44 saying, "See to it that you don't tell anybody anything, but go show yourself to the priest and make the offering that Moses commanded for your cleansing as a testimony to them."

45 But when he went out he began to talk about it so much and spread the news so widely that He no longer was able to enter a city openly, but stayed out in deserted areas, and they came to Him from all directions.

---

in this. True compassion is helping others to come into the right relationship with God.

There is a fine balance in the life of Jesus as we see Him in ministry here. He teaches, heals, casts out demons, refuses to attract more crowds, gets away from them, tells demons not to reveal who He is; but in the midst of it all, He is particularly moved to **pity** one man. Do you ever prefer to help one person rather than speak to the crowds? How well do you manage your priorities? Think hard about the problem and make the necessary adjustments.

In the healing of the leper, Jesus abides by the **Mosaic** requirements (v. 44). Christian counselors must learn to conform to the **law** so long as it does not cross biblical requirements. But there is more than that. Jesus was keen to have him go show himself to the **priests** as a **testimony** to them. Presumably, there was little opportunity otherwise to reach them. So, contrary to His policy of not advertising His work, Jesus insists that the man go to the priests so they could investigate and pronounce him clean. With all His caution, there was no end of people who heard about Him and came. Indeed, wherever He went there was not enough room in cities for His teaching because of the crowds. Like John, He had become an open-air preacher in the desert where people came to hear Him (v. 45). Jesus' adaptation to circumstances teaches the wise counselor. He did what He could do, He did what He had to do, but preeminently, He did what He had come to do. All of this He did in perfect balance. Not only is balance important in the counselor's life, it is also something he will find counselees having trouble achieving. If he, himself, is unable to achieve and maintain balance, he will hardly be able to help others do so.

CHAPTER 2

1 After some days, when He returned to Capernaum, it was reported that He was at home.

2   So many gathered together that there was no more room, not even at the door. And He spoke the Word to them.

3   Now four persons came carrying a paralytic to Him.

4   But because they weren't able to bring him in, because of the crowd, they removed the roof above Him, and when they had made an opening they lowered the stretcher on which the paralytic was lying.

5   When Jesus saw their faith He said to the paralytic: "Son, your sins are forgiven you."

6   Now some of the scribes were sitting there thinking in their hearts:

7   "Why does this man speak like this? He is blaspheming. Who can forgive sins except One—God?"

Jesus had taken an extensive preaching tour throughout the rest of Galilee. In time, when He returned to Capernaum the word soon spread that He was back; and while He was teaching in a home a crowd quickly assembled in the place (v. 1). But there was room for no more—not even at the **door** (v. 2). Then, four men, carrying a paralytic on a stretcher, finding it impossible to get through the crowd to Jesus, tore a hole in the none-too-substantial roof and lowered the sick man on his stretcher down into the courtyard before Jesus (vv. 3, 4).

These were five people who meant business. If they could not get to Jesus one way, they would find another. They did not let anything stand in their way. Occasionally, you will meet counselees like that. More often, you will meet others who greatly desire to see a loved one or friend receive counseling. Here, the **faith** of all five was evident, as Mark says. Jesus then declared openly, before all, **"Son, your sins are forgiven you."**

The **scribes**—the theologians of the day—were **thinking** inwardly "That kind of talk is blasphemy; **only God** can forgive sins" (vv. 6, 7). Of course, they were right. On this point, their theology was correct. It was in its application and its limitations that they erred. Jesus knew what they were thinking (He still knows what every counselor/counselee thinks), and confronted them: **"Why are you thinking this way?"** He asked. Then He posed the question—which is easier—to f**orgive sins** or to **heal** this sick man? They didn't answer. Of course, they were thinking "It is easy to say 'I forgive you,' but how can we know that it is for real?" In order to

> 8   Then at once, when Jesus knew in His spirit that they were thinking this way in themselves, He said to them:
>   Why are you thinking such things in your hearts?
> 9   Which is easier to say to the paralytic, "Your sins are forgiven you," or to say, "Get up and take your stretcher and walk?"
> 10   But so that you may know that the Son of Man has authority on the earth to forgive sins,
> He said to the paralytic,
> 11   "I tell you, get up, take your stretcher and go to your house."
> 12   At once, he got up and, in front of everyone, took his stretcher and left. As a result they were all astonished and glorified God, saying, "We've never seen anything like this!"

---

prove that He had the power to forgive sins, he told the sick man to **get up and take his stretcher to his house** (v. 11)—which the cripple proceeded to do. Everyone in the crowd then glorified God.

Correct theology must be correctly applied. There are many with proper theology who haven't the faintest idea how to use it to help people in trouble. They doubt that counseling can be effective because they have never seen it happen. Counselors, therefore, must *demonstrate* to them that God is doing the work of helping His people by means of those who minister His Word in the power of the Spirit. They must be brought to see that composing biblical-theological essays—right in itself, though greatly overemphasized today—is not the epitome of the use of the Scriptures. Jesus was out among the people using the Word that He preached and demonstrated to be from God. That is precisely what is needed today. You will find that some theologians, who have never been out in the rain, but have been under an academic roof all their lives since kindergarten, will object and find fault with practical ministers of the Word. There are even some who believe that in preaching, Scripture should never be applied. People like this, of course, reject counseling. They are dangerous to the cause of Christ, and their emphasis must be opposed whenever it interferes with the ministry of the Word to poor, needy Christians.

Jesus *could* **forgive sins** because He was God manifest in the flesh. He still forgives on the basis of His work on the cross. Counselors have the distinct privilege of telling counselees and those around them that this is so. Much of what counseling is all about is the continued forgiveness of sins that takes place within the heavenly family (see the footnote to the Lord's prayer). For believers, the *judicial* forgiveness of God is past, dealt with once and for all by Jesus on the cross. But *family* forgiveness by the

13 Then He went out again alongside the sea, and the whole crowd came to Him and He taught them.

14 Now while passing by He saw Levi, Alphaeus' son, sitting at the tax collector's office, and He said to him, "Follow Me." And he got up and followed Him.

15 And it happened that as He sat eating in his house many tax collectors and sinners sat with Jesus and His disciples (there were many who followed Him).

16 But when the Pharisees' scribes saw that He was eating with sinners and tax collectors, they said to His disciples, "He is eating with tax collectors and sinners!"

17 Now when Jesus heard this He said, "Those who are well don't need a doctor, but only those who are sick. I didn't come to call righteous people, but sinners."

Father continues throughout this life. Many are confused about this; help them see the difference.

Jesus was **teaching** crowds again, **alongside the sea** (v. 13). As He left there, He passed by **Levi, a tax collector**. He called him to discipleship (v. 14). He then went to Levi's home for a meal. There were tax collectors there and notorious sinners. Tax collectors were hated for three reasons: the Jews, like people in general, hated tax collectors because they did not like to pay taxes, they knew that the system virtually required a tax collector to cheat, and tax collectors were collaborators with the enemy—Rome. Notorious sinners were in the same class with tax collectors. So Jesus was with what the religious leaders would call a disreputable crowd.

Thank God He was willing to receive sinners! Jesus demonstrates by calling Levi and eating with this crowd that all who will may come to Him—regardless of their previous lives. That means that there is no Christian, however low a life he has lived in the past, who should be beyond the concern of a biblical counselor. Indeed, as here, it is often true that the outcasts are those who respond most heartily and fully.

The **scribes** of the **Pharisees** (the strictest Jewish sect) complained about Jesus' table companions. He replied to this by saying that those who are well don't need a **doctor**, only those who are **sick**. Then He said, He **came** not to call the **righteous** but **sinners** to **repentance**. This emphasis is crucial in counseling. Only those who recognize and acknowledge their sin are candidates for help. Jesus is still the great Physician (vv. 15-17). But He heals only those who know their desperate condition apart from Him. The scribes were not **righteous**—far from it—but

> **18** Now John's disciples and the Pharisees were fasting. So some people came and said to Him: "Why do John's disciples and the Pharisees' disciples fast? Your disciples don't fast."
>
> 19 Jesus replied,
>
> > Can the friends of the bridegroom fast while the bridegroom is with them? As long as they have the bridegroom with them they can't fast.
>
> 20 But the days will come when the bridegroom will be taken away from them; then, on that day, they will fast.
>
> 21 Nobody sews a patch of unshrunken cloth on an old garment. If he did, the new patch would pull away from the old material, and there would be a worse tear.
>
> 22 And nobody puts new wine into old wineskins. If he did, the wine would burst the wineskins and the wine and the wineskins alike would be ruined. Rather, new wine is put into fresh wineskins.

they believed they were. They saw no need for Jesus; they thought that they were **well** spiritually. Repentance was not for them; it was only for common sinners like those seated in Levi's house! The attitude today has not changed. Many fail to receive help because they see no need for it. It is those who come to a counselor for help, acknowledging their spiritual sickness, who alone receive Jesus' aid.

In verses 18 through 22 there is an interesting dialog between Jesus and some who noticed differences between **John's disciples** and Jesus' disciples. This leads to a brief, but important, comment by Jesus Himself. John's disciples and the Pharisees' disciples **fasted**. Jesus' disciples did not. They wanted to know why this was so. In reply, Jesus explained that you don't fast when the **bridegroom** is with you. His disciples enjoyed His daily presence. Why should they fast? But the days would come when He would leave and *then* they would **fast**. In other words, it is a joyful thing to have the Lord's presence.

Then He said, rather mysteriously, "you **don't sew a patch of unshrunken material on an old garment** because if you do, when it shrinks it will pull on the old material and cause a worse tear in the garment." In addition, He said, "you don't put unfermented wine in old, dry, rigid, unexpandable wineskins. Otherwise, when it ferments, it will burst the wineskin." No, He said, "you put new wine in new skins that will stretch with its expansion."

What did He intend by these two analogies? Well, two things were **old** and two were **new**. That much is clear. The **old garment** and the **old**

23 Now on a Sabbath it happened that He passed through the wheat fields, and as His disciples made their way they were picking some heads of wheat.

24   And the Pharisees said to Him, "Look, why are they doing something that isn't lawful on the Sabbath?"

25   And He said to them,

>   Haven't you ever read what David and those who were with Him did when they were in need and hungry?

26   He entered into God's house at the time that Abiathar was high priest and ate the presentation loaves, which nobody is allowed to eat except the priests; and he also gave them to those who were with him.

---

wineskins represent one set of circumstances; the **new patch** and the **new wine** represent the other. To what did they refer? John's ministry was useful for its time; but having achieved its purpose, it was now becoming old and was ready to be replaced by the ministry of Christ. No one was to think that he could patch it with that which Jesus is doing. The new wine of His ministry can't safely be placed in John's old wineskin. There is an advance, in what Christ is doing and saying, beyond the ministry of John. John's ministry was preparatory for Jesus' ministry. They were not the same (Acts 19:1-7 makes that abundantly clear). Jesus would give His life for His people. He is the One Who can transform counselees; John cannot. The new wine was Christ's ministry, the old wineskin was John's. The new patch was Christ's ministry; the old cloth was John's.

There are things new and old in every counseling case. People will want to mix the two in ways that are impossible. Don't allow this. What they did once in walking an aisle, for instance, is an old wineskin unfit for the current problem that must be repented of and dealt with. There was nothing wrong with John's ministry; it is just that it was now passé. The same is true of what one may have done well in the past; that will not excuse him from doing well in the present. Each problem has its own current dimensions which only fresh grace is able to solve. You can't rest on past laurels.

Finally, there is the debate over the **Sabbath** (vv. 23-28). Verses 23 through 28 record the first debate; verses 1 through 6 in chapter 3 record the continuation of the controversy. The Jews had overemphasized the Sabbath, adding rules and regulations to its observance that were never prescribed by God. Just as Jesus showed His **authority** over demons, disease and over the ministry, so, too, He now declared that He was also

27 Then He said to them,
  The Sabbath was made for man's sake, not man for the Sabbath's sake!
28 So then, the Son of Man is Lord even of the Sabbath.

Lord of the Sabbath. Obviously, plucking heads of wheat as the disciples passed through the fields was not a violation of the Sabbath, a day God made to serve man by doing him good. The example about **David** is a powerful one that demonstrates that the welfare of human beings comes before nonessential factors. Here, He declares that He is the One Who ordained the **Sabbath** and, therefore, is its **Lord**. That is to say, having ordained it for man's good, He alone has the right to determine what is and what is not a violation of it. In this chapter, therefore, Jesus has been setting forth His Lordship over everything. The Pharisees and their scribes are beginning to become annoyed by these assertions. Their objections become so strong that it is not long before they begin to determine how to **destroy Him** (3:6).

The Christian counselor will often teach things that are contrary to legalistic opinions. For instance, there are those who see no reason for divorce. That is a simplistic view of the Bible's teaching, teaching which they cannot abide. These people, like the scribes, claim to be *strict* in their interpretation; the truth is that they are not strict enough. Like every legalist, they are willing to ignore or misinterpret biblical teaching in order to maintain their legalism. They will not adhere strictly to the teaching of the Scriptures, and the Scriptures alone. Those who are truly strict in their interpretation are those who will believe and practice nothing but what the Bible teaches (for more on the issue of divorce, see my book *Marriage, Divorce and Remarriage in the Bible*).

CHAPTER 3

1 Once again He went into a synagog, and a man with a shriveled hand was there.

2   And they watched Him carefully to see if He would heal on the Sabbath, so that they might accuse Him.

3   But He said to the man with the shriveled hand, "Get up and come to the center."

4   And He said to them, "Is it lawful on the Sabbath to do good or to do evil, to save life or to kill?" But they kept quiet.

5   Then He looked around at them with anger, quite upset about the hardness of their hearts, and said to the man, "Stretch out your hand." And he stretched it out, and his hand was restored.

6   So the Pharisees went right out and plotted with the Herodians against Him about how they would destroy Him.

The issue begun at the end of the previous chapter is here continued: Jesus is accused of **Sabbath** desecration. In verses 1 through 6 we read of Jesus **healing** a man with a **shriveled hand** on the Sabbath, and the upshot of this. The **scribes** were watching Jesus to see if they would be able to catch Him in some irregularity. When He called the man to the **center** of the **synagog** where it took place, they were ready to pounce on Him. But before they could, Jesus asked them whether it was **lawful to do good or evil, to save a life or to kill**. This was a question that they could not answer the way they wanted to without condemning themselves; so they **kept quiet**.

There are times to take the initiative in counseling when persons are looking for some fault your methods in order to discourage a counselee from following a biblical course of action. It is interesting to note that His preemptive strike produced results. The kind of question that He leveled at His accusers was calculated to make them and everyone else think twice before responding. Counselors should become skilled at asking such questions. They will have numerous occasions on which to use them. When they allow the opposition to take the offensive, they, in effect, desert their counselees.

And don't miss Mark's note that Jesus **looked around at them with anger**. **Anger** is not wrong when it is aroused over matters that *ought* to elicit it and when it is exercised in a biblical manner. If Jesus became angry, it is not wrong for you to also in biblically-justified circumstances.

7 Then Jesus withdrew with His disciples to the sea, and a great crowd from Galilee followed.

8 And when they heard about the things He was doing a great crowd from Judea, from Jerusalem, from Idumea and beyond the Jordan and from around Tyre and Sidon came to Him.

9 So He told His disciples to have a small boat ready for Him in case the crowd should begin to crush Him

10 (this was because He had healed many, so that all those who had diseases were pressing toward Him in order to touch Him).

11 Now when the unclean spirits saw Him they fell down before Him and shouted, saying, "You are God's Son."

12 But He strongly warned them that they shouldn't make known Who He was.

Those who think that all anger is wrong are themselves wrong. Those who say that anger is a negative emotion fail to understand that even destructive emotions (anger is calculated to destroy) may have positive effects. Jesus' anger had the positive effect of showing up the hypocrites in the room and contrasting the truth of God to their legalism which He wished to destroy. He deals with this problem in much more depth and with utter clarity later in the book of Mark (chapter 7).

Of course, as verse 6 indicates, it is true that the long-term result of opposing the **scribes** was His death. It is altogether possible that you, too, will experience hatred and even at least a mild degree of violence from those whom you similarly silence. That, however, should not deter you from doing or saying the right thing no more than it deterred the Lord Jesus. There is a place for courage in counseling. If you have little, and are unable to muster up more, you probably have a problem to work on. Read Acts 4 about **boldness**.

The **crowds** were once more thronging about Jesus (vv. 7, 8). They became so numerous that Jesus found it necessary to ready a **boat** in which He could escape from them if necessary. It is not, as we saw earlier, possible (or necessary) to deal with everyone who seeks help. Rather, it is important to keep one's priorities in balance. Jesus did all He could in the way of teaching and healing the multitudes (cf. v. 10), but He was careful to not let matters get out of hand). And again, as demons were cast out, He forbid them to advertise **Who He was** (vv. 11, 12). Not only did He not desire testimony from such a source, He wanted to keep the people from proclaiming Him the Messiah before the proper time.

Counselors must learn prudence as well. There are many foolish

13 Then He went up into the mountain and called those whom He wanted, and they came to Him.

14 He appointed twelve[1] that they might be with Him and that He might send them out to preach

15 and to exercise authority to cast out demons.

16 Now these are the twelve that He appointed: Simon (to whom He gave the name Peter),

17 and James, Zebedee's son, and John, James's brother (to whom He gave the name Boanerges, which means "sons of thunder"),

18 and Andrew and Philip and Bartholomew and Matthew and Thomas and James, Alphaeus' son, and Thaddaeus and Simon the Zealot

---

1. Some MSS add, *whom He named apostles.*

---

actions that counselees would like counselors to take. Instead, they should act prudently and counsel others to do the same. Some inconsiderate counselees will take up all of your time, if you allow it. You fail to teach them properly when you allow them to go on being inconsiderate. If they keep on calling you at home, for instance, you may have to say, "Please write these sorts of things down and bring them to the next session. I have other matters to deal with today—and so do you."

Precautions of various sorts should be taken to forestall adverse reactions or other such problems. Holding the boat in readiness is an important factor. You also should make alternate plans (Plan B) to meet exigencies. Teach your counselees to do the same.

Verses 13 through 19 have to do with the **appointment of the Twelve** and the granting of authority to them to cast out demons as they went preaching (vv. 14, 15). Jesus had a program, and He pursued it, even in the midst of the revival that was occurring. Then notice how He relied on their help as the crowds increased. You cannot do it all. Train elders, deacons, and others who can carry a part of the counseling load when it becomes too extensive for one person. You must learn to train and trust other believers. Some think no one else is capable. Well, if Jesus wasn't afraid to leave His work in the hands of these men who were often weak and imprudent after training them, why should you be?

But how do you train them? There has been too much of the scholastic method in our educational institutions—especially in the seminaries. All would do well to learn from our Lord Who, according to verse 14, **appointed twelve that they might be *with Him* and that He might send them out to preach**. This **with Him** method of teaching is the essence of

19 and Judas Iscariot (who betrayed Him).

20 He went into a house and the crowd came together again, so that they weren't even able to eat bread.

21 But when His family heard about it they went out to take hold of Him (they said, "He is out of his mind").

---

discipleship. That it worked is plain from Acts 4:13 where we are told that in time others recognized that the apostles *had* been **with** Jesus (see also Luke 6:40). The method involves such things as letting others observe, sending them forth on missions, etc. In counseling training, it is imperative that one observe counseling, ask questions about it, try their hand at it under supervision, do it for a while and, finally, teach others. That is the discipling method in its fullest expression. Counselors should also encourage elders to sit in on counseling sessions to learn.

There will usually be one who fails you; **Judas** was one of the Twelve (v. 19). Not only did the cross make it necessary to have one who would betray Him in the group, but (perhaps as a secondary purpose) it is also encouraging for us to see that in even the best of groups, under the perfect leadership of the Savior one would have to be cast out. In time, you will find the same to be true as you work with others. There have been serious betrayals and defections from the modern biblical counseling movement. Be aware of the fact, but don't become discouraged by it.

Verse 20 is another example of Jesus' popularity. Whenever people become aware that you are able to help them, you are likely to find that you will have more people who need help than you can handle. It was so serious of a problem for Jesus and His disciples that they weren't even able to take the time **to eat** every meal. But the popularity attracted adverse criticism from Jesus' family (v. 21). Whether from envy or fear of reprisals on the family, they tried to remove Him from the crowds, saying that He had lost His mind. You will discover that there are those in the Christian world—or even your own family—who do and say similar things for various reasons. Here, this fact shows that on all fronts Jesus is beginning to receive opposition. You will also discover that as soon as you are beginning to help counselees, opposition will arise. Family opposition can be devastating if you allow it to affect you. Did it deter Jesus? Absolutely not. Should it deter you? You answer that question for yourself!

The **scribes**, who began to actively oppose Jesus, had their own explanation of the phenomenon: they said the Jesus **was possessed by Beelzebub. . . the ruler of the demons** (v. 22). They charged Him with

22 And when the scribes from Jerusalem came down they said, "He is possessed by Beelzebub," and "He casts out demons by the ruler of the demons."

23 So He called them to Him and spoke to them in parables:
   How can Satan cast Satan out?

24   If a kingdom is divided against itself, that kingdom can't stand,

25   and if a house is divided against itself, that house can't stand;

26   so if Satan stood up against himself and was divided, he couldn't stand but would come to an end.

27   Rather, nobody can enter a strong man's house to steal his property unless he first binds the strong man. Then he will steal his property.

28   Let Me assure you that all sorts of sinful acts and blasphemies spoken by the sons of men will be forgiven them,

---

casting out demons by Satan's power. This occasioned a very sharp reply on Jesus' part. First, He pointed out the stupidity of the charge. Why would the Devil lend his power to defeat his own cause (vv. 23-26)? That is foolish reasoning. Those who object to biblical ministry often level the most outrageously ridiculous charges. Get used to hearing them!

But then Jesus told them the truth of the matter in a parable: "You can't **enter a strong man's house to steal his property** (that is to cast out Satan's demons) unless you first **bind the strong man**" (that is what Jesus was doing to Beelzebub). That the devil has such absolute power, as many teach today, is an error. Sure, his time is short (Revelation 12), and he is doing all the damage he can before his final judgment; but because of Christ's triumph over him and his hosts (Colossians 2:15), he is not even able to "**touch**" the believer (I John 5:18). Those who try to get you to cast out demons fail to realize that a Christian cannot be possessed by a demon. It is almost blasphemous to believe that sort of thing (it matters little whether you call it oppression or possession; both amount to the same thing). Steer your counselee far away from it. You have no command to cast out demons. If you were to do so, you would have been commanded to do it.

Then Jesus addresses their truly **blasphemous** idea: attributing the work of the *Holy* **Spirit** to an *unclean* **spirit** is the height of blasphemy. Indeed, it is the **eternal** or unforgivable **sin** (vv. 29, 30). From time to time counselees will ask whether they have committed the unpardonable sin. If they are true Christians, of course, it is impossible for them to do so. Moreover, those who sinned this way were people who were opposed

29   but whoever blasphemes against the Holy Spirit will never be for-
        given, but rather will be held guilty for committing an eternal sin
30   (this He said because some had claimed, "He has an unclean spirit").
31   And His mother and His brothers came; and they stood outside and
sent someone to call Him.
32   A crowd was sitting all around Him. And they said to Him, "Your
mother and your brothers and your sisters[1] are outside asking for you."
33   But He replied: "Who are My mother and brothers?"

---

1.   Some MSS omit, *and your sisters.*

---

to Jesus and His work; those who fear they might have committed the
unforgivable sin are not opposed to Him. Just the opposite is true. It boils
down to this: tell counselees who inquire about this matter with concern
that their very concern proves otherwise. Then proceed to say, "Now, let's
deal with your forgivable sins!" What such people think is the unforgivable sin is not what Jesus said it was. They may think that homosexuality
or adultery or some other forgivable sin is **eternal** and, therefore, unforgivable. You are responsible to exegete the passage correctly, showing
them what the sin is really all about.

In verses 31 through 35 an additional incident regarding Jesus' family is recorded. Jesus was teaching outside (presumably, they couldn't get
to Him because of the **crowd**) and His **mother and brothers** were
attempting to get His attention. Finally, they sent someone **to call Him**
(vv. 31-32). When word of this came to Him (v. 32), He used the occasion
to teach those around Him about the family of faith (vv. 33-35). It is wonderful to know that one can call himself a brother or sister of Jesus by
faith. Remind counselees of that fact. It should encourage them to know
that their Elder Brother is looking out for them. Try not to miss opportunities that arise in counseling to teach truth that is in one way or another
connected to what you are doing. Jesus takes occasion to ring the changes
on a chance (providential) remark that enables Him to insert some nugget
of teaching that otherwise would not have arisen in His normal presentation. Counselors find that in counseling sessions, all sorts of opportunities
arise to do the same. Probably more arise than they should take advantage
of. But every now and then one is virtually served up on a silver platter
that is so important you simply must comment about it. You will find
yourself saying something like this: "Not to get off track, but let me make
a brief comment about what you just said." The danger is beginning a long
discussion that will cause an unnecessary digression. That is what you

34 Then looking around at those who were sitting about Him in a circle, He said, "Here are My mother and brothers;

35 whoever does God's will is My brother and sister and mother."

---

must avoid (note how I introduced the comment: "Not to get off track . . ."). Make it clear that you don't want to lose the thread of the discussion. Sometimes, rather than interrupting yourself, you might jot down a note about the matter and then, when you have completed whatever it was that you were discussing, you may come back to it. At any rate, don't fail to notice what Jesus did here in buying up the opportunity.

CHAPTER 4

1 Once again He began to teach by the sea, and a very large crowd gathered about Him, so He got into a boat that was out on the sea and sat in it, and the whole crowd stayed on the shore, facing the sea.
2 He taught them many things in parables, and in His teaching He told them:

Once again we see Jesus teaching **by the sea**. This would be a natural place to do so since the crowds could sit on the sloping hillside in a natural amphitheater. This time He found it necessary to use the **boat** since the **crowd** was so large that there was no place for Him to stand on the land. He **sat** (as Jewish teachers did when teaching) in the boat and spoke to the crowd on the shore. Jesus clearly was an open-air preacher whenever the requirements demanded it, as they did in this instance. We have seen Him in homes, in synagogs and in the outdoors teaching. He needed no fixed place. That should teach us a lot about the facilities we use. Nice facilities are fine to have, but not necessary. That is true not only for places of worship and preaching, but also for places in which to counsel. There was one time when I counseled in a church basement, another when I counseled in a microbus, a third when I counseled in a home, and there have been times when I have counseled in a well-appointed office. One of our early trainees once said, "I think you could counsel on a subway!" Well, I haven't tried it and don't want to, but I believe he was accurate. You do what you do in any circumstance. People who think they cannot counsel unless they have plush surroundings simply put the emphasis in the wrong place.

Jesus was teaching in **parables**. The word parable means "a throwing alongside:" a story is thrown down alongside a truth that the speaker wishes his hearer to learn. Everyone, from 9 to 99, loves a story. Moreover, a story is memorable; it sticks in the mind. And, when it is not explained, it causes one to ponder. Many of Christ's parables have a shocking or surprise twist to them (cf. Luke 15).

If you do not use parables in your counseling, you are failing to utilize one of the most powerful means of communicating truth. Learn how to compose and use them and you will be amazed at the difference it makes in comprehension and in the ability of the counselee to remember and transport truth to the home, the workplace or other places. Why not begin a notebook (loose leaf) in which you jot down at least one parable

3   Listen. A sower went out to sow seed,
4   and as he sowed it, some fell along the road, and the birds came
       and ate it up.
5   Some fell on a rocky place, where it didn't have much earth, and
       sprang up right away, because the earth didn't have any depth.
6   But when the sun rose, it was scorched, and because it didn't have
       any root it withered.
7   Some fell among thorns, and the thorns grew up and choked it,
       and it didn't bear fruit.
8   And some fell on fine earth and bore fruit, coming up and growing
       and yielding thirtyfold and sixtyfold and a hundredfold.
9   Then He said, "Whoever has ears to hear, let him hear."
   10 When He was alone, those who were around Him with the Twelve
asked Him about the parables,
11   and He told them,
       The secret about God's empire has been given to you, but to out-
       siders everything turns out to be in parables
12   so that **while they are truly seeing, they won't perceive, and
       while they are truly hearing, they won't understand, lest they
       should turn around and be forgiven**.

---

plot every day? Then on Saturdays you may flesh out the five parable
plots entered during the past week.

   In this chapter we hear Jesus telling the **parable** of the **sower**. After
the story (vv. 2-9), the disciples ask Him for its meaning, Jesus gives them
a detailed analysis of it (vv. 10-20). There are two parts to the **parable**.
The first part is about **seed sown** that did not produce fruit. The reasons
for the failure are varied (three are mentioned): some fell along the **road**
and the **birds** ate it; some fell on **shallow** soil, and because there was no
depth or moisture the **sun** dried it out; some fell among **thorns** that
choked it. Then in the second part of the parable three positive responses
are noted. The ground on which it was sown was acceptable for sowing
and yielded crops of thirty, sixty and one hundredfold.

   When Jesus explained, He first made it clear that they (believers) had
the **secret** (i.e., the understanding of it) about God's empire; but to others,
who did not believe, the parable remained simply—an unintelligible story.
Believers get the point; unbelievers do not. The latter **see**, but don't see;
they **hear** but don't hear. They learn the story but miss its truth. That will
always be true. But since we counsel only believers, we can expect them
to understand. If they continually fail to do so, it may be because their
profession of faith is not genuine. That is one reason to question it.

13 And He said to them,

Don't you understand this parable? How then are you going to understand any parable?

14 The sower sows the Word.

15 Some are those who are along the way where the Word is sown. And when they hear, Satan comes immediately and takes away the Word that was sown on them.

16 Likewise some are those who are the rocky places on which seed was sown, who when they hear the Word receive it at once with joy,

17 but since they don't have any root in themselves they are short-lived. When affliction or persecution comes about because of the Word, they stumble right away.

18 Some others are the ones sown among thorns. They are those who hear the Word,

19 but the worries of the times and the deceitfulness of riches and desires for other things come in and choke the Word, and it becomes unfruitful.

20 And some are those sown on the fine earth who hear the Word and accept it and bear fruit, thirtyfold and sixtyfold and a hundredfold.

Now, for the interpretation. Jesus is amazed at their inability to **understand** without an explanation (v. 13). You can see His expectation for believers is greater than theirs. That is often true of counselees. Their expectations may be very low. Don't counsel them until they have begun to have a biblical outlook on the matter. Jesus comments that if they are unable to interpret this simple parable, they will have greater trouble with more difficult ones. Remember, not all believers get the point immediately. Often you must explain it to them. If they still don't get it, that's when you might begin to question their faith.

The seed sown is the **Word**, the teaching He and His apostles would preach. Some fail to believe because **Satan**, by means of his many diversions, snatches it away like the birds. The second class of persons, hear and get excited about it, but because their response is purely emotional and shallow, it doesn't last. **Affliction** or **persecution** quickly separates them from God's truth. Those in the third category hear, too, but **worries**, (about money, etc.) are so important that they **choke** the new struggling plant. In none of these cases is fruit produced. Salvation is not a matter of belief alone, it is a matter of faith that leads to works (**fruit**). Faith expressed is not faith exercised. It is not genuine faith at all.

In the three responses of those who believe, some produce more than

21 He said to them,

> A lamp isn't brought in to be put under a measuring bowl or a bed, is it? Isn't it put on a lampstand?

22 > There isn't anything hidden that isn't to be disclosed; and there isn't anything that is covered up that isn't to be brought to light.

23 > Whoever has ears to hear, let him hear.

24 And He said to them,

> Be careful about what you hear. It will be measured out to you in the same measure that you measure it, and even more will be given to you.

---

others, but *all* produce fruit. Jesus doesn't work this out in any detail; so we won't either.

That is a very plain parable. Jesus explained it not only for its content, but also in order to help the disciples understand how to handle parables. Jesus then went on to say more about parabolic teaching (vv. 21-25). In verses 21 through 23 He made sure that the disciples understood the purpose of a **parable**. Like a **lamp**, it's purpose is to illumine. You don't light a lamp and then place it where it will shine (under a **bed or a bowl).** The intent of the parables is precisely the intent of all His teaching—to inform, persuade and motivate. Everything that they would need to know for the ministry to which He had called them, Jesus said, will be made known (v. 22). Nothing would be **covered up** or hidden. Like the **lamp**, it would be placed on a **lampstand**. This is an important fact. It should curb the thinking of those who have the idea that there is still more revelation to come. There is no special revelation either to the church in general or to individuals. It does not come through promptings, feelings, or signs. (For help on this see my book *The Christian's Guide to Guidance*.) *Everything* already *has* been **brought to light**. This is a passage that many do not realize teaches this and, when used properly, ought to make them pause to think matters through biblically. That is what **having ears to hear**, and using them for that purpose, means—it conveys the idea that one is to think seriously about what Jesus has just said. There are counselees who allow truth to run off their backs like water runs off the back of a duck. You tell them what God says from the Bible, but it just doesn't sink in. Whenever that happens, it is probably time to quote verse 23 to them!

Emphasizing the same thing even more intensively, Jesus went on to say that people should be **careful *how* they hear** (v. 24). If they will receive what He has to say with interest and faith, willing to put His words into practice, more and more of His teaching will be opened up to

25   To the one who has, more will be given, and to the one who doesn't have, even what he has will be taken from him.

26 And He said,

God's empire is like a person who scatters seed on the earth,

27   and he sleeps at night and rises by day, and the seed sprouts and grows, though he doesn't know how.

28   All on its own the earth bears fruit, first the blade, then the head, then the full grain in the head.

29   But as soon as the grain is ripe he sends forth the sickle, because the harvest has come.

---

them. Those who receive and retain His truth in that way will receive additional teaching; those who don't will find that even what they (thought) they had will slip away from them (v. 25). Truth will be **measured out** in proportion to the **measure** of importance that the counselee places on it and the amount of truth that he assimilates into his life (how he **measures** it for himself). In other words, he who appreciates and lives by what the Lord Jesus says will get more and more of it (but remember, *all* of it is available to *every* counselee; v. 22).

There are many counselees who are bereft of truth. That may be because they have not properly appreciated truth in the past. Through sinful negligence they may have lost what they did possess. One of your tasks is to encourage them to deal properly with this matter, to seek light from the Bible, and to measure out large portions of it for themselves. This is a powerful section of Scripture with which every counselor must become utterly familiar and with which he ought to use frequently in counseling. *How* a counselee hears (listens to) the Lord Jesus in His Word is all important to the success or failure of the counseling. For more on the points made here and on hearing, see my book *Teaching to Observe*.

Having made these vital remarks, Jesus continued revealing truth about the **empire** He had come to establish (Daniel's fifth empire). He revealed it in the form of two more **parables** (vv. 26-32). The first of these illustrates that, ultimately, God's empire is not spread by human effort. As Daniel said, it was a rock that was not quarried by human hands. We sow the **seed** but, beyond that, it is God who produces the growth **as we sleep** (that is to say, without human effort). When Jesus says **all on its own the earth bears fruit** what He means, of course, is not that the **earth** by itself does so, but the earth unaided by *human* effort (the earth is sustained and even held together by the very will and power of God) produces. The emphasis is, therefore, on the fact that this is an empire "made without hands," (Daniel 2:45). And, as soon as all of the

30 And He said,

> To what shall we liken God's empire, or by what parable shall we describe it?

31   It is like a mustard seed which, when it is sown on the earth, is smaller than all the seeds on the ground.

32   Yet when it is sown, it comes up and becomes larger than all the herbs, and grows branches so large that **the birds of the sky can nest in its shade**.

33 So with many such parables He spoke the Word to them as they were able to hear,

34 and He didn't speak to them without a parable. But privately, to His own disciples, He explained them all.

---

fruit is ready to be gathered in, the **harvest** (end of the world) will come (v. 29). This will be the last world empire—the empire of God.

The second parable (vv. 30-32) has to do with the size and *extent* of this empire. Though, like **a mustard seed,** it begins as a tiny entity, in time it grows into a bush large enough for **birds** to rest on its branches. It is **larger** than all the rest of the herbal plants. That is to say, as empires go (compare the previous four in Daniel) it is far and beyond them all. It is like Daniel's stone that grows and fills the entire earth. Moreover, unlike the four previous world empires, it will not give way to another; it will continue *until* the **harvest**.

Since all of this is true, the counselee should recognize the sort of government he is a part of. This is no mean kingdom or country. It is the worldwide empire of the King of kings and Lord of lords. Knowing that, he should think and act like the subject of a great kingdom with many resources, who is acquainted with the King and not like some impoverished peon groveling before others, not knowing where to turn for help. Try to instill proper attitudes in your counselees; when they adopt them, counseling will become more effective.

These parables are but samplings of the sorts of things Jesus spoke to the disciples about in parables (v. 33). Indeed, Mark says, from about this time, everything He said was in parables. That means that those who had ears to hear, heard; those who didn't, failed to do so. His **disciples** had all of the **parables explained** to them **privately** because they **measured out** a goodly measure of truth for themselves. They were anxious to learn, though at times slow to comprehend. They found that nothing truly would be **hidden** that would not be **disclosed**. Jesus provided them with all the data they needed. They came into "all truth." All things necessary for life and godliness were given to them. They, in turn, supplied it to us in the

35 Now on that day, when evening had come, He said to them, "Let's cross over to the other side."

36 Leaving the crowd, they took Him, just as He was, in the boat (and other boats were with Him).

37 But there arose a storm with strong winds, and the waves splashed into the boat so that the boat was already filling.

38 And He was in the stern, sleeping on the cushion. So they woke Him and said to Him, "Teacher, don't you care that we are perishing?"

39 He awoke and rebuked the wind and said to the sea, "Quiet; be muzzled!" And the wind died down and there was a great calm.

40 Then He said to them, "Why are you afraid like this? Don't you have any faith?"

41 But they were terrified and said to one another, "Who is this anyway, that both the wind and the sea obey Him?"

---

books they wrote.

In verses 35 through 41 we read more about Jesus' sovereign authority—this time over nature itself. As they crossed over to the other side to escape the crowds, a **storm** arose that threatened to swamp the **boat**. Jesus was **asleep**. They awakened Him with a mild rebuke: **"Teacher, don't you care that we are perishing?"** He, in turn, rebuked the wind, and all grew **calm**. Then, rebuking them, He asked **"Why are you afraid like this? Don't you have any faith?"** They had been with Him long enough, listening to him and watching Him heal, to know that He could control nature. But, so far, they had not seen Him do so. So, because of their lack of faith in raising the question, we now have a record of this miracle in which He demonstrates His authority over nature. This, of all the miracles, elicited the most emotional response from the disciples thus far (v. 41). Often Jesus uses occasions when we fail to teach us and others additional lessons. There are times to make that point in teaching counselees; you might say, "If in God's providence you had not failed this way, you would not have learned the truth that God wanted you to learn so graphically." In this way God can even turn our evil into good.

Counselees need not fear that their Lord will desert them or leave them to the ravages of nature. Whatever happens in this world is under His absolute control. If He does not always calm the seas immediately, knowing that at the very least He can, ought to calm their souls.

CHAPTER 5

1 So they came to the other side of the sea to the Gerasenes' country.
2 And as soon as He left the boat, a man with an unclean spirit came from the tombs to meet Him.
3 He lived among the tombs, and nobody could keep him bound any longer, even with chains.
4 The fact is that he had often been bound hand and foot with chains, but he tore apart the chains on his hands and smashed those on his feet, and nobody was strong enough to subdue him.
5 Night and day among the tombs and on the mountains he continually shouted and cut himself with stones.

The first 20 verses contain the account of the Lord's healing of the **Gerasene demoniac**. Huxley fiercely attacked this account as ludicrous, but there is no *a priori* reason for dismissing it out of hand as he did. If **demons** can possess a human being, why not an animal as well? If one human being, by means of hypnotism, may direct the actions of another, why not another personal being—such as a demon?

The accounts of healings and castings out of demons are plainly differentiated in the Gospels; they are never confused. Strange behavior or sickness may be caused by disease, by demonic possession, or by acting in a manner to make others think one is mad; all these causes are distinguished in the Bible. The concept of demon possession is not a description of primitive behavior that actually stems from another source. The counselor, then, has no reason for determining that a counselee is demon-possessed simply by observing that his behavior is bizarre or deviant. Too many do such a thing.

The demoniac lived on **the other side of the lake** where Jesus and His disciples landed after their trip across the sea of Galilee. This was a predominantly Gentile area, so there was no reason why the farmers in the area should not have been raising **pigs**. They were, of course, "unclean" for Jews. But in the context no point is made concerning their ceremonial uncleanness. What the main thrust of the narrative is we soon shall see.

This man showed interesting symptoms of the demon possession. First, he seemed to have acquired superhuman strength. He also dwelt among the **tombs** and he **cut himself with sharp stones** (vv. 1-5). He dwelt in the graveyard. Jesus commanded the demons to leave the man. The many demons within (they called themselves **Legion**, a Roman mili-

6 But when he saw Jesus from a distance, he ran and fell on his knees before Him,

7 and shouting with a loud voice, he said, "What do you want with me, Jesus, Son of the Most High God? Swear to God that you won't torture me"

8 (He was saying to him, "Come out of the man, you unclean spirit!").

9 And He asked him, "What is your name?" He said to Him, "My name is Legion, because there are a lot of us."

10 And he begged Him insistently not to send them out of the country.

11 Now there was a large herd of pigs feeding there near the mountain,

12 and they begged Him, saying, "Send us to the pigs that we may enter into them."

13 So He permitted them to do so. And the unclean spirits came out and entered into the pigs, and the herd of about two thousand rushed over the precipice, fell into the sea and were drowned in the sea.

14 The herdsmen fled and reported this to people in the city and in the fields, and they came to see what had happened.

15 But when they came to Jesus, and saw the demoniac who had been possessed by the legion sitting down, clothed and sane, they were afraid.

16 Those who had seen it told what had happened to the demoniac and about the pigs.

17 And they began to beg Him to leave their territory.

---

tary term used popularly to mean a great number of persons) brought the man to his **knees** and, using the man's voice, begged Jesus not to **torture** them. Notice that they wanted also to remain in that **country** (vv. 6-10). This is an interesting sidelight that indicates demons might travel from place to place, but not necessarily. The **demons** themselves **begged** to be sent into a **large herd of pigs feeding** nearby. Jesus allowed them to do so. Consequently, the pigs, frightened by this, rushed over the **precipice** and were drowned in the sea. What happened to the demons is an interesting question—about which we will not speculate.

Jesus has control of all things. Why He was willing to have that herd destroyed (so far as proximate causes go) we simply do not know. The bottom line, however, is that the incident once again demonstrated in a remarkable way in this heathen land His power over all things.

The **herdsmen fled into the city and fields**, told everyone about the occurrence, so they all came to see what had happened. They were afraid when they found out and **begged** Jesus to **leave their territory**. The upshot is that, in their minds (at least at this point) swine meant more than souls. That is an evaluation many still make. They would rather see Jesus

18 Now as He was getting into the boat, the man who had been a demoniac begged Him to let him go with Him,

19 but He refused and said to him instead, "Go home to your people and tell them the things that the Lord has done for you, and how He has shown mercy to you."

20 Then he left and began to preach in the Decapolis about the things that Jesus did for him, and everybody was amazed.

21 Now when Jesus had crossed over again to the other side by boat, a great crowd gathered before Him, and He was beside the sea.

22 One of the synagog rulers, named Jairus, came, and when he saw Him he fell at His feet

23 and urgently begged him in these words, "My daughter is about to die; come, lay your hands on her, so that she may be healed and live!"

---

leave than lose some of their possessions. Even Christian counselees may be in this mode of thinking. Help your counselees to take a different tack. Jesus is more important than anything else.

The former demoniac wanted to accompany Jesus as He was about to leave by **boat,** but Jesus wouldn't let him (v. 18). Instead, in contrast to His policy in Israel, Jesus told the man to return to his **people** as a missionary (v. 19). Presumably, this was because He did not intend to visit the area again. Jesus clearly shows His flexibility in all things. Don't become canned and refrigerated in your approach to people, counselor. Size up each circumstance and act accordingly. Be ready to swing with each session for what it may hold.

The man actually began to **preach** about Jesus throughout the **Decapolis** (the ten-city Gentile region of Galilee) with what seems to be positive results (v. 20). The Gentile mission of Jesus was in one sense aborted (He was asked to leave). But through this man, the mission continued. When something seems to come to an unfruitful end in counseling, don't necessarily give up on it. Think of some way to make the message you have been trying to inculcate continue to affect the counselee who tells you he wants to quit counseling. Leave behind some Scripture, some striking or memorable statement, or a person who will continue to work with him.

Jesus **crossed over** the sea again and found a **great crowd** awaiting Him. That was certainly a contrast! In your counseling you, too, will move from one sort of response to its opposite from time to time. Sometimes it will be hard to adjust, but you must learn to do so. A **synagog ruler, named Jairus**, begged Jesus to heal his **daughter** who was dying.

253

24 So he went with him.
Now a great crowd followed Him and pushed against Him.
25 And a woman who had for twelve years had a problem with bleeding,
26 and had suffered much under the care of many doctors, and had spent everything that she had, but rather than getting any better only grew worse,
27 when she heard about what Jesus was doing, came behind in the crowd and touched His clothes.
28 She said to herself, "If I can even touch His clothes, I will be healed."
29 Instantly the bleeding stopped, and she had the sensation in her body that she was cured of her trouble.
30 But Jesus immediately knew inside Himself that power had gone forth from Him, turned around in the crowd and said, "Who touched My clothes?"
31 His disciples said to Him, "You see the crowd pushing against You and You say, 'Who touched Me?'
32 But He looked around to see who had done it.
33 Now the woman, knowing what had happened to her, came and fell before Him, afraid and trembling, and told Him the whole truth.
34 Then He said to her, "Daughter, your faith has healed you. Go in peace and be healthy, now that your trouble has gone."

Jesus went home with him (vv. 23, 24). The **crowd followed and pushed** and jostled Jesus as they proceeded. And a **woman who had bleeding** that had lasted for **twelve years,** and had **spent all she had on doctors** (who could not help her; reminds you of modern psychiatry, doesn't it?) **touched His clothes. Instantly** she was healed. Jesus knew that **power had gone forth from Him** and asked, **"Who touched My clothes?"** The disciples thought, "What is He asking? All sorts of people in this crowd are touching Him!" But the woman understood the question and admitted she was the one, falling down before Him in thankful worship. Jesus said, **"Your faith has healed you."** Without **faith,** it is impossible to please God. James says that one seeking God's answers to his prayers must come in faith, believing. Doubt, unbelief or vacillation about the matter all hinder in receiving help from God. Make this clear to your counselees. If they do not exercise faith in the promises of God in the Bible, they should not expect Him to respond to their need. That does not mean that God is not sometimes better to us than our attitudes would deserve. He is a God of Grace and mercy Who often takes pity on His erring children. But it does mean that they should *expect* nothing from the Lord until they do believe (James 1:7).

As He was making that statement about faith, some people came

35 While He was still speaking, some people came from the synagog ruler's house, saying, "Your daughter has died. Why hassle the teacher any longer?"

36 But Jesus, paying no attention to their word, said to the synagog ruler, "Don't be afraid; just believe."

37 But He didn't allow anybody to go along with Him except Peter and James and John, the brother of James.

38 When they arrived at the synagog ruler's home, He saw that the situation was chaotic, with people crying and loudly wailing.

39 So when He went in, He said to them, "Why are you creating such chaos and wailing? The child hasn't died; she is sleeping."

40 But they sneered at Him. So He sent all of them outside and took the child's father and mother and those who were with Him, and went in where the child was.

41 Then, He took the child by the hand and said to her, "Talitha koum" (which, translated, means, "Little girl, I say to you, get up").

42 Immediately the little girl got up and walked (she was twelve years old). At this they were utterly stunned with amazement.

43 Then He strongly ordered them that they should let nobody know about this and told them to give her something to eat.

---

who said to Jairus, "**Your daughter has died**." But Jesus comforted him and said, "**Just believe**" (an additional emphasis on the crucial role of faith). Arriving at the synagog ruler's home, they were met by the **chaotic weeping and wailing** that usually accompanied death in that culture. The professional mourners had already taken over! Jesus told them that the child wasn't dead but **only sleeping**. In response, they **sneered at Him**. So He sent them outside and, together with the father, mother, and some close friends or relatives, went in. He said to the girl, "**get up**." Immediately she did so, and all were stunned. He ordered them not to tell anyone what He had done, and told them to **give her something to eat** (thus making it clear that it was not a spirit that they were seeing, but the flesh-and-blood girl herself). Because Jairus is named, even though people at the time didn't know, they could later check with him or his friends after this account was published.

Now what should we make of this incident? Much could be said. First, notice that it is the account of a double healing (actually, one account within another). That is how Jesus worked. He was never hurried. He took His time to do as He thought best even if it meant delaying something else. The delay, moreover, gave opportunity for Him to demonstrate His authority over death. It seems this was what He calculated.

Note, also, how Jesus picks one person out of the crowd. He is concerned with individuals who believe. You, too, should focus on those who show faith (if you must choose from among many). You cannot help everyone. If all the mentioning of crowds makes your counselee think that Jesus doesn't care about persons as individuals, then let him read this account.

Again, Jesus' **power to heal** flowed out of Him in such a way that He was aware of it. There is deep theology in that fact. (There isn't space here to examine it carefully enough.) Once more, notice the futility of the medical profession and their willingness to bleed this woman dry of all her funds while never drying up her flow of actual blood. They, of course, had none of our modern technology. But counselors, psychiatrists, and psychologists, who take money on the pretense of helping when they know that they can't, are in the same league with these doctors—or perhaps even worse. There are even Christians who counsel in unbiblical ways and take all the money they can from "patients" then drop them when they have no more money left. Some things don't change very much. Pastors counseling with the Word and the Spirit counsel freely in Christ's name as a part of their ministries.

Finally, don't miss the encouragement in the words, "**Just believe**." Without faith, it is impossible to please God. Every counselor must have faith in the Word of God and the God of the Word if his counseling is to be successful in the biblical sense of that word. You can be sure that you will convey your faith (or your lack of it) to the counselee. When things are not going well in counseling, and a counselee seems lethargic about what he is doing, check out *his* faith. That could be the problem. The chapter that we have been considering tells you about the importance of faith; don't fail to see this.

CHAPTER 6

1 Now He left there and went to His home town, and His disciples followed Him.

2   When the Sabbath came, He began to teach in the synagog, and the
large number who heard Him were astonished and said, "Where did He
learn these things? and "What is this wisdom that has been given to Him?
and "How can He do such miracles by His hands?" and

3   "Isn't this the carpenter—Mary's son, and the brother of James and
Joses and Judas and Simon?" and "Aren't his sisters here with us?" And
they stumbled over Him.

4   So Jesus said to them, "A prophet isn't without honor except in his
home town and among his relatives and in his home."

Chapter six is longer than those we have considered so far. The
chapter begins with **Jesus** and His **disciples** journeying to His **home
town**, which was Nazareth (v. 1). On the **Sabbath**, we find Him in the
local **synagog teaching**. A **large** number of people have gathered to hear
Him and are **astonished at** what they hear and see. **They** wonder where
Jesus learned all that He is setting forth. They are especially amazed at
His **wisdom and the miracles** He is performing (v. 2). They remember
that while growing up, Jesus had worked for Joseph as a **carpenter**; they
know that **Mary** is His mother and that He has other members of the family still living there. Because of this "familiarity that breeds contempt"
they stumbled over Him. That is to say, they had a difficult time respect-
ing Him for what He had become (v. 3). There are people who, instead of
saying, "Look, the home town boy has made good; how wonderful!" will
respond in the opposite manner, pooh-poohing whatever he says and does
because they "knew him *when*." You are likely to discover that same
dynamic at work if you try to minister in the place where you grew up.
Because of it, it is often wise to minister elsewhere, as Jesus did after they
rejected Him (vv. 4ff.). This idea is probably behind Jesus' comments
about *leaving* father, mother, sister or brother. It seems as though He contemplated that most who would serve Him would find it necessary to do
so. But there are always a few—a remnant—who seem to be faithful (v.
5). You may find the same true in your case.

When Jesus quoted the proverb about a **prophet** being honored
everywhere else but in his **home town**, He was hitting the nail squarely on
the head. Whether He was quoting an older proverb or coining it afresh

5   Now He couldn't do any miracles there, except to lay His hands on a few sick people whom He healed.
6   So, amazed at their unbelief, He went to the surrounding villages and taught.
7 Then He called the Twelve to Him and began to send them out in pairs and gave them authority over unclean spirits.
8   And He gave them instructions not to take anything on their trip except a staff—no bread, no wallets, no money in their belts.
9   They were to wear sandals, but not a second tunic.
10 He said to them,
        Wherever you enter a house, stay there until you leave the place.
11   And if any place won't receive you or listen to you, when you leave it, shake the dust off your feet as a testimony against them.
12 So they went out and preached that people must repent,
13 and they cast out many demons, and they rubbed oil on many sick people and healed them.

---

really doesn't matter. Because of Jesus' trenchant use of it in this context, we have come to use it ever after to summarize the truth it expresses. The large crowds of those who came for healing elsewhere, were not present here at home (indeed, only a very few were helped) because of their unbelief. So He left and ministered to those who really respected Him (vv. 5, 6).

One of the sad facts is that Jesus' **relatives** were explicitly included among those who **stumbled** (v. 4). It is probably wise not to attempt to counsel relatives or those who have been close to you over the years. It would be better to refer them to another biblical counselor whom you trust. If, however, there is no one else available, you may wish to do as I have done in such situations—tell the friend or relative something like this, "I would prefer to have someone else counsel you. But since that isn't possible, here are the ground rules that you and I will have to observe: First, you must not take anything I say as personal between you and me. And, second, I shall try as much as possible to treat you as I would any other counselee."

Jesus now sends His **disciples** out on a mission of **healing** and **teaching** (vv. 7-13). This was to be a brief, hurried trip; they were to take minimal supplies with them. Like John and Jesus, their message is described as preaching **repentance** (v. 12). Don't miss the continuity of the message throughout the New Testament. What a tragedy that so few counselors today fail to stand in that line of those who call people to

14 Now King Herod heard about Him, since His name had become well known. They were saying, "John the Baptist has been raised from the dead; that's why he is able to do miracles."

15 But others said, "He is Elijah." And still others said, "He is a prophet like one of the prophets of the past."

16 But when Herod heard these things, he said, "John, the one I beheaded, has been raised."

---

repentance. No counseling may proceed successfully if necessary repentance is neglected. Is that failure one reason why you are not having the success you would like in counseling?

The interesting thing about the orders concerning this trip is that the **disciples** were not even to take a **wallet**. That means no money. They were to live off the gratitude of the people to whom they preached. Whenever they entered a **house**, they were to remain there (they were not to move around to "better" accommodations later on). If a town refused to give them lodging and to hear their message they were to **shake the dust off their feet as a testimony against them**—and leave. That act was a very graphic way of saying, "OK, if you will have nothing to do with us, we will have nothing to with you. We won't even take the dust from your city with us; we leave everything behind *just as it was before we came.*" There are times to make a clean break with those who refuse to hear. Keep that in mind. Though there were obviously places where they did these things (or Jesus would not have given instructions to do so), there were also places where they were gladly received. In those places, they **cast out demons** and **healed** many with medicinally-aided means (v. 13).

In verses 14 through 20, we read about Jesus and **King Herod**. Herod had heard of the fame of Jesus and was afraid that He was **John the Baptist** (whom he had put to death) risen from the dead (v. 14). His guilty conscience must have driven him to this conclusion. People everywhere were speculating as to who Jesus was. Some speculated **that He was Elijah**, since Malachi had predicted his future coming (in John the Baptist, who was Elijah-*like*), others said a **prophet**, but Herod insisted that he was **John** (vv. 15, 16). Misunderstanding the Bible, a desire to speculate, or a guilty conscience all may lead to faulty interpretations of one's circumstances. Be aware of each of these possibilities and look for them when counselees begin to wildly flail about in their minds as to what is happening. Especially look at radical interpretations of the Bible (such as Herod's). Guilt could be at the bottom of them.

The story of John's **imprisonment** as the result of **Herodias'**

17 He said this because Herod himself had sent to have John seized, and had bound him in prison at the encouragement of Herodias, his brother Philip's wife, whom he had married.

18 You see, John had been saying to Herod, "It isn't right for you to have your brother's wife."

19 So Herodias had it in for him and wanted to kill him, but couldn't

20 because Herod was afraid of John, since he knew that he was a just and holy man, and he protected him. And whenever he heard him, he became very confused; yet he liked to listen to him.

21 But at last the right day came, when on his birthday Herod gave a dinner party for his nobles, the military officers, and the leading persons in Galilee.

22 When Herodias' daughter came in and danced, she pleased Herod and his guests. So the king said to the girl, "Whatever you want, ask me for it, and I'll give it to you."

---

encouragement, the **preaching** of John against Herod's adultery and the death of John, all served to strike **fear** into Herod's heart (vv. 17-20). Herod knew he had done a dastardly thing against John. The fear led to his confusion, as did the preaching of John when he was yet alive. He knew John was right, and he even enjoyed John's preaching; but at the same time he wanted to continue in his sin. Moreover, the hatred of Herodias' nagging him to get rid of John was part of what weighed heavily on Herod's mind (vv. 18-20). Here was an enormously guilty man whose conscience was wrecking havoc in him. People who imagine things are often those who have unconfessed and unforgiven guilt that is driving them to suppose unlikely scenarios. So-called paranoia is sometimes a matter of guilt driving a counselee. Whenever it is determined that counselee's strange thinking or behavior is not due to drugs or sleep loss, look into the possibility that his behavior is a result of the next most common cause, guilt.

In verses 21 through 29 the terrible story of the death of **John** is told in some depth. It is the story of a scheming, bitter and hateful woman, her use of her daughter's sex appeal and the fall of a lecherous old man. It also shows how pride and thoughtless speech can be one's downfall (vv. 23, 26). How important these verses are in showing that following one's feelings and indulging one's pride can cause him trouble! Since the story is so graphic, it may be used with great profit as a strong warning to counselees afflicted with the same problems. Those who are so afflicted are not few in number. You will meet them frequently in counseling. Sometimes the

23 And he said to her in an oath, "Whatever you ask I'll give you—up to half my kingdom!"

24 So she left and said to her mother, "What should I ask for?" And she replied, "John the Baptist's head!"

25 So right away she hurried off to the king and asked him in these words: "I want you to give me John the Baptist's head on a platter right away."

26 Now, the king became terribly upset, but because of his oaths and his guests he didn't want to go back on his word to her.

27 So immediately the king sent an executioner with orders to bring John's head,

28 and he brought his head on a platter and gave it to the girl, and the girl gave it to her mother.

29 When his disciples heard about it, they went and took his corpse and laid it in a tomb.

30 The apostles returned to Jesus and reported to Him everything that they did and that they taught.

31 Then He said to them, "Come away by yourselves to a lonely spot and rest for a little while" (many people were coming and going, and they didn't have an opportunity to eat).

---

consequences of pride and thoughtless speech are not considered seriously enough. Whenever you hear it from a counselee, warn him strongly. The consequences here are indicative of the sort of damage that can be done.

Having gone out to preach, heal and cast out demons, the **apostles** returned (note in v. 30 that the name **apostles**, "sent forth ones," is first used here of the disciples). They gave Jesus a full **report** of their activities and of the results (v. 30). Jesus recognized that they had worked hard and endured much, so He urged them to **rest** a while. They had not even had an opportunity to **eat** since they returned (v. 31). He cares about such matters. When preachers and counselors talk about "burning out for the Lord," that is not a worthy goal to set before counselees. If, indeed, providential circumstances should warrant this happening in particular cases, so be it. But to set it forth as an ideal is another thing altogether. Jesus wants His servants to recuperate from hard labor so that they may be able to work more years and more efficiently. Keep that in mind both for yourself and for some counselees who have very wrong ideas about the matter. According to verse 31, Jesus endorses the proper pursuit of rest from labor. This, of course, was set forth originally by God in His example at creation and in His ordination of the Sabbath day of rest. There are coun-

32 So they went off in the boat to a lonely spot by themselves.
33 But they saw them going, and many recognized them and together ran there on foot from all the cities, and got there before them.
34 When He got out, He saw a large crowd and had compassion on them, because they were like sheep without a shepherd. So He began to teach them many things.
35 When the hour grew late, His disciples came to Him and said,
      This is a lonely spot and the hour is late.
36   Send them away so that they may go away to the fields and villages round about and buy themselves something to eat.

---

selees who, if they were to rest a bit from the frenzied lives they live, would soon be able to get their homes and their jobs in order. Never forget this matter; Jesus didn't (v. 31). Good counselors always consider rest important to overworked counselees and do not hesitate to talk about it with them.

There are times when you will find people so desperate (and thoughtless) that they will not even allow such rest if they can get what they want. Jesus' **compassion** overcame His desire for rest (presumably He too was exhausted) and He **taught** them (v. 34). Notice, however, that the most important matter for Him was that **they were as sheep without a shepherd**. That means that their lives were disorderly, rebellious, pitiful. They were as sheep who were left by the Pharisees and other religious leaders of the day to wander into paths of sin and vanity. You are to shepherd wandering sheep in counseling. And in doing so, it is important that they be **taught**. Wandering sheep are people who have lost the way. They need to be pointed to the way of the Lord (cf. Isaiah 55:8) that is taught in His Word (see my book *Teaching to Observe*). Sometimes, today, the failure to recognize that what people need is **teaching** leads counselors into many other side issues and endeavors. Fundamentally, wandering sheep who have no one to lead them need the teaching of a true shepherd. That means that whenever you see poor, pitiful counselees wandering aimlessly in ways that displease God, you should instantly think, "What is it that they need to learn from the Bible? How may I best teach them God's way?"

Only after He ministered to their spiritual needs did Jesus minister to the material needs of the crowd (vv. 35-44). That was triggered by concern that was exhibited by the disciples for them (vv. 35, 36; and perhaps for themselves as well—cf. v. 31[b]). At any rate, it would seem that their hunger led them to mention the hunger of the crowds. It is often wise to

37   But He answered them by saying, "You give them something to eat." They said to Him, "Do you want us to go and buy two hundred denarii's worth of bread and give it to them to eat?"
38   Then He said to them, "How many pieces of bread do you have? Go and look." When they found out, they said, "Five, and two fish."
39   So He directed them to sit down on the green grass in groups by hundreds and by fifties.
40   They sat down in groups by hundreds and by fifties.
41   Then He took the five pieces of bread and the two fish, looked up to heaven, gave thanks, broke the pieces of bread and gave them to the disciples to set before them. He divided the two fish among all of them.
42   And they all ate and were satisfied,
43   and they collected twelve baskets full of broken pieces of bread and fish.
44   Now there were five thousand men who ate the pieces of bread.

---

think of your own wishes and needs when you are ministering to others; frequently theirs will parallel yours.

The disciples had been doing miracles (healing, casting out demons). Jesus now tests their faith in Him to provide all they need to minister in His Name. He says, "**You give them something to eat**" (v. 37). How could they with their meager supplies (**five loaves and two fish**) feed such a crowd as this? The answer? Only by a miracle. If Jesus so ordered, He would supply the means. They did not need to know beforehand what Jesus would do or how He would do it. They simply needed to turn to Him for the ability to fulfill His command, even as He had given them the ability previously to do so. In faith, they should have said something like, "Simply tell us what to do and we will do it Lord."

The very same *principle* is true today—even though you will not be performing miracles in Jesus' Name. The counselee may look to Jesus to supply both the wisdom and the ability to obey what He commands. You may tell counselees, with assurance, that Jesus never commands His children to do anything for which He fails to provide the resources, ability and means. It is good to know that every command of Jesus is a source of hope. If He commands His own to do something, it *can* be done!

Of course, the rest of the story is well known. Jesus feeds the five thousand [men] (v. 44). But often there is one element in the story that is forgotten: **they collected twelve baskets full of broken pieces** that were left over. Not only does this show that Jesus was thrifty and would not allow something to be wasted, but of even more significance, He demon-

263

45 Next, Jesus made His disciples get into the boat and go ahead of Him to Bethsaida on the other side while He was dismissing the crowd.

46 After He said good-bye to them, He went to the mountains to pray.

47 Now when evening came, the boat was in the middle of the sea, and He was alone on the land.

48 And He saw that they were having a hard time rowing because the wind was against them. About the fourth watch of the night He went to them, walking on the sea as if He intended to go by them.

49 But when they saw Him walking on the sea, they thought He was a ghost and screamed

50 (they all saw Him and were terrified). But then He spoke to them and said to them, "Calm down. It is I. Don't be afraid."

51 So He went up to them into the boat, and the wind stopped, and in themselves they were dumbfounded

52 because they didn't understand about the pieces of bread; rather, their hearts were hardened.

---

strated to all (but especially to the disciples who had thought that there was nothing to feed the people with) that He can do far more than is necessary to satisfy. He is the God of abundance. How important for the counselor to assure counselees that Jesus is not only able to supply all things necessary to meet their needs, but also is able to do a great deal more. Never forget that point when counseling dubious counselees (like these disciples). People who doubt need to hear that Jesus is not only adequate but also is far more than adequate.

In verses 45 through 52, again we see how Jesus is capable of transcending the nature that He, as the second Person of the Trinity, created and sustains. Not only could He calm the raging sea, but He also demonstrated that He could **walk** on it (v. 48)! The disciples, once more, mistake what is happening (v. 49); they think He is a **ghost**. But Jesus **calmed** them, told them not to **fear**, and then got into the **boat** with them. There are times when Jesus needs to strike confusion—and even fear—into counselees' hearts in order to teach them and to show them His power. The disciples had not appreciated what He was teaching them in the miracle of the multiplying loaves (see above), so they were unable to appreciate what was happening in the miracle of His walking on the water (vv. 51, 52). Their **hearts were hardened**. Obviously, this hardening was not the same as the hardening of Pharaoh or of the Pharisees; here the word refers to true but weak believers. Their hearts, it seems, were hardened so as to block the understanding that they should have had. Counsel-

53 Now when they had crossed over to the land, they came to Gennesaret and anchored.

54 And as soon as they left the boat the people recognized Him

55 and ran all around that whole area and began to bring sick people on stretchers to wherever they heard that He was.

56 So wherever He went into villages or cities or country, they laid the sick in the marketplaces and begged Him even to let them touch the edge of His clothes, and all who touched Him were healed.

---

ees, though Christians, will often fail to understand all you attempt to communicate to them because of **hard** (sluggish, as Alexander puts it) **hearts**. Since Jesus didn't give up on people like this, neither should you. Perhaps when the boat landed and multiple healings began to take place once more (vv. 53-56), their hearts began to melt.

CHAPTER 7

1 Now, when the Pharisees and some of the scribes from Jerusalem came to Jesus,

2 they saw some of His disciples eating food with common (that is, unwashed) hands—

3 This I say because the Pharisees and all the Jews hold to the elders' traditions by not eating unless they wash their hands up to the elbows.

4 And when they come from the marketplaces, they don't eat unless they sprinkle[1] first; and there are many other traditions that they hold, like the baptizing of cups, jugs and copper kettles[2]—

5 and the Pharisees and the scribes questioned Him, "Why don't your disciples walk according to the elders' traditions rather than eating food with common hands?"

---

1. Or, *baptize* (with some MSS).
2. Some MSS add, *and beds.*

In this chapter, Mark highlights the problems Jesus had with the religious leaders that ultimately would lead to His death. True, their consternation with Him and their desire to remove Him had already been manifested. But here we see the conflict etched in strong terms. One of the ways they attacked Jesus was to attack the actions of His disciples (vv. 1-13). The attacks led to some very important teaching by the Lord Jesus for which we can only be grateful. The issue presented here centered around a conflict between the truth of God and the **elders' traditions** (v. 3). These **traditions** had been designed to protect people from violating the law, but instead came to replace God's law. The one mentioned here was the ceremonial **washing of hands up to the elbows** before **eating** (v. 3). Several other foolish **traditions** are mentioned in verse 4.

Because Jesus did not require His disciples to observe these customs, the Pharisees and the scribes interrogated Him (there is no milder expression one might appropriately use) about the matter (v. 5). You, too, will run into counselees who are steeped in traditions of the modern church that have no biblical foundation at all. It should be important to you to remember how Jesus handled these situations so that you may emulate Him.

Jesus considered those who insisted on such observances **hypocrites.** He even called them such to their faces. Why? Because they made quite a show of following **human commandments** while **letting go of God's**

6   And He said to them,
        Isaiah properly prophesied about you hypocrites! As it is written:
        **These people honor Me with the lips
        but their hearts are far away from Me.**
7   **They worship Me in vain,
        teaching human commandments as their teachings.**
8   You let go of God's commandments and hold on to human tradi-
        tion!
    9   Then He told them:
        You do a fine job of setting aside God's commandment so that you
        may keep your tradition.
10   For example, Moses said, **Honor your father and your mother,**
        and **Whoever curses his father or mother must be
        stopped by death.**

(vv. 7, 8). As a result, their **worship** of God was **in vain**. Their **hearts,**
therefore, were far away from God, as Jesus pointed out in quoting the
appropriate passage from **Isaiah** (v. 6). Whenever anyone adds to God's
commandments, you may be sure that the commandments of men will
soon take over and become more important than the commandments of
God. There are legalists of all sorts out there who get themselves into
many difficulties because they attempt to follow these humanly-devised
commands and live as if God had said nothing about concocting them.
But they often get into trouble when they try to impose them on others.
You may have to do a major job of peeling off these accretions if you want
to help such counselees. This passage will be of value in doing so. The
comparison between man's and God's **commands** is stark. Verse 9 puts it
flatly: **You do a fine job of setting aside God's commandment so that
you may keep your tradition.**

Then Jesus gave an **example** (v. 10). There was a **tradition** that one
could say **corban** with reference to a **gift;** that meant that he might keep
and use for himself money that he might otherwise use to help an aged
father or mother. And by means of this practice, God's command to
honor father and mother was **set aside.** Thus, by the tradition, the Pharisee was able to **annul** the Word of God (v. 13). And, as Jesus pointed out,
this was not the only tradition of the sort; He said, **you do a number of
such things** (v. 13).

How did Jesus handle this matter? He went into it in some detail. He
gave **examples** of what He was talking about. He pointed out the **hypocrisy** in it, and He showed the seriousness of it. That is what you must do

11   But you say, "If a person says to his father or mother, 'Whatever benefit you might have received from me is Corban (that is a consecrated gift),'"

12   then you allow him from then on to do nothing for his father or mother,

13   thereby annulling God's Word by the tradition that you have received. And you do a number of such things.

   14 So He called the crowd again and said to them,
        Listen to Me, every one of you, and understand:

15   There isn't anything that enters a person from the outside that can make him common. Rather, it is the things that come out from the person that defile him.

16   [1]

17 When He left the crowd and entered a house, His disciples questioned Him about the parable.

18   He said to them:
        So, you don't understand either. Don't you know that anything that enters a person from the outside can't make him common

---

1.   Some MSS add vs. 16: *Whoever has ears to hear, let him hear.*

---

when dealing with the sort of hypocrisy you find among some types of Christians who, as I said, often come for counseling because following human traditions has landed them in great trouble. You must deal with the matter straightforwardly, as Jesus did. He was "in their faces," as we have recently learned to say.

The Lord Jesus not only made His point with the hypocrites, but He also took advantage of the occasion to speak to the crowd about the matter, setting forth a vital principle: it is not what a person ingests that **defiles** him (the person's own inner life is already **defiled**). It is the heart of man, steeped in sin and wickedness, that is his problem, not some outer observance he may fail to keep. Learn the principle in verse 15. Consider Jesus' words of admonition in verse 14 to **listen** and to **understand** it. That is an important principle for every counselor to understand and be able to state clearly for counselees whenever appropriate. Outer change alone is not enough. There must first be inner change that leads to the outer.

The denseness of the disciples once more is the occasion for a further discourse by Jesus. They ask Him the meaning of the saying, which they describe as a b. There was but one Hebrew word (*mashal)* that referred to all sorts of unusual ways of saying things. It could refer to a proverb or a

19   because it doesn't enter his heart but his stomach, and goes out
           into the drain?
(By saying this He declared all foods clean.)
20   Then He said,
           What comes out of a person makes him common.
21   I say this because from within, from people's hearts, come out evil
           thoughts, sexual sins, theft, murder,
22   adultery, greed, wickedness, deceit, lewdness, envy, blasphemy,
           arrogance and foolishness.
23   All of these wicked things come out from within and make a per-
           son common.

24   Now He got up and went away from there to the district of Tyre.[1]
And when He entered a house, He didn't want anybody to know it, but He
couldn't be hidden.
25   Rather, right away a woman who had a daughter with an unclean spirit
heard about Him and came and fell down at His feet.
26   Now the woman was a Greek of the Syrophoenician race. And she
asked Him to cast the demon out of her daughter.
27   He said to her, "Let the children be fed first; it isn't right to take the
children's bread and throw it to the pet dogs."

---

1.   Some MSS add, *and Sidon.*

---

parable, etc. That is the term used here. Jesus explains His saying (vv. 18-
23). What a person eats doesn't affect the disposition of his heart. It goes
through him and has only physical effects on him; not spiritual ones.
(vv. 18, 19). Indeed, by this, Mark points out that Jesus **declared all foods
clean** (v. 19). Mark doesn't mean that it was His intention to do so at that
very moment, but that the statement Jesus made logically would lead to
such a conclusion—as indeed is true. If food could not make one **common** (i.e., unclean, defiled), then all foods were equal (the old dietary
laws could not be applied any longer once one realized this).

     He went on to say that it is the evil words and actions that proceed
from the wicked heart that defile and make one **common** (v. 20). And then
He poured forth a list of such foul things—all of which come from the
evil heart of man. The counselor must make this clear to every counselee—if he is to cleanse his life before God, it will be not by making lists
of things to avoid saying or doing, but to have such a change of heart that
he would not think of saying or doing them. Remember, the change first
must be **within** (v. 23).

     The next section of this chapter is found in verses 24 through 30.

28 But she answered Him, "Of course, Lord, but even the pet dogs under the table eat the children's crumbs."
29 Then He said to her: "Because of what you have said, go; the demon has left your daughter."
30 So she went home and found the child lying on the bed and the demon was gone.
31 Then as He left the district of Tyre, He went through Sidon to the Sea of Galilee, up to the middle of the district of the Decapolis.
32 Now they brought a deaf person to Him, who had great difficulty speaking. And they urged Him to lay His hand on him.
33 So He took him away privately, apart from the crowd, and put His fingers into his ears and spit and touched his tongue.
34 Then He looked up into the sky and sighed, and said to him, "Ephphatha" (that is, "Open up!").

Jesus went next to **Tyre**, another Gentile area along the seacoast of Palestine. He attempted to keep His presence there unknown, but it was impossible (v. 24). A **woman whose daughter** was possessed with an **unclean spirit** came into the **house** where Jesus was and falling down before Him begged for her healing. Because she was **Greek** Jesus said, "**Let the children be fed first**," meaning let Me minister to the Jews first (vv. 25-27). She, determined to have her daughter healed, fielded His comment with the words that "**even the pet dogs under the table eat the children's crumbs**" (v. 28). We, in our day, might think the Lord harsh in what He said. But He was not. He was giving her opportunity to show her humility and faith—which is precisely what she did. And Jesus then cast out the demon (vv. 29-30).

Counselees may often find it necessary for them to be humbled in order to receive the help of the Lord. Tragically, some turn away when this happens; others turn on the counselor who may be telling them truth about their sin that they do not want to hear. But it is those who persist, acknowledging that they deserve nothing, but are willing even to have the **crumbs,** who find His blessing. God's grace is like that. But some must be taught it. You can find no better example from which to do so than the one that occurs here. Pride can turn some, like Naaman, away from help. Warn counselees about this.

In verses 31 through 37 the final episode of the chapter is recorded. After leaving the seacoast, Jesus again returned to the **Decapolis**. Some **brought a deaf person to Him** (v. 32). His deafness, presumably, had also made it difficult for him to speak properly. Everyone who comes to

35   Immediately his ears were opened and his tongue was set free and he spoke properly.

36   Then He ordered them to tell nobody; but the more He gave this order the more widely they made it known.

37   They were utterly astounded and said, "Everything He does He does well! He even makes the deaf hear and the dumb speak."

---

counseling for help will not be as easy to understand (even in trying to patch together what the story is that he is relating). Jesus **privately** healed him by putting His **fingers into his ears, and spitting and touching his tongue.** Obviously, verbal communication was not possible. So Jesus used gestures and physical, nonverbal means to reach him. The spit applied to the tongue and the fingers in the ears indicated that Jesus was going to restore both his speaking and hearing. Then, Jesus **looked up into the sky** (another nonverbal act designed to indicate that God would provide the power for Him to do so). And for the benefit of those who brought the deaf man He cried, "**Ephphatha,**" which meant "**Open up.**" Instantly, his ears were **opened** and his tongue **set free**.

There are times when you also must adapt to a situation that is out of the ordinary. If, for instance, you are attempting to communicate with a child, you may want to draw pictures that will make your meaning clearer. Sometimes a chart or diagram will help an older counselee. Learn to be flexible.

People, astounded at what Jesus was doing, spread His fame far and wide, even though He made every effort to confine His fame. It seems when people are really being helped, it will be hard to limit the number of persons who seek it. A counselor must reckon with this difficulty.

CHAPTER 8

1 At that time there was another large crowd that didn't have anything to eat. Calling His disciples, He said to them,

2   I feel sorry for the crowd, because they have spent three days with Me now, and they don't have anything to eat.

3   If I send them home with nothing to eat, they will collapse on the way (especially those who are from a long way off).

4 But His disciples replied, "Where, in this lonely place, will anybody be able to get bread to satisfy these people?"

5 So He asked them, "How many pieces of bread do you have?" And they said, "Seven."

6 Then He ordered the crowd to sit down on the ground. He took the seven pieces of bread and gave thanks and broke them and gave them to His disciples to serve the crowd, and they did it.

7 And they had a few fish. So He blessed them, and He also told them to serve these.

8 They ate and were satisfied, and they collected enough broken pieces of leftovers to fill seven baskets.

9 There were about four thousand people who ate. Then He sent them off.

The disciples never seem to learn. Aren't we glad to be able to learn of the Lord's patience with them in spite of this? And apply the fact to our own inability and that of our counselees? Here, Jesus is confronted with another instance of a crowd without food. The disciples again wonder where food will come from (v. 3). This time, there was enough left over to **fill seven baskets**. Jesus' concern for the bodies of men should be a matter of concern for counselors as well. They should always work hand-in-hand with Christian physicians to help heal bodies as well as souls. And there ought to be concern for feeding those without food and caring for the basic needs of counselees. It would seem necessary that in the church of every counselor there should be at least one deacon who would be on tap to meet such needs to whom a counselor might refer people with physical needs.

In verses 10 through 14 Jesus is confronted by Pharisees who ask Him for a **sign** that He is from God. Those today who do the same also **test** Jesus in ways that He will not accept. He absolutely refused to give any special sign to them. If they could not determine that He was the Messiah from the healings and the other miracles which He performed, then

10 Next, He got into a boat with His disciples and went to the vicinity of Dalmanutha.

11 Now, the Pharisees came out and began to argue with Him, asking Him for a sign from heaven to test Him.

12 Then, sighing from down deep inside, He said, "Why does this generation seek a sign? Let Me tell you for certain that no sign will be given to this generation."

13 So He left them, got into the boat again, and went off to the other side.

14 Now they forgot to take bread, and they didn't have more than one piece with them in the boat.

15 So He warned them, "See to it that you look out for the Pharisees' leaven and for Herod's leaven."

16 And they discussed this with each other, because they did not have bread.

17 Aware of this, He said to them,

Why are you discussing the fact that you don't have any bread? Don't you yet know or understand? Are your hearts so hardened?

18 **You have eyes; don't you see**? **You have ears; don't you hear**? Don't you remember?

19 When I broke those five pieces of bread for the five thousand, how many baskets full of pieces did you collect?

They replied, "Twelve."

20 "When I broke seven for the four thousand, how many baskets full of pieces did you collect?" And they replied, "Seven."

---

what good would an additional sign do them? Like Gideon, the **sign** never suffices; he kept asking for another!

Jesus disgust and disturbance for this asking for a sign is evidenced by His **sigh** (v. 12) which was **deep** in nature. How He must sigh today over those who fail to heed His words about generations that seek signs. What more could anyone ask than for Him to rise from the dead? If that event was not enough for that generation, clearly nothing else would be. The same is true today; if counselees will not listen to Moses and the prophets, then they will not listen to revelation through signs.

In verses 14 through 21 Jesus finally expresses His exasperation with the disciples for their denseness, failure to **understand, remember** and soften their **hearts** to the truth. Because they had forgotten to take bread with them, when Jesus spoke of looking out for the **leaven of the Pharisees and of Herod**, they misunderstood Jesus' comment to refer to the lack of **bread**. Every counselor can identify with the feelings expressed by Jesus. And it should encourage them that even He was not always suc-

21 Then He said to them, "Don't you understand yet?"

22 They came to Bethsaida. And they brought a blind man to Him and urged Him to touch him.

23 He took the blind man by the hand and led him out of the village. Then He spit on his eyes, put His hands on him, and asked him, "Do you see anything?"

24 He looked up and said, "I see people, but they look like trees walking."

25 Then again He put His hands on his eyes, and he saw clearly and was restored.

26 Then He sent him home, saying, "Don't go into the village."

---

cessful in getting through to sinful human beings. They should not expect a better record in doing this than the Lord's.

What is the **leaven of the Pharisees and of Herod**? Clearly, it is the **leaven** of unbelief. There was too little faith among the disciples. Their conduct exhibited a great deal of unbelief. Yet, there was a genuineness about the eleven that eventually emerged. It is hard at times to know whether those with whom you are working in counseling are genuine or not because of the amount of leaven that has permeated them from the unbelieving world. Warn them about the leaven that can get such a hold on them as to destroy their ability to grow and change.

In verses 22 through 26 we encounter the miracle in which Jesus healed a man of his blindness in two stages. In the first, he was able to see partially. As he himself put it, he could **see people, but they looked like trees walking** (v. 24). To see this way was to see movement that was so indistinct that you could hardly tell the difference between men and trees. Then, after a second touch, his eyesight was **restored and he saw clearly**. All of this occurred outside the village of Bethsaida into which Jesus forbade him to return (again, lest too many new people would come to swell the crowds). Why did Jesus heal in two stages? This is the only occasion on which such a thing occurred. Surely the first stage was not a failure. So why? It would seem that in this healing Jesus was enacting a parable for the dull disciples, who understood all that He said and did with such lack of clarity that it was necessary to give them truth in stages. Here, He demonstrated what their lack of faith was doing to them. Again, counselors may have to put up with slow movement on the part of counselees, even effecting change in their situations by stages. It is rare that all that needs to be done can be done instantly, more likely that it will require a period of time and, in some instances, will take more than one series of sessions.

27 Now Jesus and His disciples went to the villages of Caesarea Philippi. On the way He asked His disciples, "Who do people say I am?"
28 They responded, "Some say John the Baptist, others, Elijah, but still others say one of the prophets."
29 So He asked them, "But who do you say I am?" Peter replied, "You are the Christ."
30 He warned them not to tell anybody about Him.
31 Then He began to teach them that it was necessary for the Son of Man to suffer many things and to be rejected by the elders and the chief priests and the scribes and to be killed and after three days to rise again.
32 And He spoke openly about this. But Peter took Him aside and began to rebuke Him.
33 Then He turned around and, looking at His disciples, He rebuked Peter: "Get behind me, Satan! You aren't thinking God's way but man's way."

Jesus is now trying to bring the disciples to better understanding of Who He is and what He has come to do. As they travel, He asks, **"Who do people say I am"** (v. 27)? They repeated the conjectures they had heard (v. 28). Then He asked the question of them. Peter, always the first to speak, replied, **"You are the Christ"** (v. 29). At last, someone had come through! Doubtless, Jesus' chiding mentioned earlier in the chapter had its effect. And when you do the same for a counselee, you often will at last see a breakthrough. Again, He did not want this to be noised around so He warned them not to tell anyone else about this divinely-given insight (v. 30). If they had, that might have brought the wrath of the religious leaders down on Him prematurely.

Because they had finally—after all that had happened—come to realize Jesus' true identity, He could at last reveal His purpose in coming: to die for guilty sinners in order to save them from the consequences of sin. But Peter, whose understanding had been sharpened, is now so dumbfounded that he refuses to accept Jesus' further revelation about His death. How can it be that the Messiah, Whom he had just confessed Jesus to be, could die at the hands of the wicked elders, priests and scribes? For him it was unthinkable! He must have missed Jesus' words about rising again (v. 31). Peter **rebuked** the Lord for saying so. What he should have thought was "If He is Messiah, how can I even think to rebuke Him?" But there is little consistent thinking among sinful men. Jesus, in turn, **rebuked Peter**, calling him an adversary (the meaning of the word **Satan**). And then He uttered a statement that every counselor will fre-

275

34 Then He called the crowd, together with His disciples, and said to them,

> Whoever wants to come after Me must deny himself and take up his cross and follow Me.

35 This is because whoever wants to save his life will lose it, but whoever loses his life for My sake and for the gospel will save it.

36 Now what benefit is it for a person to gain the whole world and forfeit his life?

37 And what could a person give in exchange for his life?

---

quently find himself repeating, "**You aren't thinking God's way but man's way**." Few statements better summarize what counselors must reckon with regularly in counseling. This is totally in line with the statement of the Father in Isaiah 55:8. When people think God's way, they think His thoughts after Him. They listen to what He says, assimilate it into their thinking, and then reproduce it in their minds. That comes only from dwelling in belief on the words of Christ, today revealed only in Scripture.

Finally, so far as this chapter takes us, Jesus explains discipleship to the crowd who, for the first time, we read, **He called together with the disciples**. True disciples of His **deny** (literally, "say no to") themselves (that is, to their own thinking), **take up their crosses** (that is, put to death their desires), and **follow** Him (that is, say "yes" to His thinking and His desires). This understanding of discipleship is critical to effective counseling. Make it clear that when one denies himself, it is his *self* (with all of its selfish interests) that he denies; he does not deny himself some *thing*, as many misinterpret the verse to mean. In addition, taking up the cross does not mean that one has a hard load to carry. No, to take up the cross is to carry it to the place where one will be crucified on it. It means to crucify one's own wishes and desires in favor of Christ's. You will probably have to explain all of this to the average counselee whose thinking about the verse is all wrong.

It is because of this emphasis on death to one's self-centered interests that Jesus goes on to say in verses 35 through 37 that to try to **save** that self is actually to **lose** it. But to lose it for the sake of Christ and His gospel is the way to save it. This is not a paradox; rather, it is the straight truth of the matter. One's own ways lead to death (as the Proverb makes clear) and only Jesus' ways lead to life here and hereafter. And, as He notes in verse 37, this is the most important matter anyone could consider.

To reinforce all He had been saying, Jesus warned about the future

38   Whoever is ashamed of Me and My words in this adulterous and
      sinful generation, the Son of Man will be ashamed of him also
      when He comes in His Father's glory with the holy angels.

---

when judgment will fall, all will be gathered before Him, and all who
were ashamed of Him will be exposed before men and angels. In that day,
the tables will be turned. Always keep the ultimate, eternal state of things
before your counselees so that they will think and act in the light of eternity.

CHAPTER 9

1   And He said to them, "Let Me assure you that there are some standing here who will surely not taste death before they see God's empire come
in power."
2   Then after six days Jesus took Peter and James and John and led
them up into a high mountain privately by themselves. And in their presence He was transfigured.
3   His clothes became a glistening, brilliant white; whiter than any laun-
derer on earth could bleach them.
4   Then Elijah and Moses appeared to them; and they spoke together with
Jesus.
5   And Peter said to Jesus, "Rabbi, it is a fine thing for us to be here; let's
make three shelters, one for You, one for Moses and one for Elijah."

Having mentioned the coming of Christ **with His holy angels in
judgment upon that adulterous and sinful generation** which rejected
the **Son of Man** Who came to redeem His own (8:38), Mark now continues the discussion in the ninth chapter. He declares that **some standing
there** would not die before that judgment of apostate Judaism would
occur at the **coming** of the new **empire of God in power**. Of course, this
happened in 70 AD. Many counselees refuse to listen to warnings of this
sort about the greater judgment yet to come. If biblical warnings are
ignored it is at the peril of those in the generation when it occurs.

Verses 2 through 10 record the transfiguration. Along with the recent
revelation of Jesus' Messiahship He now shows something of that messianic glory to three witnesses, Peter, James and John. It is interesting that
these three (all former fishermen) seemed to constitute an inner circle
among the disciples. There were the disciples in general, then the twelve,
then this group of three and, closest of all to Him, the "apostle whom
Jesus loved," John. Clearly, this order of things indicates that it is not
wrong to have closer relationships with some believers than with others.
Sometimes Christians have the mistaken idea that all ought to relate in the
same way. The example of Jesus, however, contradicts this notion. Be
sure that in your teaching you do not err in this matter. Sometimes after
reconciliation people think there is a need to establish a close friendship
with the other party. That is not necessarily true. A friendship? Yes. A
close friendship? Not necessarily.

Elijah and **Moses** appeared to Jesus, two about whom something

6   He said this because he didn't know how to respond (they were terrified).
7   Then a cloud appeared and covered them, and a voice came from the cloud, "This is My dear Son: listen to Him."
8   Suddenly, as they looked around, they saw nobody with them except Jesus.
9 As they came down from the mountain, He ordered them not to tell anybody about the things they saw until the Son of Man is raised from the dead.
10   So they kept the affair a secret among themselves, debating about what "raised from the dead" meant.

---

unusual concerning their deaths occurred. They discussed the coming exodus that would take place at Jerusalem when Jesus would die. So, the transfiguration, in which Jesus' **clothes** glistened and shined like lightening, evidenced His glory as the God-man, but also prepared Him as Messiah for His coming sacrifice on Calvary.

When this happened, Peter, who always had something to say—whether or not it made any sense—offered the suggestion that three booths might be made, one for each of them. This was his reaction to **fear** (v. 6). That is an interesting interpretation of his words—fear drove him to a suggestion that made no sense. When you find nonsensical ideas floating around in a counseling session you might also look to see if they are caused by fear which is leading to confused thinking and speech. More often than not this insight will apply.

God spoke from a **cloud** telling them that they should listen to Jesus because He is God's **dear Son**. It is important to note how seldom counselors listen to Jesus. Rather, they want to hear Rogers, Freud, Skinner, Maslow, Jung or some other unbelieving theorist who hated Jesus. How is this possible for Christian counselors? Many want acceptance from their fellow psychologists. Others have been trained to hear them. Still others simply do not know how to use Scripture for the help that they need in counseling. You must not be among them. Listen to Jesus!

Jesus once more forbid the three to tell about what they had seen until after His death and resurrection (v. 9). This word was again a clear indication not only of the gospel, but of the fact that they would eventually proclaim it. Yet the disciples, hearing of the resurrection, still didn't understand (v. 10). Again, we see the difficulty they had with assimilating truth that they didn't want to hear. That this was, at least in part, involved in their lack of apprehension is clear from Peter's actions and words

> **11** And they questioned Him, "Why do the scribes say the Elijah must come first?"
> 12 He said to them,
>> Elijah is indeed to come first to restore everything. But take note of what has been written about the Son of Man, that He should suffer much and be held in contempt.
> 13 But, as a matter of fact, I tell you that Elijah has come, and they did what they wanted to him (as it has been written about him).

(8:31-33). Many counselees will either pretend not to understand, or will read things into what you teach when they don't want to hear what it is that the Bible requires. Don't be surprised at this. It is often wise, therefore, to write out assignments or other material that you want them to get straight, so that they can read and reread it throughout the days ahead. When giving an assignment, it is also wise to have the counselee repeat its substance in his own words, just to make sure that he "got it."

The appearance of **Elijah** led to questions about the prophecy of his **coming** (vv. 11-13). They wondered whether this appearance was the coming prophesied in Malachi. If so, he was late. He was supposed to precede the Lord Jesus and prepare His way. Jesus made it clear that they were right in expecting him to come beforehand and **restore everything** (by turning the fathers to the children and the children to the fathers, so that there was *agreement* between those who were faithful in past times and in the present). Jesus also made it clear that he had come in the person of John the Baptist, and that having accomplished his task, those in charge had put him to death (vv. 12, 13).

But in verse 12, He made the point that one can become too interested in prophetic fulfillments and in the sidelights of His coming and miss the heart of it: **Take note of what has been written about the Son of Man, that He should suffer much and be held in contempt**. Here again is a warning for the counselor. Counselees may have their interests in the sidelights of what you are attempting to do rather than focusing on the main concern. You can briefly answer some irrelevant question, but then **note**, as Jesus did, that the central concern should be about Him. Don't let counselees get you sidetracked.

In verses 14 through 27 we encounter another interesting event that is spelled out in some detail. When Jesus and the three disciples returned from the mountain, they encountered **a large crowd** around the rest of the disciples. In the crowd were **scribes arguing** with the nine. The argument had to do with the failure of the disciples to cast out a demon from a

14 When they came to where the other disciples were, they saw a large crowd around them, and there were scribes arguing with them.

15 But as soon as they saw Him, the whole crowd was overcome with wonder and ran to greet Him.

16 He asked them, "About what are you arguing with them?"

17 Somebody from the crowd replied,

> Teacher, I brought my son, who has a spirit that has caused him to become dumb, to you—

18   and whenever it seizes him, it knocks him down, he foams at the mouth, grinds his teeth and becomes rigid—and I asked your disciples to cast it out, but they couldn't.

19 Then He answered them, saying, "What an unbelieving generation you are! How long must I be with you; how long must I put up with you? Bring him to Me."

20 So they brought him to Him. And when the spirit saw Him, immediately it threw him into a seizure and he fell on the ground and rolled about, foaming at the mouth.

21 He asked his father, "How long has he had this problem?" And he replied, "From childhood;

22 and often it has thrown him into fire and water to destroy him. But if you can, help us; show compassion toward us."

23 Jesus said to him, "'If you can!' Everything can be done for the one who believes."

24 At once the boy's father said, "I believe; help me with my unbelief."

---

young boy who had many of the symptoms of epilepsy (which evidently the demon was able to reproduce in him; vv. 17, 18). Jesus' exasperated reply was, **"What an unbelieving generation you are!"** He was not castigating the disciples since they could hardly be addressed as a **generation.** What He meant was that just because the disciples couldn't cast out the demon was no reason to resist believing in Him. Today, the very same point needs to be made. People will criticize Christ because of the failures of His ministers or His people. That makes no sense. The Savior Himself never fails; they should look to Him and not to His disciples. That was the thrust of God's word from heaven. Make that point as often as is necessary in counseling.

Jesus demonstrated this very fact by casting out the demon. He does so after a dialog with the father who doubts Christ's ability because of the inability of the disciples; **"If you can,"** he says (v. 22). Jesus picked up on his words and in response said, **"If you can! Everything can be done for the one who believes."** The problem, all around, was doubt—lack of

25 So Jesus, seeing that a crowd was gathering rapidly, rebuked the unclean spirit, telling it, "Dumb and deaf spirit, I order you, come out of him, and don't ever enter him again."

26 Then with shouting and with a great seizure it came out, and the boy looked so much like he was dead that a number said, "He has died."

27 But Jesus took his hand and raised him up, and he stood up.

28 When He entered a house, His disciples asked Him privately, "Why couldn't we cast it out?"

29 He told them, "This kind can come out only by prayer."[1]

30 So they went from there and passed through Galilee, but He didn't want anybody to know it

---

1. Some MSS add, *and fasting.*

---

faith. Then the boy's father said, **"I believe; help me with my unbelief"** (v. 24). This statement moved the heart of Jesus. It showed the man's willingness and desire to believe—even though he had some doubt that he found difficult to clear from his mind. One need not be in any better position today to receive help from Jesus. Those who make foolish statements such as "If Jesus isn't Lord of all, He isn't Lord at all," fail to realize the great compassion and love that Christ has for His elect. He is willing to accept any genuine faith at all—even if it is small. Remember that in counseling and ask for no more than Jesus did. You will find your share of counselees who suffer from this vacillation between faith and doubt. If there is any true faith at all, that is faith deposited by the Holy Spirit of God, and thus it is acceptable.

This unclean spirit, who had done so much to ruin the life of this youngster and to harm him would not leave without one last blow—he caused a **seizure** so great that many thought he had been killed by it. But Jesus raised him up entirely cured (vv. 26, 27). The crowds are often wrong about their ideas. Never seek to please or to follow the crowds. Many counselees do, and you will find it necessary to warn them about this.

The disciples were inquisitive about their failure and asked Jesus privately why they couldn't cast out the demon (v. 28). He replied that casting out this kind of demon required prayer. That was something He had never mentioned in connection with casting out demons before. Not all ministry is alike. Some counseling cases, for instance, are more difficult than others and require more prayer than the others do. Don't classify all counseling, therefore, in the same categories.

31   because He was teaching His disciples. He told them,
> The Son of Man is to be betrayed into men's hands, and they will kill Him. But when He is killed, after three days, He will be raised.

32   But they didn't understand this saying and were afraid to question Him.

33   Then they came to Capernaum. And when He was inside the house, He questioned them: "About what were you arguing on the way?"

34   But they were silent, since on the way they had argued about who was the greatest.

35   So He sat down and called the Twelve and said to them, "If anybody wants to be first, he must be last of all and the servant of all."

36   Then He took a child, and set him in their midst, and took him in His arms and said to them,

37   Whoever receives one such child in My name receives Me, and whoever receives Me doesn't receive Me but the One Who sent Me.

38   John said to Him,
> Teacher, we saw someone casting out demons in Your name who doesn't follow along with us, so we forbade him because he doesn't follow along with us.

39   But Jesus said,

Jesus kept His presence hidden as much as possible as He traveled through Galilee, taking this time to teach His disciples (vv. 30, 31). They needed to know the essential truths of the Gospel, which He delivered to them in clear terms, but which they promptly failed to understand (vv. 31, 32).

As they traveled, rather than reflecting on the truths that Jesus had revealed to them, the disciples **argued** among themselves as to which of them would be the **greatest**. They knew that this was wrong, so when Jesus asked, **"About what were you arguing on the way?"** They kept a guilty silence (v. 34). So Jesus said in words that they could never forget, **"If anyone wants to be first, he must be last of all and the servant of all."** Then, taking up a child in His hands, Jesus illustrated this great truth for them. He said, **"Whoever receives one such child in My name receives Me** and also receives the Father" (v. 37). What did He mean? He meant that they must be willing to receive the most insignificant of persons, one who could return nothing to them. A child was helpless to do anything for them (in particular) to contribute anything to their **greatness**. In other words, they needed to think not about who was to be the greatest

Don't forbid him; nobody who does a miracle in My name can quickly speak badly about Me,

40   since anybody who isn't against us is for us.

41   I assure you that whoever gives you a cup of water to drink in My name, because you are from the Christ, certainly won't lose his reward.

42 Whoever causes one of these little ones who believe in Me to stumble, it would be better for him if he were thrown into the sea with a millstone hung around his neck.

---

among them, but who could serve others most, putting himself **last**. He would be the one who was **first**.

John, in the spirit of the arguing disciples, also mentioned forbidding someone to cast out demons in Christ's name. Christ said that this was wrong, since among those who followed Him **anybody who isn't against us is for us**. This statement should go far to relieve the tensions that exist among Christians who don't see eye-to-eye with us because they work in different contexts than we do. No one Christian—not even a disciple—has a corner on the truth. Many hurtful problems among counselees come from a very wrong view of separation much like John's. Disabuse them of it in counseling, if you can.

Not only should such a person be recognized for Christ's sake, but Jesus also goes on to say that if anyone gives them a **cup of water to drink** in His name, because they are **from the Christ**, he certainly will not lose his **reward**. That is to say, anything, however slight, that is done for Him will be acknowledged. Jesus made it clear that anyone who genuinely serves Him (or serves Him by serving His disciples) will be acknowledged for doing so. That is an assuring truth to many who wonder whether some service that they have rendered **in His Name** will be noticed. On the basis of this passage you may assure counselees that it will.

On the other hand, even the slightest negative action toward the disciples (here called "**little ones**" because of their vulnerability) will not go unnoticed. Indeed, the one who causes them to **stumble** (sin) would be better off if he were drowned! This is strong language intimating that Jesus cares deeply for His own (v. 42).

But Jesus went even further. He speaks of radical amputation—the cutting off of hand or foot and the tearing out of the eye. It is **better to enter into life crippled,** He said, than to enter into **Gehenna** (eternal punishment) with all bodily parts intact. This is of course a figure of

43 If your hand causes you to stumble, cut it off; it is better for you to enter into life crippled than, while having two hands, to go away into Gehenna, into the fire that can't be put out.

44 [1]

45 If your foot causes you to stumble, cut it off; it is better for you to enter into life lame than, while having two feet, to be thrown into Gehenna.

46 [2]

47 If your eye causes you to stumble, tear it out; it is better for you to enter God's empire with one eye than, while having two eyes, to be thrown into Gehenna,

48 **where their worm doesn't die, and the fire can't be put out**.

49 Indeed, everybody will be salted with fire.

50 Salt is fine, but if salt loses its saltiness, what will you use to salt it? Have salt among yourselves and be at peace with one another.

---

1. The better MSS omit vs. 44, which is the same as vs. 48.
2. The better MSS omit vs. 46, which is the same as vs. 48.

---

speech, and is not to be taken literally. But it is a powerful one designed to shock and to make people think and to help them to remember (vv. 43-47). Hell is likened here to the garbage dump south of Jerusalem where worms ate and fires burned the refuse. In contrast to this earthly dump, hell is a horrible place where **the worm does not dies** and the **fires are never quenched**. Carrying on the theme, He said, "**everybody will be salted with fire**." The antiseptic quality of salt was well known. Fish and meat were salted to preserve them. So, too, the eternal punishment of hell will, unlike the earthly fires that consumed, not consume those there, but will burn them for all eternity. It is a fearful picture He sketched in order to warn those who would oppose His disciples. Salt is usually thought of as good, but Jesus says in verse 50, "even though I use it here in a different way. It is no good when it loses its saltiness; however, it can be thought of in other ways as well. Nevertheless, **have** [good, salty] **salt among yourselves and be at peace with one another.** That is to say, preserve (**as though you were all salted**) **peace** among yourselves rather than argue about who is greatest as you have been."

CHAPTER 10

1 Now He left there and went into the region of Judea, beyond the Jordan. Again crowds accompanied Him, and again, as He was accustomed, He taught them.
2 Then the Pharisees approached Him and in order to test Him, asked Him if it was lawful for a man to divorce his wife.
3   He answered by saying to them,
4   "What did Moses command you?" And they said, "Moses permitted the writing of a certificate of divorce and the divorce."

In this chapter Jesus and His disciples journeyed to **Judea** from Galilee. He went through the Transjordan country on the East Bank of the river. Here He carried on a teaching ministry as He had done before. In fact, this sort of activity, Mark notes, had become customary (v. 1). But it was not long before the **Pharisees** accosted Him, throwing a question His way that they debated frequently among the various disciples of Hillel and Shammai. They asked Him, **"is it lawful for a man to divorce his wife?"** The same question is often raised today and counselors must know how to answer it. Many of the matters counselors deal with, in one way or another, involve them in discussions about divorce. Many ideas are afloat among evangelicals. In recent times even the Roman Catholic view, that there is never any valid reason for divorce, is being propagated, thus challenging the historic Protestant teaching that desertion and adultery are valid reasons for divorce. It is impossible here to discuss this matter in any depth. For a fuller discussion, see my book *Marriage, Divorce and Remarriage in the Bible.* I cannot stress strongly enough that every counselor must have these matters well in hand if he is to counsel successfully. Unfortunately, many Christians are having problems with their marriages these days. If you are not sure about the many issues concerning marriage, divorce and remarriage, you must study thoroughly until you are fully persuaded in your own mind. People going through difficult marriage problems do not need your uncertainties heaped upon their own.

Jesus then answered the question. The footnote in Matthew 19:3-9 of the *Christian Counselor's New Testament* pulls the gospel accounts' teaching on divorce together. I shall quote it here:

5   But Jesus said to them,
> It was because of your hardheartedness that Moses wrote this regulation for you.
6   > But from the beginning of creation He **made them male and female**;
7   > **for this reason a man will leave his father and mother**,
8   > **and the two will be one flesh**. So then, they aren't two any longer, but one flesh.
9   > Therefore what God has yoked together nobody must separate.

10   When the disciples were in the house, they asked Him again about this matter.

11   He told them:
> Whoever divorces his wife and marries another commits adultery against her;
12   > and if she divorces her husband and marries another, she commits adultery.

> Divorce of believers is allowed (not required) for sexual sin (cf. 5:31, 32). Marriage is not a civil contract primarily, but rather a divine covenant (v. 6). Cf. also Proverbs 2:17; Malachi 2:14. But as verse 9 makes clear, a marriage is broken by a sinful divorce (why warn against what is impossible?). To speak of divorced persons as "married in God's sight" is incorrect. In regulating the consequences of sinful activity, God does not condone the activity (vv. 8, 9). Cf. also Malachi 2:16 (cf. also the footnote on Matthew 5:31, 32 in the *CCNT*).

The matters of **adultery** against a spouse (vv. 11, 12) have to do with the fact that they *ought* to be married if they have divorced for any cause other than sexual sin. But that is not because they are still married in some sense; it is because they *should* be (see details about this in *Marriage Divorce & Remarriage in the Bible*).

In verse 4, Jesus asked about Moses' **commands** (which included loving one another). They cited what he **permitted**. But Moses was not giving permission for divorce in Deuteronomy 24; he was regulating an existing condition. That is the point of what He said in verse 5. There was no permission to divorce, but any love they had was blocked by **hard hearts,** so Moses regulated divorce. The commandment in Deuteronomy was an attempt to make a person think deeply before going through with a divorce.

13 They brought children to Him to have Him touch them; but the disciples rebuked them.

14 But when Jesus saw this, He was indignant and said to them,
Let the children come to Me and don't try to stop them since in God's empire are persons such as they.

15 Let Me assure you that whoever doesn't receive God's empire like a child certainly won't enter it.

Then Jesus went back to the creation of Adam and Eve and pointed out that God originally created one pair of persons, **male and female**, and joined them together in a **one flesh** relationship which was to be permanent. He then went on to discourage divorce by saying, "**What God has yoked together nobody must separate**."

Every biblical counselor will discourage divorce. He will do all he can to preserve the relationship that the two persons entered into when they were married—just as Jesus did. The rare conditions under which he will counsel for divorce are very carefully set forth in my book mentioned above; I shall not go into them here. Every marriage between two believers *can* be saved, and the harmful aspects of it can be turned aside. It can be successful. There is never a time when we absolutely *must* give up on two persons in whom the Holy Spirit dwells. But if one of the parties utterly refuses to do as the Bible directs and persists in this determination regardless of church discipline, he or she must be put out of the church and treated as a Gentile and a tax collector (both of whom were outside the care of the church and considered unbelievers). Then the directive about a believer and unbeliever (about which Jesus did not speak) may come into play (cf. I Corinthians 7:15).

Some persons **brought children** to Jesus to have Him **touch them** (presumably to bless them), but **the disciples rebuked them** (v. 13). Jesus was **indignant** at them for this (v. 14) and said, "**Let the children come to Me**." Jesus evidenced a love for children that ought to set the pace for every counselor. He must know how to deal with children. There is no excuse for refusing to bring them into counseling sessions in the proper way (you don't want to turn them into counseling cases!).

Jesus also made it clear on this occasion that the persons who constitute **God's empire** are childlike. He indicated that there is no other way to **enter** His **empire** than by becoming **like a child** (vv. 14, 15). What did He mean? He meant that it takes the implicit faith of a child for salvation. A child believes without questioning. For him, faith is simple and straightforward. It is neither complex nor something to be agonized over.

16   Then He took them in His arms and blessed them, putting His hands on them.

17   Now as He was setting out on His journey a man ran toward Him, fell on his knees in front of Him, and asked Him, "Good teacher, what must I do to inherit eternal life?"

18   Jesus said to him,

Why do you call Me good? Nobody is good except One—God.

Then, to demonstrate His point—*and* out of His great love for them—Jesus **blessed the children, putting His hands on them**. One implication of this act is that all children of believers ought to be a part of and *cared for* by the church. They should not be considered outside of the fold of the visible church, but as lambs *among* the flock. This care and discipline, carried on faithfully, should lead many of them to faith in Christ at an early age. The placing of hands on another is indicative of giving (or imparting) something to him. To **bless** here means to do good to another in some way. Precisely what Jesus did in blessing these children is not stated. At the very least, it was an act in which He made it clear that He and His disciples were responsible to minister to them. While very small children must be counseled through their parents, those who are of an age to understand and converse intelligently with a counselor, at some point in family counseling in which they are involved, might be profitably helped by a sympathetic counselor who can speak their language. Work at this.

Verses 17 through 22 record a very instructive incident. A man, ostensibly coming to Jesus *as* a child, willing to believe and follow all He said (notice his "humble" attitude: he **fell on his knees** before Him), asks, **"what must I do to inherit eternal life?"** In asking the question he addressed Jesus as **Good Teacher** (v. 17). Jesus picks up on this address (notice how often He uses the words of the counselee to make His point? That is a technique that you should learn to develop and employ). He asks him **why** he calls Him **good**; only **God** is **Good**. He does this because he has a superficial idea of what goodness is (as Jesus will demonstrate to him presently). In his mind, the outward keeping of the **commandments** constituted goodness (he had no idea of a heart in tune with God). So, in effect, what Jesus was saying is "unless you change your view of goodness to address Me according to the kind of goodness that is in God Himself, don't use that title for Me. I will not accept the proposition that I am good in the sense that you think you are good" (v. 18).

To show him this, Jesus mentioned some of the **commandments**

19   You know the commandments, **Don't kill, don't commit adultery, don't steal, don't give false testimony**, don't defraud,
honor your father and mother...

20   But he replied, "Teacher, I have kept all of them from my youth."

21   Then, Jesus looking at him loved him and said to him, "You lack one
thing. Go, sell whatever you have and give to the poor, and you will have
treasure in heaven. And come, follow Me."

22   But gloom spread over his face at that statement, and he went away
upset (this was because he had great possessions).

23   Then Jesus looked around and said to His disciples, "How hard it is
for those who have riches to enter God's empire!"

(v. 19). To this he responded, "**Teacher, I have kept all of them from my
youth**" (v. 20). There is no indication that he was lying. The real problem
is that he hadn't the faintest idea about what keeping God's commandments meant. Keeping them outwardly (the only way that he could make
such a claim) was not enough; one's heart also had to be right. It is not
enough to avoid committing adultery outwardly; one must not lust in his
heart. To make this clear to him, Jesus gave him a homework assignment
(see *The Christian Counselor's Manual* for extensive instructions on giving homework to counselees). Out of **love** for him (don't miss that), the
assignment was to expose his sin. Jesus told him to **sell** all he had, **give**
the money to the **poor**, store up **treasure in heaven**, and **follow** Him.
These things constitute the summary of the law: love for one's neighbor
and love for God. But, because he would not become childlike in doing all
Jesus said, "**gloom spread over his face. . . and he went away upset. . .
because he had great possessions**." The sad fact is that he loved his possessions more than he loved Jesus and his neighbor.

Obviously Jesus doesn't expect every believer to sell all he has. This
was a particular assignment, suited to deal with the problem standing in
the way of this man's salvation. And he failed to follow it. Not all of your
counseling cases will be howling successes either. But here the counselor
succeeded; it was only the counselee who failed. When your counseling
seems to fail, be sure that it is for the same reason. Notice, then, how
Jesus didn't use a canned and refrigerated approach to counselees. He
deals with each one according to his needs and problems. Never get into a
pattern that requires every counselee to submit to the same approach. Vary
your approach with each person according to the particulars of his situation. There is no "one size fits all" way that Jesus handled people. Jesus'
interpretive comment about the event was that it is very difficult for rich

24 The disciples were astounded at His words. But Jesus said to them again,

Children, how hard it is[1] to enter God's empire!

25 It is easier for a camel to go through the eye of a needle than for a rich man to enter God's empire.

26 But they were utterly dumbfounded and said to one another,[2] "Then who can be saved?"

27 Jesus looked at them and said, "With human beings it isn't possible, but that isn't true of God, since everything is possible with God."

---

1. Some MSS add, *for those who trust in riches.*
2. Some MSS read, *to Him.*

---

people to **enter God's empire**. That is because they trust in riches rather than trusting in Him like a child.

In response to what Jesus said about this rich young ruler, the **disciples** are astounded (v. 24). Wealth, to the average Jew, was a sign of God's approval. Here Jesus cut through that faulty idea. God may grant wealth to some; but neither poverty nor wealth is a sign of blessing from God. Indeed, as Jesus implied, wealth may become a curse. Never forget that fact in counseling those who seek money as their object in life. Instead, become familiar with *all* that is said about money in I Timothy 6 (a crucial passage on this subject).

Jesus continued to make His point (vv. 24, 25) giving us the great metaphor about the **camel** and the **needle** (one of the largest and smallest objects at hand). But, be sure to note, Jesus did not say that it was impossible. Using this hyperbolic metaphor, He wanted to make it clear that it is **hard for the rich** to become childlike. A child has little power. A rich man may like to control with his money. One must lay aside all his trust in riches, all his control of a situation and *truly* come to Jesus on his **knees** in repentance and faith.

The disciples still didn't get it. In astonishment they blurted out, **"Then who can be saved?"** (v. 26). That is, of course, a good question. And they received a good answer: a person cannot change his sinful heart so as to come in the right way; but it is possible for God to change him! (v. 27). That is the hope of every biblical counselor: that God will do a work in the heart of his counselee. Otherwise counseling is useless. But the Spirit uses His Word to change people. That is why we counsel and minister the Word (just as Jesus did here) in hopes that He will use it to bless our counselees.

28 Peter began to say to Him, "Look, we have left everything and have followed You."

29 Jesus said,

> I assure you that there is nobody who has left house or brothers or sisters or mother or father or children or fields for My sake, and for the sake of the good news,

30 who doesn't receive a hundred times over at this time, houses and brothers and sisters and mothers and children and fields, with persecutions; and in the coming age, eternal life.

31 But many who are first will be last, and the last first.

32 Now they were on the road going up to Jerusalem, and Jesus was going ahead of them, and they were amazed; and those who followed were afraid. So He took the Twelve again and began to tell them everything that was about to happen to Him:

From this discussion, Peter pointed out that he and the others had **left** behind their treasures and even their families to **follow** Him (v. 28). To that Jesus gave a wonderfully comforting reply that should encourage every minister of the Word who does the same. He said that God would provide a hundred times over "family" for them in this life and in the **coming age, eternal life**. God does not forget those who minister in His Name. He cares for them. Members of the church often become family to a minister who labors far away from his earthly family. This is an important word for those lonely ministers you counsel. You must tell them to find those that God has provided for them. Often, instead of doing so, they fail to see all the "family" that God brings into their lives. It is not His fault, but theirs for acting so independently (vv. 28-30).

Then, to top it off, Jesus stated another aphorism: "**many who are first will be last, and the last first**" (v. 31). What is **first** in the eyes of the world (the good life) in the end may turn out to be **last** (in reality, not so good after all)—and visa versa. Some day, what is truly valuable will become clear. For now, tell counselees, "trust and follow Jesus and you cannot go wrong, even though it may seem that you do at times."

Jesus now led the little band up toward **Jerusalem**. They were still dumbfounded over what they had heard from His lips and became **afraid** (about what would happen in **Jerusalem**, but possibly also about His words of warning concerning the difficulty of entering God's empire). Again, Jesus told His disciples what would happen in Jerusalem. In verses 33 and 34 we see that He gave them a very clear summary of all that would occur. Once more, also, He emphasized the death and resurrection

33 You see, we are going up to Jerusalem, and the Son of Man will be betrayed to the chief priests and to the scribes, and they will condemn Him to death and will hand Him over to the Gentiles,

34 and they will mock Him and will spit at Him and will lash Him and will kill Him. Yet, after three days He will be raised.

35 Then James and John, Zebedee's two sons, came to Him and said to Him, "We want You to do for us what we ask."

36 He said to them, "What do you want Me to do for you?"

37 They said to Him, "Grant that one of us may sit on Your right and one on Your left in Your glory."

38 Jesus said to them, "You don't know what you are asking. Can you drink the cup that I drink or be baptized with My baptism?"

39 But they said to Him, "We can." So Jesus said to them,

You will drink the cup that I drink, and you will be baptized with the baptism that I am baptized with,

40 but to sit on My right or left is not Mine to grant; rather it is for those for whom it has been prepared.

41 Now when they heard it, the ten became incensed about James and John.

42 So Jesus called them and said to them,

You know that those who are supposed to rule over the Gentiles lord it over them, and their great men show their authority over them.

(the two points of the gospel that they would preach).

Almost as if they had not heard—or cared to hear—about what would happen to their Lord, James and John come to Jesus with a selfish personal request. They wanted the place of preeminence with Jesus in the glorious era that would someday come. Jesus asks, **"Can you drink the cup that I drink or be baptized with My baptism?"** Here He is asking if they could endure persecution and death. That is a hard question for counselees. But, in a childlike manner, they answered, **"We can."** Jesus told them that they would do so. They, too, would endure the sorrows, pain, and sufferings that He would endure (not savingly, of course). But He would not grant their request, since that was up to the Father to determine (vv. 38-40). The others, when they heard, in a jealous rage became incensed over what James and John had requested of Jesus. So, to quell the dissension in the ranks, and to teach more to them, Jesus called them together. He said that in the pagan world **great men** hold authority over others. But in the church, things are different. To be **great**, you must

43   This isn't the way that it will be with you. Rather, whoever among you wants to become great must be your servant,

44   and whoever among you wants to be first must be the slave of all.

45   Even the Son of Man didn't come to be served but to serve and to give His life as a ransom for many.

46 So they came to Jericho. But as He was leaving Jericho, together with His disciples and a large crowd, Timaeus' son Bartimaeus, who was a blind beggar, sat by the way.

47 When he heard that it was Jesus of Nazareth, he began to shout, "Jesus, Son of David, show mercy to me!"

48 Many harshly commanded him to be quiet. But he shouted all the louder, "Son of David, show mercy to me!"

49 Jesus stood still and said, "Call him." So they called the blind man, telling him, "Cheer up! Get up; He's calling you!"

50 So he threw aside his coat, jumped up, and went to Jesus.

51 Jesus responded, saying to him, "What do you want Me to do for you?" And the blind man said to Him, "Rabbi, I want to see again."

---

become a **servant**. To be first, you must be the **slave of all**. And then He pointed to Himself: He didn't **come to be served, but to serve and to give His life as a ransom for many** (vv. 41-45). He is always the supreme Example for us.

Here is another inversion of worldly thinking. Yet, it is quite appropriate for counselees who are upset with others for denigrating them. Use this powerful passage to show them the way of greatness. But make it clear that Jesus didn't recommend trying to become great by following some formula. That was not the intent. Perhaps the joke that follows may be used to make this point. A person was given a badge for being humble, but they had to take it back when he wore it!

The chapter closes with one more incident (vv. 46-52). It is the story of the blind man, **Bartimaeus**. He was a **beggar**. **Bartimaeus** cried out for Jesus to **show mercy** on him. **Many harshly** told him **to be quiet**. There are those who will urge your counselees not to ask for help. Jesus, however, called him. Ecstatically, he went to Jesus. Jesus asked the important question that you should ask every counselee to make sure your agendas are in agreement, "**What do you want Me to do for you?**" He was explicit, "**I want to see again**." The faith that he exhibited in calling and coming, Jesus noted, had led to his healing. How important it is for counselees to come enthusiastically in faith and be clear about what they

52 So Jesus said to him, "Go, your faith has healed you." Then immediately he saw again and followed Him along the way.

---

want to accomplish in counseling. When these things are not there, you must search them out before beginning.

CHAPTER 11

1   Now at Bethphage and Bethany, on the Mount of Olives, when they drew near to Jerusalem, He sent two of His disciples
2   and said to them,

> Go into the village opposite you, and as soon as you enter it you will find a colt tied up that has never been ridden; untie it and bring it.

3   And if anybody says to you, "Why are you doing this?" tell him, "The Lord needs it and will send it back here soon."

4   So they went and found a colt that was tied outside on the street at a doorway, and they untied it.
5   And some of those who were standing there said to them, "What are you doing untying the colt?"
6   But they told them what Jesus had said, and they let them go.

7   So they brought the colt to Jesus and threw their clothes on it, and He sat on it.

Jesus was about to enter Jerusalem. At **Bethphage** and **Bethany** He paused, sending **two of His disciples** to round up a **colt** He had arranged to use. He gave them the password, in case someone objected to their taking it (vv. 1-3). In verses 4 through 6, they do all that He said, and there is no problem. There are times to arrange things ahead of time. If you want counselees to accomplish something that requires their initiative, but might need some preliminary arrangements to handle properly, it would be wise to make the arrangements and then tell them precisely what to do.

When they **brought the colt to Jesus**, they threw clothes on its back, and He got on it (v. 7). Then, many of His disciples **spread their clothes** and **straw** on the **road** before Him. By this they greatly honored Him as He rode into Jerusalem. People anticipating His coming and those who accompanied Him shouted, "**Hosanna!**" which means "Save now!" Many (perhaps most) who did so thought Jesus was coming to save them from the power of Rome. However, in God's providence, they were unwittingly calling on Him to save by His death on the cross. They were expecting Jesus to reestablish the earthly reign of **David**, not realizing that He was coming to do just that by bringing in the worldwide **empire** of God—a spiritual kingdom that is "not of this world (John 18:36)."

Many times God brings about events in accord with His will by unexpected means. Look for such providential happenings to point them out to your counselees.

8   Many spread their clothes on the road and others spread straw that they had cut from the fields.

9   Both those who went ahead and those who followed shouted,

> Hosanna! **Happy is the One Who comes in the Lord's name**!

10   Happy is the coming empire of our father David! Hosanna in the highest places!

11 Then He entered Jerusalem and went into the temple. After He looked around at everything, He left for Bethany with the Twelve, because the hour was late.

12 Now the next day, as they left Bethany, He became hungry,

13   and when He saw at a distance a fig tree with leaves, He went to see if He could find something on it, but when He came close, He found nothing but leaves (it was not the season for figs).

14   In response to this He said to it, "May nobody ever eat fruit from you again!" And His disciples heard him.

15 Then they came to Jerusalem, and He entered into the temple and began to eject those who were selling and those who were buying in the temple, and He upset the moneychangers' tables and the seats of the dove merchants

16   and wouldn't let anyone carry a load through the temple.

Entering **Jerusalem**, Jesus went to the **temple**, sized up the situation there, and then returned to **Bethany**. On the next day, traveling from Bethany to Jerusalem, Jesus became **hungry**. He saw a **fig tree** with **leaves**. But when He went up to it, there were no figs. Because it was **not the season for figs**, the tree should not have had fully formed leaves that would advertise that it did. Jesus cursed the fig tree, saying that it would never again bear fruit. This act was symbolic of what God was going to do to a rebellious people who bore no fruit. They would be utterly rejected so that never again would they do so.

Counselors could use actions in the experience of the counselee to symbolize significant truth that he needs to learn. For example, a counselee has accumulated debt through credit cards. He then loses his wallet with all his cards. The counselor who has been dealing with his irresponsible behavior may say, "Let that be symbolic of what you should do—dispose of all your credit cards until you learn to be responsible in your use of money. Thank God in His providence that He has given you this example by which to remember that resolution."

Having sized up the temple situation the day before, Jesus went back and ejected those who were making it **a den of thieves**. He also refused to allow people to take short cuts through its grounds as a walkway for busi-

17   Then He taught them: "Hasn't it been written that **My house will be called a house of prayer for all the nations**? But you have made it a den of thieves."

18   Now, the chief priests and scribes heard this, and they looked for a way to destroy Him because they were afraid of Him, since the whole crowd was astounded at His teaching.

19   And when it began to get late they[1] went outside the city.

20   Early the next morning as they went along, they saw the fig tree withered from the roots.

21   Then Peter remembered and said to Him, "Look, the fig tree that You cursed has withered."

22   Jesus answered by saying to them,
Have faith in God.

23   Let Me assure you that whoever says to this mountain, "Be lifted up and thrown into the sea," and doesn't doubt in his heart but believes that what he is saying will happen, he will have it.

24   So then, I tell you, in everything that you pray and ask for, believe that you have received it, and you will.

---

1.   Some MSS read, *He.*

---

ness (vv. 15-17). Jesus' actions of this sort hardly endeared Him to the **priests and scribes** who were getting a cut of the profits by allowing the merchandisers space within the temple environs. They looked for **a way to destroy** Him after this. Moreover, they became **afraid** of Jesus. Would He ruin their businesses? Would He upset the status quo? It certainly seemed so. After all, He was gathering the favor of the crowds.

Fear will lead to drastic action. Here, it led to the determination to do away with Jesus. When you deal with fear in a counselee, you are dealing with the most powerful emotion your counselee ever experiences. Because of this, he is likely to engage in foolish and harmful activities and may make very bad decisions. You must know how to deal with fear. For more information, see the sections on fear in my *Christian Counselor's Manual.*

Coming back into Jerusalem the following day, the disciples saw the fig tree **withered** up. Once more Jesus had exercised His power over nature. They then remembered what Jesus had said to it (vv. 20, 21). In response to their amazement Jesus urged them to also **have faith in God.** After all, it was God Who had accepted the curse as valid and had then validated it for them. He went on to point out that, as apostles, they too would do remarkable works by the power of God working through them if

25 And when you stand praying, if you have something against anyone, forgive him, so that your Father in the heavens also may forgive you your trespasses.

26 [1]

27 And they came to Jerusalem again. Now as He was walking in the
temple, the chief priests and the scribes and the elders came to Him.

28 And they said to Him, "By what authority are you doing these things?"
and "Who gave you the authority to do these things?"

29 Jesus said to them,

I am going to ask you one question; answer Me, and I will tell you
by what authority I am doing these things.

30 John's baptism—was it from heaven or was it from men? Answer
Me.

---

1. Other MSS add vs. 26: *But if you don't forgive, your Father Who is in the heavens won't forgive your trespasses.*

---

they asked in faith, without **doubting** (vv. 23, 24). Your counselees also
should be encouraged to pray in faith. But, of course, they have no such
promise of performing miracles (what the illustration about the **mountain**
indicated) like the apostles did.

Then Jesus spoke about **prayer** concerning **forgiveness**. Of course,
whenever they prayed, they were to have a forgiving attitude—a willingness to forgive anyone who repented. They were never to carry resentment
in their hearts toward anyone. If they failed to forgive, God would not forgive them. There is no requirement here to forgive those who fail to
repent. In this instance, they are pictured as talking only to God, not to
anyone else. There are many wrong ideas about forgiveness—a matter
that every counselor must understand thoroughly since in so many
instances counsel concerning forgiveness is necessary. Please see my
book *From Forgiven to Forgiving* for more details.

In verses 27 through 33 the important question of **authority** is
raised. After all, Jesus not only had taught, but He also had upset the status quo in the temple. So the **chief priests and scribes and elders** confronted Him about it (vv. 27, 28). Jesus answered their questions with one
of His own (a good way to meet objections from counselees or others).
Jesus asks, in effect, "Where did **John** get his authority to baptize? Was it
a heavenly conferred authority or was it initiated by men?" By this question, Jesus impaled them on one or the other horn of the dilemma (vv. 31,
32). Either way they answered, they were in trouble. So they refused to

31 Now they argued with one another, saying, "If we say, 'From heaven,' he will say, 'Then why didn't you believe him?'
32 But suppose we say, 'From men!'..." (They were afraid of the crowd, because everybody believed that John really was a prophet.)
33 So they answered Jesus, "We don't know." And Jesus said to them, "Then I won't tell you by what authority I am doing these things."

---

answer. Jesus likewise refused to answer their question (v. 33). It is not always necessary to answer the questions of a counselee or others. Frequently, when the question is asked for purposes of entrapment, the very best way to respond is with another question of your own—as Jesus did. It is particularly useful, if possible, to ask a question that will expose the motives of those who are asking. This kind of question may often come from one who is not the primary counselee, but from one who wants to queer the counseling process. This is a powerful method for dealing with him.

CHAPTER 12

1 Then He began to speak to them in parables:
   A man **planted a vineyard, placed a hedge around it, dug a wine press, built a tower**, rented it to farmers, and went away.
2 When it was time, he sent a slave to the farmers to get some of the fruits of the vineyard from them.
3 But they took him, beat him, and sent him away with nothing.
4 Again, he sent another slave to them, but this one they wounded in the head and dishonored him.
5 So he sent another, and they killed that one, and a number of others—they beat some and killed others.
6 He had still one more, a dear son; he sent him last to them, saying, "They'll respect my son."

The chapter opens with Jesus once more speaking in **parables**. There were people who, given the opportunity, would put Him to death on the spot. Therefore, His message had to be put in the form of parables so that those who wanted to hear would understand, and those whose hearts were hardened against what He would say would not. Parables, remember, enlighten so long as the hearer places them on a lampstand and refuses to put them under a bushel! A counselor may use parables or illustrations for the same reason. However, it is largely for the sake of the enlightenment, shock value and mnemonic qualities of parables that he will be using them. Why not construct a half dozen or so parables to handle the most common counseling situations that you encounter from day to day, and have them ready to use in the future?

In verses 1 through 12 Jesus told the parable of the **vineyard** and the vine dressers. The story is simple. Everything was done to make the work profitable. There could be no complaint about the preparations or the provisions (v. 1). But at the time when the **owner sent for some of the fruits**, the **farmers** refused to send anything to him, and to add insult to injury (or perhaps the other way around) they beat his **slave** and threw him off the property. The slave the owner sent next was even more severely manhandled (v. 4). A third was **killed** along with others that he sent (v. 5). Finally, he sent his dear son. But, recognizing him to be the heir, the farmers said, "**Come on, let's kill him, and the inheritance will be ours.**" Which they did. In verse 9, Jesus asks the question, "**What will the owner of the vineyard do?**" The answer to that question is the point of

7	But those farmers said to each other, "This is the heir. Come on, let's kill him, and the inheritance will be ours."
8	So they took him and killed him and threw him out of the vineyard.
9	What will the owner of the vineyard do? He will come and will destroy the farmers and will give the vineyard to others.
10	Haven't you read this Scripture: **The Stone that the builders rejected** **became the Head of the corner**;
11	**This was from the Lord,** **and it is amazing in our eyes**?

12   Then they looked for a way to seize Him (but they were afraid of the crowd), because they knew that He had spoken the parable about them. So they left Him and went away.

---

the parable: **He will come and destroy the farmers and give the vineyard to others.**

The message of the parable was that the Jews who had treated God's prophets and apostles as they did would lose the kingdom, and it would be given to another people. Jesus quoted Psalm 118:22 in order to reinforce the point, to show that this was no glitch in the plans of God, but rather was the fulfillment of prophecy.

The principle for counselors is clear. Those who have been given privileges are expected to produce. Tell them so. If and when they reject, despise, and misuse the counsel that they are given, they will ultimately be rejected. Your patience should be like that of God, Who over and over gave the Jews opportunities to repent and bear **fruit**. But there is a time—when Jesus and His Word are ultimately rejected—that the "counselee" must be also. Your time may be spent more profitably in counseling others who truly want help.

By this time His enemies were becoming more adept at understanding Jesus' parables. While they surely didn't understand all (nor did the disciples understand about the handing over of the kingdom to the Gentiles), they understood enough to know that **He had spoken the parable about them** (v. 12), and they began to determine which was the best way to seize and kill Him—thereby fulfilling the prophecy of the parable!

Don't expect every counselee who rejects Christ's way to leave quietly. If you have exposed his sin, have pointed to the way of repentance, and he refuses to take it, you, too, may find yourself in trouble. Be ready to encounter it!

13 But they sent some Pharisees and some Herodians to Him to trap Him in a discussion.

14 They came and said to Him,

> Teacher, we know that you are genuine and aren't influenced by people, because you don't care about their positions, but teach God's way according to the truth. Is it lawful to pay taxes to Caesar or isn't it? Are we allowed to pay or aren't we?

15 But He understood their hypocrisy and said to them: "Why are you testing Me? Bring Me a denarius to look at."

16 So they brought it. Then He said to them, "Whose picture and inscription is this?" And they said to Him, "Caesar's."

17 Then Jesus said to them, "Give to Caesar what is Caesar's, and to God what is God's." And they were astounded at Him.

In verses 13 through 17 we read of the efforts of the **Pharisees** and the **Herodians** to **trap** Jesus. Lying through their teeth, they told Him that they knew He was **genuine** and **not influenced by people**, intimating that they would get an honest answer from Him. Then they put the question that they thought would gore Him on one or the other horns of a dilemma whichever way He answered: "**Is it lawful to pay taxes to Caesar?**" He then asked for a denarius. Either answer—yes or no—would bring down somebody's wrath on His head. On one side of the coin was the head of Caesar and on the other a statue of a goddess. Then, showing them the picture of Caesar, He asked, "**Whose picture and inscription is this?**" And they answered, "**Caesar's.**" Then Jesus said, "**Give to Caesar what is Caesar's and to God** (not the goddess) **what is God's.**" This so unexpected, yet appropriate reply **astounded** them.

From time to time you also will be tested, even led toward traps, by counselees who have been brought to counseling under duress. Learn to give oblique answers, as Jesus did. He answered in unanticipated, but effective, ways.

These Pharisees and Herodians, according to Mark, were hypocrites (v. 15). A hypocrite is a person who misrepresents himself to others. He works on making the outside look good when, inwardly, he is full of treachery. There are hypocrites today who wash the outside of the cup, but not the inside. Hypocrites sometimes come for counseling today. They will come, for instance, in order to look good in someone else's eyes. They do not really want to change, even though they pretend that they do. They come only to say that they were there and "that the counselor couldn't help me, even though I went." Of course you can't help people

303

18 Then some Sadducees came to Him (they are the ones who say that there won't be a resurrection), and they questioned Him, saying,

19   Teacher, Moses wrote for us that **if a man's brother dies** and leaves a wife but **doesn't leave a child, the brother must take his wife and raise up children for his brother**.

20   There were seven brothers. The first married and died leaving no children.

21   So the second married her, and he died leaving no children. Then the same thing happened to the third,

22   and all seven, who left no children. Last of all the wife also died.

23   In the resurrection, when they rise again, whose wife will she be? Each of these seven had her for a wife.

24 Jesus said to them,
       It's because you don't know the Scriptures or God's power that you are going wrong, isn't it?

25   The fact is that when they rise again, they neither marry nor are given in marriage. Rather, they are like the angels in the heavens.

26   Now concerning the dead that will be raised, haven't you read in the book of Moses how God said to him at the bush, **I am the God of Abraham and the God of Isaac and the God of Jacob**?

27   He isn't the God of the dead but of the living. You are quite wrong.

---

who will not let you. When you recognize that you have one of these persons present in the counseling room, it is wise to expose his hypocrisy by throwing the problems he presents to you back at him, as Jesus did here.

Next, in verses 18 through 27 we are introduced to an attempt by the **Sadducees** to impale Jesus. Because they did not believe in the resurrection (v. 18), they had a number of seemingly impossible scenarios to present to the Pharisees who did. So they pulled out one and handed it to Jesus. It was a situation in which **seven brothers,** in succession, **married** the same **woman**. When they all rise **in the** [supposed] **resurrection,** they asked, **whose wife will she be** (v. 23)? Probably, the Pharisees had never been able to answer this question. For Jesus it was not difficult to answer. Jesus chided them for **not knowing the Scriptures or God's power**. He told them that they erred because of that. This is probably the most prevalent cause of error today. Often you will find yourself up against counselees who, because they have misinterpreted (or simply failed to study) the Bible, are in trouble in their thinking and their living. The error here came from not recognizing the Old Testament teaching about the **resurrection** (a problem that many supposedly sophisticated commentators still have

28 Then one of the scribes approached Him and heard them debating. Knowing that He answered them effectively, he asked Him, "Which commandment is the first of all?"

29   Jesus answered,

The first is **Hear, Israel, the Lord our God is one Lord,**

30   **and you must love the Lord your God with all your heart, with all your soul, with all your mind and with all your strength.**

31   The second is this: You must **love your neighbor as yourself.** There isn't any commandment that is greater than these.

32   The scribe replied, "Well put, Teacher! You are right in saying that **He is One and that there is no other beside Him,**

---

today). Jesus then assumed the resurrection is a fact (He says, "**when they rise again**") and then explained that there will be no marriage in heaven, but risen believers will be like the **angels**. Then, He gave them a Bible lesson on the resurrection from a passage they had never thought about in that way before. When God at the burning **bush** called Himself the **God of Abraham, Isaac and Jacob**, He observed, that was an affirmation of the fact that these men were still alive, not annihilated. How did He reason to that conclusion? "Well, God," He said, "**is not the God of the dead, but of the living.**" Then He straightforwardly told them, "**You are quite wrong**" (v. 27).

Be prepared to do Bible study with counselees. Be ready to prove your statements from passages in the Scriptures as Jesus did. Be ready to state that a counselee is dead wrong when it is clear that he is and needs to hear it. Counseling is neither a matter of mere listening, as Rogers taught, nor is it a matter of allowing the counselee to guide you, as Freud thought. It is a matter of stating the truth as it is found in the Scriptures and calling the counselee to submit to it in thinking and in living.

Next a **scribe,** who understood that Jesus had gotten the better of the Pharisees, the Herodians and the Sadducees, came to Jesus. He asked, "**Which commandment is the first of all?**" (a matter that seems to have been troubling him). Jesus immediately replied that it was the commandment to **love God**, and secondly to **love one's neighbor as himself**. These two commands sum up all the rest. Rather than pitting one commandment against another, as people were prone to do, Jesus summed them all up in His teaching about love.

The scribe was deeply impressed with Jesus' reply (v. 32) and understood that Jesus' emphasis on love was **more basic than all burnt offerings and sacrifices**. That, contrary to the teaching of the day, was an

33 **and to love Him with all the heart, with all the understanding and with all the strength, and to love one's neighbor as oneself** is much more basic than all burnt offerings and sacrifices."

34 Then, when Jesus saw that he had answered sensibly, He replied, "You aren't far from God's empire." After that, nobody dared to question Him.

35 When Jesus was teaching in the temple, He inquired,
> How can the scribes say that the Christ is David's Son?

36 David himself said by the Holy Spirit,
> **The lord said to my Lord,**
> **Sit at My right hand**
> **till I put your enemies under Your feet.**

37 David himself calls Him Lord; how is it that He is his Son?
And the large crowd heard Him with pleasure.

38 Now in His teaching He said,
> Watch out for the scribes who like to walk around in long robes and receive greetings in the marketplaces,

39 and like to have the best seats in the synagogs and the best seats at dinners;

40 these are the people who devour widows' houses and pray long prayers for a show! They will receive a greater judgment.

---

insight that up till then had not been expressed. Jesus was pleased with the reply and declared that the scribe wasn't **far from God's empire**. What He meant, of course, is that his answer showed that he was concentrating on the right thing—the inner man—rather than on an outer conformity to rituals and ceremonies. By thinking that way, he was approaching faith in Him. There comes a time in counseling when you recognize that someone is beginning to "get it". That is the time to observe, as Jesus did, that he is on the right road.

We now skip to a time when Jesus was teaching in the temple (vv. 35-40; 41-44). The first point He made had to do with teaching not in response to questions from others, but in connection with those Jesus Himself asked. He raised the question, **"How can the scribes say that the Christ is David's Son?"** He then answered His own question by saying that the Holy Spirit spoke through David telling us so. In other words, if God by His Spirit said so, that settles the matter. The inspiration, inerrancy, and authority of the Bible are all asserted in this reply. You, too, may point out that if God says something in the Bible, it is authoritative and ought to be sufficient. Actually, He never answered His own question beyond raising an additional one (v. 37). He left these questions dangling in the air for people to think about. That isn't a bad method for teaching.

41 Then He sat down opposite the offering chest and watched how the crowd put money into the chest. Many rich people put in a lot.

42 Then one poor widow came and put in two lepta, that together were worth one fourth of a cent.

43 So He called His disciples to Him and said to them,

Let Me assure you that this poor widow has put in more than all those who are putting money into the offering chest.

44 They all gave out of their abundance, but this woman out of her poverty put in everything, all that she had to live on.

Next, Jesus issued a warning about the **scribes** who sought notoriety and wealth (we have our share in the ministry today too!). He warned the **crowd** not to follow or praise them. Indeed, He made it clear that these hypocrites **would receive a greater judgment**. It is not always easy to do, but part of your task is to warn counselees about those who would mislead them. People don't like you to do this, but it is necessary.

The next word—growing out of Jesus' comment about the **devouring of widow houses**—had to do with the **poor widow** who gave **more** (proportionately) than those who gave great amounts, because she gave all that she had to God (vv. 41-44). The teaching here is about the heart of a person when he gives It is not about the total amount. The former, not the latter, is what counts to God. The principle can be utilized in counseling to refer to the use of gifts as well as to resources. It is a principle that you should remember when one claims that he has so little with which to serve God. It is not so much what he has as what he does with it that is of importance.

CHAPTER 13

1 Now as He left the temple one of His disciples said to Him, "Teacher, look how large these stones are and how great these buildings are!"

2   But Jesus said to him, "You see these great buildings, do you? There won't be one stone left on another; they'll all be thrown down!"

3   When He sat down on the Mount of Olives, opposite the temple, Peter and James and John and Andrew asked Him privately,

4   "Tell us when these things will happen and what will be the sign that all these things are about to take place."

5   And this is what Jesus began to tell them:
       Watch out so that nobody will lead you astray.

6   Many will come in My name, saying, "I am He," and they will
       lead many astray.

The teaching in this chapter is prophetic. There are varying interpretations of its content ranging from those who believe it is entirely of future application to us, to those who believe that the prophecies have all been fulfilled, to those who hold to some of both. The view set forth in this book is that Jesus was speaking of events, prophetic at the time when He spoke, but all of which would take place within the lifetime of those to whom He spoke.

The occasion for Jesus' discourse on the Mount of Olives was the disciples' comment about the remarkable size and quality of the **stones** in the **temple** and the adjacent **buildings** (v. 1). His response is that **not one stone would be left on another** when their destruction came. That phrase means *complete* destruction. He **sat down** to teach in full view of the temple. The four who were His students on this occasion are listed in verse 3. They ask Jesus two questions:

When will this overthrow take place?

What sign will God give us that it is about the take place?

Jesus responded to those questions in His discourse. In addition, He warned about those events that were *not* signs and by which they might be led astray if they wrongly interpreted them as such (vv. 1-13). Precisely what He warned against sadly has happened; many, not heeding the warning, have wrongly interpreted them as the **signs** of the coming of Christ.

It would be easy to be led astray, Jesus said, since **many would come in His Name**, declaring that they—not He—are the Christ (the **Name,**

7	But when you hear of wars and rumors of wars, don't be disturbed. This must happen, but it isn't the end.
8	Nation will rise against nation and kingdom against kingdom; there will be earthquakes here and there and famines. These are the beginning of birth pangs.
9	But watch yourselves. They will hand you over to councils, and you will be beaten in synagogs: you will stand before leaders and kings for My sake, as a witness to them.
10	So the good news must be preached to all the nations first.

"Messiah" that He rightly bore). The problem has not ceased. In Jewish history, there have been such persons before and after the destruction of Jerusalem. Even in our lifetime a man, purporting to be the Messiah, has arisen among the Jews.

The ease with which people are led astray and leave the true Messiah for someone or something else, ought to alert the wise counselor to the phenomenon. The Bible is full of warnings about false teachers and those who follow them to their peril. Counselors, whose counsel is being challenged and opposed by such, must be able to refute them so as to help shield counselees—who are frequently in a weakened frame of mind—from their wiles. Are you aware of the current heresies? Can you correct counselees' errors and help them steer clear of them? You ought to be able to assist in this way. No small amount of counselees' problems (or at least failure to solve problems) is due to false concepts that they have accepted and are trying to follow. With modern communication it is so easy to widely spread *any* belief—no matter how bizarre—within a very short time. If you have never studied the cults or heresies before, I urge you to bone up on them so that you will be prepared when you run into people influenced by them.

Well, not only would religious problems arise, but international conflicts and **rumors** of them, along with "natural" disasters, would also dominate the forty-year period before the destruction of the temple (vv.7, 8). But as Jesus said at the end of verse 7, they would **not** be the **sign** of the **end** of the temple and the city. The apostles would also find themselves hailed up before leaders and kings for their faith. This would give them opportunity to witness about Christ all around the Mediterranean world (vv. 9, 10). But **first** (that is before the end would come) the good news would be preached all over this world (as indeed, Paul in Colossians 1:6 and 23 said it had been in his day. How far the other apostles went and to whom they preached is largely unknown to us. But, you may be

309

> **11** Now when they arrest you and bring you to trial, don't worry beforehand about what you will say. Rather, say whatever is given to you in that hour (it won't be you speaking, but the Holy Spirit).
>
> 12 A brother will turn in his brother to be put to death, and a father his child; and children will rise up against parents and have them put to death.
>
> 13 Everybody will hate you because of My name. But whoever endures to the end will be saved.
>
> **14** Now, when you see the **abomination that leads to desolation** standing where it shouldn't (let the reader understand), then those who are in Judea should flee to the mountains:
>
> 15 whoever is on the roof of a house shouldn't come down or go in to take anything out of his house,
>
> 16 and whoever is in the field shouldn't go back to get his coat.

---

assured, Paul had good reason to write as he did.). Verses 11 through 13 are a "footnote" in which Jesus tells the apostles not to prepare for those occasions when they would defend themselves and when they would have a chance to witness for Christ because in that hour the Holy Spirit would speak through them, giving them the very words they were to speak. That means that these defenses and sermons were inspired. That is one reason why preachers and counselors ought to study the sermons and the speeches in the Book of Acts which Luke gives as examples of this inspired preaching that carried the good news from Jerusalem to Rome. From that sort of study, the minister of Jesus Christ may learn much about what the Spirit thinks is essential and about how to present it.

From verse 14 onward, Jesus began to describe what would occur immediately prior to the destruction of Jerusalem. The **abomination of desolation** was the true sign about which they had asked. That was the coming of Titus and his Roman army to the city. The pagans would first mound up a wall around Jerusalem to create a siege. When the siege was successful, and they could finally enter the city, they would literally push the stones of the temple off one another (see Josephus for details).

There is a time to **flee. The abomination** (or thing loathsome to God and all His true worshippers) that would lead to the **desolation** of the city was the presence of Gentiles in the temple itself. The description is borrowed from **Daniel**, as Jesus pointed out, to give them some idea of what He was talking about. In Daniel's prophecy, it referred to the coming of Antiochus Epiphanes into the temple where he erected a statue of Zeus, sacrificed a pig on the altar, and sprinkled pig juice all over the place. Few

17	Woe to pregnant women and to nursing mothers in those days.
18	Pray that it won't happen in winter!
19	I say all of this because the affliction of those days will be of a sort that hasn't happened from the beginning of God's creation until now, and never will happen again.
20	Indeed, if the Lord hadn't shortened those days, nobody would survive. But for the sake of His elect people whom He chose, He shortened those days.
21	At that time if anybody tells you, "Look, here is the Christ," or "There He is," don't believe it.
22	False Christs and false prophets will arise, and they will perform great signs and wonders to mislead (if it were possible) the chosen ones.
23	But you must watch out. I have told you everything beforehand.

things could be more abominable in the sight of a pious Jew. A similar circumstance would occur, Jesus explained. The Gentiles would raze the temple and the holy ground would be profaned. When it was apparent that the city had been surrounded, the believers were to head for the hills beyond Pella (which Eusebius says that they did) to escape. The historians tell us that after the city was surrounded, for some unknown reason (apart from the providence of God) the army withdrew temporarily, and the Christians in Jerusalem who heeded this prophecy fled. Then the army took up the siege once more never to leave again until the destruction was completed.

A counselor may advise a counselee to **flee** when it is appropriate. In most situations that might be poor advice. But when the inevitable is coming, it is appropriate. The advice to neither return from the field nor come down from the housetops graphically emphasizes the importance of immediate flight. It is those, who like Lot's wife linger and look back with longing, who miss future opportunities and find themselves in trouble.

Verses 17 and following stress the urgency of fleeing and also the difficulties that would arise on that occasion. This would be a major catastrophe—one greater than had ever been experienced before. Indeed, it would be so severe that if God had not mercifully **shortened** the devastation, even the **elect** would not have been able to endure. Once more, Jesus warned about false Christs who would arise during the invasion and would **mislead** many. In times of crisis, people are inclined to follow bad leaders who take advantage of the situation. Be aware that many counselees are in crisis. Instead, Jesus commands His own to **watch**—to be alert,

> **24** But in those days, after that affliction,
> **The sun will grow dark,**
> **and the moon will not give her light;**
> 25   **the stars will fall from the sky,**
> and the powers in the heavens will be shaken.
> 26   At that time they will see **the Son of Man coming in clouds** with great power and glory.
> 27   And at that time He will send out His angels and they will gather together His chosen ones from the four winds, from the end of the earth to the end of the sky.
> **28** Now learn a parable from the fig tree: Whenever its branch has already become tender and shoots forth leaves, you know that summer is near.
> 29   So also with you—when you see these things happening, know that He is near, at the door.

---

not sleepy, but ready for all such things.

What about verses 24 and 25? Are these verses to be taken literally? No. These figures of speech were used to describe great political upheavals. They implied that orders which were seemingly as permanent as the stars and other heavenly bodies would fall (cf. Acts 2:19ff. where Joel is quoted to indicate the change of the Old Testament order into the New by using such figures. The prophets frequently used these sorts of figures of speech to speak of the downfalls of nations).

It is then that Jesus would **come in great power and glory** (v. 26). That Jesus was the One He claimed to be would be recognized by those who rejected Him. His words would be fulfilled and He would destroy the temple and the city in **great power and glory**. This **coming** of Jesus is not to be confused with His second coming at the final judgment. This would be His judgment-coming on Jerusalem. Not all comings are the same.

Verse 27 refers to the sending out of the apostles (**angels** ="messengers," as is the primary meaning of the Greek word) to the ends of the earth to **gather** the **elect** into the newly ordered empire of God.

In verse 28, Jesus began to answer the disciples' other question: *when* would these things take place? He was specific as to the **generation** (it would happen in the lifetime of many who were then alive; cf. v. 30) but nonspecific as to when in the generation (vv. 32-37). Because of this uncertainty, they were to be alert at all times watching for His **coming** in judgment.

All interpreters face difficulties in these verses. But the time ele-

30	Let Me assure you that this generation surely will not pass away until all these things take place.
31	Heaven and earth will pass away, but My words won't pass away.
32	But about that date or hour—nobody knows it; not the angels in heaven, or the Son. Only the Father does.
33	Watch out. Be alert because you don't know when that time will be.
34	It's like a man leaving his house on a trip, who puts his slaves in charge of things, each with his task, and orders the doorkeeper to watch.
35	So then, you must watch—because you don't know when the owner of the house will come, whether it will be in the evening, or at midnight, or when the rooster crows or in the morning—
36	so that if He comes suddenly He won't find you sleeping!
37	Now what I say to you, I say to all—watch!

ments are clear—it would be in that **generation** that **all** these predictions would be fulfilled. There are some who would like to read **generation** as "race" in order to relieve themselves of the great difficulties that their interpretation presents, but this meaning is impossible in the light of the use of the word (see Alexander's commentary on this). The key message of the chapter is the command to be **alert** and to **watch**. Just as they were to watch for the judgment coming on Jerusalem, so we too are to watch for the final judgment which could happen in our lifetime. Too many get caught up in the arguments about this and that in prophecy, only to miss this major thrust of Scripture. Don't let counselees get you debating prophecy or other matters to the detriment of their lives and their readiness to serve Christ as He commands! When they do so, it can often be a dodge to get away from difficult or embarrassing discussions. Be aware of this tendency and don't get caught up in it.

CHAPTER 14

1 Now the Passover and the Feast of Unleavened Bread were to begin in two days. And the chief priests and the scribes were looking for some deceptive way to seize Him so they could kill Him.

2   But they said, "Not during the feast, or the people may riot."

3 When He was in Bethany at Simon the leper's house, while He was sitting at the table, a woman came with an alabaster jar of pure nard perfume that was very expensive. And she broke the jar and poured the perfume over His head.

4   Now some angrily said to one another, "Why has this waste occurred?

5   This perfume could have been sold for over three hundred denarii, and then given to the poor." And they were furious with her.

We approach a very long chapter at this point (72 verses! One wonders, at times, on what principle the chapters were divided. As you are aware, there were no chapters or verses in the original. These were added later for convenience in locating material). Once more we are told that His enemies were **looking for some way to seize** Jesus (v. 1). However, they could not do so openly because of the crowds that followed Him. This would cause a **riot**, they supposed, with bad consequences to themselves. So they sought an underhanded way to accomplish their nefarious designs. The **Passover Feast** and the **Feast of Unleavened Bread** drew great crowds to Jerusalem from all over the Mediterranean world, and possibly even beyond. Whenever counselees want to be **deceptive** about how they carry out something or other, not only reprove them for their deceptions but also look for what it is they fear. Often, it is because of fear that they cook up such ways and means. While handling the obvious, don't miss the less obvious.

The story of the **woman** with the **alabaster jar of perfume** who **broke** it above Jesus' **head** is recorded in verses 3 through 9. This was expensive ointment; pouring it over Him showed her love for and gratitude to Jesus. Judas and some other apostles remarked about the supposed waste in this act (vv. 4, 5). But Jesus was of another mind. He said, "**She has done a fine thing for Me.**" There are those who will make complaints about money spent in the cause of Christ to honor Him. You will hear such things in counseling. Remind them that if the money is truly given to honor Him, it is a **fine thing**. Be careful before agreeing with a critical counselee that an expenditure is a waste of money that might be spent

6   But Jesus said,

     Let her alone. Why are you giving her a hard time? She has done a fine thing for Me.

7   You're always going to have the poor with you, so whenever you want to you can do good for them, but you won't always have Me.

8   She did what she could. She has anointed My body for burial beforehand.

9   I tell you for certain that wherever the good news is preached in the whole world, what this woman did also will be related in memory of her.

10   Then Judas Iscariot, one of the Twelve, went off to the chief priests to betray Him to them.

11   When they heard what he had to say, they were delighted and promised to give him money. So he looked for an opportunity to betray Him.

12   Now on the first day of unleavened Bread, when they sacrificed the Passover lamb, His disciples said to Him, "Where do You want us to go and make preparations so that You may eat the Passover?"

13   So He sent off two of His disciples, saying to them,

     Go into the city, and a man carrying a jar of water will meet you. Follow him,

14   and wherever he enters, tell the person who is in charge of the place that the Teacher says, "Where is My guest room in which I shall eat the Passover with My disciples?"

---

more profitably elsewhere. Probe gently to see if there might not be more behind it. And on what basis, you must ask, can anything done for Christ be judged as extravagant? Think this one through carefully.

The excuse that the perfume could have been sold and used for the poor is countered by Jesus' words that the poor would always be with them to do good for, but that He was about to leave. He went on to declare that she had **anointed [His] body beforehand for burial**. He continued by saying that wherever the gospel was preached in all the world her deed would be remembered. Once again, Jesus made it clear that He would soon die.

An account of **Judas'** bargain with the chief priests is given in verses 10 and 11. The promise of money, in the end, was a bitter disappointment—as, indeed, all promises of profit from harming another always will be. In dealing with avaricious counselees, don't forget **Judas**!

In verses 13 through 16 we read of Jesus' **preparation** for the **Passover**. The arrangements, unlike those having to do with the securing of the colt, seem not to have been made beforehand. Yet they probably were.

15   And he will show you a large upper room with the seating arranged and ready; make preparations for us there.

16   So the disciples went out and came into the city and found just what He had told them, and they prepared the Passover.

17   When it was evening, He came with the Twelve.

18   And as they were reclining at the table and eating, Jesus said, "Let Me tell you that it is certain that one of you will betray Me, one who is eating with Me."

19   They began to get upset, and one after another said to Him, "It isn't I, is it?"

20   He said to them,

It is one of the Twelve, one who dips together with Me in the dish.

21   On the one hand this will happen because the Son of Man will go exactly as it has been written about Him, but on the other hand, woe to that man by whom the Son of Man will be betrayed. It would be better for that man if he hadn't been born!

Though it might not seem to be a matter of preparation for one to be carrying a **water jar**, that is precisely the reason why I say it could be. It was *women* who normally carried water. To find a *man* doing so may be unusual enough to call attention to itself. The phrase, **the Teacher**, also seems to be one that would be known to both parties in the transaction.

Why was there so much circuitous action? Because Jesus did not want it leaked beforehand where they would be celebrating the Passover. He wanted no interruptions by the religious officials or the often unruly crowds. Many times you will have to caution your counselees about how they should go about doing things that might be hindered by outside interference. Keeping matters fairly confidential will be one way of averting interference. Some unwisely speak too much, to too many persons about their intentions, so that nothing can be done privately.

In the evening, as they partook of the Passover meal, Jesus revealed that there was one who would **betray** Him (vv. 17-21). This was a terrible thought to those present (and Judas must have wondered if the game was up). The basic insecurity, uncertainty, and instability of the disciples are revealed as they all wonder out loud, saying, **"It isn't I, is it?"** Jesus indicated to them that it was **Judas** who would **dip in the dish** with Him. He once more indicates that everything will happen to Him exactly as it was written in the prophetic passages that refer to His death. But in verse 21 (and this is crucial) where He says this, He makes it clear that prophecy does not excuse those who fulfill it from their responsibility. Judas will

22 Now as they were eating, He took a piece of bread, blessed it, broke it and gave it to them and said, "Take it; this is My body."

23 Then He took a cup, gave thanks and handed it to them, and they all drank from it.

24 And He said to them:

This is My blood of the[1] covenant that is poured out for many.

25 Let Me assure you that it is certain that I won't drink of the fruit of the vine again until that day when I drink the new wine in God's empire.

26 Now after they sang a hymn, they went out to the Mount of Olives.

---

1. Some MSS add, *new*.

---

receive unbelievable punishment for his terrible deed. The plan and purpose of God, often expressed beforehand in prophecy, does not cancel out man's responsibility, because it is through the responsible actions of those who fulfill it that the prophecy takes place. For a fuller discussion of this issue see my book *The Grand Demonstration* (in which I devote a chapter to the problem).

The uncertainty of the disciples is, perhaps, as telling of man's fundamental sense of his sin and guilt as you could find anywhere. They knew, as they sat there, that they were capable of gross acts of sin. Counselees who fail to admit this—a fact they know full well—might profit from having it pointed out in this passage.

Next comes the institution of the Lord's supper, which grew out of the Passover (vv. 22-25). This ordinance is given to the church in such simplicity that it is astounding what suspicion, bitterness, and controversy has arisen over it throughout the centuries. Jesus, in the well-known words of the Lord's supper said, **"This is My body and this My blood of the covenant that is poured out for many."** The disciples certainly had no idea of the elements turning into true body and blood. After all, the One who said it was seated there in their midst in that body through which the blood was flowing. What Jesus said is the same as if I held up a photograph of her and said, "This is my wife." No one would imagine that I meant that paper was the real life person. Or, since it was a symbolical act, it would be as if a person seated at a table, explaining to a friend how to get to a certain location, were to say (as he placed the salt cellar in one spot and the pepper in another), "This is the bank and this is the post office." Using symbols is useful in the counseling room as well, but you must be sure that the counselee doesn't take your words and distort the

317

27 And Jesus said to them,
> You will all stumble and fall, because it is written, **I will strike the Shepherd, and the sheep will be scattered**.

28   But after My resurrection I will go before you into Galilee.

29 Then Peter said to Him, "Even if everybody stumbles and falls, yet I won't!"

30 Then Jesus said to him, "Let Me assure you, today—this very night—before the rooster crows twice you will deny Me three times."

31 But all the more insistently he said, "If I have to die with you, I will never deny you." And they all also said the same thing.

32 Then they went to a place that was called Gethsemane. And He said to His disciples, "Sit here while I pray."

---

symbol into something literal. 9According to the custom to conclude the Passover, they sang a hymn.)

The uncertainty of the disciples, mentioned above, now gave way to a false security—indeed it turns out to be a proud boast. Quoting the Old Testament (v. 27), Jesus predicted that all the disciples would sin (**stumble**) by denying that they were a part of His band. Yet (v. 28) He intimated that they would be forgiven and restored after His resurrection when He met them again in **Galilee** (cf. 16:7). That would be when He would **again drink of the fruit of the vine** with them—in the **empire** which would have fully come by then (v. 25). He ate with the disciples after the resurrection on several instances.

But Peter (followed by all the disciples, v. 31) proudly declared that even if the others forsook Him, he would not (v. 29). But Jesus assured them that he would do so three times—before the **rooster crowed** twice. Yet in spite of the Scripture quoted, and the assurance of the Lord, they persisted in their unfounded assertion of fealty. Later events proved them all wrong.

Sometimes it is best to warn a counselee that he is likely to fall, and assure him that pride always goes before such a fall. But if he persists, back off (as Jesus did), and let him *experience* the truth of what you have been telling him. Some won't listen; they will have to learn the hard way. Of course you might always be wrong; Jesus cannot be. So you must qualify the terms in which you speak "It surely *looks like* you will fail if you do that at this point. I *doubt* if you are ready to. . ." The italicized words (or words to that effect) are significant for a human counselor to use. He does not possess special revelation. When a counselee thinks he can get away with doing what the Bible expressly forbids, however, the counselor

33 Then He took Peter and James and John with Him, and became greatly distressed and agitated.

34 Then He said to them, "I am so upset I am at the point of death. Stay here and watch."

35 When He had gone forward a short distance, He fell upon the ground and prayed that if it were possible that hour might pass away from Him.

36 He said, "Abba (Father), everything is possible for You; remove this cup from Me. Yet don't do what I want, but what You want."

37 Then He came and found them sleeping and said to Peter,

> Simon, are you sleeping? Couldn't you watch for one hour?

38 > You all must watch and pray, so that you won't enter into temptation. The spirit is eager enough, but the flesh is weak!

39 Then He went away again and uttered the same prayer.

40 When He came again He found them sleeping, because their eyes were heavy. And they didn't know what answer to give Him.

41 Then He came a third time and said to them,

> Are you still sleeping and resting? That's enough. The hour has come. See, the Son of Man is betrayed into the hands of sinners.

---

may be every bit as certain as the Lord Jesus Himself.

Next, we journey with the little band that left the upper room to the Garden of Gethsemane. Here Jesus told them to watch and pray as He went off for a little while and did so Himself. Three times He found them **sleeping**. It was probably because they had failed to prepare for what was coming in prayer (as Jesus did) that they were caught off guard when it happened and ended up denying Him. That seems to be the import of verse 38 where Jesus speaks of the **temptation** (test, trial) that they were going to face.

In His own prayer, the Lord struggles in His human nature with the coming ordeal in which He would become sin for His elect and endure the wrath of God for them all. But His willingness to do God's *will* rather than His own was exemplary of what all prayer should be. There are many things to learn here about trials, prayer, sleeping when one ought to be praying, and watching alertly. The counselor who cannot see these facts when they are mentioned to him probably is not going to counsel well anyway.

In verse 41 Jesus said, "**the hour has come.**" Jesus knew *when* He was to do *what*. We, who are created in the image of God, like Him, must plan our work and then work our plan. Many counselees fail, at least in part, from poor planning—or planning (good enough in itself) that is never carried out. This has to do with a lack of discipline.

42   Get up; we must go. See, the one who is betraying Me is near by.

43 And right then, while He was still speaking, Judas (one of the Twelve) came, together with a mob, carrying swords and clubs, sent by the chief priests and scribes and elders.

44   Now His betrayer had given them a signal: "The one I kiss is the one; grab Him and lead Him away securely."

45   So he came and, immediately going to Him, said, "Rabbi," and kissed Him with a show of affection.

46   Then they laid their hands on Him and arrested Him.

47   Now one of those who stood by drew his sword, struck the priest's slave and cut his ear off.

48   But Jesus responded to them with these words:

Have you come out with swords and clubs to arrest Me as you would a robber?

49   Every day I was with you, teaching in the temple, but you didn't seize Me. Nevertheless, this is in order to fulfill the Scriptures.

50 Then, they all left Him and fled.

51   Now a certain young man who was following Him was wearing only a linen garment over his naked body. And they grabbed him,

52   but he left behind the linen garment and fled naked.

53 Then they led Jesus away to the high priest, and all the chief priests and elders and scribes came together.

A crowd of rabble (not official soldiers or police) gathered together in a hurry, was sent by the chief priests to arrest Him. Judas signaled Who He was by kissing Him (thereby aggravating his sin). And Peter unsheathed his sword and cut off the ear of the high priest's slave.

Jesus reprimanded them for coming for Him as though He were a common criminal (v. 48) and pointed out that they didn't have the courage to take Him in public (v. 49). Then in verse 50, the significant verse that bears upon the disciples' proud boasting, we read that **they all fled**. We also read about a young man (probably Mark himself) who lost his linen nightshirt when he was grabbed and, consequently, fled naked. This is an embarrassing footnote that adds a note of pathos to the rest of the account.

Verses 53 through 65 tell of Jesus' illegal trial (by law, trials could not be held at night) before the high priests and the Sanhedrin. Mixed in with this account is the beginning of **Peter's** three denials leading to his sorrow and remorse for what he had done. It was difficult to trump up charges against Jesus because the so-called **witnesses'** testimonies conflicted (v. 59). Because of this, the high priest turned to the real issue (Jesus had not deigned to reply to the false charges leveled against Him).

54 And Peter followed Him at a distance, right into the courtyard of the high priest. And he sat with the guards and was warming himself by the fire.

55 Now the chief priests and the whole council searched for testimony against Jesus so that they could put Him to death, but they couldn't find any.

56 A number gave false testimony against Him, but their testimonies weren't consistent.

57 Some rose up and falsely testified against Him, saying,

58 "We heard him say, 'I will destroy this temple that is made by hands, and in three days I will build another not made by hands.'"

59 Yet their testimony wasn't consistent either.

60 Then the high priest stood up in the midst and questioned Jesus, "Aren't you going to reply to what these people are testifying against you?"

61 But He was silent and made no reply at all. Again the high priest questioned Him and said to Him, "Are you the Christ, the Son of the Blessed One?"

62 Then Jesus said,

> I am. And you will see **the Son of Man sitting at the right hand of the Almighty One and coming with the clouds of the sky**.

63 Then the high priest ripped his clothes apart and said, "What more need is there for witnesses?

64 You heard the blasphemy; what do you think we should do?" And they all condemned Him as deserving of death.

He asked, "**Are you the Christ, the Son of the Blessed One?**"

There was no longer a need to veil His identity. In unmistakable terms He declared "**I am**," and went on to say that (as Daniel had prophesied) they would see Him **sitting on the right hand of the Almighty One and coming with the clouds of the sky** (v. 62). That is to say **coming** (not to earth, but) to the Ancient of Days to receive the Empire from God (cf. Daniel 7:13, 14). In effect, Jesus was saying that He is the One Who would fulfill Daniel's prophecy. This, of course, was the admission they wanted. Witnesses were unnecessary; they had heard what they needed from Jesus' own lips. They called it **blasphemy**, which it would have been, if it were not true (a possibility they would not entertain). They all determined, therefore, that He should die for this claim. Then they treated Jesus with utter contempt and injustice (v. 65).

Peter's denials of Jesus follow in verses 66 through 72. How sad that even a servant girl could bring terror into the heart of a guilt-ridden disciple. It does not take much to set off the angry denials of a Christian who is

65   And some of them began to spit at Him and to blindfold Him and to punch Him and to say to Him "Prophesy!" And the guards greeted Him with slaps.

66   Now when Peter was below in the courtyard, one of the high priest's servant girls came along,

67   and seeing Peter warming himself, she looked him over and said, "You were with Jesus the Nazarene."

68   But he denied it, saying, "I don't know or understand what you are talking about." And he went outside into the entrance.[1]

69   But the servant girl, seeing him, began to say again to those who were standing by, "This man is one of them."

70   But he denied it again. And after a little while those who were standing by said to Peter, "It's true; you are one of them—indeed, you're a Galilean."

71   But he began to take a curse on himself and swear, "I don't know this man that you're talking about!"

72   Just then, the rooster crowed the second time.[2] And Peter remembered Jesus' word, how He had said to him, "Before the rooster crows twice, you will deny Me three times." And as he thought he wept.

---

1.   Some MSS add, *and the rooster crowed.*
2.   Some MSS omit, *the second time.*

---

being pursued and is fearful of the consequences. The more angry the denial and the more it is punctuated by curses or oaths, the more likely that you are dealing with a lie. (i.e. He protests too greatly!) Every good counselor understands this sort of response and its roots.

Ultimately, Peter came to his senses as he thought more calmly about the matter, **remembered Jesus' word—and wept.**

CHAPTER 15

1 Now as soon as morning came, the chief priests, together with the elders and scribes and the entire council, held a conference. Binding Jesus, they led Him away and handed Him over to Pilate.

2   Pilate questioned Him, "Are you the King of the Jews?" Answering him, He said, "You are the one who said it."

3   The chief priests accused Him of a number of things.

4   So Pilate questioned Him again, "Aren't you going to answer? See how many accusations they are making against you!"

5   But Jesus didn't give any other answer, and this surprised Pilate.

6 Now at the feast he used to release to them one prisoner that they requested.

7   There was one named Barabbas, who was imprisoned with the rebels who had committed murder in the insurrection.

8   So they went up and began to ask him to do as he used to do for them.

9   And Pilate answered them by saying, "Do you want me to release the King of the Jews?"

10   (He knew that it was because of envy that the chief priests had handed Him over.)

11   But the chief priests stirred up the crowd to request him to release Barabbas to them instead.

In this chapter we tread on holy ground. It is here that we see the Lord crucified. Since they were unable to exercise capital punishment, the religious leaders led Jesus away to Pilate, the Roman governor. To some initial questioning by Pilate Jesus said, "You were the one who said I am the King of the Jews." He was letting Pilate think about his own answer. **You are the one who said it** (v. 2) is a powerful answer for counselors to give to counselees at the right time. Think deeply about it, then pack this away in your counseling kit somewhere near the top to be used from time to time.

Pilate was surprised that Jesus said nothing more (v. 5). Why He was silent is a matter of speculation. Pilate had doubtless heard many plead for their lives before and was surprised that Jesus was so silent in this situation where His life was hanging in the balance.

The story of Barabbas and what it tells about Pilate and the Jews is recounted in verses 6 through 15. Pilate recognized that the religious leaders had arrested Jesus out of **envy** and wanted to release Him (v. 10). So rather than stand firmly against such injustice, he sought a way out that he

12 So Pilate, answering again, said to them, "What then should I do with the one that you call the King of the Jews?"

13 But they shouted again, "Crucify him!"

14 Pilate said to them, "Why? What has he done wrong?" But they shouted all the more, "Crucify him!"

15 So Pilate, deciding to satisfy the crowd, released Barabbas to them, and after he had Him whipped, he handed Jesus over to be crucified.

16 Then the soldiers led Him away to the inside of the court (that is, the Praetorium), and they assembled the entire cohort.

17 They put a purple robe on Him and crowned Him with a crown of woven thorns.

18 And they began to greet Him, "Hail, King of the Jews!"

19 And they struck Him repeatedly on the head with a reed, and spit on Him, and they knelt down, and worshiped Him.

20 Then, after they had mocked Him, they took the purple robe off and put His clothes on Him. And they led Him out to be crucified.

---

hoped would still please the Jews. He made them choose between the cut-throat Barabbas and Jesus thinking that they couldn't possibly choose Barabbas. But they surprised him and asked that Barabbas be released according to the annual custom rather than Jesus. Pilate, once he had begun to compromise, was on the slippery slope. This is a marvelous example to hold before counselees who are tempted to try to please everyone in some issue. He acted against his conscience. Finally, having called Jesus the King of the Jews, he asked them what he should do with their King. They shouted, **"Crucify Him!"** When he protested that Jesus had done nothing worthy of death, they shouted all the more. So **to satisfy the crowd**, he had Jesus **whipped and crucified**. This was the final cave in that was begun in his first compromise.

In verses 16 through 20 we read of how Jesus was treated by the **soldiers** of Pilate. They mocked Jesus as **"king,"** by placing on Him the **robe of purple** (possibly scarlet; the royal color), by **kneeling** before Him, and then by crowning Him with **a crown of thorns**. They thus made sport of the loving Lord who had come to save men from such sinful behavior! In addition to this cruel treatment, they **struck Him on the head with** a **rod, spit** on Him, and gave Him **mock worship**. Then they **led Him to be crucified**. In these things every counselor is brought close once again to the sinful heart of men turned against their Creator. Let him never minimize the power and the depth of sin.

In verses 21 through 26 we read of the journey to the cross and the

21 And they forced a certain Simon of Cyrene, the father of Alexander and Rufus, who was passing by as he came in from the country, to carry His cross.

22 Then they brought Him to the place called Golgotha (which, when translated, means "The Place of the Skull").

23 And they offered Him wine mixed with myrrh, but He wouldn't take it.

24 Then they crucified Him. And they divided His clothes, casting lots on them to determine who got what.

25 It was nine o'clock when they crucified Him.

26 The official text of the charge against Him was written on top: THE KING OF THE JEWS.

27 And they crucified two robbers with Him, one on His right and one on His left.

28 [1]

29 Those who passed by blasphemed Him, shaking their heads and saying, "So! You are the one who was going to destroy the temple and rebuild it in three days!

30 Save yourself! Come down from the cross!"

31 So too the chief priests together with the scribes mocked Him, saying to each other, "He saved others, but he can't save himself!

---

1. Some MSS add vs. 28: *And the Scripture that says, "He was counted with transgressors," was fulfilled.*

---

actual **crucifixion** itself. Simon was forced to help **carry the cross**. When they came to **Golgotha**, that place where a hill looked like a **skull**, they offered to stupefy Him with **wine** that pious women provided for the purpose, but He Who would feel the full force of sin in His own body, refused to mitigate His suffering (v. 23). Having crucified Him, they divided Jesus' clothes and cast lots for them. Jesus was crucified at nine o'clock. Over His head was placed a sign that read THE KING OF THE JEWS. Again, we see the providence of God at work. Pilate's spite at being forced to crucify Jesus is shown for all to see in the placard he insisted be placed over His head. In spite of men and their sin, God has His way. Often, He uses that sin, as we see here, to spread His truth.

In verse 27 we are told that Jesus was not crucified alone, but (according to prophecy, like so much else that happened on that day) He was crucified in the company of robbers. Those who passed by also made fun of Him (as prophecy had declared they would) saying, "**Save yourself!**" as if He could not. And the religious leaders joined in the mockery and scorn (vv. 31, 32). Even those who were crucified with Him

32 Let the Christ, Israel's King, come down from the cross now so that we may see and believe." And those who were crucified with Him reproached Him.

33 Now when it was twelve noon, darkness spread over the entire land until three o'clock.

34 At three o'clock Jesus shouted with a loud voice, **"Eli, Eli, lama sabachthani?"** (which, when translated, means, **My God, My God, why have You forsaken Me?**).

35 Some of those who were standing by, hearing Him, said, "Listen, He is calling Elijah!"

36 One person, having filled a sponge with vinegar, put it on a reed and ran to give Him a drink, saying, "Wait! Let's see if Elijah comes to take him down."

37 But Jesus let out a loud shout, and breathed His last.

38 And the veil of the temple was torn in two from the top to the bottom.

39 When the centurion who stood facing Him saw how He expired, he said, "Truly this man was God's Son!"

40 Now there were also women watching from a distance, among whom were Mary Magdalene, Mary the mother of James the younger and of Joses, and Salome,

41 who, when He was in Galilee, followed Him and served Him. And there were also a number of other women who came up to Jerusalem with Him.

---

reproached Him (though one, later on, repented and believed). There was hope even at this late hour, just as there is for a counselee. Remember that. Be sure that you have very good reason before you write anyone off.

Now at noon, great, supernatural **darkness spread over the land**. It lasted till **three** in the afternoon. This was the hour of punishment for the sins of God's people. At three, Jesus shouted the opening lines of Psalm 22 about God's **forsaking** Him so that He would not have to forsake His elect. As throughout His life, He was misunderstood here also (v. 35). They gave Him a refreshing drink, and then, with a **loud shout**, Jesus died (v. 37).

In the temple, the **veil** was torn from the top to the bottom, signifying God's hand at work demonstrating that the **temple** ceremonies were at an end. The sacrifice that they typified had been slain; they were no longer needed. The **centurion**, who had been observing everything, came to faith in Christ (v. 39). Though the disciples had fled, the **women** were there at the cross (vv. 40, 41).

That evening, Joseph of Arimathea, **who had been expecting God's**

42 Now, when evening came (since it was the preparation day, that is, the day before the Sabbath),

43 Joseph of Arimathea, a respected councilman, who also was expecting God's empire, courageously went in to Pilate and asked for Jesus' body.

44 But Pilate wondered whether He was dead already, so he called the centurion and asked him if He had died some time before.

45 And when he learned from the centurion that He had, he let Joseph have the corpse.

46 So he brought a linen sheet, and when he had taken Him down he wrapped Him in the sheet and placed Him in a tomb that had been hewn from rock. Then he rolled a stone across the door of the tomb.

47 And Mary Magdalene and Mary the mother of Joses saw where He had been laid.

---

empire predicted by Daniel, John and Jesus Himself, showing more **courage** than the disciples, went to Pilate and **asked** for the body. Hearing from the **centurion** in charge that Jesus was already dead, he granted Joseph permission to bury the body, which he did in **a rock hewn tomb**. A **stone** was **rolled** across the opening that served as a door. The location was marked by the women.

CHAPTER 16

1 Now when the Sabbath had passed, Mary Magdalene and Mary the mother of James, and Salome bought spices so that they might go and rub them on Him.

2   So very early, on the first day of the week, they went to the tomb, just at sunrise.

3   They were saying to one another, "Who is going to roll the stone from the door of the tomb for us?"

4   Then, as they looked up, they saw that the stone, which was a very large one, had been rolled away.

5   As they went into the tomb they saw a young man sitting on the right side, who was clothed in a white robe. And they were terribly upset.

6   But he said to them,

> Don't be so upset. You are looking for Jesus of Nazareth, Who was crucified. He has risen; He isn't here. Take a look at the place where they laid Him.

7   But go, tell His disciples—and Peter—that He is going before you into Galilee. You will see Him there, just as He told you.

8   Then they went out and fled from the tomb, because they were trembling and shocked. But they didn't tell anybody anything, because they were terrified.

This chapter (remember that they were divided by men, not by God) is but eight verses long in the better manuscripts. I shall not argue this point; the commentaries do so fully.

After the **Sabbath the two Marys and Salome brought spices** to the tomb. They were wondering how they could get into the tomb with the **stone** rolled across it. As they approached and looked up at the tomb, they saw that the **large stone** had been removed. There was **a young man sitting on the right side of the tomb, clothed in a white robe**. This appearance of an angel terrified them.

Then he told them to calm down. He told them that he knew they were **looking for Jesus**, and that He had **risen** from the dead. Then he urged them to look at the place where Joseph had laid His body. Finally, he ordered them to **go tell the disciples** (specifically including **Peter**, who had given up after his denial), and that He would meet them in **Galilee**, just as He had said He would. They went out terrified and told no one else what had happened.

This is a short, but powerful gospel of the Lord Jesus. Because of its

9-20[1]

---

brevity and the wealth of material it contains appropriate to counseling, it might be wise to memorize which events are mentioned in each chapter so that you may easily turn to them when needed in counseling sessions. It is easier to remember chapters than hundreds of verses. This, then, should help you, if you endeavor to do it.

www.ingramcontent.com/pod-product-compliance
Lightning Source LLC
Chambersburg PA
CBHW071406090426
42737CB00011B/1368